Java Developer's Guide to E-Commerce with XML and JSP

Java™ Developer's Guide to E-Commerce with XML and JSP

Bill Brogden

Chris Minnick

Leroy Gonzalez
NYC
September 2003

SYBEX®

San Francisco • Paris • Düsseldorf • Soest • London

Associate Publisher: Richard Mills
Contracts and Licensing Manager: Kristine O'Callaghan
Acquisitions and Developmental Editor: Denise Santoro Lincoln
Editors: Jeff Gammon, Susan Hobbs
Production Editor: Leslie E.H. Light
Technical Editor: John Zukowski
Electronic Publishing Specialist: Franz Baumhackl
Graphic Illustrator: Tony Jonick
Proofreaders: Camera Obscura, Yariv Rabnovich
Indexer: Ted Laux
CD Coordinator: Kara Eve Schwartz
CD Technician: Kevin Ly
Book Designer: Robin Kibby
Cover Designer: Design Site
Cover Illustrator/Photographer: Jack D. Myers

*To my wife, Rebecca,
my unfailing support
through many years.*

Bill Brogden

ACKNOWLEDGMENTS

I would like to thank the following people for their help:

As always, to my wife, for her support over many, many years.

To my fellow LANWrights, Inc. employees Ed Tittel and Dawn Rader for their guidance and editorial expertise, respectively.

Thanks to Toivo Lainevool for his contributions of Chapters 5 and 6.

Finally, to all the wonderful people at Sybex for being a great group of people to work with!

Bill Brogden

I'd like to thank Ed Tittel and William Brogden for their expert advice and guidance. Thanks also to Dawn Rader for making me look good. A very special thanks to my family (you know who you are), my wife Margaret (who also knows who she is), and to Roger Smith (who sometimes knows who he is) for the inspiration and assistance they've given me over the years.

Chris Minnick

CONTENTS AT A GLANCE

CONTENTS

INTRODUCTION

Many years ago, I (Bill Brogden) attended a conference on environmental data management. One of the reasons for the conference was to address the extreme difficulty that scientists had in exchanging data, especially between countries. Between the different computer brands, tape formats and data storage formats, any researcher trying to coordinate data from different sources felt like he was dealing with a real Tower of Babel.

One of the environmental department heads (with a liberal arts background) at this meeting started the meeting by expressing how utterly astonished he was when he found out that tapes of scientific data had no built-in information describing what was on the tape. If you didn't get detailed information from a separate source, a tape of data was utterly useless. We scientists admitted that it was a bad situation, but we didn't know what to do about it.

The idea of data that carries along a plain language description of itself is now a reality with XML. The widespread acceptance of the Extensible Markup Language (XML) since the 1998 publication of the first standard by the World Wide Web Consortium (W3C for short) indicates that many areas in science and industry were ripe for a revolution in data description.

One reason for the rapid spread of XML is that the Internet has allowed so many people to become familiar with HTML, the standard markup language for Web pages. HTML introduced many potential users to the idea of using tags to impart extra information in plain text. With that base, it is a fairly short (but non-trivial) step to using XML tags for data description.

The most obvious advantage of XML is the user's ability to extend the language as needed for specific tasks. This provides a great attraction when you are struggling to cope with the variety of data types in a particular field. A second advantage, which is not so immediately obvious, is that no matter what extensions are added, XML tools can continue to be used to validate and process any data as long as the XML language rules are followed.

It has turned out that this flexibility is exactly what is needed for many practical applications. Businesses that must communicate data with other businesses are rapidly discarding old Electronic Data Interchange (EDI) formats for XML. These so-called B2B (business-to-business) applications are expected to be the largest volume of XML encoded data on the Internet.

There are now many Web sites of interest to users of Java and XML. For reference material and news, `oasis.oasis-open.org` is a great place to start. This site belongs to the Organization for the Advancement of Structured Information Standards. The world's largest independent, non-profit organization dedicated to the standardization of XML applications.

XML and Java

If you are at all interested in Java, you have probably been exposed to a lot of news about XML because Java has been involved with XML from the very beginning. One of the prime movers of the initial XML standardization effort, Jon Bosak, works for Sun, and most of the early work on XML parsers was done with Java.

However, enthusiasm for XML spread throughout the entire computer industry, from giant corporations such as IBM and Microsoft to informal working groups at all levels. Individuals and small groups have accomplished many of the most significant advances. For example, the informal "XML Deviant" group organized around an Internet mailing list was responsible for developing the Simplified API for XML known as SAX. The development work for this project was first done in Java.

Java Servlets and JavaServer Pages

In this book, we will be using Java servlets and JavaServer Pages (JSP) to implement Web-based applications with XML data. Servlets provide a way to extend Web servers with functionality that was previously accomplished with CGI scripts. JSP allow you to combine elements of HTML markup with fragments of Java code in the same page. Servlet and JSP technology has been evolving about as rapidly as XML.

During development of this book, the current Java Servlet API has been version 2.2, the final release version of December 1999. This API incorporates many changes over the previous version, particularly in the areas of integration into Web applications and standardized configuration using XML.

Standardization of JavaServer Pages technology has occurred much more slowly. The API was stuck at version 0.92 for quite a while. In the absence of a clear path from Sun, many software companies developed their own technologies for combining custom tags in HTML with database search and similar capabilities.

As Sun developed what would become the Java 2 Enterprise Edition, it became clear that JSP had a big part to play in the overall Web application picture, so API development proceeded rapidly to version 1.0 and then 1.1. With the publication of the Java 2 Enterprise Edition, it appears that Java Servlets and JSP have become well integrated into the bigger picture of Web application development with Java. Another important feature of J2EE is heavy dependence on XML for description of Web applications.

A most significant event occurred in October 1999. Sun turned over all Servlet 2.2 and JavaServer Pages 1.1 code to the Apache organization for further development of reference implementations of open-source Java servlet and JSP engines. This development is independent of the J2EE specifications and ensures that there will always be a free and up-to-date implementation of the servlet and JSP APIs.

Who Should Buy This Book

We assume that you have basic familiarity with HTML, Web servers, and the Java language, and that you have access to a computer capable of running a small-scale Web server, the standard Java compiler, and other utilities. Editing XML data can be done with any text editor, or you can use one of the many commercial and open-source editors designed to support XML.

Beyond those requirements, just about anybody who has to deal with data in any form is a potential XML user. It is hard to think of any area of human endeavor that doesn't have some XML related project going on somewhere on the Internet.

What You Will Need

The small-scale Web server we have used for many projects is the free Jakarta-Tomcat development kit (`http://jakarta.apache.org`). Tomcat is a good place to start if you don't already have a Web server. We have also used the JRun server (`www.allaire.com`) both freestanding and as an add-on for Microsoft's PWS and IIS Web servers. Another server you might look at is the Orion server (`www.orionserver.com`), which has a nice JSP tag library tutorial.

Utility programs and toolkits for dealing with XML in Java are proliferating like mushrooms after a rain. For the sake of standardization, we have stuck with Sun's standard JAXP (Java API for XML Parsing) version 1.0 parser toolkit. This toolkit can be downloaded from the `java.sun.com` Web site. The next version of this toolkit is currently in beta testing and is expected to be available soon after this book is released.

What's in the Book

The purpose of this book is to introduce Java developers to the techniques for using XML in Java programs. Rather than taking a theoretical approach, we jump right into practical applications usable on a commercial Web site.

Chapter1—This is an introduction to XML with an explanation of all the tricky bits, and discussion of typical uses. There is also a survey of both the DOM and SAX approaches to processing XML with Java.

Chapter 2—This chapter takes you through the design decisions involved in using XML in a product catalog. XML is so flexible that it is sometimes hard to choose between many different ways to represent data. The catalog design we finally choose illustrates many of the important problems you would face in your own design. We build a catalog file with over 100 items that is used in the following chapters.

Chapter 3—In this chapter, we start with a survey of the Java servlet and JavaServer Pages APIs for creating dynamic Web pages. Next, we survey the standard Java API for extracting data from XML and then put it all together with a Java servlet to extract information from the catalog and present it in HTML. Neat features include a keyword search capability.

Chapter 4—Here we expand the presentation classes from Chapter 3 and create a functioning shopping cart for taking online orders. This process introduces the concept of session tracking as implemented in Java servlets.

Chapter 5—Now that we have a full shopping cart, we need to take the customer's money and record the order (using XML of course). This example of presentation of information to the customer uses JavaServer Pages technology.

Chapter 6—Here we explore the problem of updating the XML formatted catalog via an online interface.

Chapter 7—A vital part of a commercial site is the ability to gather information about your customer. This chapter presents an XML-driven questionnaire system with branching capability. The problem of analyzing accumulated survey results gives us a chance to demonstrate how to use SAX when processing large XML documents.

Chapter 8—Every commercial site needs a way to show the current company news. This chapter designs a flexible XML system for company news and develops servlets and JavaServer Pages to support it.

Chapter 9—These days, a lot of commercial sites include current events news listings in an attempt to induce users to visit frequently. You don't need a staff of reporters to provide the current news in literally hundreds of topic areas, just XML and Java, as demonstrated in this chapter.

Chapter 10—Previous chapters glossed over the details of organizing the resources for Java-based Web applications. In this chapter, we review Sun's standard as published in the v2.2 servlet API and look ahead into the next generation of APIs for Java and XML.

What's on the CD

Naturally, a book on XML and Java must have working examples. For Chapters 3, 4, 5, and 6, we created an XML catalog of over 100 rather amazing products for an imaginary commercial Web site. Other chapters also include sample XML files for the applications.

This book contains a great deal of working Java and JavaServer Pages code. The source code for all these is on the CD-ROM in directories following the chapter organization. Because the CD is one of the very last parts of the book to be finalized, files on the CD may have improvements or additions that don't appear in the chapter text.

If we come up with additions and improvements after the book is published, they will be posted at

```
www.lanw.com/books/javaxml/
```

Conventions Used Within the Book

We have tried to keep the layout as simple as possible. Typography convention will be familiar to all readers, with all code in a `monospace` font as in the following method declaration example:

```
public void _jspService( HttpServletRequest request, HttpServletResponse response )
```

NOTE   Occasionally we will use this Note format to present an aside from the main text.

WARNING   This is the warning style that is used to call your attention to possible problems, such as a deviation from standards.

Contacting the Authors

I (Bill Brogden) would be delighted to hear from any reader. You can reach me at wbrogden@ bga.com in Cyberspace. My real-space address is William Brogden, 130 Woodland Trail, Leander, TX, 78641.

Reports of errata or other problems should be sent to me so I can post corrections. Errata will be posted at this Web site:

`www.lanw.com/books/errata`

About the Authors

William (Bill) Brogden (author of Chapters 3, 4, 7, 8, 9, and 10) has been working with Java since version 1.0 was released. His first big Java project was an applet that presented animated near-real-time major league baseball games. Bill is employed by LANWrights, Inc., where he has been using Java technology for online courseware. Bill has written several books about Java, including *Java Developer's Guide to Servlets and JavaServer Pages*, from Sybex.

In his spare time, Bill reads science fiction and trains Basset hounds. He lives in the woods near Austin, Texas, with his wife, Rebecca, and numerous hounds.

Chris Minnick (author of Chapters 1 and 2) is the president of Minnick Web Services (`www.minnickWeb.com`). He has co-authored several Internet-related books, and he is a contributing editor for Software Development Magazine and a judge for the annual Software Development Jolt Product Excellence and Productivity Awards. Chris has been writing and teaching about Web applications since 1996. He founded Minnick Web Services in San Francisco in 1996 and relocated to Austin, Texas, in 1999. Minnick Web Services specializes in developing database-driven Web applications for small- to medium-sized businesses, and project-oriented Web applications for large consulting and law firms.

In his spare time, Chris trains in martial arts, writes fiction, produces television shows for Austin's cable access channels, and publishes an online humor and travel 'zine (`www.motelmag.com`) with his wife, Margaret.

Toivo Lainevool (author of Chapters 5 and 6) has been developing software professionally since 1990. He is currently a Senior Infrastructure Specialist at ObjectSpace Inc., where he creates object-oriented distributed systems using a variety of technologies including Java and XML. He is also the creator of the XMLPatterns.com Web site, which catalogs known solutions to recurring problems in XML schema development.

In his spare time, Toivo likes to read, ski, take trips back home to Toronto, Canada, and go for hikes in the hills of Los Angeles with his wife, Michele, where they currently live.

XML for Data Description

- Introduction to XML

- What XML has to do with commerce

- The rules of XML

- When and why you should use XML

- Available APIs for interfacing with XML

As a Java programmer, you've surely heard quite a bit about XML in the last couple of years. This chapter will get you up to speed on the technology and the lingo as quickly as possible so you can start realizing the benefits of XML. Once you've started developing applications that use XML, the "XML at a Glance" and "Rules of XML" sections of this chapter will serve as quick XML references.

What Is XML?

Extensible Markup Language (XML), created in 1996 by the World Wide Web Consortium (W3C), is a subset of the Standard Generalized Markup Language (SGML). XML was designed to be a flexible, yet formal, metalanguage for use on the Internet.

A *metalanguage* is a language for describing languages. For example, you could say that an English dictionary and an English grammar book together make up a metalanguage for English.

In the case of XML, its purpose is to describe markup languages. A *markup language* uses tags to identify structure in data. Hypertext Markup Language (HTML), the most common markup language in use today, was originally written in SGML but can be, and has been, written using XML.

HTML was designed to be used for the specific task of marking up scientific and academic papers. As you are well aware if you have done any Web development, HTML is stretched beyond its limits and is busting at the seams from all of the attempts over the years to make it fit the Webmaster's every need. Many people have called XML a replacement for HTML. This is not exactly accurate.

Whereas HTML contains a fixed set of tags, XML does not contain any tags. Instead, XML gives you the ability to create markup languages that actually fit your specific application. In this book, we'll be creating an e-commerce application. The markup language that we use for this application will contain tags (such as `<price>` and `<quantity>`) that are meaningful to e-commerce.

XML applications typically have the following types of data and auxiliary functions:

- The XML data file itself, which follows a rigid structure
- Optionally, a Document Type Definition (DTD), which defines the structure of the XML file
- Optionally, style sheet information, which tells how the data should be formatted for output
- An XML processor and various utilities for manipulating and reformatting the data

XML and E-Commerce

Web developers are used to thinking about what tags do to text. We expect that HTML's bold tag, <b> (font), will make text bold. In actuality, though, <b> (font) has no inherent meaning at all. How text inside of tags is displayed is entirely up to the program that parses the data. In the case of HTML, this program is usually a Web browser. Because HTML documents are usually created to be read by humans using Web browsers, many HTML tags specify how data should be formatted rather than identify information. The purpose of XML is to make it possible to separate the data in a document from the code that specifies how the data should be displayed, in order to make it easy to extract data programmatically.

For example, imagine that you are a light bulb reseller, and your Web site features the latest price information from various lighting manufacturers. Rather than check the manufacturers' sites for updated prices, you decide to write a program to read the product information from the various sites, add 10 percent to the manufacturer's price for yourself, and display the product information on your own site. One of your suppliers is ABC Lighting. Listing 1.1 is a part of an HTML product information table from ABC Lighting's Web site.

Listing 1.1: An HTML Table Containing Product Information

```
<table>

<tr>
  <th>Product Name</th>
  <th>Description</th>
  <th>Price</th>
</tr>

<tr>
  <td><b>Flashlight</b></td>
  <td>Portable light, without fire!</td>
  <td>$9.95</td>
</tr>

<tr>
  <td><b>Neon Light</b></td>
  <td>Nothing says "class" like Neon lighting.</td>
  <td>$14.75</td>
</tr>
  ...
</table>
```

The HTML document specifies only how the text should be formatted. Extracting information from a static HTML page is a tricky business at best. If you want to get the price of the flashlight from the preceding example, you can look for the text in the third column of the row that has Flashlight in the first cell, but you're risking that your program will fall apart the next time the site's design is changed or the product's name is changed.

There is a chance that some of the lighting manufacturers are dynamically generating their Web pages from a database. In that case, you might be able to work with the Webmasters of each site to create an interface to their data, but this can be a time-consuming and confusing process that could be different for each database from which you need to get data. It would be much easier if the document itself contained all of the information needed to extract meaningful information.

Listing 1.2 demonstrates how the same information can be presented in an XML document.

Listing 1.2: An XML Document Containing Product Information

```
<?xml version="1.0" standalone="no"?>
<!DOCTYPE ABC_Lighting:catalog SYSTEM "catalog.dtd">

<ABC_Lighting:catalog xmlns:ABC_Lighting = "http://www.abclighting.com">

<ABC_Lighting:product>
<ABC_Lighting:name>Flashlight</ABC_Lighting:name>
<ABC_Lighting:description>Portable light, without fire!
</ABC_Lighting:description>
<ABC_Lighting:price>$9.95</ABC_Lighting:price>
</ABC_Lighting:product>

<ABC_Lighting:product>
<ABC_Lighting:name>Neon Light</ABC_Lighting:name>
<ABC_Lighting:description>Nothing says "class" like Neon lighting.
</ABC_Lighting:description>
<ABC_Lighting:price>$14.75</ABC_Lighting:price>
</ABC_Lighting:product>

</ABC_Lighting:catalog>
```

The first line in this document is the XML declaration, and provides information to XML parsers. The *XML declaration* indicates the type of the document and the version of XML that it is written for. This statement is not required, but it is standard practice to begin XML documents with this line. The `standalone = "no"` attribute indicates that this document has a DTD. The next line is the Document Type Declaration. This statement specifies which DTD the document conforms to—in this case, the DTD is called `catalog.dtd`. Note that although they have the same initials, there is a big difference between a Document Type Definition (commonly called a DTD) and a Document Type Declaration. A Document Type Declaration is used to indicate to which Document Type Definition an XML document conforms.

The Document Type Declaration also tells what the root element of the document is. The *root element* is the element that encloses everything else in the document. In this case, the root element is `ABC_Lighting:catalog`. The part of the element name before the colon is the tag's namespace. Namespaces are not required, but they can be used to ensure uniqueness of tags. If ABC Lighting were to start selling products manufactured by other companies on its Web site, namespaces would eliminate the possibility of errors caused by identically named, but differently structured, elements from the outside data.

Here is what `catalog.dtd` might look like:

```
<!ELEMENT ABC_Lighting:catalog (product)*>
<!ELEMENT ABC_Lighting:product (name, description?, price+)>
<!ELEMENT ABC_Lighting:name (#PCDATA)>
<!ELEMENT ABC_Lighting:description (#PCDATA)>
<!ELEMENT ABC_Lighting:price (#PCDATA)>
```

This DTD specifies the elements that can appear in a catalog, the order in which they must appear, and the number of times they can or must appear. Using the XML data and the DTD, programmatically identifying and extracting useful information from an XML document is simple, as you will see in the rest of this book.

XML Resources

Check the following additional resources for the latest developments, insights into future plans for XML, and tools for working with XML:

- World Wide Web Consortium (`www.w3c.org`).
- O'Reilly & Associates, Inc.'s XML.com (`www.xml.com`)—one of the best commercial XML information sites on the Web.
- The XML Industry Portal (`www.xml.org`).
- xmlhack (`www.xmlhack.com`)—a news site for XML developers.
- Enhydra (`www.enhydra.org`)—home of the Enhydra Java/XML application server.
- The Unicode Consortium (`www.unicode.org`).

The Many Uses of XML

XML can be deployed on the client side or on the server side. The following sections explore each approach. Additionally, XML can be used for data storage, which is also discussed following the client and server sections.

XML on the Client

On the client side, XML enables a level of customized data presentation that is very difficult or impossible to achieve using HTML. For example, Web-enabled devices, such as Personal Digital Assistants (PDAs) or mobile phones, require that pages be formatted differently than standard Web browsers. The typical way to deliver a site to small-screen devices has been to create an entirely different version of the site. By using structured data in XML documents, however, the data is separated from the formatting, and all you need to do to customize the display of your site on different types of devices is to apply a different style sheet to the data.

XML on the Server

XML is having the biggest impact today on the server. One application of XML on the server side is messaging. *Messaging* is the exchange of data between applications or computers. In order for applications, computers, and businesses to share information, they must decide on a message format. To understand the potential impact that XML could have in messaging, it's important to know a little about the history of messaging. Deciding on a standard for sending messages has been a problem ever since humans began to communicate, but I'll only go back about 30 years.

Electronic commerce, or e-commerce, as defined by the European Workshop on Open System's Technical Guide on Electronic Commerce (EWOS TGEC 066), covers such diverse activities as marketing, contract exchange, logistics support, settlement, and interaction with administrative bodies (e.g., tax and custom data interchange). Electronic Data Interchange (EDI) dates back to the 1970s, when it was introduced by the Transportation Data Coordinating Committee (TDCC). In industries such as finance, which have been networked for over 30 years, EDI has been the standard electronic commerce messaging format. EDI grew out of the need for businesses to be able to exchange commercial data in a standard format. The problem with EDI systems is that they are expensive to set up and maintain and often require dedicated networks.

In the 1980s, electronic mail for workgroups began to spring up and be implemented in corporations. As vendors attempted to establish their e-mail solutions as the standard, a much larger number of businesses began to rely on electronic messaging. Packages such as Microsoft Mail and Lotus cc:Mail allowed smaller companies to exchange intraoffice messages, but they did not generally scale well and became difficult to manage. Providing connectivity with the world outside of the local area network (LAN) proved to be difficult as well. The bottom line, though, was that, as with the rest of computing, messaging was becoming increasingly decentralized. The movement of electronic messaging away from centralized, tightly controlled, dedicated networks opened up the technology to more users and uses. Decentralization also resulted in compatibility nightmares, duplication of effort, and an inability to leverage organizational shared knowledge.

By the time the Internet emerged, companies were all too familiar with the need for standard, flexible ways for businesses and people to communicate and conduct electronic commerce. A freely available, standardized electronic messaging format would have the power to impact every type of communication, whether commercial or not.

The first step, though, was to agree on a language. This is where XML comes in. The chief reason that XML is perfect for designing messaging formats is its simplicity. XML has no optional features, it's not tied to any one operating system or vendor, and it's compatible with a large base of tools and applications that have been developed over the years for SGML. XML's strict enforcement of its well-formedness rules ensures that any XML parser will be able to read and comprehend any XML document. In addition, many more people are familiar with using markup languages than are familiar with the message formats required to build EDI systems. Using XML, message formats can be created by anyone who can write a well-formed XML document.

Another use for XML in Web documents is to specify metacontent. *Metacontent*, or content about content, can make it possible for search engines to retrieve much better results. For example, if you were looking for news stories that took place in Austin, Texas, you might search for *Austin Texas News*. Because most search engines today simply index all of the content in a site, chances are very good that many of the results returned from this search would not really be what you were looking for. If news articles from Austin were written as structured XML documents, you would be able to perform much less ambiguous searches, such as `City = Austin, State = TX, StoryType = News`.

XML for Data Storage

XML can also be used to create databases. XML stores data in a tree structure. Although XML documents are not (by a long shot) the most efficient way to store data, they do have their advantages. As with messaging, the most important advantage is simplicity. Tree structures are an intuitive and familiar way to organize data. In addition, almost any type of data structure can be represented by an XML data tree—from relational databases to object-oriented databases to hierarchical structures. Another important advantage of using XML for data storage is that XML supports the Unicode character set. As a result, any international character you're ever likely to use is legal in XML documents.

Unicode is the official way to implement the Universal Character Set (UCS) defined by the International Standards Organization (ISO); it is the universal character encoding standard used for representation of text for computer processing. Unicode uses UCS Transformation Formats (UTFs) to change character encodings to actual bits.

The XML Specification requires that XML processors must support two UTFs: UTF-8 and UTF-16. UTF-16 uses two bytes to represent every character. UTF-8 uses the one-byte ASCII character encodings for ASCII characters and represents non-ASCII characters using variable-length encodings. UTF-8 is useful if you need to maintain compatibility with ASCII. The downside to UTF-8 is that it uses anywhere from 1 to 3 bytes to represent non-ASCII characters. If your text is mostly ASCII, UTF-8 saves space. If you are using non-ASCII characters, UTF-8 wastes space. The default encoding in XML is UTF-8. The character encoding you wish to use for a document is specified in the XML declaration using the encoding attribute, as in the following example:

```
<?xml version="1.0" standalone="no" encoding="UTF-8"?>
```

Rules of XML

Today's HTML browsers will generally attempt to display anything, no matter how odd or poorly formed the HTML markup may be. XML processors, on the other hand, are required to generate a fatal error when they come across a markup error. A *fatal error* means that the application will halt processing and display an error message. This strictness is often referred to as *draconian error-handling*. Although this type of all-or-nothing error handling may seem primitive to HTML writers, and possibly even to SGML authors, it is necessary to help ensure that XML documents will be interpreted the same way in every XML processor.

An XML document that follows the rules of XML syntax is said to be *well formed*. XML's authors wrote well-formedness into the specification to prevent XML from becoming a victim of something like the browser wars. The end result of the so-called browser wars between Microsoft and Netscape was that HTML writers today have to constantly worry about compatibility. If this type of fragmentation were to happen to XML, it would be worthless.

An *XML processor* is a software module that provides applications with access to data stored in XML documents. XML processors can be either validating or non-validating. A validating processor will check the structure of the document against the rules specified in a DTD, and a non-validating processor will only check to make sure that the document conforms to the rules of XML.

Defining a Well-Formed XML Document

All of the text in an XML document can be divided into two broad categories: character data and markup. *Markup* is anything that begins with a < and ends with a > or that begins with a & and ends with a ;. *Character data* is everything that is not markup. Character data can further be divided into two categories: parsed and unparsed character data. *Parsed character data*, or PCDATA, is parsed by an XML processor. *Unparsed character data*, naturally, is not parsed.

Listing 1.3 shows an example of a well-formed XML document.

Listing 1.3: A Well-Formed XML Document

```xml
<?xml version="1.0" standalone="yes"?>

<beverage>
  <name>Canned Water</name>

  <manufacturer>
    <name>Extra Good Beverages</name>
    <url href = "http://www.extragoodbev.com"/>
  </manufacturer>

  <nutrition_facts serving_size="1 can">

    <calories>
      <amount unit="g">0</amount>
    </calories>

    <fat>
      <amount unit="g">0</amount>
    </fat>

    <sodium>
      <amount unit="mg">0</amount>
    </sodium>
```

```
<carb>
  <amount unit="g">0</amount>
</carb>

<protein>
  <amount unit="g">0</amount>
</protein>

</nutrition_facts>

</beverage>
```

The first thing you should notice about this document is the `standalone="yes"` attribute in the XML declaration. This indicates that this document does not use a DTD. XML documents are not required to use DTDs. In fact, applications that use XML data will often not use a DTD in order to increase performance in cases where structure and reusability are not as important.

Following the XML declaration are elements. *Elements* are the most common form of markup; they are delimited by angle brackets, and they describe the data they surround. Elements are made up of a starting tag and an ending tag (`<beverage>`...`</beverage>`, for example). The name of an element is called its *generic identifier (GI)* or its *type*. The text between the start and end tag is called the element's *content*. For example, the following element's type is `book`, and the name of the book is the element's content.

```
<book>Java Developer's Guide to XML</book>
```

An element that has no content is called an *empty element*. You can combine the start tag and end tag of an empty element by putting the slash at the end of the start tag: `<br/>`. XML also allows you to write empty elements using a starting tag and an ending tag, for example: `<br></br>`.

There are actually two types of empty elements: those that are defined as empty and can never have content, and those that just happen to not have content. To distinguish between the two, it is recommended that you use a start-tag/end-tag pair for elements that contain no data, and the empty element tag format for elements that are defined as empty.

For example, HTML's `br` element cannot contain data and should be written as `<br/>`. If, on the other hand, your XML document has an instance of an element that currently has no content but may have content at some point, you should use the standard element syntax, like this:

```
<cupboards></cupboards>
```

Elements can have attributes. *Attributes* are name-value pairs inside of the start tag of an element. In the following example, `src`, `width`, and `height` are attributes of `img`.

```
<img src = "balloons.gif" width="100" height="100"/>
```

TIP If you want to start writing your HTML code to be compatible with XML, you may notice that the HTML break tag is particularly troublesome. Some browsers won't understand **
** and will interpret **
</br>** as two line breaks. To overcome this problem, put a space between the **br** and the slash: **
**.

In XML, attribute values must be in either single or double quotes. A list of the well-formedness rules that XML documents must adhere to can be found at the end of this chapter.

DTDs and Validity

A DTD, or Document Type Definition, is a means for you to explicitly define the structure of a class of XML documents. For example, a DTD for a catalog of animals might specify that each animal must have a name, an animal type, and a sound. The DTD for this animal catalog would look like this:

```
<!ELEMENT animal-list (animal)*>
<!ELEMENT animal (name,type,sound)>
<!ELEMENT name (#PCDATA)>
<!ELEMENT type (#PCDATA)>
<!ELEMENT sound (#PCDATA)>
```

If this were the standard zoology DTD (it isn't), any zoologist could be sure that his or her data would be usable by any other zoologist and that they were working with the same rules for lists of animals. An XML document that conforms to the rules of the DTD for which it was written, as well as to the rules of XML in general, is considered well formed and valid. Here is an example of a well-formed XML document that conforms to the preceding DTD:

```
<?xml version="1.0" standalone="no"?>
<!DOCTYPE animal-list SYSTEM "zoology.dtd">
<animal-list>
  <animal>
    <name>Bessie</name>
    <type>cow</type>
    <sound>moo</sound>
  </animal>
  <animal>
    <name>Rover</name>
    <type>dog</type>
    <sound>woof</sound>
  </animal>
</animal-list>
```

NOTE The words that are in all-capital letters in the preceding examples. These are XML keywords. Writing them in all caps is actually not just a stylistic choice. As a result of XML's case-sensitiveness, an XML processor will produce an error if a keyword is not in all caps. As far as XML is concerned, DOCTYPE and Doctype are no more similar than DOCTYPE and EGGDROP.

Element Declarations

The most basic type of declaration in a DTD is the <!ELEMENT> declaration. The format for an element declaration is <!ELEMENT elementname rule>.

Every element that is used in your XML document must be defined in the DTD, if you're using one. There are several rules that you need to follow when naming elements:

- Element names should not contain < or >.

- The name of an element must begin with a letter or an underscore. After the first character, it can contain any number of letters, numbers, hyphens, periods, or underscores.

- Element names cannot start with the string xml (in any combination of uppercase or lowercase letters).

- Colons are forbidden, unless you are using namespaces.

Content Specification

In the rule portion of an element declaration, you specify what can appear in the contents of the element. If you want to declare an element that cannot contain any data, you can use the EMPTY type (for example, <!ELEMENT img EMPTY>).

A good example of an empty element is the HTML img element. To make this element valid in an XML document, you write it using the empty element syntax, as in the following example:

```
<img src="mycar.jpg"/>
```

If you only want to allow parsed character data in an element, use the following declaration:

```
<!ELEMENT mymemoirs #PCDATA>
```

You can also specify which element types may appear inside of an element, in what order they must appear, and how many times they can appear, as in the following example:

```
<!ELEMENT mymemoirs (title, author, philosophizing, sad_story,
    funny_story, lesson, conclusion)>
```

In this example, each of the element types listed must appear once (and only once) inside of the mymemoirs element, in the order that they are listed in the declaration.

NOTE The elements that appear inside of the `mymemoirs` element are called its children, and `mymemoirs` can be referred to as their parent. Any element can be a child of any number of other elements in a document. Elements that are more than one level separated from each other are referred to as grandchildren, great-grandchildren, and so forth (or as grandparents, great-grandparents, and so forth in the other direction). You can also just talk about relationships between elements in terms of ancestors and descendants.

You can write more flexible rules by using *occurrence operators*. The following shows the three possibilities.

Symbol	Meaning
?	Must occur zero or one time
+	Must occur one or more times
*	May appear any number of times or not at all

Here is the `mymemoirs` declaration again, rewritten using occurrence operators:

```
<!ELEMENT mymemoirs (title, author, philosophizing+, sad_story*,
    funny_story*, lesson+, conclusion)>
```

You can specify that a choice needs to be made between elements by using the vertical bar (|), as in the following example:

```
<!ELEMENT mymemoirs (title, author, philosophizing+, sad_story*,
    funny_story*, lesson+ | conclusion)>
```

In this declaration, `mymemoirs` is allowed to have one or more `lesson` or `conclusion` elements—but not both. Even more complicated rules can be defined by using nested parentheses. Listing 1.4 shows how the complete `mymemoirs.dtd` might look.

Listing 1.4: A Complete Version of *mymemoirs.dtd*

```
<!ELEMENT mymemoirs (title, author, philosophizing+, sad_story*,
    funny_story*, (lesson+ | conclusion)*)>
<!ELEMENT title (#PCDATA)>
<!ELEMENT author (#PCDATA)>
<!ELEMENT philosophizing (paragraph)*>
<!ELEMENT sad_story (paragraph*, letter*,(lesson | conclusion)*)>
<!ELEMENT funny_story (paragraph*, letter*,(lesson | conclusion)*)>
<!ELEMENT letter (paragraph)*>
<!ELEMENT lesson (paragraph)*>
<!ELEMENT conclusion (paragraph)*>
<!ELEMENT paragraph (#PCDATA)>
```

The least strict rule, of course, is "anything goes." You can use ANY as the rule to specify that parsed character data or elements can appear inside of this element, as in the following example:

```
<!ELEMENT mymemoirs ANY>
```

Such a broad rule as the ANY element type really doesn't seem to fit in the rigid structure of XML. Generally, if you write a DTD that uses the ANY keyword, you're probably doing something wrong, and you should see if there's a better way.

Attribute Declarations

Attributes are used to associate name-value pairs with elements. Attributes are defined using attribute declarations. The format for an attribute declaration in a DTD is:

```
<!ATTLIST target_element name type default_value ?>
```

Attributes are used to provide additional information about elements. It is sometimes difficult to decide whether a piece of data should be an attribute or an element. For example, both of the following pieces of XML could be used to accomplish the same goal:

```
<dog name = "Snuggles"></dog>
```

or

```
<dog>
    <name>Snuggles</name>
</dog>
```

Although the choice is up to you, you can follow certain guidelines. We'll talk about those in Chapter 2, "A Catalog in XML." For now, just be aware that this is a conundrum faced by all XML authors.

The following are some examples of attribute declarations (their meaning will be explained shortly):

```
<!ATTLIST dog name CDATA #REQUIRED>
<!ATTLIST dog gender (male | female) #IMPLIED>
<!ATTLIST dog species #FIXED "Canis familiaris">
```

There are nine different types of attributes, and they fall within three different categories: string, tokenized, and enumerated. String attributes are defined using the CDATA keyword as the type, as in the following example:

```
<!ATTLIST dog name CDATA>
```

The value of this string can be any valid character string.

There are several tokenized attribute types. The most important of these are ID and IDREF. Attributes with the IDREF type can be used for a simple form of linking. Attributes of type ID can be used to uniquely identify elements. ID attributes must uniquely identify the element in which they are used. For example, the following attribute declaration creates a required product ID tag:

```
<!ATTLIST product id ID #REQUIRED>
```

IDs and IDREFs can be used much like anchors in HTML. The value of an IDREF attribute must be the value of the ID attribute of another element. For example, the following piece of a DTD declares an element with an ID attribute and an element with an IDREF attribute that refers to the first element:

```
<!ELEMENT product (name,description,price)>
<!ATTLIST product id ID #REQUIRED>
<!ELEMENT featured_products (product_reference)*>
<!ELEMENT product_ref (#PCDATA)>
<!ATTLIST product_ref link IDREF #IMPLIED>
```

An XML file that uses this DTD might have a section that looks like this:

```
<product id= "X4343">
  <name>rock</name>
</product>
<featured_products>
  <product_ref link = "X4343">a rock</product_ref>
...
</featured_products>
```

Enumerated attribute types list possible values that the attribute can contain. For example, if you wanted to declare an attribute called angle_type for an element called triangle, you could specify the possible values as follows:

```
<!ATTLIST triangle angle_type (obtuse | acute | right) #REQUIRED>
```

Attribute defaults can be used to declare that an element must contain a particular attribute, and even what the value of the attribute must be. The following mini-table shows the three keywords that may be used and what they mean. If you don't specify a default value, IMPLIED is implied.

Attribute Default	Definition
#REQUIRED	Every occurrence of the named element must have this attribute.
#IMPLIED	No default is specified.
#FIXED	The element must have this attribute, and the attribute value must be the value specified.

Entity Declarations

Declaring entities allows you use entity references. An *entity reference* is a series of characters that substitute for a different series of characters. A common use is to denote symbols that might otherwise be mistaken for markup. If you've written much HTML, you've probably come across entity references. The most common type of entity is the general entity. *General entities* are entities that can substitute for characters inside of an XML document. The format for general entity declarations is:

```
<!ENTITY name "replacement characters">
```

Entity references take the form **&***entityname*;. There are five built-in general entities in XML. You do not need to declare these in your DTD, although the XML specification recommends that you do anyway, for interoperability. The five built-in entities are shown in the following mini-table.

Entity Reference	Replacement Text	Character
&amp;	&#38;	&
&lt;	&#60;	<
&gt;	&#62;	>
&apos;	&#39;	'
&quot;	&#34;	"

You can declare these entities using the following declarations:

```
<!ENTITY lt    "&#38;#60;">
<!ENTITY gt    "&#62;">
<!ENTITY amp   "&#38;#38;">
<!ENTITY apos  "&#39;">
<!ENTITY quot  "&#34;">
```

NOTE   The < and & characters in the declarations of lt and amp are doubly escaped to meet the requirement that entity replacement be well formed. In other words, the & symbol and the < symbol are the two symbols that signal to an XML processor that the text that follows is a new XML markup statement. If these characters weren't doubly escaped in these entity declarations, the XML processor would interpret them as the beginning of a new piece of markup before the entity declaration ends and would generate an error.

The built-in entity references are essential for creating XML documents in which you want to use any of these characters as character data rather than as part of the markup. General entity references that you define yourself are useful for assigning names to character codes that you need to use frequently. For example, to declare an entity reference to represent the trademark symbol (™), you could use the following declaration:

```
<!ENTITY tm "&#8482">
```

The trademark symbol could then be inserted into any XML document that uses a DTD with this declaration. For example:

```
<product_name>
Super Drink&tm;
</product_name>
```

Although entities may be used in the definitions of other entities, an important rule to keep in mind is that you may not make circular references.

Invalid:

```
<!ENTITY myentity "please see &myotherentity; ">
<!ENTITY myotherentity "please see &myentity; ">
```

Valid:

```
<!ENTITY tm "&#8482">
<!ENTITY myentity "I enjoy Super Drink&tm; ">
```

Declaring Parameter Entities

You can also declare entity references that will be replaced by their entity definitions in the DTD. This type of entity is called a parameter entity. *Parameter entity* references begin with a percent sign and may not be used in XML documents—only in the DTD in which they are defined. Here is an example of a use for a parameter entity:

```
<!ENTITY % actors " (Joe, Mary, Todd, Bill, Jane)* ">
<!ELEMENT dialog %actors;>
```

Declaring External Entities

External entities are a way of including external files in your XML documents. They are declared as follows:

```
<!ENTITY latest_prices SYSTEM
    "http://www.getthepricesofthings.com/today.xml">
```

After declaring an external entity, you can include the XML content specified into your document by using an entity reference—&latest_prices; in this case.

Declaring Unparsed Entities

Unparsed entities can be used to include non-XML data in an XML document. The keyword NDATA is used to define an entity as unparsed. For example:

```
<!ENTITY bookcover SYSTEM
    "http://www.sybex.com/books/xml/javadevguide.gif" NDATA gif>
```

Immediately following NDATA is the *notation data keyword*. This keyword is declared using a notation declaration. *Notation declarations* (or notations/plural) provide additional information (such as identifying information) or, in this case, format information for unparsed data. Notation keywords are defined using <!NOTATION> declarations. For example:

```
<!NOTATION gif SYSTEM
  "-//CompuServe//NOTATION Graphics Interchange Format 89a//EN">
```

Unparsed Character Data: CDATA, Comments, and Processing Instructions

Parsed character data does not contain markup. Therefore, if you want to include the characters < or & in the contents of an element, you need to escape them. One way to escape these characters is to use their numeric character references (< and &, respectively), or you can use XML's built-in entity references (&#lt; and &#amp;, respectively). If you don't want to worry about escaping these characters, you can use a *CDATA section* to designate a block of text as unparsed character data—as explained in the following section.

CDATA Sections

CDATA sections start with the string <![CDATA[and end with]]>. None of the characters in a CDATA section will be parsed, except for the string]]>. If you wanted to include an XML example inside of an XML document, rather than escaping every < and & by using < and &, you could include the entire block that contains these characters inside of a CDATA section. For example:

```
<example>
Here is an example of a well-formed XML document:
<!CDATA[
<?xml version="1.0" standalone="yes"?>
<beverage>
  <name>Super-Drink</name>
  <manufacturer>
    <name>Extra Good Beverages</name>
    <url href = "http://www.extrasuperbev.com"/>
  </manufacturer>
</beverage>
]]>
</example>
```

Using XML Comments

XML *comments* work the same as HTML comments, as the following demonstrates:

```
<!--this text is commented out. -->
```

Comments may appear anywhere inside a document, outside of other markup. They are not part of a document's character data and cannot be used by an XML parser.

In HTML, comments are often used to contain text that is available to programs but is not part of the document. For example, CGI commands and JavaScript are often put inside of comments in HTML documents. XML parsers are allowed to completely ignore comments, so this trick should not be used. Instead, XML features processing instructions for this purpose.

WARNING   In my experience, Internet time is not really faster; it's actually much like daylight saving time. Just as the borrowed hour of daylight always bites you back by throwing off your schedule for a week when "normal time" resumes, neglecting to comment your code in the interest of saving time will result in much bigger problems later on.

Processing Instructions

Processing instructions (PIs) are used to include information in your document that is intended to be used by applications. Like comments, processing instructions are not considered to be part of the character data of a document. Unlike comments, XML parsers must pass processing instructions through to applications.

Processing instructions begin with <? and end with ?>. The first word in a PI is the name of the application the processing instruction is intended for. You may also use a notation name to associate a URI (Universal Resource Identifier) with an application name. Following the identifying information, a PI may contain any type of character data that you like. The following is an example of a PI:

```
<?playsounds sounds.mp3?>
```

This PI might cause an application that knows what to do with it to play the mp3 file that is indicated.

XML Schema

Although DTDs are currently the standard for defining XML document types, they do have several serious limitations. DTDs were inherited from SGML, where they were originally designed for defining markup languages for documents, not for creating database schemas. The biggest limitation of DTDs is that they don't give you enough control over the contents of elements. For example, DTDs provide no way to specify that

```
<todaysdate>09/01/2000</todaysdate>
```

is valid, whereas

```
<todaysdate>Eggs, Toast, Coffee</todaysdate>
```

is not valid. Occasionally, you may also want to specify more exact limits on the number of times elements can occur. This also isn't possible using DTDs.

As a result of the limitations of DTDs and the increasing use of XML for data storage, several alternatives are being considered. The front-runner among these is currently the XML Schema Definition language (XSD).

NOTE   As I am writing this, XML Schema is still a W3C working draft. This means that it may undergo significant changes between now and when it gets a blessing as an official recommendation. The XML Schema specification can be found at **www.w3.org/XML/Schema.html**.

XML schemas have the same purpose as DTDs: to define classes of XML documents. The main difference is that XML schemas divide elements into two types: complex and simple.

Elements that contain other elements or attributes as well as character data have *complex types*, and elements that only contain character data have *simple types*. Attributes always have simple types. Listing 1.5 shows an XML schema for a product catalog. Listing 1.6 shows an XML document that uses this schema.

Listing 1.5: The Catalog Schema (*catalog.xsd*)

```
<xsd:schema xmlns:xsd="http://www.w3.org/1999/XMLSchema">

<xsd:element name="Catalog" type="CatalogType"/>

<xsd:complexType name="CatalogType">
<xsd:element name="product" type="ProductType"/>
<xsd:attribute name="onSaleDate" type="xsd:date"/>
<xsd:attribute name="partNum" type="Sku"/>
</xsd:complexType>

<xsd:complexType name="ProductType">
<xsd:element name="productName" type="xsd:string"/>
<xsd:element name="quantity_in_stock">
<xsd:simpleType base="xsd:positiveInteger">
<xsd:maxExclusive value="500"/>
</xsd:simpleType>
</xsd:element>
<xsd:element name="price" type="xsd:decimal"/>
<xsd:element name="description" type="xsd:string"  minOccurs="0"/>
</xsd:complexType>
```

```
<xsd:simpleType name="Sku" base="xsd:string">
<xsd:pattern value="\[A-Z]{3}-[A-Z]{3}d{3}"/>
</xsd:simpleType>

</xsd:schema>
```

Listing 1.6: A Catalog (*mycatalog.xml*)

```
<?xml version="1.0"?>
<catalog>
  <product partNum="ABC-PRO336" onSaleDate="12/12/2004">
    <productName>BigSoft Xtreminator 3.36</productName>
      <quantity_in_stock>20</quantity_in_stock >
      <price>195.99</price>
  <description>Managing your life has never been so easy.</description>
    </product>
<product partNum="ABC-PRO343" onSaleDate="12/12/2004">
<productName>E-Dev ProntoWorks</productName>
      <quantity_in_stock>35</quantity_in_stock >
      <price>299.99</price>
<description>The premier integrated rapid e-development suite
  for busy e-professionals.</description>
    </product>
</catalog>
```

Elements that have complex types are defined using the `complexType (font)` element. Elements with complex types contain other elements and attributes. The elements and attributes contained within complex elements are defined using the `element` and `attribute` elements, respectively. For example, in Listing 1.5, `item product` is defined as a complex type. Inside of the definition of the product type are five elements: `productName`, `quantity_in_stock`, `price`, `comment`, and `partNum`.

Elements with simple types have no attributes and do not contain any other elements. XSD contains a set of built-in simple types, which includes such types as `string`, `binary`, `boolean`, `double`, `float`, and so forth. Additional simple types can be derived from the built-in types. For example, the preceding example defines the simple type `Sku`, which is based on the `string` type.

The process used to derive new simple types from existing ones is called *restriction*. Note that the definition of the `Sku` data type uses a regular expression to define a pattern that the contents of any element or attribute that uses this type must follow.

XML Schemas have much more flexible occurrence constraints than DTDs. DTDs only allow you to specify that elements must occur zero, one, one or more, or any number of times. In addition to these constraints, XML Schema allows you to specify a minimum or a maximum number, a value, or a range of values, as well as even more complicated constraints.

Creating Style Sheets with XSL

Extensible Stylesheet Language (XSL) is a language for expressing style sheets. XSL *style sheets* are used to specify the presentation of XML documents that are to be read by people.

For example, a designer may create a style sheet for an XML product catalog. This style sheet could say what fonts, font sizes, borders, and so forth will be applied to the document when it and the style sheet are combined using an XSL style sheet processor.

There are two steps that a style sheet processor goes through to apply a style sheet to XML data. The first is *tree transformation*. You could, for example, write a style sheet that would put the products in your catalog in alphabetical order, or number them before outputting them. Transformation can also move and perform computations on XML data.

The second step involved in the presentation process is *formatting*. Formatting is the actual process of applying style, font sizes, page breaks, and so forth to data.

To allow you to accomplish these two tasks, the XSL Specification consists of three separate languages:

XML Path Language (XPath)   A language for referencing parts of an XML document

XSL Transformations (XSLT)   The language used to generate a result tree

Extensible Stylesheet Language (XSL)   XSLT plus a description of a set of Formatting Objects and Formatting Properties

Suppose that you have information about your music library in an XML document, as shown in Listing 1.7.

Listing 1.7: Sample Music Library (*MyMusic.xml*)

```
<?xml version="1.0"?>
<library>
  <cd>
    <title>Just Singin' Along</title>
    <artist>The Happy Guys</artist>
    <description>A lovely collection of songs that the whole family
```

```
    can sing right along with.
  </description>
  <song><title>I'm Really Fine</title></song>
  <song><title>Can't Stop Grinnin'</title></song>
  <song><title>Things Are Swell</title></song>
  <purchase_date>2/23/1954</purchase_date>
</cd>
<cd>
  <title>It's Dot Com Enough for Me: Songs From Silicon
    Somewhere</title>
  <artist>The Nettizens</artist>
  <description>A collection of the best folk music from Internet
companies.</description>
  <song><title>My B2B Is B-R-O-K-E</title></song>
  <song><title>Workin' in a Cubicle</title></song>
  <song><title>Killer Content Strategy</title></song>
  <song><title>She Took the Bricks, I Got the Clicks</title></song>
  <purchase_date>7/12/2000</purchase_date>
</cd>
</library>
```

Say you want to create a printable list of everything in your library. One way to do this would be to apply a style sheet to the document that transforms it into HTML. Listing 1.8 is a style sheet that does just that.

Listing 1.8: A style sheet for HTML output (*CDstyle.xsl*)

```
<?xml version="1.0"?>
<xsl:stylesheet xmlns:xsl="http://www.w3.org/TR/WD-xsl">
<xsl:template match="/">
<TABLE STYLE="border:1px solid black; width:300px">
<TR STYLE="font-size:10pt; font-family:Verdana; font weight:bold;
    text-decoration:underline">
<TD>Title</TD>
<TD>Artist</TD>
</TR>
<xsl:for-each select="library/cd">
<TR STYLE="font-family:Verdana; font-size:12pt; padding:0px 6px">
<TD><xsl:value-of select="title"/></TD>
<TD><xsl:value-of select="artist"/></TD>
</TR>
```

```
</xsl:for-each>
</TABLE>
</xsl:template>
</xsl:stylesheet>
```

You can link to XSL style sheets from XML documents using a processing instruction. For example:

```
<?xml-stylesheet href="CDstyle.xsl" type="text/xsl"?>
```

And you can use Cascading Style Sheets (CSS) to apply format to XML data. In that case, you would link to the style sheet using a processing instruction more like this one:

```
<?xml-stylesheet href="CDstyle.css" type="text/css"?>
```

Listing 1.8 shows a basic example of the template-driven transformation of XML data using XSL. The XSLT finds data that matches a pattern and inserts it into a point in a template. Pattern matching is a very important part of XSL. Take a look at the pattern being applied in the second part of this example:

```
<xsl:for-each select="library/cd">
```

This line will loop through each instance of the cd element inside of the library element. If you wanted to create a comma-separated list of the songs on each cd, you could create another loop inside of this loop, as in the following example:

```
...
<xsl:for-each select="library/cd">
<TR STYLE="font-family:Verdana; font-size:12pt; padding:0px 6px">
<TD><xsl:value-of select="title"/></TD>
<TD><xsl:value-of select="artist"/></TD>
<TD>
<xsl:for-each select="song">
    "<xsl:value-of select="title"/>"
<xsl:if test="context()[not(end())]">, </xsl:if>
</xsl:for-each>
</TD>
</TR>
</xsl:for-each>
...
```

When opened in a Web browser that supports XSL, the XML document will look like the example shown in Figure 1.1.

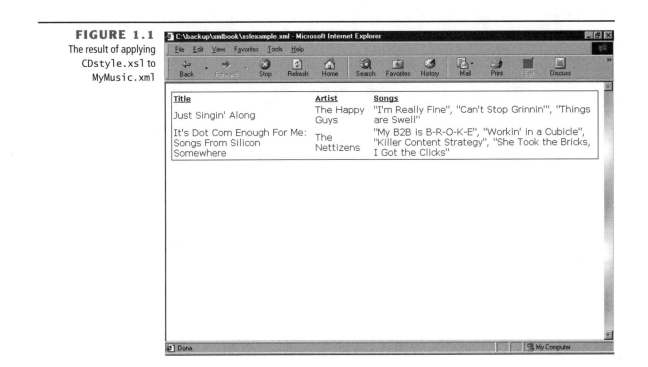

FIGURE 1.1
The result of applying
CDstyle.xsl to
MyMusic.xml

Using XML in Applications

In this book, we will use an XML database to store a product catalog for a fictitious store. Although we expect that accessing data directly from an XML data store is adequately fast for most applications of this program, this application's XML database could be imported into a high-performance relational database. Every major database vendor now provides, or has plans to provide, means for transferring data between a relational database and XML documents, and numerous third-party and other tools are also available. Data can easily be retrieved from any database and converted to XML for use by this application without having to modify the application. This is perhaps the biggest advantage of writing your application to use XML data: The use of a standard into which any type of data can be converted ensures that your application will be easily usable with legacy and future data.

Now that you are convinced that XML is the way to go for creating a catalog, let's look at the two approaches to writing Java programs that process XML.

The DOM and SAX Programming Models

The orientation of SGML is a complete document, so it is hardly surprising that XML started out thinking in Document Object Model (DOM) terms. All DOM processing assumes that you have read and parsed a complete document into memory so that all parts are equally accessible. This approach is shown symbolically in Figure 1.2.

FIGURE 1.2
Document Object Model
processing

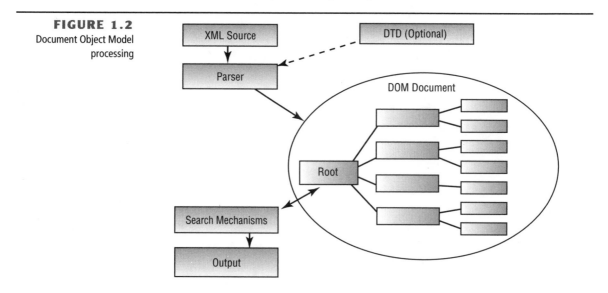

As people started programming with the DOM, it was found to be pretty clumsy if all you wanted to do was to pick out a few elements. Furthermore, the memory requirements could get restrictive, if not downright impossible. Thus, the Simplified API (application programming interface) for XML (SAX) was born of necessity. Both the DOM and SAX specify application programming interfaces that have been implemented in a number of languages in addition to Java.

As shown in Figure 1.3, a SAX parser makes a single pass through an XML file, reporting what it has parsed by calling various methods in your application code. The SAX documentation uses the term *event* for what happens when the parser decides it has identified an element in the XML document, so these methods are called *event handlers*. When the parser reaches the end of the document, the only data in memory is what your application saved.

As mentioned earlier, and as shown in Figures 1.2 and 1.3, the use of a DTD is optional in XML.

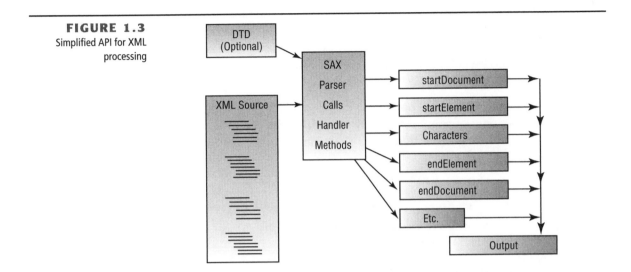

FIGURE 1.3
Simplified API for XML processing

Both models can be useful for servlet and JSP programming, as I demonstrate in upcoming examples. First, let's look at the Java tools for both DOM and SAX. These are tools for the "level 1" DOM and SAX version 1. Just to keep things complicated, SAX version 2 and DOM level 2 are in the works. By the time you read this, parsers implementing these new versions will probably be available.

Programming with the DOM

The definitive API for working with the Document Object Model is provided by the org.w3c .dom package, a recommendation of the World Wide Web Consortium. This API consists entirely of interface definitions plus a single exception class. The basic idea is that an XML document is turned into a DOM consisting of Java objects that implement these interfaces. Every part of the document becomes an object, and the connections between the objects reflect the hierarchy of the document.

Parsing XML to Create a DOM

From the programmer's standpoint, creating a DOM is simplicity itself because all the work is done by the parser. All the programmer has to do is create an input stream, select a parser, and stand back. Listing 1.9 shows a skeleton of a method to read from a file using utility classes from the com.sun.xml.parser package and to return a com.sun.xml.tree.XmlDocument object. The XmlDocument class implements the Document interface as specified in the W3C recommendation.

If you are using parser utilities from a different supplier, the names would be different but the general flow control would be similar. This particular example uses classes released by Sun as "Java API for XML Parsing" or JAXP and is currently used in the Tomcat servlet engine. However, note that the Tomcat project will eventually use whatever Sun's current parser is.

An astonishingly large number of different XML parsers have been created in the last few years, but only a few are completely compliant with the W3C DOM recommendations. The most recent compliance tests as of this writing indicate that the Sun parser has the highest compliance rating.

Listing 1.9: Skeleton of a Method to Create an XML Document

```
public XmlDocument exampleDOM(String src ) {
  File xmlFile = new File( src ) ;
  try {
    InputSource input = Resolver.createInputSource( xmlFile );
    // ... the "false" flag says not to validate
    XmlDocument doc = XmlDocument.createXmlDocument (input, false);
   return doc ;
  }catch(SAXParseException spe ){
    // handle parse exception here
  }catch( SAXException se ){
    // handle other SAX exceptions here
  }catch( IOException ie ){
    // handle IO exceptions here
  }
  return null ;
}
```

Once you have a DOM in memory, you manipulate it using methods provided in the DOM interface recommendation as embodied in the `org.w3c.dom` package plus additional methods as provided by the available toolkit.

Programming with SAX

The basic steps required to process an XML document with SAX can be summarized as:

- Create one or more custom classes to handle the events that the SAX parser detects
- Create an object to provide an input stream of characters

- Create a parser from one of the toolkits
- Attach the event-handling classes to the parser
- Attach the input stream to the parser, and start parsing
- Handle all of the events in your custom classes to capture the data you are interested in, to detect errors, and so on

As you can see, SAX processing of XML involves a programming philosophy that is completely different than using the DOM. Deciding which approach to use for a particular application is your most important design decision. Table 1.1 summarizes the important considerations.

TABLE 1.1: Comparison of DOM and SAX Programming

Programming Factor	DOM Style	SAX Style
Memory requirements	May be quite large	Only as large as the items retained in memory
Startup time	Slower because every element is parsed	Faster, especially if the elements of interest are easy to locate
Repeated search time	Faster because everything is in memory	Slower because every search involves a new parsing run
Modification capability	Very flexible	Limited to writing a new XML document with every pass

XML at a Glance

This section can be used as a guide to the most common rules of XML. For the complete XML specification, please visit www.w3c.org.

Well-Formedness Rules

- Each element must have a start tag and an end tag, except in the case of empty elements, which can use the empty-element syntax.
- The names of start tags and end tags must match. Remember that XML is case sensitive.
  - Incorrect: <Name></name>
  - Correct:
- Elements must be properly nested.
  - Incorrect: <p><b>some text</p></b>
  - Correct: <p><b>some text</b></p>
- Element names should not contain < or > and must start with a letter or underscore.

- Element names cannot start with the string xml (in any combination of upper or lower-case letters).

- Colons are forbidden in element names, unless you are using namespaces.

- No attribute may appear more than once in the same start tag or empty-element tag.

- Attribute values must be enclosed in quotes.

- Attribute values cannot contain direct or indirect entity references to external entities.

- The replacement text of any entity referred to directly or indirectly in an attribute value (other than <) must not contain a <.

Elements

Here we summarize XML elements and the way they are declared. This discussion includes usage and declaration syntax for elements.

Usage

Example elements:

```
<tag/>
<tag attribute="value" />
<tag attribute="value">some text</tag>
```

Element Declarations

Syntax:

```
<!ELEMENT elementname rule>
```

Element Types	Example Declaration
EMPTY	`<!ELEMENT url EMPTY>`
#PCDATA	`<!ELEMENT name #PCDATA>`
ANY	`<!ELEMENT contacts ANY>`
Mixed	`<!ELEMENT list (#PCDATA | item)*>`
Children	`<!ELEMENT co-worker (title, name, address)>`

Attributes

Here we summarize the format for attribute declarations. This discussion includes attribute syntax, type, declarations, and defaults.

Syntax:

```
<!ATTLIST target_element name type default_value ?>
```

Attribute	Types	Example Declaration
String	CDATA	`<!ATTLIST image url CDATA ?>`
Tokenized	ID	
	`<!ATTLIST id ID #REQUIRED ?>`	
	IDREF	
	IDREFS	
	ENTITY	
	ENTITIES	
	NMTOKEN	
	NMTOKENS	
Enumerated		`<!ATTLIST list type (ordered | bullet) "bullet" ?>`

Attribute Default	Definition
`#REQUIRED`	Every occurrence of the named element must have this attribute.
`#IMPLIED`	No default is specified.
`#FIXED`	The element must have this attribute, and the attribute value must be the value specified.

Entities

Here we summarize entity usage and declarations. This discussion includes usage examples, declaration information, and syntax.

Usage

Examples:

```
Copyright &copy; 2001 Sybex Inc.
while( a %lt; b ) // to present Java code in HTML
```

Entity Declarations

Syntax:

```
<!ENTITY name "replacement characters">
```

Type of Entity	Example	Description
General	`<!ENTITY publisher "Sybex">`	Can be used only in XML data
Parameter	`<!ENTITY %cdata "#CDATA">`	Can be used only in DTD
External	`<!ENTITY stockquotes SYSTEM "quotes.xml">`	Used for including external XML files
Unparsed	`<!ENTITY picture SYSTEM "picture.jpg" NDATA jpg>`	Used for including non-XML files

CHAPTER 2

A Catalog in XML

- Design an XML Document Type Definition

- See the process of constructing a product catalog using XML

- Create functional and flexible Document Type Definitions

- See examples of some of the problems, perils, and limitations of DTD design

In Chapter 1, you learned what XML is and how to create markup languages using XML. You now have the tools to create XML documents and DTDs. There is a big difference, however, between having the tools and knowing how to use them. As you know, learning to use a language takes hands-on experience.

To give you a good feel for the kinds of decisions that you'll need to make when designing XML documents and XML document types, this chapter walks through the entire process of creating an XML product catalog for a fictitious e-commerce company. Most aspects of how to do this are covered, including requirement gathering, DTD design, and the actual catalog creation.

What You Want from a Web Site

Our fictitious company, Xtreme Mega-Large Gifts (XMLGifts), is a retailer of rare musical recordings, books, and miscellaneous widgets. The market for the items sold by XMLGifts is extremely limited in the small town where the store is located. The owners of XMLGifts are certain, though, that people would buy these wares if only potential buyers knew about the products. Therefore, the company has decided to create a Web site called XMLGifts.com.

As with any project, the first and possibly most important step is information gathering. Therefore, the following section explores the requirements and constraints of creating such a Web site.

Site Requirements

High-level, or *business*, *requirements* are the overall objectives that XMLGifts.com has in developing its e-commerce Web site. Now that the decision has been made to create a Web site, these high-level requirements must be laid out clearly in a document describing the vision of management.

User requirements are the tasks that the user of the site should be able to accomplish. The business and user requirements for XMLGifts.com are as follows:

- People should be able to search an online catalog, add products to a shopping cart, and purchase items.
- The catalog must be easy to update and expand.
- The store should be able to handle moderate amounts of traffic. As the site grows, it should be possible to improve the site's performance and features without rebuilding the site.

- The site should support an affiliate program, where other sites can display information about and link to XMLGifts.com's products.

- The site must be built quickly to take advantage of the upcoming holiday shopping season.

- The site must contain ways for XMLGifts.com to get feedback from its customers, as well as to collect data about customers and products.

- Finally, all of this must be accomplished on a limited budget.

With these requirements in hand, and after thoroughly interviewing various people at the company, we can make a new list of more detailed functional requirements, as follows:

- Future additions and expansions will likely require that the site's user interface be redesigned and that the data source be modified. To make these changes as painless as possible, the site's business logic should be as independent as possible of both the data source and the presentation.

- The client does not want to be tied to any particular server platform or database. Currently, various operating systems and data formats are in use throughout the company. Like every company, XMLGifts.com has a long-term goal to tie all of these different data sources and applications together into some sort of comprehensive application that works without a lot of hassle.

- The catalog created for the store should be able to serve as a central database throughout the company. For example, it should be possible and fairly easy to generate the printed catalog from the same data source as the Web site.

- The site should have an easy-to-understand method for other Web sites to retrieve data from the catalog.

- A rather extensive database will be necessary to track customer information. The application should have a way to capture certain customer preferences. It must then be possible to generate reports and personalized content from the customer database and the product database.

Site Constraints

Perhaps more important than the requirements are the constraints: namely, the limited budget combined with a tight schedule. This situation occurs often enough in Web development that it merits a detailed discussion of the possible solutions.

A fundamental rule of the universe is that "faster, better, and cheaper" is *not* attainable. Most consultants and developers have learned this lesson the hard way. When clients are dead-set on having all three, it often means that the project is doomed to failure, or the consultant ends up doing more work for less money. To maximize this project's chances of success, the client is presented with the options covered in the following three sections, basically requiring them to pick one set of options to ensure success.

Pre-built Application (Faster-Cheaper)

Purchasing a pre-built e-commerce package and customizing it to your needs can sometimes save development time. More often than not, though, this method locks you into particular technologies and a shopping application that may work now but probably isn't exactly right for your site and may not scale up well.

If the site you're developing is a pretty standard store, and if the primary goal is to get it up and running as quickly as possible, this may be the way to go. Do your homework to make sure you're really getting something that will do the job. This is the *faster-cheaper* method.

WARNING If you're not careful when using this method, you'll end up attempting to modify or to tack on additions to make the pre-built application into what you need, and the project could end up costing more and taking longer than most other solutions.

Custom Built Using Standard Parts (Better-Cheaper)

Another way to develop a site is to do it from scratch. Although this method generally takes longer than simply purchasing a solution and customizing it, the functionality will be exactly what the client wants.

Because everything needed to program a site from the ground up is freely available, much more of the project's budget can be used to create exactly the functionality that the client desires. This method is called *better-cheaper*.

Web Application Server (Faster-Better)

To speed up development time while still having all of the benefits of a custom-built site, you could use a Web application server. Web application servers typically contain a set of pre-built objects for many of the most common tasks of Web application development. Your application can access these objects and other services provided by the application server. The services provided by application servers often include load balancing, data caching, scheduling and workflow tools, and server management tools.

This functionality often comes at a hefty price, and you'll likely end up paying for functionality you'll never use, though. This is the *faster-better* method.

Why Choose XML?

The dilemma developers frequently face is that the client cannot give in on *faster* or *cheaper* but still requires custom functionality that can't be provided using a pre-built application. In this case, it's up to the developer to figure out how to compromise on *better* while still meeting the client's needs.

One way to accomplish this is this: Don't build a system that is more robust than is needed today. The XMLGifts.com site, for example, is expected to have moderate traffic for the first year or so. Rather than building in functionality that will be needed later, you can just build the application they need now and provide ways to easily scale it up when it becomes necessary.

One result of this strategy is that the requirements and the client's expectations may need to be trimmed a bit, but the more important goals of staying within budget and delivering on time can be realized. If you remember that you can't have all three (faster, better, and cheaper) and you figure out where the compromise will be, your projects will stand a greater chance of success. If you build a Web application correctly, adding onto or expanding the site in the future should be easy.

After weighing the pros and cons of several different approaches, XMLGifts.com decided to write the business logic in Java and to use XML data. But, with a quick glance at the cover of this book, you probably could have guessed that this would be the approach.

NOTE   In the real world, unlike in this book, Java and XML will not always be the ideal solution. Weigh your priorities, requirements, and available resources carefully before deciding on the technologies to use for an application.

A few of the reasons for the company's decision are:

- Tool availability
- Tool flexibility
- Tool compatibility
- Unicode support

Each of these broad reasons is examined in more detail in the sections that follow.

Tool Availability

XML and Java have both benefited greatly, in terms of number of users and popularity, from being based upon open and freely available standards, which makes them somewhat of a natural match for each other.

A large number of inexpensive or free tools exist for developing Java applications that work with XML data. These tools include XML parsers, XML editors, XML validators, XML conversion tools, and XML middleware.

Until recently, the missing link between XML and Java was a standard for exchanging data among applications on the Internet using XML. Simple Object Access Protocol (SOAP) is changing that. With support from heavyweights such as Microsoft and IBM, SOAP is certainly generating quite a bit of excitement.

SOAP

SOAP is an XML-over-HTTP remote procedure protocol. It was submitted to the Worldwide Web Consortium (W3C) by DevelopMentor, Microsoft, and UserLand Software as an Internet Draft in December of 1999.

SOAP method requests are sent using HTTP POST requests. The SOAPMethodName HTTP header indicates the method you want to invoke. For example, the following header indicates the namespace of the method being invoked (sybex-com) and the name of the method (getPrice):

```
POST /xmlstore.jsp HTTP/1.1
Host: www.sybex.com
SOAPMethodName: urn:sybex-com:SybexStore#getPrice
Content-Type: text/xml
Content-Length: nnnn
```

The payload of a SOAP message is written in XML, as follows:

```
<?xml version='1.0'?>
<SOAP:Envelope
  xmlns:SOAP='urn:schemas-xmlsoap-org:soap.v1'>
  <SOAP:Body>
    <ns1:getPrice
      xmlns:ns1=' urn:sybex-com:SybexStore '>
      <ISBN>x-xxxx-xxxx-x</ISBN>
    </ns1:getPrice>
  </SOAP:Body>
</SOAP:Envelope>
```

This request simply sends all of the data necessary to invoke the method. Note that the first element inside of SOAP:Body must have a namespace-qualified tag name that is identical to the SOAPMethodName in the header.

If everything goes right (the method requested actually exists and the remote server accepts SOAP requests), some action will be taken. Once the requested action has been completed, an HTTP response will be sent back to the client.

SOAP is not yet an official W3C recommendation, but if you wish to begin working with it today, IBM and DevlopMentor have created Java libraries that implement SOAP. IBM has turned its reference implementation over to the Apache Organization for open source development (http://xml.apache.org/soap/index.html). You can also download the Develop-Mentor version in both Perl and Java from www.develop.com/SOAP.

Tool Flexibility

Although our store's data is initially stored in XML documents, it could be stored in a binary relational or object database to improve performance and then be converted to XML as it is requested by the application.

Various middleware applications exist for just this purpose. The higher-end XML data servers provide features such as caching, replication, and load balancing. XML servers are typically Java applications that can use data from any data source for which you have a Java Database Connectivity (JDBC) driver.

Both XML and Java are *portable standards*. This means that the underlying platform does not matter. With the application layer written in Java, it can run on any Java virtual machine. An application that uses XML data can easily interface with any type of data source. If you need to change the data source of an XML application, it won't require changes to the application.

Tool Compatibility

Developing in Java and XML makes it possible to easily create relationships with other stores and Web sites. Any relationship or data transfer between Web sites is a messaging problem. You do not want to give anyone else access to your database, but at the same time, you need to give them data they can understand.

Many so-called affiliate programs today work by requiring the consumer application (the affiliated site) to fetch HTML code from the provider. The downside of this is that the for-matting of the information is preset. By using XML data, the consumer can format the data any way they please. The more important advantage to using XML data for sharing information between sites is that XML, unlike HTML, can be reliably parsed and used by the consumer application for more than just displaying information.

Unicode Support

XMLGifts.com would like to eventually publish its catalog in several languages. XML and Java's built-in support for Unicode will help to make this job easier.

As Web site developers continue to become more concerned with creating content and user interfaces that aren't language specific, Unicode support will become an increasingly important feature for any Internet technology. Unicode support has been added to other popular Web programming languages, such as Perl and Tcl. Because Java was designed with Unicode support from the ground up, processing international characters does not add any complexity to applications, as it might with other platforms.

The Product Catalog and DTDs

Once the requirements have been gathered and analyzed and the decision to use XML has been made, the next steps in creating the XML catalog are to examine the existing data and to convert it to a usable format.

At the beginning of the project, XMLGifts.com's catalog is stored as a spreadsheet. A portion of this spreadsheet is shown in Table 2.1.

TABLE 2.1: A Sampling of XMLGifts.com's Catalog

SKU	Product Name	Description	Category	Price	Quantity in Stock	Author
bk0022	*Guide to Plants*	Everything you've ever wanted to know about plants.	Books	$12.99	4	William Smith
cd0024	*Just Singin' Along*	A lovely collection of songs that the whole family can sing right along with.	CDs	$10.00	100	
Wz0027	Percussive Interface Unit	Communicate with your favorite electric calculating machine— through tapping!	Widgets	$109.99	7	

From our experience, this type of data store is typical of many brick-and-mortar businesses that are just starting to develop an online presence. The actual spreadsheet may go on for quite a while to the right of what we can show here, but the point is that the catalog has one product per line, and a column for every possible piece of data that anyone might need to know about a product. This type of single-table organization of an entire catalog is usually the result of a product line that has grown faster than the technical skills of the staff. Needless to say, it needs an overhaul. The next decision to be made is how to best organize this data.

Organizing Your Data

Tables are perhaps the most common way to organize data. Storing data in rows and columns provides great flexibility to create views and relationships. A single table, though, is a very inefficient way to organize data.

If a relational database were to be used for the shopping application in our example, the first step in improving the data model would be to create a table for each product line. This would help to eliminate the obvious waste that is caused by product line–specific information, such as author. Still, if one book had an editor but no author listed, another field would have to be added to the database for this single book. If another book were to have more than one author, you would need to either create another field, perhaps called `author2`, or create a separate table for authors.

Figure 2.1 is one way that the relationships between these tables could be shown.

FIGURE 2.1
Diagram of relationships between tables

Figure 2.2 shows a portion of the previous figure with some of the field names from the `authors` table added in.

FIGURE 2.2
Relationships between tables and fields

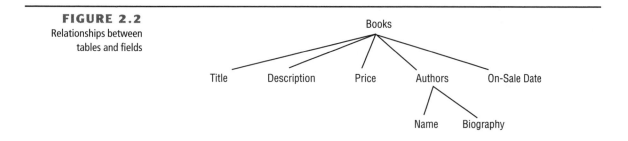

In Figure 2.3, we've added in some actual values and organized the data as an outline.

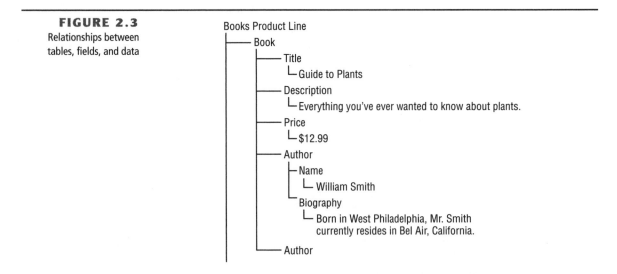

FIGURE 2.3
Relationships between tables, fields, and data

Does everything in the three previous figures look familiar? These diagrams show a relational database as hierarchical data. *Hierarchical data structures*, such as those that are created using XML, are very good for organizing data because they have a single point of view. For example, in Figure 2.3, everything is shown as it relates to the Books product line. The single point under which everything else is organized in an XML document is called the *root element*. Remember that every XML document must have a root element.

Whereas relational databases use key fields to create relationships, markup languages show relationships using nesting. For example, the author of a book can be shown by nesting an Author element inside of a Book element.

Relationships and semantics that would be very complex to show using a relational database can be shown easily and intuitively using markup. Here is a piece of well-formed XML that shows the same information as Figure 2.3:

```
<Products>
<Book>
    <Title>Guide to Plants</Title>
    <Description>Everything you've ever wanted to know about plants.
  </Description>
    <Price>$12.99</Price>
    <Author>
```

```
  <Name>William Smith</Name>
      <Biography>Born in West Philadelphia, Mr. Smith currently resides in
Bel Air, California.
      </Biography>
    </Author>
  </Book>
</Products>
```

As shown in the preceding example, relational data can often be converted to XML by declaring a root element that has the same name as the database, then creating elements from the table names and mapping the columns of each table as children of those elements.

Converting from relational databases to XML does not have to be done manually, though. A large number of tools exist for this purpose as well as for converting in the other direction (from XML to tables).

You can also automate the process by using SQL queries. The basic method for converting tabular data to hierarchical data is to use a SQL outer join. An *outer join* merges two tables while preserving all of the data from only one of them. The resulting table shows the two tables from the point of view of one of the input tables. For example, assume that we have two tables, Books and Author. To create a hierarchical view of this relational data, you can use something like the following SQL statement:

```
SELECT *
FROM Books LEFT JOIN Authors ON [Authors].[Book_ID]=[Books].[ID];
```

This SQL statement will merge the Books and Authors tables while preserving all of the rows from the Books table, even when there is no matching record in Authors. Because this is a view of Books, rows from the Authors table that are not associated with any records from Books will not be selected. The resulting table shows the data from the point of view of Books, as shown in Table 2.2.

TABLE 2.2: The Books View

Book Title	Author Name
For Whom the Bell Tolls	Ernest Hemingway
Java Developer's Guide to E-Commerce with XML and JSP	William Brogden
	Chris Minnick
Crime and Punishment	Fyodor Dostoyevsky

To convert this table to XML data, you can simply make each column a child of a Book element, as shown in Listing 2.1.

**Listing 2.1: The Relational Books Database Converted to an XML Document
(*BookView.xml*)**

```
<BookView>
  <Book>
      <Title>For Whom the Bell Tolls</Title>
      <Author>
      <Name> Ernest Hemingway</Name>
      </Author>
  </Book>
  <Book>
      <Title>Java Developer's Guide to E-Commerce with XML and JSP</Title>
      <Author>
      <Name>William Brogden</Name>
      </Author>
      <Author>
      <Name>Chris Minnick</Name>
      </Author>
  </Book>
  <Book>
      <Title>Crime and Punishment</Title>
      <Author>
      <Name> Fyodor Dostoyevsky</Name>
      </Author>
  </Book>
</BookView>
```

Writing a DTD

Regardless of how you convert data into XML, the process of writing a DTD (Document
Type Definition) is certain to give you valuable insight into potential problems with the data.
A DTD will also specifically define how elements in the catalog in our example are related to
each other and make it possible to enforce the validity of data that is added to the catalog in
the future.

One way to create a DTD is to start with a well-formed XML document and derive a DTD
from it. To create a DTD from an XML document, simply step through the document and
create declarations for each piece of markup you encounter. This process can be (more or
less) automated. This method is often a good start, but the resulting DTD will not be as logical or as useful as a DTD that is crafted from the ground up and based on extensive research.

Another method for designing a DTD is to write the DTD before writing any XML documents. This method is a more formal way of designing DTDs and requires careful planning. If you're starting from scratch, with no existing data to be converted, this could be the way to go.

Most often, though, you'll write DTDs using a combination of these two methods. For example, if we wanted to write a DTD for my interoffice memos, we might start by looking at a typical memo and marking it up as XML, as follows:

```
<memo>
    <from>Chris Minnick</from>
    <to>Staff</to>
    <body>Take the day off. Go to the lake.</body>
</memo>
```

A DTD for this simple document might look like this:

```
<!ELEMENT memo (from,to,body)>
<!ELEMENT from (#PCDATA)>
<!ELEMENT to (#PCDATA)>
<!ELEMENT body (#PCDATA)>
```

Revising Your DTD

After examining this DTD, its inadequacies become apparent, and we realize that some revisions are in order. The first problem is that there is no way to uniquely identify this memo. Second, we probably should specify more specifically what can be contained in the From and To elements. Third, there are occasions when memos are sent from more than one person or to multiple people. After thinking about the types of memos that are actually sent in the office, we've changed the DTD into the one shown in Listing 2.2.

Listing 2.2: An Improved DTD for Memos (*memo.dtd*)

```
<!ELEMENT memo (from, to, cc?, body)>
<!ATTLIST memo
  id ID #REQUIRED
  date CDATA #REQUIRED
    subject CDATA #IMPLIED>
<!ELEMENT from (name,department)*>
<!ELEMENT to (name,department)*>
<!ELEMENT cc (name,department)*>
```

```
<!ELEMENT name (#PCDATA)>
<!ELEMENT department (#PCDATA)>
<!ELEMENT body (#PCDATA,important_part?)>
<!ELEMENT important_part (#PCDATA)>
```

Using this DTD, anyone at XMLGifts.com (or any XML-enabled application) can know exactly what is meant by the word "memo." Listing 2.3 shows a well-formed and valid memo.

Listing 2.3: A Well-Formed and Valid Memo (*memoexample1.xml*)

```
<?xml version="1.0" standalone="no"?>
<!DOCTYPE memo SYSTEM "memo.dtd">
<memo id = "cm0001"
date = "8/2/2000"
subject = "your task for today">
    <from>
    <name>Chris Minnick</name>
    </from>
    <to>
      <department>All</department>
    </to>
    <body>
  Congratulations on the completion of the XMLGifts.com project.
Let's <important_part>take the day off and go to the lake</important_part>.
    </body>
</memo>
```

This method of looking at a sample of existing data and then revising the DTD for possible future needs is the one we will use for XMLGifts.com.

Listing 2.4 shows a first draft XML document describing a few products from the XMLGifts .com catalog. The XML in Listing 2.4 was written without a DTD. It is well formed, but because it does not conform to any DTD yet, it is not valid and is not self-describing.

Listing 2.4: A First Draft Attempt to Describe Products

```
<?xml version="1.0"?>

<catalog>
<product_line name="Books">
```

```
<product id="bk0022">
<name>Guide to Plants</name>
<description>Everything you've ever wanted to know about plants.
</description>
<price>$12.99</price>
<quantity_in_stock>4</quantity_in_stock>
<image width="234" height="400"
src="images/covers/plants.gif">
<caption>
This is the cover from the first edition.
</caption>
</image>
<onsale_date>12/23/1999</onsale_date>
</product>

<product id="bk0035">
<name>Writing Fake Catalogs</name>
<description>Chris Minnick's latest book explains, in agonizing detail,
 the process of thinking up fake products for a demonstration catalog.
</description>
<price>$59.95</price>
<quantity_in_stock>30</quantity_in_stock>
<onsale_date>09/01/2000</onsale_date>
</product>

</product_line>

<product_line name="CDs">

<product id="cd0024">
<name>Just Singin' Along</name>
<description>A lovely collection of songs that the whole family can sing
right along with.</description>
<price>$10.00</price>
<quantity_in_stock>100</quantity_in_stock>
<onsale_date>2/23/2000</onsale_date>
</product>

<product id="cd0025">
<name>It's Dot Com Enough for Me: Songs from Silicon Somewhere</name>
```

```
<description>A collection of the best folk music from Internet companies.
</description>
<clip format="mp3" length="4.32" size="4.0 Mb"
src="track2.mp3">
<title>Track 2: My B2B Is B-R-O-K-E</title>
</clip>
<onsale_date>4/12/2000</onsale_date>
</product>

</product_line>

<product_line name="widgets">

<product id="wi0026">
<name>ElectroThermal Oxidizor</name>
<description>This amazing gizmo uses electricity to produce heat that
can be used for oxidization purposes.</description>
<price>$24.95</price>
<quantity_in_stock>10</quantity_in_stock>
<image width="200" height="200" src="/images/toaster.gif">
</image>
<onsale_date>6/2/2000</onsale_date>
</product>

<product id="wz0027">
<name>Percusive Interface Unit</name>
<description>Communicate with your favorite electric calculating machine--
 through tapping!</description>
<price>$109.99</price>
<quantity_in_stock>7</quantity_in_stock>
<onsale_date>6/23/2001</onsale_date>
</product>

</product_line>
</catalog>
```

Creating a First-Draft DTD

To create a rough first draft of a DTD to define the class of data to which the preceding XML document belongs, we used the CLIP! XML Editor from Techno2000USA, Inc. This editor has the handy capability to create a DTD from a well-formed XML document. The DTD in Listing 2.5 is the result. Many XML editors can be used to automate the process of creating the first draft of a DTD. XML Spy (available at www.xmlspy.com), for example, can generate a DTD (as well as several other types of XML schemas) from any well-formed document. Unfortunately, this editor is no longer available commercially.

Listing 2.5: The First Draft DTD

```
<!ELEMENT catalog (product_line)* >
<!ELEMENT product_line (product)* >
<!ATTLIST product_line
name CDATA #IMPLIED>
<!ELEMENT product
(name|description|price|quantity_in_stock|image|onsale_date|clip)* >
<!ATTLIST product
id CDATA #IMPLIED>
<!ELEMENT name (#PCDATA)* >
<!ELEMENT description (#PCDATA)* >
<!ELEMENT price (#PCDATA)* >
<!ELEMENT quantity_in_stock (#PCDATA)* >
<!ELEMENT image (caption)* >
<!ATTLIST image
width CDATA #IMPLIED>
<!ATTLIST image
height CDATA #IMPLIED>
<!ATTLIST image
src CDATA #IMPLIED>
<!ELEMENT caption (#PCDATA)* >
<!ELEMENT onsale_date (#PCDATA)* >
<!ELEMENT clip (title)* >
<!ATTLIST clip
format CDATA #IMPLIED>
<!ATTLIST clip
length CDATA #IMPLIED>
<!ATTLIST clip
size CDATA #IMPLIED>
<!ATTLIST clip
src CDATA #IMPLIED>
<!ELEMENT title (#PCDATA)* >
```

Refining the First Draft

The preceding DTD accurately describes the XML document, but it's also very vague. To make the DTD more accurately reflect the reality of our product catalog, we'll need to tighten it up a bit. Let's step through this DTD in the next several sections and make improvements and modifications as we go.

The *catalog, product_line,* and *product* Elements

The first element declaration is for the root element, `catalog`.

```
<!ELEMENT catalog (product_line)* >
```

This declaration is straightforward enough: It says that a `catalog` consists of any number of `product_line` elements.

The `product_line` element is similarly simple, but it also has an attribute called `name`.

```
<!ELEMENT product_line (product)* >
<!ATTLIST product_line
name CDATA #IMPLIED>
```

The declaration for the `name` attribute of `product_line` indicates that this attribute is implied, meaning that it's not required. Because knowing that a `product` belongs to a `product_line` is not useful unless we know which product line it belongs to, we will make the `name` attribute required. This is a simple enough change, as follows:

```
<!ATTLIST product_line
name CDATA #REQUIRED>
```

The next element declaration is the real meat of this DTD:

```
<!ELEMENT product (name|description|price|quantity_in_stock|photo|
onsale_date|clip)* >
```

As it stands, this declaration says that a `product` may contain any number of any of the enumerated elements. This rule does not jive with XMLGifts.com's actual catalog. Also, we neglected to account for the authors of books or for CDs whose artist will be listed. This sort of major oversight can often happen if you don't use a large enough sample of the data you're creating a Document Type Definition for. The final `product` element declaration looks like this:

```
<!ELEMENT product name,author*,artist*,
description,price,quantity_in_stock,image*,
onsale_date?,clip*>
```

NOTE Notice in this revised product element declaration that only one `name`, `description`, `price`, and `quantity_in_stock` are permitted per `product`. Note also that each of these elements is also required. Also notice we've renamed `photo` as `image` to be more general.

Although this `product` declaration is not perfect and probably doesn't account for every possible product, it is a good start. Because this DTD is being designed for a very specific purpose, and not as a general purpose DTD, we can afford to come back and revise the DTD as the catalog changes. It is always preferable, and easier in fact, to start with a broad Document Type Definition and add elements to it as they are needed. This method is called *additive refinement*. The opposite method of revising a DTD, by removing declarations, is referred to as *subtractive refinement*.

After the `product` element is defined, the DTD goes on to define `product`'s `id` attribute.

```
<!ATTLIST product
id CDATA #IMPLIED>
```

As with `product_line`'s `name` attribute, our application must have a unique `id` for each product, so we'll make this attribute required. Also, this attribute should use the ID type to ensure that the value of each product's `id` attribute will be unique. The rewritten `product id` attribute looks like this:

```
<!ATTLIST product
id ID #REQUIRED>
```

Besides being able to identify a product by its unique `id`, we also want to be able to find products by keywords. To help facilitate this, we'll add another attribute, `keywords`, to the `product` element.

```
<!ATTLIST product
keywords CDATA #IMPLIED>
```

Our idea for the `keywords` attribute is that its value will be a comma-separated list that can be used for searching and categorizing the products.

The *description*, *paragraph*, and *general* Elements

The next part of the DTD defines each of `product`'s child elements. The child of the product element called `name` may currently contain any type of parsed character data, which will work fine for our purposes. The `description` element is defined the same way. A product's `description` is intended to be read primarily by humans, but it also may contain a certain amount of data that we would like to make use of programmatically.

To make `description`'s content easier to read and to apply styles to at a later point, we should provide a way to divide the `description` into paragraphs that can contain elements to show bolded text, italicized text, and so forth. The first step is to allow the `description` element to contain `paragraph` elements and to define a `paragraph`, as follows:

```
<!ELEMENT description (paragraph*)>
<!ELEMENT paragraph (#PCDATA|bold|italics|quote|link)*>
<!ELEMENT bold #PCDATA>
<!ELEMENT italics #PCDATA>
<!ELEMENT quote #PCDATA>
<!ATTLIST quote
attrib CDATA #IMPLIED>
<!ELEMENT link (#PCDATA)>
<!ATTLIST link
href CDATA #REQUIRED
alt CDATA #IMPLIED>
```

There is a good chance that the same list of text-markup elements used by `paragraph` will be used elsewhere in the DTD (for example, in a `title` or a `footnote` element). To reduce typing and complexity, we'll declare a `parameter` entity with this list of text-markup elements, as follows:

```
<!ENTITY % running_text "(#PCDATA|bold|italics|quote|link)*">
```

> **TIP**
>
> Remember that entities are simply stand-ins for their replacement value and that both kinds of entities, general and parameter, must be declared before they are used. Because `parameter` entities are used only in the DTD, it is customary to group them together at the beginning of DTDs. Putting this `parameter` entity declaration at the beginning of the DTD in our example will also make it easier to find if we should need to add a type of markup to `paragraph` in the future.

Once this parameter entity is in place, the `paragraph` tag declaration can be rewritten:

```
<!ELEMENT paragraph %running_text;>
```

If used correctly, a `parameter` entity can increase the readability of a DTD and encourage reuse. But be careful! Just as you should avoid making elements unnecessarily complex, you also should resist the urge to overuse `parameter` entities. If used excessively or incorrectly, `parameter` entities can decrease the readability of a DTD.

Our second goal in revising the `description` element is to be able to extract meaningful data from descriptions programmatically. To achieve this, we must be allowed to use other elements inside of description. For example, suppose that we have the following description element in our catalog:

```
<description>
<paragraph>Sounding like a cross between Iggy Pop and the Spice Girls, this
hot new band from Belgium is taking the world by storm.</paragraph>
</description>
```

It would be nice if our schema made it possible for the application to use the various pieces of data in that description to link to related products. The problem that we encounter at this point is that there are thousands of types of data that can be included in a description. We could try to create a detailed list of possible pieces of data that could be in a description, but this would create an enormous element declaration that would be flawed from the start and would just confuse whoever is marking up the description.

A good work-around for this problem is to use a generic and meaningless element with an attribute called type. By putting identifying information in the value of the attribute, we can give maximum flexibility to the author and the person who marks up the description element, as in the following:

```
<!ELEMENT general #PCDATA>
<!ATTLIST general
type CDATA #REQUIRED>
```

Using the general element and the paragraph element, our example description can now be marked up for human as well as for machine interpretation.

```
<description>
<paragraph>Sounding like a cross between
<general type="artist">Iggy Pop</general> and
<general type = "artist">the Spice Girls</general>, this hot new band from
<general type="country">Belgium</general> is taking the world by storm.
</paragraph>
</description>
```

An application can then fairly easily convert elements with the general type into name-value pairs.

After all of that, the description element declaration and its children look like the following:

```
<!ELEMENT description (paragraph|general)* >
<!ELEMENT paragraph %running_text;>
<!ELEMENT bold #PCDATA>
```

```
<!ELEMENT italics #PCDATA>
<!ELEMENT quote #PCDATA>
<!ATTLIST quote
attrib CDATA #IMPLIED>
<!ELEMENT link (#PCDATA)>
<!ATTLIST link
href CDATA #REQUIRED
alt CDATA #IMPLIED>
<!ELEMENT general #PCDATA>
<!ATTLIST general
type CDATA #REQUIRED>
```

The *price, quantity_in_stock,* and *image* Elements

The next element to be declared is `price`. It would be nice if prices were as simple as the current DTD makes them out to be.

```
<!ELEMENT price (#PCDATA)*>
```

The truth, though, is that there cannot be just one simple price. Various products have various discount amounts in the real world, and products, or categories of products, are sometimes on sale. To accommodate discounts, we'll need to add an attribute called `discount` onto the price element.

```
<!ELEMENT price #PCDATA>
<!ATTLIST price
discount CDATA #IMPLIED>
```

Our catalog database does not need to account for how a user got a discount (whether by being part of a group or through a sale). These factors will be controlled by the application and the customer database. Discounts given to specific customers or groups of customers will be stored in the customer information database.

All that our `price` element needs to be concerned with is how much an item costs. Because there is no way to specify the data type of an element in a standard DTD, the application will be responsible for making sure that only valid prices are entered into the price field.

The next element in our DTD, `quantity_in_stock`, doesn't need much modification.

```
<!ELEMENT quantity_in_stock (#PCDATA)*>
```

With the elimination of the superfluous asterisk, this element should be just fine.

```
<!ELEMENT quantity_in_stock (#PCDATA)>
```

The `image` element will not actually contain images. XML documents, being simply text files, cannot easily contain binary data. Instead, it is much simpler (and much more compact) for the `image` element and its sub-elements to just provide an address and other information about an image, as follows:

```
<!ELEMENT image (caption)>
<!ATTLIST image
width CDATA #IMPLIED>
<!ATTLIST image
height CDATA #IMPLIED>
<!ATTLIST image
src CDATA #IMPLIED>
<!ELEMENT caption (#PCDATA)*>
```

Some of the products in XMLGifts.com's catalog do not have images at all. In cases in which a picture of a product is not available, many online stores will display a default image indicating that the image is not available. We could code this rule into our DTD at this point by using a default value for the `src` attribute. After considering this possibility for a moment, though, XMLGifts.com has decided in favor of just handling this bit of logic in the application if it becomes necessary. The reason for this is that a default "image not available" image really doesn't contain any data about a product. This image is typically used in online catalogs just to keep the design from falling apart if no image is present. Because it's more closely related to presentation than to actual product description, the default-image rule has no place in a DTD.

Although products are not required to have images, if an `image` element is present it must have an `src` attribute, and it can optionally have a caption.

```
<!ELEMENT image (caption?)>
<!ATTLIST image
width CDATA #IMPLIED>
<!ATTLIST image
height CDATA #IMPLIED>
<!ATTLIST image
src CDATA #REQUIRED>
<!ELEMENT caption (#PCDATA)>
```

One addition to the `image` element that needs to be made is a way to specify the format of the image. To make sure that product images are in a format that can be displayed by most Web browsers, we will limit the possible formats. We've decided that the allowed image formats will be GIF, PNG, and JPG. The format limitations can be written in the following new attribute:

```
<!ATTLIST image
format (gif|png|jpg) #REQUIRED>
```

The `image` element now has one child and four attributes, two of which, `src` and `format`, are required.

The image's caption may contain only character data. This seems like a perfect opportunity to reuse the `paragraph` element that we created for the `description` element.

```
<!ELEMENT caption (paragraph*)>
```

Although the `image` element and its children don't actually contain an image, they do provide all of the information that our application will need to use images of products.

```
<!ELEMENT image (caption?)>
<!ATTLIST image format (gif|png|jpg) #REQUIRED
    width CDATA #IMPLIED
    height CDATA #IMPLIED
    src CDATA #REQUIRED>
<!ELEMENT caption (paragraph*) >
```

The *onsale_date*, *time*, *clip*, and *title* Elements

The next element declared in the DTD is `onsale_date`. The primary purpose of this element is to allow us to enter products into the database before we actually begin selling them. Other uses for this element may appear in the future. For example, we may want to give the user the option of viewing new products, or we may use the on-sale date in preparing sales reports for internal use.

As discussed in Chapter 1, "XML for Data Description," there is no way to specify in a DTD that an element must contain a date. You can, however, create several child elements of the `onsale_date` element to more clearly explain what type of data is expected and to make the date more flexible, as follows:

```
<!ELEMENT onsale_date
(day_of_week?,month?,day_of_month?,year?,(hour,minute, seconds?)?)>
<!ELEMENT day_of_week (#PCDATA)>
<!ELEMENT month (#PCDATA)>
<!ELEMENT day_of_month (#PCDATA)>
<!ELEMENT year (#PCDATA)>
<!ELEMENT hour (#PCDATA)>
```

```
<!ELEMENT minute (#PCDATA)>
<!ELEMENT seconds (#PCDATA)>
```

Things are starting to get a little complicated here. What this declaration says is that each of onsale_date's child elements can occur zero or one times. The time elements are optional, but both hour and minute must occur if the time elements are used. Another improvement we can make here is to define a parameter entity for the date-time rule so we can reuse it in other elements.

```
<!ENTITY % date_time
"(day_of_week?,month?,day_of_month?,year?,(hour,minute, seconds?)?)">
<!ELEMENT onsale_date %date_time;>
```

For our application to be able to give the shopper samples from music recordings, our original XML document and its generated DTD uses the clip element. The idea behind this element is that it functions similarly to the image element: It simply provides a reference to multimedia files that are stored outside of the XML database.

```
<!ELEMENT clip (title)* >
<!ATTLIST clip
format CDATA #IMPLIED>
<!ATTLIST clip
length CDATA #IMPLIED>
<!ATTLIST clip
size CDATA #IMPLIED>
<!ATTLIST clip
src CDATA #IMPLIED>
<!ELEMENT title (#PCDATA)* >
```

You may notice that title is defined as an element whereas format, length, size, and src are attributes. A good argument could also be made for making title an attribute. Our rationale for writing the document this way is that format, length, size, and src are all primarily used by the application, while title is meant to be read by humans. It's also a matter of consistency: In the image element, caption was defined as an element.

As with previous element declarations in this DTD, several changes can be made to make clip, its attributes, and its children more specific. The first is to change the rule for the clip element itself. Although it's understandable that there would be multiple clips per product, we can't think of any time we would need to have multiple titles for any one clip. We can rewrite the clip element declaration to reflect this, as follows:

```
<!ELEMENT clip (title)>
```

In addition, there may be times when a particular media clip will need some explanation. We can allow the `clip` element to contain a description for this purpose.

```
<!ELEMENT clip (title,description?)>
```

As with `image`'s `format` attribute, `clip`'s `format` attribute should also only allow certain values.

```
<!ATTLIST clip
format (mp3|mpeg|mov|rm) #REQUIRED>
```

The `src` attribute of `clip` should also be required. The `length` and `size` attributes can be left pretty much as they are for now. We don't imagine that we'll be doing too much with `length` and `size` at first, except for displaying their values next to the link to the media file. There's really not much that we can do in terms of specifying units or constraints for these fields anyway. We'll let the application handle the validation for these attributes.

The *shipping* Element

Finally, we need an element to describe the shipping requirements for each product. Although our initial catalog is mostly made up of items typically shipped by parcel services, we need to make this element open-ended in case we get into electronic distribution or are sending unique items for which special arrangements must be made.

```
<!ELEMENT shipping_info >
<!ATTLIST shipping_info
type CDATA #REQUIRED>
<!ATTLIST shipping_info
value CDATA #IMPLIED>
```

Rather than supplying a weight for each item, we have chosen the more general term `value`. This can easily be applied to different types of distribution; for example, if we start selling downloadable electronic books, value could supply the size in megabytes.

The Final Version

After all of these changes have been made to the first draft, we are ready to finalize the `catalog.dtd` file and create a `catalog.xml` example. It looks quite a bit different from the first draft, and is (we hope) much better suited to our needs. Listing 2.6 shows the latest version of our DTD.

Listing 2.6: The Revised *catalog.dtd*

```
<!ENTITY % running_text "(#PCDATA|bold|italics|quote|link|general)*">
<!ENTITY % date_time "(day_of_week?,month?,day_of_month?,year?,
(hour,minute,seconds?)?)">
<!ELEMENT catalog (product_line*) >
<!ELEMENT product_line (product*) >
<!ATTLIST product_line
name CDATA #IMPLIED>
<!ELEMENT product (name,author*,artist*,description,price,
quantity_in_stock,image*,onsale_date?,clip*)>
<!ATTLIST product
    id ID #REQUIRED>
<!ELEMENT name (#PCDATA)>
<!ELEMENT author (name)>
<!ELEMENT artist (name)>
<!ELEMENT description (paragraph|general)* >
<!ELEMENT paragraph %running_text;>
<!ELEMENT bold (#PCDATA)>
<!ELEMENT italics (#PCDATA)>
<!ELEMENT quote (#PCDATA)>
<!ATTLIST quote
    attrib CDATA #IMPLIED>
<!ELEMENT link (#PCDATA)>
<!ATTLIST link
    href CDATA #REQUIRED
    alt CDATA #IMPLIED>
<!ELEMENT general (#PCDATA)>
<!ATTLIST general
    type CDATA #REQUIRED>
<!ELEMENT price (#PCDATA)>
<!ATTLIST price
    discount CDATA #IMPLIED>
<!ELEMENT quantity_in_stock (#PCDATA)>
<!ELEMENT image (caption?)>
<!ATTLIST image format (gif|png|jpg) #REQUIRED
    width CDATA #IMPLIED
    height CDATA #IMPLIED
    src CDATA #REQUIRED>
<!ELEMENT caption (paragraph)* >
```

```
<!ELEMENT onsale_date %date_time;>
<!ELEMENT day_of_week (#PCDATA)>
<!ELEMENT month (#PCDATA)>
<!ELEMENT day_of_month (#PCDATA)>
<!ELEMENT year (#PCDATA)>
<!ELEMENT hour (#PCDATA)>
<!ELEMENT minute (#PCDATA)>
<!ELEMENT seconds (#PCDATA)>
<!ELEMENT clip (title,description?)>
<!ATTLIST clip
    format (mp3|mpeg|mov|rm) #REQUIRED
    length CDATA #IMPLIED
    size CDATA #IMPLIED
    src CDATA #REQUIRED>
<!ELEMENT title (#PCDATA)>
```

Listing 2.7 shows a well-formed and valid document that uses `catalog.dtd`. This is a sub-set of the complete example `catalog.xml` file that you will find on the CD.

Listing 2.7: An Example *catalog.xml*

```
<?xml version="1.0" standalone="no"?>
<!DOCTYPE catalog SYSTEM "catalog.dtd">

<!-- Begin Catalog -->

<catalog>

<!-- Book Product Line -->

  <product_line name="Books">


  <product id="bk0022" keywords="gardening, plants">
  <name>Guide to Plants</name>
  <description>
  <paragraph>
  <italics>Everything</italics> you've ever wanted to know about plants.
  </paragraph>
  </description>
```

```
 <price>$12.99</price>
 <quantity_in_stock>4</quantity_in_stock>
 <image format="gif" width="234" height="400" src="images/covers/plants.gif">[
   <caption>
    <paragraph>This is the cover from the first edition.</paragraph>
    </caption>
  </image>
 <onsale_date>
<month>4</month>
<day_of_month>4</day_of_month>
<year>1999</year>
</onsale_date>
 <shipping_info type="UPS" value="1.0" />
</product>
<product id="bk0023" keywords="gardening, plants">
 <name>Guide To Plants, Volume 2</name>
 <description>
<paragraph>Everything else you've ever wanted to know about plants.
</paragraph>
</description>
 <price>$12.99</price>
 <quantity_in_stock>4</quantity_in_stock>
 <image format="gif" width="234" height="400"
     src="images/covers/plantsv2.gif">
    <caption>
    <paragraph>This is the cover from the first edition.</paragraph>
    </caption>
  </image>
 <onsale_date>
<month>4</month>
<day_of_month>8</day_of_month>
<year>2000</year>
</onsale_date>
 </product>
<product id="bk0024" keywords="how-to, technology">
 <name>The Genius's Guide to the 3rd Millenium</name>
 <author><name>Christoph Minwich</name></author>
  <description><paragraph>Learn to convert your replicator into a
transporter...and other neat tricks.</paragraph></description>
  <price>$59.95</price>
```

```
<quantity_in_stock>0</quantity_in_stock>
<image format="gif" width="234" height="400"
src="images/covers/millenium.gif">
</image>
<onsale_date>
<month>1</month>
<day_of_month>1</day_of_month>
<year>2001</year>
</onsale_date>
</product>
<product id="bk0025" keywords="how-to, art">
<name>Dryer Lint Art</name>
<description><paragraph>A new book about the new folk art that's
catching on like wildfire.</paragraph></description>
<price>$5.95</price>
<quantity_in_stock>34</quantity_in_stock>
<image format="gif" width="200" height="200" src="images/covers/
dryerart.gif">
</image>
<onsale_date>
<month>11</month>
<day_of_month>3</day_of_month>
<year>1971</year>
</onsale_date>
<shipping_info type="UPS" value="1.5" />
</product>

</product_line>

<!-- end Book Product Line -->

<!-- begin CDs Product Line -->

<product_line name="CDs">

<product id="cd0023" keywords="music,easy listening">
<name>Music for Dogs</name>
<description><paragraph>Keep your pets calm while you're away from
the house! Each of the 15 tracks on this CD has been scientifically
shown to relax pets of all kinds.</paragraph></description>
<price>$14.99</price>
```

```
<quantity_in_stock>50</quantity_in_stock>
<image format="gif" width="200" height="200"
src="http://www.musicfordogs.com/images/cover.gif">
</image>
<onsale_date>
    <month>3</month>
<day_of_month>2</day_of_month>
<year>1990</year>
</onsale_date>
<clip format="mp3" length="2:12" size="1.6 Mb"
 src="http://www.musicfordogs.com/sounds/track1.mp3">
<title>Track 1: Fetching the Stick</title>
<description><paragraph>An exciting and playful melody.
    </paragraph></description>
</clip>
</product>
<product id="cd0024" keywords="music,easy listening">
<name>Just Singin' Along</name>
<description><paragraph>A lovely collection of songs that the whole family
 can sing right along with.</paragraph></description>
<price>$10.00</price>
<quantity_in_stock>100</quantity_in_stock>
<onsale_date>
    <month>2</month>
<day_of_month>23</day_of_month>
<year>2000</year>
</onsale_date>
   <shipping_info type="UPS" value="0.5" />
</product>
<product id="cd0025" keywords="music,folk">
<name>It's Dot Com Enough for Me: Songs from Silicon Somewhere</name>
<description><paragraph>A collection of the best folk music from Internet
 companies.</paragraph></description>
<price>$12.99</price>
<quantity_in_stock>4</quantity_in_stock>
<onsale_date>
<month>4</month>
<day_of_month>12</day_of_month>
<year>2000</year>
</onsale_date>
 <clip format="mp3" length="4.32" size="4.0 Mb" src="track2.mp3">
```

```
      <title>Track 2: My B2B Is B-R-O-K-E</title>
    </clip>
    <shipping_info type="UPS" value="0.5" />
    </product>


    </product_line>
<!-- end CDs product line -->

<!-- begin Widgets product line -->

  <product_line name="widgets">

    <product id="wg0026" keywords="appliance,electronics">
    <name>ElectroThermal Oxidizor</name>
    <description><paragraph>This amazing gizmo uses electricity to
    produce heat that can be used for oxidization purposes.</paragraph>
    </description>
    <price>$24.95</price>
    <quantity_in_stock>10</quantity_in_stock>
    <image format="jpg" width="208" height="178" src="/images/toaster.jpg">
    </image>
    <onsale_date>
<month>6</month>
<day_of_month>2</day_of_month>
<year>2000</year>
</onsale_date>
      <shipping_info type="UPS" value="10" />
    </product>
    <product id="wg0027" keywords="computing,electronics,input device">
     <name>Percusive Interface Unit</name>
     <description><paragraph>Communicate with your favorite electric
     calculating machine--through tapping!</paragraph></description>
     <price>$109.99</price>
     <quantity_in_stock>7</quantity_in_stock>
     <onsale_date>
<month>6</month>
<day_of_month>23</day_of_month>
<year>2001</year>
</onsale_date>
    </product>
    <product id="wg0028" keywords="outdoors">
```

```
<name>Umbrella</name>
<description><paragraph>Imagine going out into the rain and NOT
getting wet! The amazing umbrella makes it possible.</paragraph>
</description>
<price>$10.99</price>
<quantity_in_stock>7</quantity_in_stock>
<onsale_date>
<month>7</month>
<day_of_month>2</day_of_month>
<year>2000</year>
</onsale_date>
<shipping_info type="UPS" value="8" />
</product>

</product_line>

<!-- end widgets product line -->

<!-- end catalog -->
</catalog>
```

DTD Design Principles

If you didn't skip to this section but actually followed us through the complexity of refining the product catalog, you may be ready to throw up your hands and say goodbye to XML and DTDs. Don't give up; there are some helpful generalizations we can make about designing a DTD. This section discusses some of the most useful ones.

In Chapter 1, you saw two different languages for defining classes of XML documents: the Document Type Definitional language that is defined in the XML 1.0 specification, and XML Schema. Other methods are currently being considered for adoption as standards for defining document types, including: XML-Data and Document Content Description (DCD).

NOTE   Although we will be creating our document type using the language in the XML 1.0 Specification, many of the concepts in this section are not specific to Document Type Definitions designed using that particular document-type description language.

Some form of computer text markup language has existed for several decades. Over the years, a few things have been learned about marking up documents. The creators of XML took a look at the problems that SGML authors and standard-makers were running into and purposefully made XML less prone to some of these problems. They did this by making XML simpler and more verbose than SGML, while making sure that it was still compatible with SGML.

During the last few years, many new XML authors have run into the same types of issues faced by SGML authors, as well as several that are particular to XML. The following tips are designed to help you avoid and understand some of the problems you may face while designing DTDs.

A Representative Sample of the Data

A trick in designing general purpose DTDs is to analyze a large enough sample of data in planning your DTD that you don't leave out anything vital, but don't go into such great detail that you create an unmanageable monster.

You'll never account for everything. If you try, it will bog you down in endless meetings and arguments. History has shown us that any time people try to decide on "standards," whether they're metalanguage standards, markup language standards, or plumbing standards, the potential exists for things to degenerate into long-winded discussions of semantics with very little being decided. By deciding to create an imperfect and possibly over-generalized DTD that can be added to when it becomes necessary, you'll at least get the horse out of the gate.

Avoid Subtractive Refinement

Subtractive refinement is much more difficult than additive refinement, as HTML authors know. Browser manufacturers have made many additions (or extensions) to HTML over the years. Many of these additions filled a specific need at the time that they were introduced, but today they are holding the language back and need to be removed from the specification as well as from general use.

The most notorious of the HTML extensions is the `font` element. When `font` was introduced, there was no viable alternative for specifying how text should be formatted. Today, we have Cascading Style Sheets (CSS), and, increasingly, XSL for applying presentation logic. Still, many (if not the majority) of Web designers still use `font` for formatting text. The problem is that Web designers know how to use `font`, and they know exactly what it will do to text in each of the major browsers. CSS, although much more flexible, is more complicated, and the various glitches and quirks of each browser's implementation of CSS are not widely known.

The W3C has been in the process of removing the font element from HTML for several years now. Because so many Web pages use it, and because so many Web designers rely so heavily on it, there is still a long way to go. It would be nice if subtractive refinement could always be avoided, but that's not realistic. You can, however, minimize the potential for future removal of markup from a document type.

The first step in being able to minimize the necessity for subtractive refinement is to understand why subtractive refinement becomes necessary. The main reason to remove declarations from a DTD, for instance, is that they specify data types or rules that don't fit with, or that run counter to, the actual business entities that they are meant to show. For example, imagine that you have a DTD for marking up invoices. Your company always charges a flat fee for services. The DTD, though, may be from the days when you also performed services on an hourly basis. The relevant declarations might look like this:

```
<!ELEMENT invoice (service*,total_due)>
<!ELEMENT service (description,(duration,rate)?,fee?)>
<!ELEMENT description (#PCDATA)>
<!ELEMENT duration (hours,minutes)>
<!ELEMENT rate (#PCDATA)>
<!ELEMENT fee (#PCDATA)>
<!ELEMENT total_due(#PCDATA)>
```

Because you no longer perform services on an hourly basis, these declarations have become ambiguous. For example, if you agreed to perform a service for a customer for a flat fee of $300, and if the project takes you three hours, there are at least two ways to write that, as follows:

```
<!--first way to write invoice-->

<invoice>
<service>
  <description>Installed fuel pump</description>
  <duration>
<hours>3</hours>
<minutes>0</minutes>
</duration>
<rate>$100</rate>
<fee>$300</fee>
</service>
...
</invoice>
```

```
<!--second way to write invoice-->

<invoice>
<service>
  <description>Installed fuel pump</description>
  <fee>$300</fee>
</service>
...
</invoice>
```

According to the DTD, either of these methods is correct. Only the second method accurately reflects your actual business. To prevent this DTD from being used incorrectly, the rate and duration elements should be removed, as in the second method.

Simplify Your DTDs

Don't make your DTDs so complex that they can't be easily and quickly read. The more widely a DTD can be read and understood, the more useful it becomes. If you are designing a DTD for a highly specialized industry, your DTD can certainly contain a higher level of complexity than a general product catalog. In the Listing 2.8 example, both DTDs define an element and attributes that can be used for the same purpose.

Listing 2.8: Two Possible Phone-Call DTDs

```
<!--phone_call DTD-->

<!ENTITY % valid_phone_digits "
(1|2|A|B|C|3|D|E|F|4|G|H|I|5|J|K|L|6|M|N|O|7|P|R|S|8|T|U|V|9|W|X|Y|0)">
<!ELEMENT phone_call (from*,to*,content)>
  <!ELEMENT from (phone_number)>
  <!ELEMENT phone_number ((digit?,digit?,digit?,dash?)?,
digit,digit,digit,dash,digit,digit,digit,digit)>
  <!ELEMENT digit EMPTY>
<!ATTLIST digit number
%valid_phone_digits; #REQUIRED>
  <!ELEMENT dash EMPTY>
  <!ATTLIST dash
  value CDATA #FIXED "-">
  <!ELEMENT to (phone_number)>
<!ELEMENT content (caller|answerer)*>
<!ELEMENT caller (#PCDATA)>
<!ELEMENT answerer (#PCDATA)>
```

```
<!--simplified phone_call DTD-->

<!ELEMENT phone_call (from*,to*,content)>
  <!ELEMENT from EMPTY>
<!ATTLIST from
phone_number CDATA #REQUIRED>
  <!ELEMENT to EMPTY>
  <!ATTLIST to
phone_number CDATA #REQUIRED>
  <!ELEMENT content (caller|answerer)*>
<!ELEMENT caller (#PCDATA)>
<!ELEMENT answerer (#PCDATA)>
```

The first declaration is too specific for most purposes. How long would it take someone to figure out that all of the confusing declarations are just asking for a standard phone number? The limits of the capabilities of a DTD are really being stretched here. Do we really need to have each digit of the phone number marked up separately? This example may be over the top, but it does illustrate the basic point: Don't go overboard in creating DTDs or XML documents. There is a point where too much detail can be harmful.

Elements versus Attributes

Perhaps the most frequently asked, and the most hotly debated, question about DTD design is the question of when to use an element and when to use an attribute. For example, given a book and its title, how do you know which of the following ways to show this data is correct?

```
<Book>
  <Title>Guide to Plants</Title>
</Book>
```

Or:

```
<Book Title="Guide to Plants">...</Book>
```

The truth of the matter is that it's largely a personal choice. As with most things, there are extremists on both ends of the spectrum. Some people claim that using only attributes makes it easier to access data in XML documents. The side effect of using only attributes, though, is decreased human readability. Others claim that data should only be stored in elements. Most people's views are somewhere in the middle.

Several rules have been developed by SGML and XML writers over the years that you can follow for determining whether a piece of data should be an element or an attribute. These can take some experience to know how to apply. Keep in mind, also, that there are always exceptions to these rules.

- Attributes should be used for information about content (metadata), whereas elements should be used for the actual content itself. (For example, the color of a book could be considered to be metadata. A paragraph in the book would be considered the actual content.)

- An attribute should be used for enumerated values (such as a product number or a unique ID).

- Use attributes for values that are meant to be read by machines and elements for values that are for humans.

- If the order of values is important, use elements. (The reason for this is that it is not possible to prescribe the order of an element's attributes, but you can model the order of elements.)

Design for Business Processes

When designing DTDs, think about requirements in terms of business processes rather than in terms of a specific application. If you don't make any assumptions about how or by whom the document will be processed, your DTD will be much more flexible. For example, even though the DTD for our e-commerce store will probably be read and manipulated by the application much more often than by humans, we are not taking that into account in the DTD. If we were to design a DTD purely to be manipulated by machines, we could save considerable space by making names as short as possible and by using more parameter entities, for example. This defeats the purpose of XML, though. XML code ought to be easily readable by humans as well as by machines. The sacrifice in disk space and speed is outweighed by the usefulness and the flexibility of correctly marked up data.

XML Design Patterns

Design patterns are solutions to common problems that arise in particular contexts. Patterns have been getting a lot of attention lately as a way to improve the software development process and to reuse knowledge both within companies and in the software development industry as a whole.

Despite the number of books and articles being written about design patterns lately, they are nothing revolutionary. The idea behind design patterns is the same idea behind self-help and diet books; similar problems often have similar solutions. A design pattern simply states a context, a problem, and then a solution. Design patterns are typically written in similar ways, to make them easy to read and understand.

If you were to only apply design patterns when making DTD design decisions, you probably wouldn't go too wrong, but you should keep in mind that design patterns are not always the right solution. More often than not, though, someone else has experienced the same problem you're struggling with, or are about to struggle with, and a repository of design patterns can save you the agony of reinventing the wheel.

The following sections discuss the generic element design pattern for a Web document. This pattern and many others can be found at www.xmlpatterns.com.

Abstract

To provide flexibility to users of a document, designers can provide an element type that is very generic. The use of an element is not well specified by the document's type. This allows for authors to use the document type in ways that may not have been foreseen.

Problem

The designer does not know exactly what the users of the document intend to do with the document but needs to add flexibility to the document type.

Context

This is useful in general-purpose document types, when flexibility is needed.

Forces

Flexibility is required to make some document types useful. This pattern can affect the ease of processing of the document type.

Solution

This provides a new element that does not have a specific meaning.

Examples

Here's the example code:

```
<Paragraph>
Albert Camus's <General type="book">The Stranger</General>
  is an existentialist novel.
</Paragraph>
```

Discussion

Not providing enough flexibility can make document authors use the wrong element for markup. This can lead to documents that are difficult to understand, and mistakes in processing occur.

The need for flexibility can make processing software difficult to create. Adding `Role Attributes` to the generic element can help provide the processing software some clues as to how to process the element.

Related Patterns

A `Role Attribute` is often used in conjunction with generic elements.

Known Uses

The `div` and `span` elements in XHTML are common uses for this document type.

References

The Fielded Text example from *The XML and SGML Cookbook: Recipes for Structured Information*, by Rick Jelliffe (published as part of the Charles F. Goldfarb series on information management; March, 1998; ISBN: 0136142230) uses generic elements.

Moving toward DTD Standardization

Many applications that use XML today don't bother with creating a DTD. This is especially true of applications that just use XML for messaging and not for data storage. Even if you don't formally define a DTD, you still need to think about the best way to mark up your application's data. The process of deciding how to mark up data can often be frustrating and time consuming.

The hope of many XML authors is that in the future we won't need to worry as much about designing DTDs. Once a schema language that is better suited for describing data is agreed upon, it will become much easier for the reuse and the standardization of Document Type Definitions to occur.

Although a custom-developed DTD, such as the one we have created for XMLGifts.com, can be a very powerful tool, the real strength of XML will be realized as more industries agree on standard schemas.

As the following list details, several XML schemas for electronic commerce are being pushed today by various vendors and organizations:

- According to Commerce One, the Common Business Library (CBL) is an "open XML specification for the cross-industry exchange of business documents such as purchase orders, invoices, product descriptions, and shipping schedules."

- EbXML is being developed by The United Nations body for Trade Facilitation and Electronic Business (UN/CEFACT) Organization for the Advancement of Structured

Information Standards (OASIS). According to the Web site at www.ebxml.org, EbXML is a globally developed, open XML-based standard for global electronic commerce.

- According to IBM, its Business Rules Markup Language (BRML) is an "XML Rule Interlingua for Agent Communication, based on Courteous/Ordinary Logic Programs." BRML is used in conjunction with IBM's CommonRules, a Java library that provides functionality for business rules.

- IBM's Trading Partner Agreement Markup Language (tpaML) is a language for creating electronic contracts between trading partners.

- The Internet Open Trading Protocol (OTP) is a payment-system-independent framework for Internet commerce. OTP was developed by various banks and Internet payment-processing companies, including SET, Mondex, CyberCash, DigiCash, and GeldKarte.

Flexible, reusable data is the key to developing manageable XML applications. Careful DTD design, or, if possible, agreement upon an industry-standard DTD, should therefore be the first step in any serious XML application development effort. As we move forward in this book into actually manipulating XML data using Java, the DTD will always be there (although it may need to be occasionally revised) to provide structure and to ensure data integrity.

CHAPTER 3

Presenting an XML Catalog Online

- The API for presentation with Java servlets

- The API for presentation with JavaServer Pages

- The API for working with the Document Object Model

- Java classes for presenting XML catalog data

In this chapter, we survey the APIs for Java servlets, for JavaServer Pages, and for the manipulation of XML elements. These are the essential programming tools for creation of dynamic Web pages from XML data. Using these APIs, we then explore various approaches for online presentation of the catalog items created in Chapter 2, "A Catalog in XML."

Presentation Technologies

When creating a commerce-oriented site on the Internet, Java programmers have a tremendous number of options to choose from. All of these options operate within the basic constraints of Web protocols. The most basic of these constraints is that the user's Web browser and the Web server conduct a very simple conversation: A single user request elicits a single server response. This conversation is said to be stateless because there is no requirement in the protocol for the Web server to remember anything about the transaction after the response has been sent.

The HTTP Conversation

The World Wide Web Consortium (W3C) organization (`www.w3.org`) maintains the current standard for Web servers: HTTP version 1.1. (This is a refinement over the previous HTTP version 1 standard, which has many problems.) The standard defines the required format for browser requests and Web-server responses.

The Browser Request

The request message from browser to Web server starts with a header consisting of one or more ASCII text lines terminated by carriage-return–line-feed (crlf) characters. The first line is required to specify a method, a Uniform Resource Identifier (URI), and an indicator of the HTTP version being used. The standard methods in the HTTP 1.1 protocol are `OPTIONS`, `GET`, `HEAD`, `POST`, `PUT`, `DELETE`, `TRACE`, and `CONNECT`, but for commercial sites, `GET` and `POST` are the ones we usually have to deal with. A header may or may not be followed by a body of additional data.

A request for a plain HTML page uses the `GET` method. Simple search requests typically also use `GET`, whereas form submission requests, such as "shopping cart" applications, typically use the `POST` method. The practical difference is that in `GET` method requests parameters (such as search terms) are passed as part of the URI line in the header, but `POST` method requests pass data in the body of the message.

The header also contains lines that give additional information about the kinds of data the browser will accept, the browser version, and the type of connection desired. Listing 3.1 shows an example request resulting from clicking the Send button on a simple HTML page with a form using the POST method and having a hidden variable named action and a value of showkeywords. Note that the Accept: line has been broken to fit this page.

Listing 3.1: A POST Message from Browser to Web Server

```
POST /servlet/cattest HTTP/1.1
Accept: application/msword, application/vnd.ms-excel, image/gif,
image/x-xbitmap, image/jpeg, image/pjpeg, */*
Referer: http://localhost/XmlEcommBook/CTestSnoop.html
Accept-Language: en-us
Content-Type: application/x-www-form-urlencoded
Accept-Encoding: gzip, deflate
User-Agent: Mozilla/4.0 (compatible; MSIE 5.0; Windows NT; DigExt)
Host: localhost:9000
Content-Length: 19
Connection: Keep-Alive

action=showkeywords
```

The Web-Server Response

The response message from Web server to browser also requires a header. The header always starts with a status line that contains the protocol being used, a numeric status code, and a text version of the status code. Subsequent lines provide additional information in the keyword: value format, followed by a single blank line.

Information passed in the response header typically includes the type and size of the content body of the message. The response header can also contain lines that attempt to set "cookie" values in the browser. The following is the header received in response to the request shown in Listing 3.1. This was followed by a blank line and then the HTML body of the message.

```
HTTP/1.0 200 OK
Server: Microsoft-PWS/2.0
Date: Mon, 25 Sep 2000 14:15:55 GMT
Content-Type: text/html
```

The body of the server response can be anything, from a standard HTML page to the binary data making up an image (or any number of other specialized data formats). In the preceding header, note that the content type is specified as `text/html`.

NOTE   For more in-depth coverage of HTML, we recommend Sybex's *HTML Complete, Second Edition*, or check out `www.sybex.com` for a detailed listing of related titles.

The API for Java Servlets

Java servlet technology operates at the most basic level of a Web server and is essential to all Java-based server functions. Servlet technology can be used to handle all Web-server functions, or servers based on other technologies can be configured to pass certain types of requests to add-on servlet engines.

NOTE   A complete discussion of the servlet API would take a whole book (for example, the *Java Developer's Guide to Servlets and JSP*, by Bill Brogden and published by Sybex, ISBN 0-7821-2809-2). This section presents a quick review.

As this chapter is being written, the current API for servlets is version 2.2, with version 2.3 entering the public review stage. By the time this book is published, the version 2.2 API should be widely supported by stand-alone Web servers and add-ons for existing Web servers.

In a Web server with an add-on servlet engine, the server has configuration settings that tell it which requests are handled by servlets. Sun Microsystems maintains a list of add-on servlet engines and Web servers at the following site:

    `http://java.sun.com/products/servlet/industry.html`

Examples of 100% Pure Java Web servers include those in the following list:

Tomcat   An open-source project at The Apache Software Foundation (`http://jakarta.apache.org`).

Enhydra   A low-cost, commercial, Java-based application server (`www.lutris.com`) supporting servlets, JavaServer Pages, and Enterprise JavaBeans.

Orion   A commercial application server (`www.orionserver.com`) but with a free development/noncommercial license. It supports all of the latest Java technology, including E2EE and Enterprise JavaBeans.

Resin   A 100% Pure Java server (`www.caucho.com/index.xtp`). Designed as an Enterprise-scale application server with emphasis on the use of XML and XSL.

In Sun's nomenclature, a Web server handling Java servlets acts as a "servlet container," similar to the way a browser acts as a container for applets. A servlet depends on this container to load and initialize the required classes and to conduct the basic parts of an HTTP transaction. The servlet container creates an `HttpServletRequest` object, which contains a convenient representation of the user's request, and an `HttpServletResponse` object, which provides the methods needed for the servlet to send a response.

The servlet container also provides a `Thread` to execute the servlet code in response to a user request. Each request gets its own `Thread` that executes the servlet methods independently, but typically only one servlet instance is created. This means that the programmer must be very cautious in using instance variables.

Because a servlet instance typically stays loaded in the Web server memory for extended periods, the response to a request directed to a servlet can be very rapid. This approach is much faster than technologies that have to spawn a new process and load an application each time a request arrives.

The Classes and Interfaces for the Java Servlets

The `javax.servlet` and `javax.servlet.http` packages contain the classes and interfaces used in servlet creation. The basic classes and interfaces in `javax.servlet` are generalized, whereas the classes in `javax.servlet.http` are specialized for working with the HTTP protocol. Table 3.1 summarizes the `javax.servlet` interfaces.

TABLE 3.1: Interfaces in the *javax.servlet* Package

Interface	Description
Servlet	This interface defines the methods that all servlets must implement. The `Generic-Servlet` class implements the `Servlet` interface.
ServletRequest	All information about a client request is accessed through an object implementing this interface. Creating a `ServletRequest` object is the responsibility of the servlet engine.
ServletResponse	Objects implementing this interface must be created by the servlet engine and passed to the servlet's `service` method to be used for output to the client.
RequestDispatcher	This powerful interface permits you to forward a request from the current servlet to another servlet or a JSP page for additional processing.
ServletConfig	Objects using this interface are used to hold information that helps configure the servlet during servlet initialization.

TABLE 3.1:   Interfaces in the *javax.servlet* Package *(continued)*

Interface	Description
ServletContext	Objects using this interface let a servlet locate information about the servlet engine the servlet is running in and the servlet's environment.
SingleThreadModel	This interface contains no methods. It is a marker that forces the servlet engine to ensure that only one `Thread` executes an instance of the servlet at once. The servlet engine can do this either by restricting access to a single instance of the servlet or by creating a separate instance for every `Thread`.

The classes in the `javax.servlet` package (see Table 3.2) provide basic, bare-minimum functionality. In general, programmers work with classes that extend these for more specific applications.

TABLE 3.2:   Classes in the *javax.servlet* Package

Class	Description
GenericServlet	This class provides bare-minimum functionality.
ServletInputStream	A class for reading a stream of binary data from the request.
ServletOutputStream	A class for writing a stream of binary data as part of a response.

Only two exceptions are defined in the `javax.servlet` package. The `ServletException` class is a general-purpose exception used in servlet classes, whereas the `Unavailable-Exception` is to be thrown when a servlet needs to indicate that it is temporarily or permanently unavailable. These classes do not descend from `RuntimeException`, so if a method declares that it throws `ServletException`, a calling method must provide for catching it.

The `javax.servlet.http` package adds the interfaces shown in Table 3.3 and the classes shown in Table 3.4. These are the interfaces and classes you, as a programmer, will be dealing with when creating a Web application with servlets.

TABLE 3.3:   Interfaces in the *javax.servlet.http* Package

Interface	Description
HttpServletRequest	This extension of the `ServletRequest` interface adds methods specific to HTTP requests, such as getting cookie settings.
HttpServletResponse	An extension of the `ServletResponse` interface, this interface adds methods specific to the HTTP protocol, such as setting cookies and header values.
HttpSession	Objects implementing this interface are an essential part of shopping-cart applications because they allow the programmer to store information about a user between individual page visits or transactions.
HttpSessionBindingListener	Objects implementing this interface can be notified when they are added to or removed from an `HttpSession`.

TABLE 3.4:   Classes in the *javax.servlet.http* Package

Class	Description
HttpServlet	This abstract class is the one you will usually extend to create useful Web servlets.
Cookie	These objects are used to manipulate cookie information that is sent by the server to a browser and returned on subsequent requests. Cookie information in a request is turned into `Cookie` objects by the `HttpServlet-Request`.
HttpUtils	Static methods in this class are useful occasionally.
HttpSessionBindingEvent	The class of events sent to objects implementing `HttpSessionBinding-Listener`.

Servlet Request Handling

In a typical commerce application, user requests are processed in the following sequence:

1. The user's request data is used to create an `HttpServletRequest` object, which contains information from the request headers plus any additional data.

   An `HttpServletResponse` object is also created in preparation for the creation of a response.

2. The servlet `service` method is called with references to these two objects. By examining the request type, the service method determines which of the request-handling methods should be called. Custom servlets typically do not override the default `service` method but instead override the `doPost` and/or `doGet` methods.

3. The `doPost` or the `doGet` method examines the request and determines the application function required. For all but the simplest application, the servlet class typically makes use of other objects to carry out database queries or calculations.

A Simple Servlet Example

A typical servlet application program includes a class that extends `HttpServlet` and implements the methods that will respond to the various types of requests that the application must handle. The simple example shown in Listing 3.2 only has to respond to GET requests, so it only implements the `doGet` method. Note that the output is written to a `PrintWriter` object named `out` that is obtained from the `HttpServletResponse` object.

Listing 3.2: A Simple Servlet Handling a *GET* Request (*DateDemo.java*)

```java
import java.io.*;
import java.util.* ;
import javax.servlet.*;
import javax.servlet.http.*;

public class DateDemo extends HttpServlet
{
  public void doGet(HttpServletRequest req,
       HttpServletResponse resp)
  throws ServletException, IOException
  {
    resp.setContentType("text/html");
    PrintWriter out = resp.getWriter();
    String username = req.getParameter("uname");
    if( username == null ) username = "unknown person" ;
    out.println("<HTML>");
    out.println("<HEAD><TITLE>Date Demo</TITLE></HEAD>");
    out.println("<BODY>");
    out.println("Hello " + username + "<br>");
    out.println("Date and time now: " + new Date().toString()
             + "<br>");
    out.println("</BODY>");
    out.println("</HTML>");
    out.close();
  }
}
```

In this example, the doGet method attempts to locate a parameter named "uname" in the HttpServletRequest object to be used in the response. Also, note the use of the setContentType method to set the response content type to "text/html".

Servlet Initialization

When a servlet container loads servlet code and creates an instance of the servlet class, the API guarantees that the init method will be the first method called and that it will be executed before any user request is processed. The servlet API provides for passing initialization parameters to the newly created instance using an object of the ServletConfig class.

Prior to the 2.2 version of the servlet API, each vendor had a different approach to configuring these initialization settings. Now that Sun has decided on XML-based configuration nomenclature, we can expect configuration to become standardized.

Listing 3.3 shows the XML used to set initialization parameters for servlets we will be discussing in Chapter 7, "Using Surveys to Know Your Customer."

Listing 3.3: The XML Configuration with Initialization Parameters (*web.xml*)

```
<web-app>
  <servlet><servlet-name>Questionnaire</servlet-name>
  <servlet-class>com.XmlEcomBook.Chap07.QuestionnaireServ</servlet-class>
    <init-param>
     <param-name>homedir</param-name>
     <param-value>e:\\scripts\\questionnaire</param-value>
    </init-param>
  </servlet>
  <servlet><servlet-name>Qanalysis</servlet-name>
  <servlet-class>com.XmlEcomBook.Chap07.QanalysisServ</servlet-class>
    <init-param>
     <param-name>homedir</param-name>
     <param-value>e:\\scripts\\questionnaire</param-value>
    </init-param>
  </servlet>
</web-app>
```

In the `init` method of the `QuestionnaireServ` servlet, the parameter named `homedir` is used to set the value of a `String` named `homedir` with the following code, where `config` is the `ServletConfig` passed to the `init` method or acquired from `getServletConfig()`:

```
homedir = config.getInitParameter("homedir") ;
```

Other things that are usually accomplished in the `init` method include establishing connections to databases and opening logging files.

Servlet Response Generation

All of the resources required to control the response are encapsulated in the `ServletResponse` and `HttpServletResponse` interfaces. For example, the following calls to the `setHeader` method can be used to ensure that the browser will not cache the page that is being sent:

```
response.setHeader("Expires", "Mon, 26 Jul 1990 05:00:00 GMT");
response.setHeader("Cache-Control" ,"no-cache, must-revalidate");
response.setHeader("Pragma", "no-cache"); // for HTTP/1.0
```

The `ServletResponse` object provides an output stream for your servlet program to write the page content. This output stream can be either a `PrintWriter` type, which can carry out Unicode translation, or a plain binary stream of the `ServletOutputStream` type that writes bytes without translation.

The Role of JavaBeans

Java has had great success with a simple component architecture called JavaBeans. Although initially planned as an architecture for graphical-user-interface components, it has also been found very useful in non-graphical applications. A *JavaBean* is simply a Java class that meets the following criteria:

- The class must be public and implement `Serializable`.
- The class must have a no-arguments constructor.
- The class must provide `set` and `get` methods to access any variables used by other classes.

By creating classes and naming methods according to these simple JavaBean conventions, it is possible to partially automate many program construction functions, especially in JavaServer Pages. You will also hear the term Enterprise JavaBeans used a lot in connection with Web application servers. An *Enterprise JavaBean* is distinctly different from a JavaBean, and much more complicated.

The API for JavaServer Pages

There have been numerous attempts to develop systems that allow an author to write static HTML content that incorporates dynamic data by means of special tags embedded in the HTML—the idea being that when transmitting a page, the static file data will be passed through a special processor that recognizes the tags and uses them to insert data dynamically as the page is transmitted. Frequently, the file type is set to a unique name as a clue to the Web server that special processing is required.

Examples of highly successful implementations of special tag processing include the Cold-Fusion server (`www.allaire.com`) and Microsoft's Active Server Pages, ASP (`http://msdn.microsoft.com/workshop/server/default.asp`).

Sun's approach to incorporating dynamic Web-page generation is the JavaServer Pages (JSP) API. This standard, at version 1.1 as of the publication of this book, is considered to be an essential part of the Java approach to Web application servers, as embodied in the Java 2 Enterprise Edition platform.

JSP technology is based on servlet technology. Essentially, the JSP processor turns static Web-page elements and dynamic elements defined by JSP tags into the Java source code for a servlet class. When a user request that addresses a JSP page comes to the Web server, this class is executed to create a response. As long as the static elements of the JSP page remain unchanged, the response to a request can be very rapid, because the class remains in memory just like servlet classes.

Benchmark tests comparing Active Server Pages applications with similar JSP applications have been conducted by one of the major vendors. Recent results have the Orion JSP implementation much faster than ASP. You can see the most recent results at `www.orionserver` `.com/benchmarks/benchmark.html`.

The Language of JSP Tags

In the following JSP page code, the JSP tag starts with <%= and ends with %>. When compiled into a Java class, a request for this page will result in the output of the HTML tags and text plus the `String` created by the `toString` method operating on a new `Date` object.

```
<HTML>
<HEAD><TITLE>JRun Date Demo</TITLE></HEAD>
<BODY>
<H2>Date And Time <%= new java.util.Date().toString() %></H2>
<hr>
</BODY>
</HTML>
```

Because of major changes in the JSP API between early versions and the current version 1.1 API, JSP tags occur in two styles. The old style tags, as shown in Table 3.5, are still available.

TABLE 3.5: JSP Tags Using the "<%" Style

Tag	Used for	Example
<%-- --%	Comments	<%-- this is never shown --%>
<%= %>	Expressions (evaluated as `String`)	<%= new Date() %>
<%! %>	Declarations	<%! Date myD = new Date() ; %>
<% %>	Code fragments	<% for(int i = 0 ; i < 10 ; i++ { %>
<%@ %>	Directives	<%@ page import="java.util.*" %>

As shown in Table 3.6, the new style tags obey XML tag-formatting rules. In general, Sun is trying to move to an all-XML style for JavaServer Pages.

TABLE 3.6: New JSP Style Tags Use an XML Style

JSP Tag	Description
`<jsp:include />`	Incorporates bulk text from a file
`<jsp:forward />`	Forwards the request to a servlet, another JSP, or static Web page
`<jsp:param />`	Used inside a **forward, include,** or **plugin** to add or modify a parameter in the **request** object
`<jsp:getProperty />`	Gets the value of a Bean property by name
`<jsp:setProperty />`	Sets the value of a Bean property
`<jsp:useBean />`	Locates or creates a Bean with the specific name and scope
`<jsp:plugin />`	Provides full information for a download of a Java plugin to the client Web browser

Custom Tag Libraries

An elegant feature of the JavaServer Pages API is its capability to define a library of custom action tags. This is a very powerful concept that enables you to use specialized toolkits as easily as you use the standard tags.

Custom tags use interfaces and classes in the `javax.servlet.jsp.tagext` package. This capability has great potential for simplifying the authoring of JavaServer Pages.

JSP Request Handling

Here is the sequence of events that occurs when a user request names a JSP page:

1. The request naming a JSP page is directed to the JSP engine by the Web server.

2. The JSP engine looks for the corresponding servlet based on the page name. If the servlet exists and is up to date, the request is passed to the servlet `_jspService` method using `HttpServletRequest` and `HttpServletResponse` objects, just like with a regular servlet.

3. If the source page has been changed or has never been compiled, the page compiler parses the source and creates the equivalent Java source code for a servlet implementing `HttpJspPage`.

4. This code is then compiled, and the new servlet is executed. The servlet object can stay in memory, providing a very fast response to the next request.

The `request` and `response` objects are exactly the same ones used in normal servlets; the difference here is that the creation of the `service` method is accomplished by the JSP engine.

Default Variables in a JSP

Table 3.7 shows the variables that are automatically available in a JSP page.

TABLE 3.7: The Default JSP Page Variables

Variable Name	Type	Description
`request`	An implementation of `HttpServletRequest`	Represents the user's request
`response`	An implementation of `HttpServletResponse`	Creates the output response
`pageContext`	A `javax.servlet.jsp.PageContext` object	Contains attributes of this page
`session`	A `javax.servlet.http.HttpSession`	Contains arbitrary variables attached to this user's session
`application`	A `javax.servlet.ServletContext` object	Contains attributes for the entire application and affects the interpretation of several other tags
`out`	A `javax.servlet.jsp.JspWriter` object	Determines the output stream for the response
`config`	A `javax.servlet.ServletConfig` object	Contains servlet initialization parameter name-value pairs and the `Servlet-Context` object
`page`	An `Object` reference pointing to `this`	The current servlet object
`exception`	A `java.lang.Throwable` object	Contains only pages designated as error pages in the page directive

Organizing the Catalog

The catalog of products as created in the XML document has only a sequential organization. However, we want customers to have flexible access to the catalog items, rather than having to page through the entire catalog in the original order to locate products. In this section, we consider Java techniques for organizing access to the elements of the XML catalog.

The W3C Document Object Model API

We will generally be using Sun's JAXP (Java API for XML Parsing) toolkit for XML in this book. The basic API for manipulating parts of XML documents follows the formal Document Object Model (DOM) recommendation by the W3C. This API gives the most complete access to all elements of an XML document at the expense of considerable complexity. There are simpler APIs supporting DOMs, but the W3C version is the most widely accepted and supported.

You can download the current JAXP toolkit from Sun's Web site, or use the version provided in the Tomcat download from `jakarta.apache.org`. The toolkit consists of Java packages that represent the W3C API plus packages that provide implementation of various parsers and utilities. As of this writing, this package was not yet part of the Java standard extensions library, so you will have to download it from the developer site:

```
http://developer.java.sun.com/developer/products/xml/
```

Creating the Catalog DOM

As we mentioned in Chapter 1, the initial creation of a DOM in Java is very simple because the toolkit parser does all the work. Listing 3.4 shows part of the code for a class to represent the catalog as an `org.w3c.dom.Document` object. The bulk of the constructor code is in catching the various possible parsing errors.

Listing 3.4: An Example of Parsing a Document (*TheCatalog.java*)

```
]
import javax.xml.parsers.* ;
import org.xml.sax.* ;
import org.w3c.dom.* ;

public class TheCatalog… {

org.w3c.dom.Document catDoc ;

public TheCatalog( File f  ){
  try {
    timestamp = f.lastModified();
    DocumentBuilderFactory dbf = DocumentBuilderFactory.newInstance();
      // statements to configure the DocumentBuilder would go here
```

```
    DocumentBuilder db = dbf.newDocumentBuilder ();
}catch(ParserConfigurationException pce){
    lastErr = pce.toString();
    System.out.println("constructor threw " + lastErr );
}catch(SAXParseException spe ){
    StringBuffer sb = new StringBuffer( spe.toString() );
    sb.append("\n  Line number: " + spe.getLineNumber());
    sb.append("\nColumn number: " + spe.getColumnNumber() );
    sb.append("\n Public ID: " + spe.getPublicId() );
    sb.append("\n System ID: " + spe.getSystemId() + "\n");
    lastErr = sb.toString();
    System.out.print( lastErr );
}catch( SAXException se ){
    lastErr = se.toString();
    System.out.println("constructor threw " + lastErr );
    se.printStackTrace( System.out );
}catch( IOException ie ){
    lastErr = ie.toString();
    System.out.println("constructor threw " + lastErr +
        " trying to read " + f.getAbsolutePath() );
}
}
```

The DOM data structure is organized in memory with the same hierarchy as the XML document. Java objects represent the various parts of the XML document and are linked by references to their neighboring elements, as suggested by Figure 1.2 in Chapter 1. The programming interfaces for the Java objects that represent the various parts of the document are defined in the `org.w3c.dom` package. Every part of an XML document, including the root element, is represented as an object implementing an interface that is an extension of the fundamental `Node` interface.

The *Node* Interface

The primary set of methods for the entire `org.w3c.dom` package is provided by the `Node` interface. There are 13 sub-interfaces in the `org.w3c.dom` package derived from `Node` to represent various parts of a document. Although they all extend `Node`, certain methods don't make any sense in some sub-interfaces.

Table 3.8 summarizes the methods in the `Node` interface. Note that the interpretation of the `nodeName` and `nodeValue` return values depends on the type of node.

TABLE 3.8: The *Node* Methods

Method	Returns	Description
getNodeName	NodeName	The `String` name of the **Node**; interpretation depends on type.
getNodeValue	NodeValue	The `String` value of the **Node**; depends on type.
setNodeValue	Void	
getNodeType	short	A code defined in the **Node** interface, representing the **Node** type.
getParentNode	A **Node** reference	The parent of this **Node** in the document hierarchy. Not all types have parents.
getChildNodes	A **NodeList** reference	**NodeList** objects provide for accessing an ordered list of **Node** references.
getFirstChild	A **Node** reference	The first child of this **Node**, or `null` if none exists.
getLastChild	A **Node** reference	The last child of this **Node**, or `null` if none exists.
getPreviousSibling	A **Node** reference	The **Node** immediately preceding this one, or `null` if none exists.
getNextSibling	A **Node** reference	The **Node** immediately following this one, or null if none exists.
getAttributes	A **NamedNodeMap** reference	**NamedNodeMap** methods provide for access to attributes by name. Returns `null` if the **Node** has no attributes.
getOwnerDocument	A **Document** reference	The **Document** this **Node** belongs to, or `null` if this **Node** is a **Document**.

The type of **Node** that we will generally be manipulating is called an **Element**; these objects use the `org.w3c.dom.Element` interface. The **Element** interface adds a number of methods for dealing with attributes and for dealing with named **Nodes** contained within an **Element**.

NOTE   To simplify the discussion, we will be talking about objects implementing the **Node**, **Element**, and other interfaces as **Node**, **Element**, etc. objects. The actual type of the object implementing the interfaces does not matter because we will be using only interface methods.

Because we don't have space to formally lay out the `org.w3c.dom` API, let's examine how a product entry from the catalog is represented in Java objects. Listing 3.5 shows the XML for a single product; the **Element** object for this item will contain a hierarchy of **Node** objects that represent the XML.

Listing 3.5: The XML for a Single Product (*catalog.xml*)

```
<product id="bk0022" keywords="gardening, plants">
  <name>Guide to Plants</name>
  <description>
    <paragraph>
    <italics>Everything</italics> you've ever wanted to know about plants.
    </paragraph>
  </description>
  <price>$12.99</price>
  <quantity_in_stock>4</quantity_in_stock>
  <image format="gif" width="234" height="400"
      src="images/covers/plants.gif">
    <caption>
    <paragraph>This is the cover from the first edition.</paragraph>
    </caption>
  </image>
  <onsale_date>
    <month>4</month>
    <day_of_month>4</day_of_month>
    <year>1999</year>
  </onsale_date>
</product>
```

For example, if you were to execute the getFirstChild method of the product Element you would get a reference to the Node that represents the name Element. The name Element contains a child Node of the Text type; the value of this Node is the String Guide to Plants.

The XML attributes attached to the product Element can be accessed with the get-Attribute method, which takes the name of an attribute and returns a String with the attribute value, as in this example:

```
String id = product.getAttribute("id")
String keywords = product.getAttribute("keywords");
```

All of the first level of the hierarchy of Nodes attached to the product Element can be accessed with the getChildNodes method. This returns an object implementing the NodeList interface. A NodeList object differs from other Java collection types in that it holds a dynamic representation of the XML document. This means that if another Node were inserted into the hierarchy of Nodes contained in the product Element it would show up in the NodeList of child nodes automatically.

The *NodeList* Interface

This interface has only the following two methods:

int getLength()   This method returns the current number of Nodes, which may be zero.

Node item(int n)   This returns a reference to the nth Node in the list or null if there is nothing at this position.

The *Document* Interface

The Java object that encapsulates an entire XML document in memory implements the Document interface extension of the Node interface. Most of the methods in this interface are concerned with creating or modifying a DOM in memory. The method we will be using most often simply returns an Element reference for the document, as follows:

```
Element rootE = catDoc.getDocumentElement();
```

For example, to obtain a NodeList of all of the product Elements in the catDoc document, you would use the following:

```
Element rootE = catDoc.getDocumentElement();
NodeList nl = rootE.getElementsByTagName("product");
```

Creating Indices for Product Lookup

With the preceding quick survey of the Java interfaces for accessing the DOM, we are now ready to look at how to create various indexes that will speed up catalog presentation while still leaving the product information in DOM format. Here are some of the data and functionality we need:

- A list of the names of the product_line divisions of the catalog
- A list of all products in a particular product_line
- A quick lookup of the product Element from the product id
- A list of all keywords in use so we can present keywords for the user to choose from
- A quick lookup for products from selected keywords

The scanCatalog method, as shown in Listing 3.6, creates the data structures to fulfill these requirements. These data structures are String arrays named productLineNames, keywords, and Hashtable objects named productLineHT, productHT, and prodByKeyHT. We are using collection classes compatible with both Java 1.1 and Java 1.2 JDKs because, as of this writing, some servlet engines still use Java 1.1 libraries.

The scanCatalog method is called immediately after the XML file is parsed by the constructor for this class (Listing 3.4). Note that in scanCatalog the first method called on the root Element is normalize(). The reason for this is that the Sun parser tends to turn the carriage returns and extra spaces (which XML authors like to use to make the text document easily scanned) into multiple Text nodes. The normalize method lumps all adjacent Text node content together into a single Text node.

Listing 3.6: The *scanCatalog* Method Initializes Various *Hashtables* (*TheCatalog.java*)

```java
public void scanCatalog(){
  Element rE = catDoc.getDocumentElement(); // the root
  rE.normalize();
  productLineNL = rE.getElementsByTagName("product_line");
  productLineHT = new Hashtable();
  productHT = new Hashtable();
  prodByKeyHT = new Hashtable();
   // note that in contrast to other get methods, getAttributes
   // returns "" if the attribute does not exist
  int i,j, ct = productLineNL.getLength();
  productLineNames = new String[ ct ];
  for( i = 0 ; i < ct ; i++ ){
    Element plE = (Element)productLineNL.item(i);
    productLineNames[i] = plE.getAttribute("name");
    NodeList prodNL = plE.getElementsByTagName("product");
    productLineHT.put( productLineNames[i], prodNL ); // node list
    int pct = prodNL.getLength();
    System.out.println( productLineNames[i] + " ct " + pct );
    for( j = 0 ; j < pct ; j++ ){
      Element prodE = (Element)prodNL.item(j) ;
      String id = prodE.getAttribute("id");
      if( id == null ){
        System.out.println("No id - productLine " +
          productLineNames[i] + " product " + j );
      }
      else { productHT.put( id, prodE ); // product by id
        String keys = prodE.getAttribute("keywords");
        if( keys != null ){
          addProdByKey( keys, prodE );
        }
      }
    }
  }     // end loop over product lines
  ct = prodByKeyHT.size();
  keywords = new String[ ct ];
  i = 0 ;
```

```
Enumeration en = prodByKeyHT.keys();
while( en.hasMoreElements()){
    keywords[i++] = (String)en.nextElement();
}
shellSortStr( keywords );
}
```

Creating the prodByKeyHT is accomplished in the addProdByKey method, as shown in Listing 3.7. This method has to cope with the fact that the keywds String may have more than one word or phrase separated by commas. The StringTokenizer class was designed for this sort of work, but note that we have to use the trim method to trim leading and trailing spaces off the String parsed by the StringTokenizer. The Vector we are storing the Element references in preserves the original order of products in the XML file.

Listing 3.7: The *addProdByKey* Method (*TheCatalog.java*)

```
// separate and clean up list, creating/adding to Vector in prodByKeyHT
    private void addProdByKey( String keywds, Element pE ){
        StringTokenizer st = new StringTokenizer( keywds, "," );
        while( st.hasMoreTokens() ){
          String key = st.nextToken().trim();
          Vector v = (Vector)prodByKeyHT.get( key );
          if( v == null ){
            v = new Vector();
            prodByKeyHT.put( key, v );
          }
          v.addElement( pE );
        }
    }
```

Information Flow for Presentation Generation

Generally speaking, the information that ends up being displayed on the user's browser has gone through several steps to organize the presentation. The basic element of the DOM that is manipulated is an Element representing a product. The steps in creating a presentation from the XML catalog follow:

1. Start with the full catalog DOM, represented as a NodeList of product elements.

2. Apply selection rules to the NodeList of product elements. Possible selection rules include the product id, keyword, or product line.

3. Apply sorting to the array of elements, if necessary.

4. For each element, generate the HTML presentation format and add it to the page under construction.

Presenting Choices

Because we have gone to the trouble of coding keywords for each product in the catalog, we certainly want the user to be able to search for products by keyword. Recall from the preceding section that the scanCatalog and addProdByKey methods create a String array of keywords and also maintain a Hashtable that keeps a Vector of product Element references keyed by the keywords.

Rather than having the user type words into a search form to see if certain words are in the keyword list, we can present an HTML form using the SELECT input type and having all of the keywords and phrases set in it. The resulting display is shown in Figure 3.1.

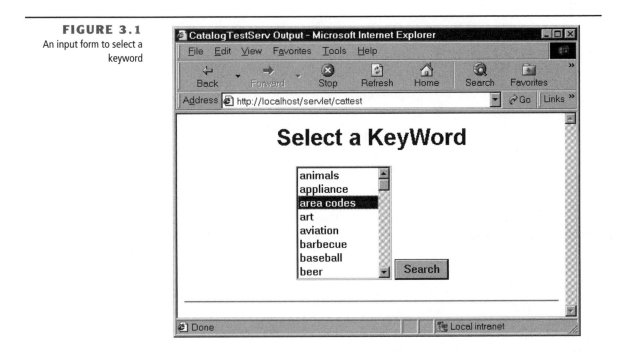

FIGURE 3.1
An input form to select a keyword

The HTML code that created this figure is shown (with only a few of the keywords) in Listing 3.8. Note that in addition to the keyword options we also include a hidden variable named action, with the value of keywdsearch.

Listing 3.8: The HTML to Create the Keyword Selection Form

```
<center><h2>Select a KeyWord</h2>
<form method="POST" action="http://localhost/servlet/cattest" >
<input type="HIDDEN" name="action" value="keywdsearch" >
<select name="keyword" size="8">
<option value="animals" > animals
<option value="appliance" > appliance
<option value="area codes" > area codes
<option value="art" > art
<option value="aviation" > aviation
<option value="barbecue" > barbecue
<option value="baseball" > baseball
<option value="beer" > beer

<option value="writing" > writing
</select>
<input type="SUBMIT" value="Search" >
</form>
</center><hr>
```

To encapsulate catalog-formatting functions in a class that are usable with both servlets and JavaServer Pages, we have written a `CatalogBean` class. By putting as much as possible of the formatting functions into `CatalogBean`, the servlet code becomes greatly simplified. The following code in the servlet is sufficient to generate the keyword selection form:

```
public void doKeywordSelect( PrintWriter out ){
    CatalogBean cb = new CatalogBean();
    cb.setHidden( "action","keywdsearch");
    out.println("<center><h2>Select a KeyWord</h2>");
    out.print( cb.doKeywordSelect( alias ) );
    out.println("</center><hr>");
}
```

The call to the `setHidden` method tells the `CatalogBean` to format all forms with a hidden variable tag. In this case, the result is the following:

```
<input type="HIDDEN" name="action" value="keywdsearch" >
```

By having the `doKeywordSelect` method return a `String`, as opposed to passing a `PrintWriter` to the method, we avoid tying the `doKeywordSelect` method to any particular output stream type. As shown in Listing 3.9, we use a `StringBuffer` to construct the complete form text. Note that the call to `getKeywords` gets the `String` array created by the `scanCatalog` method (Listing 3.6).

Listing 3.9: A Method to Format a String Array as a Selection Form (*CatalogBean.java*)

```java
public String doKeywordSelect(String alias ){
  StringBuffer sb = new StringBuffer( "<form method=\"POST\" action=\"" );
  sb.append( alias ); sb.append("\" >\r\n");
  String[] kwd = getKeywords();
  int i ;
  int ct = hiddenNames.size();
  if( ct > 0 ){
      for( i = 0; i < ct ; i++ ){
        sb.append("<input type=\"HIDDEN\" name=\"");
        sb.append( hiddenNames.elementAt(i) );
        sb.append("\" value=\"");
        sb.append( hiddenVals.elementAt(i) );
        sb.append( "\" >\r\n");
      }
  }
  sb.append("<select name=\"keyword\" size=\"8\">" );
  for( i = 0 ; i < kwd.length ; i ++ ){
      sb.append("<option value=\"" );
      sb.append( kwd[i] );
      sb.append( "\" > " );
      sb.append( kwd[i] ); sb.append("\r\n");
  }
  sb.append("</select>\r\n");
  sb.append("<input type=\"SUBMIT\" value=\"Search\" >\r\n" );
  sb.append("</form>\r\n" );
  return sb.toString();
}
```

Formatting Product Descriptions

When trying to decide how to present product descriptions, we determined that our design criteria should emphasize the following:

Flexibility of Styles   It is essential to separate considerations of style, such as colors and font sizes, from the code that creates the display.

Flexibility of Content   A method is needed that enables the Web-page designer to select the content of any part of the XML product description, without requiring a redesign of the Java classes.

Flexibility of Styles

The obvious choice for achieving flexibility of style is to use Cascading Style Sheets (CSS) to set style parameters for the various components of a Web page. CSS is currently the most widely supported standard and is an official part of the HTML 4 specification.

Placing style information in a separate file (called a *style sheet*) greatly reduces the amount of text your servlet has to generate. If the same style sheet is used for all pages on your site, the user's Web browser can cache it, thus reducing the response time for all of your site.

Listing 3.10 shows a simple style sheet that sets styles for the HTML <body>, <h1>, <h2>, and <p> tags and for four named styles that we use in the next example.

TIP   You can find an excellent tutorial on style-sheet usage at www.htmlhelp.com/reference/css.

Listing 3.10: An Example Style Sheet (*catalog.css*)

```
body{font-family:Arial font-size:10.0pt}
h1{font-size:30pt; font-family:Arial; color:red ;}

h2{font-size:20pt; font-family:Arial; color:navy; }
p {font-size:10pt; font-family:Arial, Helvetica; background-color:#fef6df ;}

.ch1{font-size:30pt; font-family:Arial; color:red ;}
.ch2{font-size:20pt; font-family:Arial; color:navy ;}
.ch3{font-size:15pt; font-family:Arial; color:purple ;}
.ch4{font-size:10pt; font-family:Arial; color:black ;}
```

A style sheet can be attached to an HTML page with a link tag placed in the <head> area of a page, as in this example:

```
<head><title>Catalog Test Servlet Output</title>
 <link rel="stylesheet"
   href="http://localhost/XmlEcommBook/catalog.css" type="text/css"
   media="screen" >
</head>
```

With the style sheet attached, setting the style for any element can be as simple as adding the style="ch2" attribute to a tag. The style then overrides the browser's default for that tag. That this is more efficient can be seen by comparing these HTML lines, which accomplish the same thing. Compare the following lines (which include style-sheets classes):

```
<a class="ch3" href="http://localhost/servlet/cattest?action=showproduct">
   Guide to Plants </a><span class="ch4">price ea = $12.99 </span>
```

with the following version (which includes font tags):

```
<font face="Arial" SIZE="15pt" color="purple" >
<a class="ch3" href="http://localhost/servlet/cattest?action=showproduct">
   Guide to Plants </a></font>
<font face="Arial" SIZE="10pt" color="black" >price ea = $12.99 </font>
```

Flexibility of Content

To provide for flexibility of content, we are going to use a formatting class named Product-Formatter. This class will output the data from an XML product Element in a format controlled by a list of field names with a matching list of styles to be applied to the text of the field.

As a simple example, to create a presentation in which the display for each product consists of the product name in the "ch3" format followed by the price in the "ch4" format, we define the following two String arrays:

```
String[] elem = { "prname", "price" };
String[] shortSt = { "ch3", "ch4"
```

We also require that the product name is formatted as a clickable link that will bring up a complete display for the selected product. This is accomplished by setting the aLink String to incorporate this value, as in the following line:

```
"http://localhost/servlet/cattest?action=showproduct
```

We also define an int variable named linkN that gives the index of the field that will become the clickable link. In this case, linkN is 0 so that the product name will become the clickable link. With these parameters set, the doOutput method, as shown in Listing 3.11, will format the data for a particular product Element into a String ready for output to an HTML page.

Listing 3.11: The *doOutput* Method (*ProductFormatter.java*)

```
public String doOutput( Element el ){
    StringBuffer sb = new StringBuffer( );
    String pid = null ;
    if( aLink != null ){
      pid = "id=" + el.getAttribute("id");
    }
    for( int i = 0 ; i < elem.length ; i++ ){
      if( i == linkN && pid != null ){
        sb.append( "<a class=\"" );
        sb.append( style[i] );
        sb.append("\" href=\"");
```

```
          sb.append( aLink );
          sb.append("\">");
          addText( sb, elem[i], el );
          sb.append( " </a>");
        }
        else {
          sb.append( "<span class=\"");
          sb.append( style[i] ); sb.append("\">");
          addText( sb, elem[i], el );
          sb.append( " </span>");
        }
      }
    }
    return sb.toString();
  }
```

For the product Element shown in Listing 3.12, the output of the doOutput method will be as follows:

```
<a class="ch3" href="http://localhost/servlet/cattest?action=showproduct">
Guide to Plants </a><span class="ch4">price ea = $12.99 </span>
```

Listing 3.12 A Single *product Element* from *catalog.xml*

```
<product id="bk0022" keywords="gardening, plants">
  <name>Guide to Plants</name>
  <description>
    <paragraph>
    <italics>Everything</italics> you've ever wanted to know about plants.
    </paragraph>
  </description>
  <price>$12.99</price>
  <quantity_in_stock>4</quantity_in_stock>
  <image format="gif" width="234" height="400" src="images/covers/plantsv1.gif">
  <caption>
  <paragraph>This is the cover from the first edition.</paragraph>
  </caption>
  </image>
  <onsale_date>
  <month>4</month>
    <day_of_month>4</day_of_month>
    <year>1999</year>
  </onsale_date>
  <shipping_info type="UPS" value="1.0" />
</product>
```

That takes care of formatting the data for a single product; now let's look at how to create a list of products. The `CatalogBean` has an array of `Element` references named `selected`. In the `setInitialSelect` method (Listing 3.13), this array can be set to either the complete list of products or the products in a single product line.

Listing 3.13: The *setInitialSelect* Method in CatalogBean (*CatalogBean.java*)

```java
public boolean setInitialSelect(String s){
    boolean ret = false ;
    if( s.equals("all") ){
      selected = cat.getAllProduct(); ret = true ;
    }
    else {
      selected = cat.getProductsByPL( s );
      if( selected != null ) ret = true ;
      else {
        System.out.println("selection problem");
      }
    }
    return ret ;
  }
```

`CatalogBean` also has the `doOutput` method, which simply calls the `ProductFormatter` class `doOutput` method with an `Element` in the `selected` array, as follows:

```java
public String doOutput( int n ){
    return pf.doOutput( selected[n] );
  }
```

Now we can put all of these parts together to get a formatted HTML page displaying the complete catalog. Listing 3.14 shows a simplified servlet `doPost` method. This method sets the response header, then writes the `<head>` and `<title>` tags, followed by a `String` containing the `<link>` tag pointing to a style sheet, as described earlier. Next, it writes the `<body>` tag and then calls the `completeCatalog` method. Finally, it writes the closing tags and closes the `PrintWriter`.

Listing 3.14: The *doPost* Method in a Servlet for Display of the Complete Catalog (*CatalogTestServ.java*)

```java
public void doPost(HttpServletRequest req, HttpServletResponse resp)
    throws ServletException, IOException
{
  resp.setContentType("text/html");
```

```
PrintWriter out = new PrintWriter(resp.getOutputStream());
String action = req.getParameter("action");
out.println("<html>");
out.println("<head><title>CatalogTestServ Output</title>");
out.println( cssLink );
out.println("</head>\r\n<body>");
try {
  if( "showcatalog".equals( action )){
    completeCatalog( out );
  }
  else if( "selectkeyword".equals( action )){
    doKeywordSelect( out );
  }
}catch( Exception e ){
    e.printStackTrace( out );
}
out.println("</body>");
out.println("</html>");
out.close();
}
```

As shown in Listing 3.15, the `completeCatalog` method writes the HTML tags to create a table with three columns. Each column is filled with the product information formatted by the `doOutput` method shown in Listing 3.11.

Listing 3.15: This Method in the Servlet Writes the Complete Catalog (*CatalogTestServ.java*)

```
public void completeCatalog( PrintWriter out ){
   CatalogBean cb = new CatalogBean();
   out.println("<h2>Complete Catalog</h2>");
   out.println("<table width=\"90%\" border=\"3\" align=\"center\" >");
   out.println("<thead><tr><th>Books</th><th>CDs</th><th>Gadgets</th>"
          + "</tr></thead>");
   out.println("<tbody><tr valign=\"top\"><td>");
   String link = alias + "?action=showproduct" ;
   cb.setInitialSelect("Books");
   int ct = cb.getSelectedCount();
   out.println("We have " + ct + " titles." + brcrlf );
   cb.setOutput("short", link);
   for( int i = 0 ; i < ct ; i++ ){
     out.println( cb.doOutput(i) );
```

```
        out.println( brcrlf );out.println( brcrlf );
    }
    out.println("</td><td>");
    cb.setInitialSelect("CDs");
    ct = cb.getSelectedCount();
    out.println("We have " + ct + " CD titles." + brcrlf );
    cb.setOutput("short", link);
    for( int i = 0 ; i < ct ; i++ ){
        out.println( cb.doOutput(i) );
        out.println( brcrlf );out.println( brcrlf );
    }
    out.println("</td><td>");
    cb.setInitialSelect("widgets");
    ct = cb.getSelectedCount();
    out.println("We have " + ct + " kinds." + brcrlf );
    cb.setOutput("short", link );
    for( int i = 0 ; i < ct ; i++ ){
        out.println( cb.doOutput(i) );
        out.println( brcrlf );out.println( brcrlf );
    }
    out.println("</td></tr></table>");
}
```

Listing 3.16 shows the text of the first part of the resulting HTML page. Note that many of the lines have been wrapped to fit this page. In spite of all of the space-saving use of a style sheet, the full page takes 17,213 bytes.

Listing 3.16: The First Part of the HTML Page Generated by the Servlet

```
<html>
<head><title>CatalogTestServ Output</title>
<link rel="stylesheet" href="http://localhost/XmlEcommBook/catalog.css"
    type="text/css" media="screen" >
</head>
<body>
<h2>Complete Catalog</h2>
<table width="90%" border="3" align="center" >
<thead><tr><th>Books</th><th>CDs</th><th>Gadgets</th></tr></thead>
<tbody><tr valign="top"><td>
We have 28 titles.<br />
```

```
<a class="ch3" href="http://localhost/servlet/cattest?action=showproduct">
  Guide to Plants </a><span class="ch4">price ea = $12.99 </span>
<br />

<br />

<a class="ch3" href="http://localhost/servlet/cattest?action=showproduct">
  Guide to Plants, Volume 2 </a><span class="ch4">price ea = $12.99 </span>
<br />

<br />

<a class="ch3" href="http://localhost/servlet/cattest?action=showproduct">
  The Genius's Guide to the 3rd Millenium </a><span class="ch4">price ea = $59.95
</span>
  <br />
```

Now for the end result of all of this effort. Figure 3.2 shows the browser display of the catalog.

FIGURE 3.2
The complete catalog display

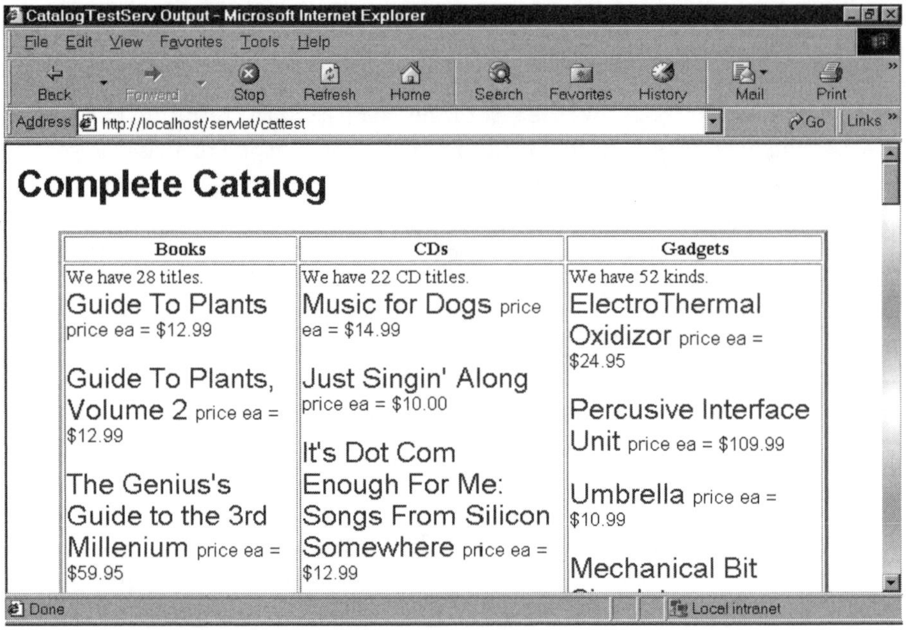

In the next chapter, we will add even more functionality and flexibility to the CatalogBean and ProductFormatter classes to create the displays needed for a shopping-cart application.

Filling a Shopping Cart

- Options for session tracking

- The HttpSession solution

- Classes to implement a shopping cart

You want to make it as easy as possible for your Web site users to locate items to buy, add them to a "shopping cart," and pay for them in a "seamless" experience. Unfortunately, basic HTML and Web protocols are not designed for this. This chapter examines the behind-the-scenes work needed to make it easy for the user to buy stuff!

The Shopping Cart Problem

Online commerce users instinctively understand the shopping cart analogy. It seems only natural that when shoppers visit a retail store they can toss articles in a container that stays with them until they decide to check out. Unfortunately, what might appear to an online shopper as browsing around a store in one continuous trip can be seen by the Web server as a disconnected series of requests and responses. That is because the basic Web HTTP protocol is stateless and has no way to determine that the present request should be associated with a previous request because they come from the same person.

The problem of keeping data for a particular user during an extended visit to a Web site is generally referred to as the *session-tracking* problem. There are three possible approaches to solving this problem: cookies, hidden form variables, and URL rewriting.

A *cookie* is a chunk of text information that a browser associates with the address of a particular Web site. The Web server sends cookie data with a response and the Web browser stores the text. Every time the browser sends a request to the Web server, this chunk of text is attached to one of the message headers where the server can find and interpret it. Cookie text takes the familiar form of `attribute=value`, just like XML attribute name and values.

One nice feature of cookies is that the programmer has control over the life span of the data. You can create cookies that will only be in effect for the duration of a single visit to a site, expire after a fixed number of days, or never expire. Commercial Web sites frequently remember repeat visitors by means of cookies having a long life span.

The Java servlet API offers facilities for sending and receiving cookie data, and this approach can solve many session-tracking problems. However, Web browsers impose a limit on the amount of text a cookie can store and the total number of cookies from a given site. This makes it impractical to store a full shopping cart as cookie text, so the usual approach is to store a unique customer ID with the cookie and use that as a key to look up the required customer information on the server.

To use hidden form variables for session tracking, your program must write hidden data into every form or link on every HTML page. For example, if we need to track the value of a customerid variable, every form should have the following:

```
<input type="hidden" name="customerid" value="124c41" >
```

and every link would have to include something like the following, in which the "?" separates the URL from the query string:

```
href="http://localhost/servlet/catalog?customerid=124c41"
```

The value of customerid would then be recovered in the servlet doGet or doPost method with code like:

```
String customerid = req.getParameter("customerid");
```

The technique called URL rewriting adds extra information to every URL that is the target of a form or link. The format chosen must not prevent the Web server from sending the request to the right servlet but still must be detectable by the servlet. The Java approach to URL rewriting results in URLs that use the semicolon character so that the rewritten URL looks like this:

```
href="http://localhost/servlet/catalog;jsessionid=124c41"
```

For session tracking in the ShoppingCart servlet, we are going to use the HttpSession class in the Java servlet API. This class allows the servlet engine to manage the details of session tracking with minimal effort on the part of the programmer.

Using *HttpSession* Objects

With this approach, the Java servlet engine (sometimes called the servlet *container*) manages a collection of objects that implement the HttpSession interface. Our program can use one of these objects to store any information required to create a shopping cart. Each HttpSession object has an id that is simply a String created when the object is created, and guaranteed to be unique.

This unique ID is tracked by one of two possible methods:

- **Cookie tracking**. The value of the id is sent to the user's browser as a cookie header generated by the HttpServletResponse object. The standard name for this cookie is "jsessionid" and a typical value would be: "9717879996250188366," simply a random number generated by the servlet engine. This value is picked up automatically from the next user request so our program simply asks for the HttpSession that belongs to a user.

- **URL rewriting**. The value of the ID is attached to every URL that a customer might use to submit a request to the server. Because this may involve URLs that are part of static templates or dynamically generated text, the programmer must make an extra effort to ensure that every URL gets rewritten.

For the sake of keeping our example code simple, our shopping cart servlet relies on the cookie tracking approach. These simple lines in the **doPost** method get the current **HttpSession** for this user. The **req** variable is the **HttpServletRequest** object. The **boolean** constant **true** in the call to **getSession** tells the servlet engine to create a new session object if the user request did not supply one. The second line illustrates how you can tell if the session is a new one.

```
HttpSession session = req.getSession(true);
if( session.isNew() ){
        System.out.print("Session is new " + session.getId() );
}
```

In the JavaServer Pages API, the name for the implicit **HttpSession** variable is **session**, so using that name consistently is a good habit in both servlets and JSP. Now let's take a quick look at the API you use when dealing with an **HttpSession** object.

The *HttpSession* API

The **HttpSession** interface is in the **javax.servlet.http** package. Table 4.1 summarizes the methods in the interface as of the version 2.2 API. There were several changes from the 2.1 API that we need to point out because some older servlet engines and books use the earlier version.

The **getAttribute** and **setAttribute** methods replace the earlier **getValue** and **setValue** methods. The **getAttributeNames** method replaces the earlier **getValueNames** method. These changes were done as part of a general cleanup of nomenclature in the servlet classes.

Storing an object reference in an **HttpSession** and recovering it is done with a **String** name, as in the following example where **session** is the **HttpSession**:

```
ShoppingCart cart = (ShoppingCart)session.getAttribute("cart");
if( cart == null ){ // presumably the first pass
    cart = new ShoppingCart();
    session.setAttribute( "cart",cart );
}
```

Security considerations led to some additional changes in the API from earlier versions. In the 2.1 version of the API, it was possible to use a **getSessionContext** method to get the associated `HttpSessionContext` object. This method and the `HttpSessionContext` interface are deprecated and will be removed from future versions of the library.

The 2.2 API emphasizes the restriction of essential Web application information within an application. The `ServletContext` interface defines methods that a servlet can use to communicate with the servlet container and share objects with other servlets in the same application. A particular `HttpSession` object can be used by more than one servlet, but only if the other servlets are part of the same application context. Membership of a servlet or JavaServer Page in a particular application is established by initialization parameters used by the servlet engine.

TABLE 4.1:   Summary of Methods in the *HttpSession* Class

Returns	Method	Return Value Use
Object	getAttribute(String name)	Returns the object attached with the specified name, or `null` if no object has the name.
void	setAttribute(String name, Object obj)	Attach the object to this session, with this name. Any previous reference with this name is lost.
Enumeration	getAttributeNames()	An Enumeration of `String` objects containing the names of all the objects attached to this session.
void	removeAttribute(String name)	Removes the object with this name from the session.
long	getCreationTime()	The system time when this session was created, as in `System.currentTimeMillis()`.
long	getLastAccessedTime()	The last time the client sent a request associated with this session—same scale as `getCreationTime`.
int	getMaxInactiveInterval()	The maximum time interval, in seconds, that the servlet container will keep this session open between client accesses.
void	setMaxInactiveInterval (int interval)	Sets the time, in seconds, between client requests before the servlet container will invalidate this session.
void	invalidate()	Invalidates this session and unbinds any objects bound to it.
boolean	isNew()	Returns `true` if the client does not yet know about the session or if the client chooses not to join the session. This is usually called right after calling the `getSession` method of an `HttpServletRequest` object.
String	getId()	Returns the unique identifier assigned to this session.

If the `HttpSession` mechanism just accepted attributes and didn't provide for a way to dispose of them, a servlet engine would run out of memory in a hurry. Fortunately there are several ways to design an application to avoid memory problems.

The default behavior for the servlet engines we are using for these examples (JRun and Tomcat) is for the engine to dispose of HttpSession objects that have not been used for 30 minutes. This time delay can typically be set in servlet engine initialization parameters for each application. You can set this period with the setMaxInactiveInterval method, as shown in Table 4.1. A setting of –1 prevents the HttpSession from ever being expired by the servlet engine. In that case it will be up to the programmer to explicitly remove the object with the invalidate method.

You can also explicitly remove particular objects from the HttpSession with the remove-Attribute (was removeValue in 2.1 API) method. The programmer must think very carefully before storing objects in a session. Keep in mind that you have no control over when the session might be accessed next. It would not be a good idea to store objects, such as database connections, that consume lots of system resources.

The *HttpSessionBindingListener* Interface

As an aid to managing system resources that may be involved with sessions, and as a debugging tool, the servlet API defines the HttpSessionBindingListener interface and the HttpSessionBindingEvent class. This interface defines two methods:

> **void valueBound(HttpSessionBindingEvent event)**   When an object implementing the interface is attached to an HttpSession, this method is called. The event carries two kinds of information—the name that was used to attach the object to a session, and the session id String.

> **void valueUnbound(HttpSessionBindingEvent event)**   This method is called when the object is about to be removed from the session. Normally this will be when the HttpSession invalidate method is called due to inactivity.

In the CatalogServ servlet, we demonstrate the use of this interface for simple debugging.

The Shopping Cart in Java

The example servlet we have created for this chapter is limited to catalog presentation and ordering functions. In a real commercial site, these functions would be only a small part of the user's experience. In this example, a new HttpSession object is created when a user enters the CatalogServ servlet for the first time. In a real site, the session might have been created in another part of the site.

Possible entry points for a user could be viewing the entire catalog, viewing the complete listing for a product line, or viewing the results of a keyword search. In any case, we don't create a `ShoppingCart` object until the user is sufficiently interested in a particular product to view the full product description. At that point we create a `CartItem` for that product directly from the XML representation of that product and store it in the `ShoppingCart`.

As the user browses the catalog items, we keep the `CartItem` objects for each product that the user has decided to purchase and discard those that the user decides not to purchase. At every page, the user has the option to view other parts of the catalog, search, view the current cart contents, or check out. Now let's look at the details of how this is accomplished.

The *CartItem* and *ShoppingCart* Classes

The minimum requirement for an object to represent a product in the user's shopping cart would just be to have a product `id` code and the number purchased. The product name, price, and other details could be looked up through the catalog XML. For the actual `CartItem` class, we added name, price, and shipping information variables as shown in Listing 4.1.

There are several important points to note about the `CartItem` class. First, the constructor works directly from the DOM `Element` object representing the product. This makes it simpler to add any additional variables to the XML catalog. Second, the class implements the `Serializable` interface. This makes it feasible to send the collection of `CartItem` objects representing an order to another Java program by serialization. Serialization is also required if the servlet engine has to store the session or transmit it to another server. Finally, the access methods, such as `getId` and `setNumberOrdered`, follow the JavaBean naming convention to facilitate using a `CartItem` object in JavaServer Page code.

Listing 4.1 The *CartItem* Class (*CartItem.java*)

```
package com.XmlEcomBook.catalog;

import java.util.* ;
import java.io.* ;
import org.xml.sax.* ;
import org.w3c.dom.* ;

public class CartItem implements java.io.Serializable
{ // be sure to change this if substantive variables change
  static final long serialVersionUID = 3260689382642549142L;

  // these are set from the constructor
  private String id ; // from product element
```

```
private String name ; // from name element
private String price ; // from price element
private String shippingType ; // from shipping_info element
private String shippingValue ; // may be null if type is special

private int numberOrdered ; // changes

 public String getId(){ return id ;}
 public String getName(){ return name ; }
 public String getPrice() { return price ; }
 public String getShippingType() { return shippingType ; }
 public String getShippingValue() { return shippingValue ; }

 public void setNumberOrdered( int n ){ numberOrdered = n ;
  // System.out.println("setNumberOrdered " + n );
 }
 public int getNumberOrdered(){ return numberOrdered ; }

 // constructor uses a <product> org.w3c.dom.Element
 public CartItem( Element pe ){
   id = pe.getAttribute("id");
   NodeList nl = pe.getElementsByTagName( "name" );
   name = nl.item(0).getFirstChild().getNodeValue() ;
   nl = pe.getElementsByTagName( "price" );
   price = nl.item(0).getFirstChild().getNodeValue() ;
   nl = pe.getElementsByTagName( "shipping_info" );
   Element ship = (Element) nl.item(0);
   shippingType = ship.getAttribute("type");
   shippingValue = ship.getAttribute("value"); // may be ""
 }

 // handy for debugging
 public String toString() {
   StringBuffer sb = new StringBuffer("CartItem name:");
   sb.append( name ); sb.append(" numberOrdered: ");
   sb.append( Integer.toString( numberOrdered ));
   return sb.toString();
 }
}
```

The ShoppingCart class turns out to be quite simple because all it has to do is provide for manipulating CartItem objects. As shown in Listing 4.2, we store CartItem references in both a `Vector` and a `Hashtable`. The reason for using both is that the order of objects in a `Hashtable` is unpredictable and may even change as more objects are added. It seems reasonable for the cart to maintain the items in a predictable and reproducible order in the `Vector` while allowing access by means of the product `id` through the `Hashtable`.

Note that the `ShoppingCart` class implements the `Serializable` interface so a complete `ShoppingCart` can be transferred between Java programs or written to a file by serialization.

Listing 4.2 The Start of the *ShoppingCart* Class (*ShoppingCart.java*)

```
package com.XmlEcomBook.catalog;

import java.io.*;
import java.util.* ;

public class ShoppingCart implements java.io.Serializable
{
  private Vector items ;  // maintains order of selection of items
  private Hashtable itemsById ;

  public ShoppingCart(){
    items = new Vector();
    itemsById = new Hashtable();
  }

  // items vector may be empty
  public Vector getItems(){ return items ; }

   // returns CartItem for this id or null if not in list
  public CartItem getProdById(String s ){
    return (CartItem) itemsById.get( s );
  }

  // CartItem is assumed to be unique
  public int addItem( CartItem x ){
    items.addElement( x );
    itemsById.put( x.getId() , x );
    return items.size();
  }
```

Listing 4.3 shows the remaining methods in the `ShoppingCart` class. Because we are keeping a reference to a `CartItem` in two collections, the `removeById` method has to use the product id to get the CartItem reference from the Hashtable, and then call the removeElement method in the items Vector.

Listing 4.3 The Remainder of the *ShoppingCart* Class (*ShoppingCart.java*)

```java
// remove an item from the cart by product id
public CartItem removeById( String s ){
  CartItem ret = (CartItem)itemsById.get( s );
  if( ret == null ) return null ;
  itemsById.remove(s); // remove by key
  items.removeElement( ret );
  return ret ;
}

// remove all CartItem for which the numberOrdered is zero
// returns the count of items left
public int removeEmptyItems(){
  Enumeration keys = itemsById.keys();
  while( keys.hasMoreElements()){
    String key = (String)keys.nextElement();
    CartItem ci = (CartItem)itemsById.get(key);
    if( ci.getNumberOrdered() == 0 ){
      removeById( key );
    }
  }
  return items.size();
}

// mainly for debugging
public String toString()
{ StringBuffer sb = new StringBuffer( "ShoppingCart has " +
      items.size() + " items.\r\n" ) ;
  Enumeration e = items.elements();
  while( e.hasMoreElements()){
    sb.append("Item: ");
    sb.append( e.nextElement().toString() );
    sb.append("\r\n");
  }
  return sb.toString();
}

}
```

The *CatalogServ* Class

The class we have written to demonstrate presentation of catalog items and managing the user's `ShoppingCart` is called `CatalogServ`. We use improved versions of the presentation classes from Chapter 3, "Presenting an XML Catalog Online," and add session tracking and shopping cart capabilities. This servlet provides for the following functions:

- Presenting compact listings of the catalog items using selection criteria, such as
  - The full catalog
  - A product line
  - Items associated with a particular keyword
- Presenting an item in detail with controls
  - Add the item to the cart
  - Change the number purchased
- Presenting a list of the current shopping cart items

To simplify things, the only display that allows adding an item to the cart or changing the number of items purchased is the detailed display.

In addition, the servlet does not attempt to demonstrate any other functions of a commercial Web site. As you can see in Figure 4.1, the servlet simply generates "Your Site Navigation Could Go Here" where a normal commercial site would put logos and site navigation features.

FIGURE 4.1

Presenting the complete catalog with *CatalogServ*

Before delving into the source code for `CatalogServ`, let's look at some of the other displays it generates. Figure 4.2 shows the keyword selection display as part of the complete screen. This is the same basic form shown in Chapter 3, Figure 3.1, but the `CatalogServ` servlet adds additional active areas at the bottom of the page for "Full Catalog," "Books," "CDs," "widgets," and "Search."

FIGURE 4.2
Presenting the keyword
selection form

Table 4.2 shows a list of the "action" parameters that the `CatalogServ` servlet responds to. The action command is typically modified by additional parameters.

TABLE 4.2: The Action Commands Recognized by *CatalogServ*

action	Modified by	Resulting Display
showcatalog	select parameter = "all" or one of the product lines	A table of all product lines. Example Figure 4.1.
showcatalog	select parameter = a product line	A list of products in a particular product line. Example Figure 4.3.
selectkeyword	select parameter = "all"	The keyword selection form. Example Figure 4.2.
showproduct	id parameter from form	A complete product information display. Example Figure 4.4.

TABLE 4.2: The Action Commands Recognized by *CatalogServ* (continued)

action	Modified by	Resulting Display
keywdsearch	keyword parameter from form	A list of products with that keyword.
setcart	id and itemct parameters from form	A complete product information display with a changed number ordered. Example Figure 4.5.
showcart	none	A list of all products in the user's shopping cart including the number ordered. Example Figure 4.6.

Servlet Initialization

As shown in Listing 4.4, the CatalogServ class has a number of static variables that define various resources. We have shown typical values from a working example in the listing. Normally these values will be replaced by system-specific values stored in a catalog.properties file and read by the init method. We will be using the Properties class, an extension of Hashtable found in the java.util package, which has very convenient methods for loading text parameters from a file.

Listing 4.4 The Static Variables and *Init* Method of *CatalogServ* (*CatalogServ.java*)

```java
package com.XmlEcomBook.catalog;

import java.io.*;
import java.util.* ;
import javax.servlet.*;
import javax.servlet.http.*;

public class CatalogServ extends HttpServlet
{
  static String brcrlf = "<br />\r\n" ;
  static String version = "1.03 Oct 17, 2000";
  static String cssLinkA =  "<link rel=\"stylesheet\" href=\"" ;
  // following is part of a web server URL for the style sheet
  static String cssLinkB = "XmlEcommBook/catalog/catalog.css" ;
  static String cssLinkC = "\" type=\"text/css\" media=\"screen\" >" ;
  static String resourcepath = "XmlEcommBook/catalog/" ;
  static String host = "http://localhost/";
   // these are servlet engine aliases
  static String servlet = "servlet/catalog" ;
  static String checkout = "servlet/checkout" ;
```

```
    // these are complete webserver paths
    static String cssLink = cssLinkA + host + cssLinkB + cssLinkC ;
    static String alias ; // for catalog servlet
    static String checkoutalias ;
    static String resources ; // for images, style sheets, etc

    // now for instance variables
    String catPath = "e:\\scripts\\XMLgifts" ; // for xml

    String catName = "catalog.xml" ;
    Properties catProp = new Properties();

    public void init(ServletConfig config) throws ServletException
    { try {
......super.init(config);

        System.out.println("CatalogTestServ init called, version "
            + version );
        String tmp = config.getInitParameter("workdir");
        if( tmp != null ) catPath = tmp ;
        File f = new File( catPath, "catalog.properties");
        if( f.exists() && f.canRead() ){
            FileInputStream fis = new FileInputStream(f) ;
            catProp.load( fis );
            fis.close();
            tmp = catProp.getProperty("csspath");
            if( tmp != null ) cssLinkB = tmp;
            tmp = catProp.getProperty("host");
            if( tmp != null ) host = tmp ;
            tmp = catProp.getProperty("resourcepath" ) ;
            if( tmp != null ) resourcepath = tmp ;
            tmp = catProp.getProperty("catalogservlet");
            if( tmp != null ) servlet = tmp ;
            tmp = catProp.getProperty("checkoutservlet" );
            if( tmp != null ) checkout = tmp ;
        }
        else { System.out.println("CatalogServ can't read catalog.properties");
        }
        resources = host + resourcepath ;
        alias = host + servlet ;
        checkoutalias = host + checkout ;
```

```
        System.out.println( "resources:" + resources );
        System.out.println("servlet: " + alias );
        System.out.println("checkout: " + checkoutalias );
        CatalogBean.setTheCatalog( catPath, catName );
        CatalogBean.setResourcePath( resources );
      }catch( Exception e ){
        System.out.println("CatalogTestServ init " + e );
      }
    }
```

Note that the `init` method calls two static methods in the `CatalogBean` class. The `set-TheCatalog` method call causes the XML file representing the products to be read in, and the `setTheResourcPath` method sets the path which will be used to address resources such as product images. You'll find the `CatalogBean` class defined later in the chapter in the section on "The `CatalogBean` Class."

The *doGet* and *doPost* Methods

All GET requests are simply forwarded to `doPost`, as shown in Listing 4.5. The `doPost` method puts together a finished page by combining a standard HTML HEAD section with output from three methods—`doPageTop`, `doPageMid`, and `doPageEnd`. Note that the call to `getSession` with a parameter of `true` always creates a new `HttpSession` if one does not exist for this user.

As a demonstration of debugging techniques, we check the session to determine if it is a new one. If the session is new, we attach a `CartListener` object and print the `id` of the new session. The function of the `CartListener` is discussed later. These debugging statements would probably be removed when the application is completely debugged as the `Date` object is rather time consuming to construct and print.

Listing 4.5 The *doGet* and *doPost* Methods (*CatalogServ.java*)

```
public void doGet(HttpServletRequest req, HttpServletResponse resp)
    throws ServletException, IOException   {
  doPost( req, resp );
}

public void doPost(HttpServletRequest req, HttpServletResponse resp)
  throws ServletException, IOException
{
  resp.setContentType("text/html");
```

```
    PrintWriter out = new PrintWriter(resp.getOutputStream());
    outputHead( out );
    HttpSession session = req.getSession(true);
    if( session.isNew() ){
       // session.putValue( "listener", new CartListener() );
       session.setAttribute( "listener", new CartListener() );
       System.out.print("Session is new " + session.getId() +
             " " + new Date().toString() );
    }
    try {
      doPageTop( req, resp, out, session );
      doPageMid( req, resp, out, session );
      doPageEnd( req, resp, out, session );
    }catch( Exception e ){
      e.printStackTrace( out );
    }
    out.println("</body>");
    out.println("</html>");
    out.close();
  }

  private void outputHead( PrintWriter out ){
    out.println("<html>");
    out.println("<head><title>Catalog Information</title>");
    out.println( cssLink );
    out.println("</head>\r\n<body>");
  }
// compose and output all material at the top of the page
  public void doPageTop( HttpServletRequest req, HttpServletResponse resp,
        PrintWriter out, HttpSession session ){
    out.print("<h1>XMLgifts</h1>");
    out.print("<h2>Your Site Navigation Could Go Here</h2>\r\n");
  }
```

In this example, the doPageTop method is very simple. In a real commercial Web site, this method could be used to display general site navigation components and other functions.

The *doPageEnd* Method

In this example, the doPageEnd method (Listing 4.6) simply creates a bunch of active links at the bottom of the page. The links for various kinds of catalog access are always generated, but some links appear only when the user's ShoppingCart contains items. Note that we call the removeEmptyItems method in ShoppingCart to ensure that the nitem variable correctly reflects the current contents of the cart.

Listing 4.6 The *doPageEnd* Method (*CatalogServ.java*)

```
public void doPageEnd( HttpServletRequest req, HttpServletResponse resp,
      PrintWriter out, HttpSession session ){
//ShoppingCart cart = (ShoppingCart)session.getValue("cart");
ShoppingCart cart = (ShoppingCart)session.getAttribute("cart");
String a1 = "<a href=\"" + alias + "?action=" ;
int nitem = 0  ; // permit checkout if cart has any items
out.print("<center>");
if( cart != null &&
    (nitem = cart.removeEmptyItems()) > 0 ){
  // out.print( cart.toString());  // debugging
  out.print( brcrlf );
  out.print( a1 +"showcart\" > Show Cart (" + nitem +
      " items)</a>   " );
  out.print("<a href=\"" + checkoutalias +
      "?action=initial\" >Checkout Now</a>   \r\n");
}
out.println( a1 + "showcatalog&select=all\" >Full Catalog</a>   ");
String[] prodL = CatalogBean.getCat().getProductLineNames();
for( int i = 0 ; i < prodL.length ; i++ ){
  out.print( a1 + "showcatalog&select=" + prodL[i] + "\" >");
  out.println( " " + prodL[i] + " </a>   ");
}
out.print( a1 + "selectkeyword&select=all\" > Search </a>" );
out.print("</center>\r\n");
out.println("<hr><center>" + version + "</center>\r\n");
}
```

The *doPageMid* Method

This is the method that determines how the servlet responds to the user's request. The value of the action parameter controls the selection of an output method that in turn generates the required presentation. As shown in Listing 4.7, a series of if statements determines which method is called.

Listing 4.7 The *doPageMid* Method (*CatalogServ.java*)

```java
public void doPageMid( HttpServletRequest req, HttpServletResponse resp,
        PrintWriter out, HttpSession session ){
    String action = req.getParameter("action");
    String select = req.getParameter("select");
    if( "showcatalog".equals( action )){
        if( select == null || select.equals("all") ){
            completeCatalog( out );
        }
        else {
            productLineCatalog( out, select );
        }
    }
    else if( "selectkeyword".equals( action )){
        if( select == null || select.equals("all") ){
            doKeywordSelect( out );
        }
    }
    else if( "keywdsearch".equals( action )) {
        String keyword = req.getParameter("keyword");
        if( keyword != null ){
            keywordCatalog( out, keyword );
        }
    }
    else if( "showproduct".equals( action ) ||
            "setcart".equals( action) ){
        doShowProduct( req, resp, out, session, action );
    }else if( "showcart".equals( action ) ){
        doShowCart( req, resp, out, session, action );
    }
}
```

The completeCatalog (Listing 4.8) and productLineCatalog (Listing 4.9) methods take a similar approach to generating a table populated with a short item listing. The main difference being that in the completeCatalog, as seen in Figure 4.1, the table has three columns reflecting the three product lines in our catalog. Each product line is selected by calling the setInitialSelect method of CatalogBean. Handling more than four product lines with this table layout would probably look pretty bad, so a different approach would be needed.

The HTML text that is written for each product is similar to the following:

```
<a class="ch3"
href="http://localhost/servlet/catalog?action=showproduct&id=bk0022">
Guide to Plants </a><span class="ch4">price ea = $12.99 </span>
```

This makes the product name an active link that will send the `action` and `id` parameters to the servlet and cause display of full product information. The `class` attributes control the font and color used for the different chunks of text by selecting styles from the catalog.css style sheet.

Listing 4.8 The *doKeywordSelect and completeCatalog* Methods (*CatalogServ.java*)

```java
public void doKeywordSelect( PrintWriter out ){
    CatalogBean cb = new CatalogBean();
    cb.setHidden( "action","keywdsearch");
    out.println("<center><h2>Select a KeyWord</h2>");
    out.print( cb.doKeywordSelect( alias ) );
    out.println("</center><hr>");
}

public void completeCatalog( PrintWriter out ){
    CatalogBean cb = new CatalogBean();
    out.println("<h2>Complete Catalog</h2>");
    out.println("<table width=\"90%\" border=\"3\" align=\"center\" >");
    out.println("<thead><tr><th>Books</th><th>CDs</th><th>Gadgets</th>"
          + "</tr></thead>");
    out.println("<tbody><tr valign=\"top\"><td>");
    String link = alias + "?action=showproduct" ;
    cb.setInitialSelect("Books");
    int ct = cb.getSelectedCount();
    out.println("We have " + ct + " titles." + brcrlf );
    cb.setOutput("short", link);
    for( int i = 0 ; i < ct ; i++ ){
        out.println( cb.doListOutput(i) );
        out.println( brcrlf );out.println( brcrlf );
    }
    out.println("</td><td>");
    cb.setInitialSelect("CDs");
    ct = cb.getSelectedCount();
    out.println("We have " + ct + " CD titles." + brcrlf );
    cb.setOutput("short", link);
```

```
for( int i = 0 ; i < ct ; i++ ){
  out.println( cb.doListOutput(i) );
  out.println( brcrlf );out.println( brcrlf );
}
out.println("</td><td>");
cb.setInitialSelect("widgets");
ct = cb.getSelectedCount();
out.println("We have " + ct + " kinds." + brcrlf );
cb.setOutput("short", link );
for( int i = 0 ; i < ct ; i++ ){
  out.println( cb.doListOutput(i) );
  out.println( brcrlf );out.println( brcrlf );
}
out.println("</td></tr></table>");
}
```

The productLineCatalog method, as shown in Listing 4.9, produces a table that is one column wide. After setting up the start of the HTML table, the variable line is used in the call to the CatalogBean method setInitialSelect to select a single product line. Then we just iterate through the selected list, using the doListOutput method to output the HTML markup for each product. Finally, we finish off the single table row. A typical result is shown in Figure 4.3.

Listing 4.9 The *productLineCatalog* Method (*CatalogServ.java*)

```
public void productLineCatalog( PrintWriter out, String line ){
    CatalogBean cb = new CatalogBean();
    out.println("<h2>" + line + " Catalog</h2>");
    out.println("<table width=\"90%\" border=\"3\" align=\"center\" >");
    out.println("<thead><tr><th>" + line + "</th>" + "</tr></thead>");
    out.println("<tbody><tr valign=\"top\"><td>");
    String link = alias + "?action=showproduct" ;
    cb.setInitialSelect( line );
    int ct = cb.getSelectedCount();
    out.println("We have " + ct + " items." + brcrlf );
    cb.setOutput("short", link);
    for( int i = 0 ; i < ct ; i++ ){
      out.println( cb.doListOutput(i) );
      out.println( brcrlf );out.println( brcrlf );
    }
    out.println("</td></tr></table>");
}
```

FIGURE 4.3
The display for a single
product line

The keywordCatalog method (Listing 4.10) takes a similar approach, but the selection is set by the keyword variable in the call to the setKeywordSelect method of CatalogBean.

Listing 4.10 This Method Shows Items Having a Selected Keyword (*CatalogServ.java*)

```java
public void keywordCatalog( PrintWriter out, String keyword ){
    CatalogBean cb = new CatalogBean();
    out.println("<h2>Selected by " + keyword + " Catalog</h2>");
    out.println("<table width=\"90%\" border=\"3\" align=\"center\" >");
    out.println("<thead><tr><th>" + keyword + "</th>" + "</tr></thead>");
    out.println("<tbody><tr valign=\"top\"><td>");
    String link = alias + "?action=showproduct" ;
    cb.setKeywordSelect( keyword );
    int ct = cb.getSelectedCount();
    out.println("We have " + ct + " items." + brcrlf );
    cb.setOutput("short", link);
    for( int i = 0 ; i < ct ; i++ ){
      out.println( cb.doListOutput(i) );
      out.println( brcrlf );out.println( brcrlf );
    }
    out.println("</td></tr></table>");
}
```

Creating a Full Product Display

The doShowProduct method of the CatalogServ class is responsible for controlling the display of full information on a single product item. There are several variations on the form of the display, depending on whether or not there is an image that is attached to the product Element in the XML, and also on whether the item is in the user's shopping cart.

Figure 4.4 shows a typical display generated for an item that is not yet in the user's cart and has an image. The button in the lower right will generate a request to the servlet with an action parameter value of setcart and an itemct value of 1. This will add this item to the user's cart with a quantity ordered of one.

FIGURE 4.4
Product display with an associated image

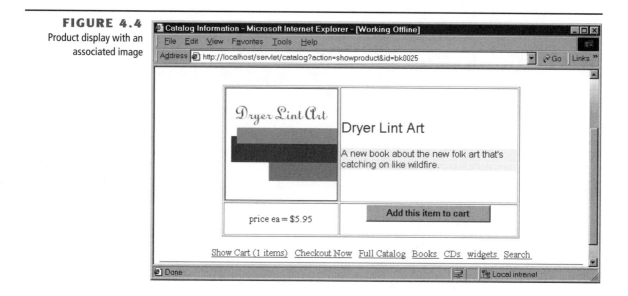

If the product is in the user's ShoppingCart object, the display includes a field that shows the present value of numberOrdered and provides for changing that number. An example of this display when an image is not attached to the product is shown in Figure 4.5. If the user clicks the "Change" button, the request to the servlet has an action parameter value of set-cart and an itemct value of the contents of the text field.

FIGURE 4.5
Product display without an
image

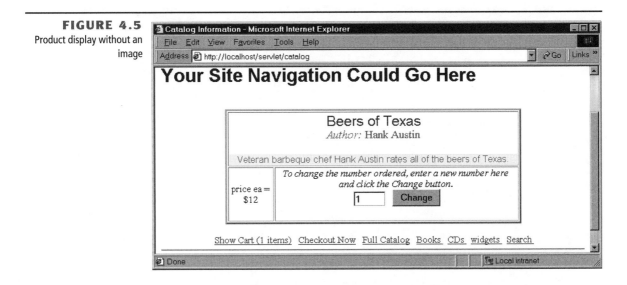

Now let's look at the details of the doShowProduct method, as shown in Listing 4.11. This method shows detailed information for a single product and supports adding the product to the user's shopping cart. The first thing this method has to do is to get an instance of the ShoppingCart class. The code shown uses the getAttribute method of the HttpSession class, which is preferable to the deprecated getValue method. The commented-out line shows how getValue would be used if you have a servlet engine based on the 2.1 API.

When doShowProduct is called, the HttpServletRequest will always have an id parameter identifying the product to be displayed.

The doShowProduct method is called with an action value of setcart when the user has clicked a button in a display, such as that in Figure 4.4 or 4.5. In that case, the itemct parameter must be interpreted as a new value for the number of items ordered.

When doShowProduct is called with an action value of showproduct, the value of the numberOrdered in the corresponding CartItem will not be changed.

Listing 4.11 Showing a Single Product Item with *ShoppingCart* Capability (*CatalogServ.java*)

```
public void doShowProduct( HttpServletRequest req, HttpServletResponse resp,
        PrintWriter out, HttpSession session, String action ){
    // ShoppingCart cart = (ShoppingCart)session.getValue("cart");
    // older servlet engines use getValue
```

```
ShoppingCart cart = (ShoppingCart)session.getAttribute("cart"); // API 2.2
if( cart == null ){ // presumably the first pass
    cart = new ShoppingCart();
    //session.putValue("cart", cart ); // older
    session.setAttribute( "cart",cart ); // API 2.2
}
out.print( brcrlf );
CatalogBean cb = new CatalogBean();
String id = req.getParameter( "id" );
if( "setcart".equals( action ) ){
  String tmp = req.getParameter("itemct");
  int itemct = 0;
  try {
    itemct = Integer.parseInt( tmp );
  }catch(NumberFormatException e){
      System.out.println("doShowProduct " + e );
  }
  CartItem item = cart.getProdById( id );
  if( item == null ){
      item = cb.createCartItem( id );
      cart.addItem( item );
  }
  item.setNumberOrdered( itemct );
  cart.removeEmptyItems();
}
out.print("<table width=\"70%\" border=\"3\" align=\"center\" >\r\n");
cb.doFullItem( id, out, cart, alias );
out.print("</table>\r\n");
}
```

The showcart action causes the doShowCart method to be called. As shown in Listing 4.12, this method writes the HTML tags that create the start and end of a table. The rows of the table are written by the doCartList method in CatalogBean.

Listing 4.12 The *doShowCart* Method (*CatalogServ.java*)

```
public void doShowCart( HttpServletRequest req, HttpServletResponse resp,
      PrintWriter out, HttpSession session, String action ){
  // ShoppingCart cart = (ShoppingCart)session.getValue("cart");
  // older servlet engines use getValue
  ShoppingCart cart = session.getAttribute("cart"); // API 2.2
```

```
    if( cart == null ){
        out.println("Serious problem with session data" + brcrlf );
        return ;
    }
    CatalogBean cb = new CatalogBean();
    String link = alias + "?action=showproduct" ;
    cb.setOutput("short", link);
    out.print("<table width=\"90%\" border=\"3\" align=\"center\" >");
    cb.doCartList( out, cart );
    out.print("</table>\r\n");
}
```

Using the *CartListener* Class

Because the servlet engine manages so much of the behavior of an `HttpSession` object, debugging problems related to sessions can get tricky. The servlet API provides the `HttpSessionBindingListener` interface and `HttpSessionBindingEvent` to help deal with debugging and with managing resources that might be attached to an `HttpSession`.

Listing 4.13 shows a simple use of this interface in the `CartListener` class, an inner class in `CatalogServ`. In this example we simply record the system time when the object is attached to an `HttpSession` and then print the lifetime of the object when the session is destroyed. A `CartListener` object is attached to the `ShoppingCart` object when it is first created in the **doPost** method (Listing 4.5).

Listing 4.13 The *CartListener* Inner Class (*CatalogServ.java*)

```
class CartListener implements
    HttpSessionBindingListener {
  long created ;
  public void valueBound( HttpSessionBindingEvent evt ){
     created = System.currentTimeMillis();
  }
  public void valueUnbound( HttpSessionBindingEvent evt ){
     long del = System.currentTimeMillis() - created ;
     System.out.println( "Session lifetime: " + ( del / 1000 )
         + " seconds ");
  }
 }
}
```

The *CatalogBean* Class

As you have seen in the `CatalogServ` class methods, the job of creating formatted output for a product is handled by methods in the `CatalogBean` class. One reason for moving output formatting out of the servlet class was to make it easy to implement catalog functions in JavaServer Pages instead of a servlet. We don't have space in this chapter to work up a JSP version of the catalog, but you can see JSP in action in Chapter 5, "Billing and Order Confirmation."

Most of the methods in `CatalogBean` as used in this chapter remain unchanged from the version of Chapter 3. The most important changes are related to working with a `Shopping-Cart` and with `CartItem` objects. Recall that `CatalogBean` has a static variable for the `TheCatalog` object that manages the DOM created from the catalog XML file. In the current version of `CatalogBean`, we made this variable private and provided an access method as follows:

```
private static TheCatalog cat ;

static void setTheCatalog( String path, String name ){
  File f = new File( path, name );
  cat = new TheCatalog( f, null, null );
  cat.scanCatalog();
}
static TheCatalog getCat(){ return cat ; }
```

We have also added a static `resourcePath` variable and a method to set it when the servlet is initialized as follows:

```
private static String resourcePath ; // as used for images, sounds, etc
  static void setResourcePath( String s ){ resourcePath = s ; }
```

Working With *CartItem* and *ShoppingCart*

As shown in Listing 4.14, `CatalogBean` handles creation of a `CartItem` for a product by getting the `Element` that contains product information from the `cat` instance of `TheCatalog`.

The `doCartList` method, shown in Listing 4.14, controls output of all of the `CartItem` objects held in a `ShoppingCart` instance. The formatting to create the start and end of the display table is provided by the `doShowCart` method in `CatalogServ`. The `doCartList` method provides formatting to make each item a row in an HTML table and display the current value of the `numberOrdered`. A typical resulting display is shown in Figure 4.6.

Listing 4.14 ShoppingCart Related Methods in *CatalogBean* (*CatalogBean.java*)

```java
public CartItem createCartItem( String id ){
  Element pE = cat.getProductElByID( id );
  return new CartItem( pE );
}

// we are in a <table>.. </table> pf was created with setOutput
public void doCartList( PrintWriter out,
    ShoppingCart cart  ){
  Vector v = cart.getItems();
  int ct = v.size();
  for( int i = 0 ; i < ct ; i++ ){
    CartItem item = (CartItem)v.elementAt(i);
    out.print("<tr><td>");
    String id = item.getId();
    out.print( pf.doListOutput( cat.getProductElByID(id)));
    out.print( "</td><td>");
    out.print( "Number ordered: " + item.getNumberOrdered() );
    out.print( "</td></tr>\r\n");
  }
}
```

FIGURE 4.6
Display of shopping cart contents

The complicated formatting of a full item display, as shown in Figures 4.4 and 4.5, is controlled by the doFullItem method shown in Listing 4.15. Basically, we build a table with three or four sections, depending on the presence of an image. This table organizes the product image, name, descriptive information, price, and number ordered. A ProductFormatter object is created with the "full" style to handle output of the various chunks of text taken from the product XML.

Normally a CartItem corresponding to the product id will have already been attached to the cart. However, if one does not already exist in the cart, a new one is created.

The presence or absence of an image tag in the product XML controls the formatting of the top row of the table. If there is no image, we allow the description to take up the entire top of the table.

Listing 4.15 The *doFullItem* Method (*CatalogBean.java*)

```java
// we are in a <table>.. </table>
public void doFullItem( String id, PrintWriter out,
     ShoppingCart cart, String alias ){
  pf = new ProductFormatter( "full" );
  pf.setResourcePath( resourcePath );
  Element pE = cat.getProductElByID( id );
  // out.print( cart.toString() );  // debugging
  if( pE == null ){
     out.print("Bad Product ID " + id ); return ;
  }
  CartItem ci = cart.getProdById( id );
  if( ci == null ){
    ci = new CartItem( pE );
    System.out.println("Create CartItem " + ci.toString() );
  }
  String imgS = pf.doImageTag( pE );
  if( imgS != null ){
     out.print("<tr><td align=\"center\">");
     out.print(pf.doImageTag( pE ));
     out.print("</td><td align =\"left\" >");
  }
  else{ // no image, spread description
    out.print("<tr><td align=\"center\" colspan=\"2\" >");
  }
```

```
out.print(pf.doProdName( pE ));
out.print(pf.doAuthorArtist( pE ));
out.print(pf.doDescription( pE ));
out.print("</td></tr>\r\n");
out.print("<tr><td align=\"center\" >");
out.print(pf.doPrice( pE ));
// lower right cell contains form
out.print("</td><td align=\"center\" ><form method=\"POST\" action=\"");
out.print( alias ); out.print( "\" >\r\n" );
out.print("<input type=\"HIDDEN\" name=\"id\" value=\"");
out.print( id ); out.print("\" >");
out.print("<input type=\"HIDDEN\" name=\"action\""
   + " value=\"setcart\" >");
if( ci.getNumberOrdered() == 0 ){
  out.print("<input type=\"HIDDEN\" name=\"itemct\" value=\"1\" >");
  out.print("<input type=\"SUBMIT\" value=\"" );
  out.print("Add this item to cart\" >");
}
else {
  out.print( "<i>To change the number ordered, enter a new number here "
     + "and click the Change button.</i><br />" );
  out.print("<input type=\"TEXT\" name=\"itemct\" size=\"5\"" +
       " value=\"" + ci.getNumberOrdered() + "\" >   ");
  out.print("<input type=\"SUBMIT\" value=\"");
  out.print("Change\" >");
}
out.print("</form></td></tr>\r\n");
}
```

The *ProductFormatter* Class

We have added many methods to the ProductFormatter class introduced in Chapter 3. In general these methods simply expand the capability along the previous lines. Listing 4.16 shows the static variables that define two styles. The short style is used in list outputs and the full style is used in the doFullItem method of CatalogBean. We also create the fieldHash collection that relates names of product data to integer constants.

Listing 4.16 Static Variables in the *ProductFormatter* Class (*ProductFormatter.java*)

```java
package com.XmlEcomBook.catalog;

import java.util.* ;
import java.io.* ;
import org.xml.sax.* ;
import org.w3c.dom.* ;

public class ProductFormatter
{
  static String brcrlf = "<br />\r\n" ; // xhtml style br
  static String[] shortEl = { "prname", "price" // for product name
  };
  static String[] shortSt = { "ch3", "ch4"
  };
    // as used in doListOutput
  static String[] fullEl = { "prname",
    "author","artist","description",
    "price" // for product name
  };
  static String[] fullSt = { "ch3",
    "au1", "au1", "ch4", "ch4"
  };

  static Hashtable fieldHash ;
   // field names for lookup
  static String[] fields = { "id", "keywords",
    "prname", "price", "author", "artist", "description",
    "image", "caption", "quantity_in_stock", "onsale_date",
    "shipping_info"
  } ;

  static { fieldHash = new Hashtable() ;
    for( int i = 0 ; i < fields.length ; i++ ){
      fieldHash.put( fields[i], new Integer( i ) );
    }
  }
```

Listing 4.17 shows the start of the instance methods and variables and the Product-Formatter constructor. Note that the constructor sets the formatting that will be used according to the frmt supplied.

Listing 4.17 Start of Instance Methods and Variables (*ProductFormatter.java*)

```
      String[] elem, style ;
      String resourcePath ;
      String aLink  ;
      int linkN ;
// when aLink is supplied, it should be something like
// "/servlet/catalog?action=showproduct", then the doListOutput will build a
// complete link adding &id=xxxxxx to attach to the first parameter

   public void setALink(String s, int pos  ) { aLink = s ; linkN = pos ;}

   public void setResourcePath( String s ){ resourcePath = s ; }

   // throws exception if unknown frmt
   public ProductFormatter( String frmt ){
     if( frmt.equals("short")){
       elem = shortEl ; style = shortSt ;
     }
     else if( frmt.equals("full")){
       elem = fullEl ; style = fullSt ;
     }
     else { throw new IllegalArgumentException("ProductFormatter: " + frmt );
     }
   }
```

Methods Called by *doFullItem*

Now let's look at the methods used in the full description of a product. These methods, shown in Listing 4.18, are called by the doFullItem method of the CatalogBean class.

Listing 4.18 The Methods Used to Do Full Descriptions (*ProductFormatter.java*)

```
      public String doImageTag( Element el ){
        NodeList nl = el.getElementsByTagName( "image" );
        int ct = nl.getLength();
        if( ct == 0 ) { return null ;
        }
        Element img = (Element)nl.item(0);
```

```
    StringBuffer sb = new StringBuffer( );
    addText( sb, "image", img );
    return sb.toString();
}

// element is the complete product
public String doProdName( Element el ){
    NodeList nl = el.getElementsByTagName( "name" );
    if( nl.getLength() == 0 ) return "";
    StringBuffer sb = new StringBuffer( );
    sb.append( "<span class=\"" );
    sb.append( "ch3" ); sb.append("\">");
    addText( sb, "prname", (Element)nl.item(0) );
    sb.append( " </span><br />");
    return sb.toString();
}

// element is the complete product
public String doAuthorArtist( Element el ){
    NodeList unl = el.getElementsByTagName( "author" );
    NodeList rnl = el.getElementsByTagName( "artist" );
    if( rnl.getLength() == 0 &&
        unl.getLength() == 0 ) return "";
    StringBuffer sb = new StringBuffer( );
    int i ;
    int ct = rnl.getLength();
    if( ct > 0 ){
      sb.append("<span class=\"au1\" >" );
      if( ct == 1 ) sb.append( "<i>Artist:</i> " );
      else sb.append("<i>Artists:>/i> ");
      for( i = 0 ; i < ct ; i++ ){
        addText( sb, "artist",(Element) rnl.item(i) );
        if( ct > 1 && ( i + 1) < ct ) sb.append(", ");
      }
      sb.append("<br />");
    }
    ct = unl.getLength();
    if( ct > 0 ){
      sb.append("<span class=\"au1\" >" );
```

```
      if( ct == 1 ) sb.append( "<i>Author:</i> " );
      else sb.append("<i>Authors:</i> ");
      for( i = 0 ; i < unl.getLength() ; i++ ){
        addText( sb, "author",(Element) unl.item(i) );
        if( ct > 1 && ( i + 1) < ct ) sb.append(", ");
      }
      sb.append("<br />");
    }
    return sb.toString();
  }

  // element is the complete product
  public String doDescription( Element el ){
    NodeList nl = el.getElementsByTagName( "description" );
    if( nl.getLength() == 0 ) return "No Description Available";
    StringBuffer sb = new StringBuffer( );
    addText( sb, "description",(Element) nl.item(0) );
    return sb.toString();
  }

  public String doPrice( Element el ){
    NodeList nl = el.getElementsByTagName( "price" );
    if( nl.getLength() == 0 ) return "Contact XMLgifts";
    StringBuffer sb = new StringBuffer( );
    addText( sb, "price", el );
    return sb.toString();
  }
```

The *doListOutput* Method

The doListOutput method (Listing 4.19) is called from a CatalogBean to create a String with formatted data for a single product. This is used when building a table, such as that shown in Figure 4.3. Note that we create a StringBuffer to build the String in because adding to a StringBuffer is much more efficient than concatenating String objects. Note also that if an aLink variable has been supplied, the method makes the text corresponding to linkN into the HTML to create a clickable link.

Listing 4.19 The *doListOutput* Method (*ProductFormatter.java*)

```
// create a String with single product data as used in various listings
// presentation determined by the contents of elem and style
// usually with attached link for more detail
public String doListOutput( Element el ){
  StringBuffer sb = new StringBuffer( );
  String pid = null ;
  if( aLink != null ){
    pid = "&id=" + el.getAttribute("id") ;
  }
  for( int i = 0 ; i < elem.length ; i++ ){
    if( i == linkN && pid != null ){
      sb.append( "<a class=\"" );
      sb.append( style[i] );
      sb.append("\" href=\"");
      sb.append( aLink );    // typically "http://xxxhost/servlet/serv
      sb.append( pid );
      sb.append("\">");
      addText( sb, elem[i], el );
      sb.append( " </a>");
    }
    else {
      sb.append( "<span class=\"");
      sb.append( style[i] ); sb.append("\">");
      addText( sb, elem[i], el );
      sb.append( " </span>");
    }
  }
  return sb.toString();
} // end doListOutput
```

The *addText* Method

The addText method as shown in Listing 4.20 is called by several other methods in Product-Formatter. It is called with a StringBuffer to which text is added, a name parameter identifying the text to be added, and an Element for the product being formatted. The name is used to look up an integer that controls the switch statement.

Listing 4.20 The *addText* Method (*ProductFormatter.java*)

```
    // note that in most cases the node value is what we want
    private void addText(StringBuffer sb, String name, Element el ){
      Object obj = fieldHash.get( name );
      if( obj == null ){
          sb.append( "no " + name + " found " ); return ;
      }
      switch( ((Integer)obj).intValue()){
        case 0 : // "id",
          addID( sb, el ); break ;
        case 1 : // "keywords",
        case 2 : // "prname", product name
          addProductName( sb, el ); break ;
        case 3 : // "price"
          addPrice( sb, el ); break ;
        case 4 : // "author",
          addAuthor( sb, el ); break ;
        case 5 : // "artist",
          addArtist( sb, el ); break ;
        case 6 : // "description",
          addExtendedText( sb, el ); break ;
        case 7 : // "image",
          addImageTag( sb, el ); break ;
        case 8 : // "caption"
          addExtendedText( sb, el ); break ;
        case 9 : // "quantity_in_stock",
        case 10 : // "onsale_date"
      }
    }
```

The source for the various methods called by addText appears in Listings 4.21 and 4.22. These methods extract text from the product Element and add it to the StringBuffer.

Listing 4.21 Various Methods Called by *addText* (*ProductFormatter.java*)

```
    // Element is a product
    private void addID(StringBuffer sb, Element e ){
      String id = e.getAttribute("id" );
      sb.append("product code: ");
      if( id.length()== 0 ){ sb.append("not assigned");
      }
```

```
  else { sb.append( id );
  }
}

// element is either a <product> or <name> as child of a product
private void addProductName( StringBuffer sb, Element e ){
  if( !e.getNodeName().equals("name") ){
    NodeList nl = e.getElementsByTagName( "name" );
    e = (Element) nl.item(0);
  }
  sb.append( getChildrenText( e ) );
}

// element is <author> tag
private void addAuthor( StringBuffer sb, Element e ){
  NodeList nl = e.getElementsByTagName( "name" );
  sb.append( getChildrenText( (Element) nl.item(0)) );
}

private void addArtist( StringBuffer sb, Element e ){
  NodeList nl = e.getElementsByTagName( "name" );
  sb.append( getChildrenText((Element) nl.item(0)) );
}

// known to have price
private void addPrice( StringBuffer sb, Element e ){
  NodeList nl = e.getElementsByTagName( "price" );
  sb.append("price ea = ");
  sb.append( nl.item(0).getFirstChild().getNodeValue() );
}
```

The utility method getChildrenText, shown in Listing 4.22, collects the text from all child nodes in a given Element.

Listing 4.22 The *getChildrenText* Utility Method (*ProductFormatter.java*)

```
private String getChildrenText( Element e ){
  StringBuffer sb = new StringBuffer();
  NodeList nl = e.getChildNodes();
  for( int i = 0 ; i < nl.getLength() ; i++ ){
```

```
         sb.append( nl.item(i).getNodeValue() );
      }
      return sb.toString();
   }
```

The `addImageTag` method, shown in Listing 4.23, uses the information inside an image tag. Here is an example from the `catalog.xml` file:

```
<image format="gif" width="234" height="400" src="images/covers/plants.gif">
<caption>
  <paragraph>This is the cover from the first edition.</paragraph>
</caption>
</image>
```

In addition to creating the `<img>` tag that will bring the image into the HTML page, it also parses and displays the caption.

Listing 4.23 The Method That Creates Image Tags (*ProductFormatter.java*)

```
private void addImageTag( StringBuffer sb, Element img ){
   String format = img.getAttribute("format");
   String width  = img.getAttribute("width");
   String height = img.getAttribute("height");
   String src    = img.getAttribute("src");
   String desc = "image ";
   sb.append("<img src=\"");
   // detect option for image source to point off site
   if( !src.toUpperCase().startsWith("HTTP")){
      sb.append(resourcePath );
   }
   if( sb.charAt( sb.length() - 1 ) == '/' &&
       src.charAt(0) == '/' ){
      sb.append( src.substring(1) );
   }
   else  sb.append( src ) ;
   sb.append( "\" alt=\"" );
   NodeList imgNL = img.getElementsByTagName("caption");
   if( imgNL.getLength() > 0 ){
      addText(sb, "caption", (Element) imgNL.item(0) );
   }
   else  sb.append( desc );
   sb.append( "\" width=\"" );
```

```
      sb.append( width ); sb.append( "\" height=\"" );
      sb.append( height ); sb.append( "\" >" );
      //NodeList imgNL = img.getElementsByTagName("caption") ;
      if( imgNL.getLength() == 0 ) return ;
      Element caption = (Element) imgNL.item(0);
      addText( sb, "caption", caption );
      return ;
   }
```

Our catalog XML format provides for a "running_text" style used in captions and product descriptions. The addExtendedText and doExtendedTextElement methods, shown in Listing 4.24, can concatenate all of the text in a description or caption with the appropriate HTML markup to create paragraph, italics, or bold text styles.

Listing 4.24 The *addExtendedText* Method ()

```
      // possible contents include straight text, <paragraph>
      private void addExtendedText( StringBuffer sb, Element e ){
        NodeList nl = e.getChildNodes();
        int ct = nl.getLength();
        // sb.append("child count " + ct + brcrlf );
        for( int i = 0 ; i < ct ; i++ ){
          Node n = nl.item(i);
          switch( n.getNodeType() ){
            case Node.TEXT_NODE :
              sb.append( n.getNodeValue().trim() ); break ;
            case Node.ELEMENT_NODE :
              Element en = (Element) n ;
              // sb.append("Element Name " + en.getNodeName() );
              doExtendedTextElement(en.getNodeName(), sb, en );
              break ;
            default :
              sb.append("default Name " + n.getNodeName() );
              sb.append(" Value " + n.getNodeValue() );
          }
          sb.append(' ' ); // because values get trimmed
          //sb.append( brcrlf );
        }
      }
      //
```

```java
private void doExtendedTextElement( String name, StringBuffer sb, Element e){
  if( name.equals("paragraph") ){
    sb.append("<p>"); addExtendedText( sb, e );
    sb.append("</p>");
  }
  else if( name.equals("italics")){
    sb.append("<i>" ); addExtendedText( sb, e );
    sb.append(" </i>");
  }
  else if( name.equals("bold")){
    sb.append("<b>" ); addExtendedText( sb, e );
    sb.append(" </b>");
  }
  else { addExtendedText( sb, e );
  }
}
public String toString()
{ StringBuffer sb = new StringBuffer("ProductFormatter ");
  return sb.toString();
}

}
```

CHAPTER 5

Billing and Order Confirmation

- Accept customer information
- Accept credit card information
- Process payment
- Order processing

In the last chapter, we showed how shopping cart functionality could be implemented for our store. Next, we need to actually allow the customer to purchase the items they have selected. This is the area where Internet-based customers have the least confidence in the Internet, so we need to make sure that this process goes smoothly. Many Internet sales are lost at this point in the interaction with the customer, mostly due to user's reluctance to give sensitive credit card information over the Internet.

The Payment Process

It is common practice for retail Web sites to accept credit card payments. Making electronic payments by credit card either in person or through a mail-order vendor is something that predates the Web by many years. On a retail level, the process put in place to complete these transactions has been well established, and any Web site needs to follow this same process. We will review this process before we get into the details of the implementation.

Making a credit card or electronic payment involves many different parties: the client, the store, the client's bank, the store's merchant provider, and the processing service provider. The client's and the store's roles in the payment are relatively obvious. The client's bank is the financial institution that issued the credit card to them. The next two paragraphs detail the remaining two parties involved.

The store's merchant provider is often a bank, but can be some other financial institution, such as a credit card company itself. To accept credit cards, a merchant must set up an account with a bank. Each bank's requirements and fees vary, but usually there are at least three fees involved. First, a fee called the discount rate is taken on each payment accepted by the merchant. The discount rate is typically 2.5% to 5%. The second fee is called a transaction fee and is a small charge for each transaction that takes place, typically 30 to 50 cents per transaction. Finally, the merchant bank usually charges a monthly fee. The store and the bank negotiate all of the fees before the store can accept credit cards.

The final party involved in the payment is a processing service provider. This is also known as a *clearinghouse*. The processor is responsible for accepting requests from the store, verifying account validity and funds availability, and handling the transfers of money between banks.

The actual process of making a payment occurs in two parts. In the first part, the store sends an authorization request to the processing service provider. This request contains the amount of the purchase, the credit card number, and the address of the cardholder. The processor checks the account, makes sure there are sufficient funds, and optionally verifies that the address is correct. If everything checks out, the processor sends back an authorization code. At this point, no funds have been transferred, but a hold for the amount of the purchase has been put on the cardholder's account.

The next phase of the payment process occurs when the store has finished fulfilling the order, and the customer's account is charged. A second transaction, known as a *capture* or *settlement*, is sent to the processor. In a brick and mortar store, this occurs when the customer walks out of the store with the merchandise. Typically, non-virtual stores send all of their capture transactions in a batch at the end of the shift or day. The capture can, however, also be sent as an individual transaction. In an online store that sells merchandise, the capture event should not be sent until the merchandise actually ships. This prevents the customer's account from being charged too early, or improperly charged if an item is out of stock.

In addition to payment authorization and capture, there are other transactions that can take place through the processing service provider. One of these is a void transaction. If an authorization has taken place, but the order cannot be fulfilled for some reason, such as the merchandise is out of stock or the customer cancels the order, a void transaction can be used to remove the hold on the funds in the customer's account.

Another transaction that can take place is a refund transaction. This occurs when the customer returns merchandise that was purchased on a credit card. The refund transaction places the funds back into the customer's account.

For small Web stores, it might not make sense to try and set all of this up to be an automated process. For a small number of transactions, it might be more economical to perform these transactions manually. This may cause longer delays to customers when getting their credit cards verified, but it is something to consider for a small Web site just starting up.

There are many companies set up to help with the whole process for Web sites wanting automated, online payment processing. These companies are either processing service providers or act as middlemen between a store and the processing service provider. The capabilities and requirements of these services vary a great deal, so you are encouraged to investigate a wide variety of them before choosing one. Some of the companies to consider are Cyber-Source (`www.cybersource.com`), Verifone, (`www.verifone.com`), Authorize.net (`www.authorize.net`), and ClearCommerce (`www.clearcommerce.com`). Most of these companies not only provide the service, but also provide software that runs on a merchant's Web site to make the communication with the service provider easier.

Security

Security is very important at any e-commerce Web site. To ensure that security is implemented properly at a Web site, a security policy should be put in place. All risks need to be assessed and a plan put in place to try to reduce these risks. Having an overall policy put in place allows a site to maintain security even in a rapidly changing environment. Among the things that need to be considered are:

- **Information Confidentiality** - Protecting information that is stored or transported
- **Authentication** - Verifying identification of users
- **Authorization** - Limiting the scope of what users can do within the system
- **Data Integrity** - Assuring that data is not changed accidentally or intentionally
- **Non-Repudiation** - Providing proof of the source and integrity of the data
- **Availability** - Assuring that the system is accessible at the times it should be

It is outside the scope of this book to go into detail in all of these areas, but there are some specific issues that we will mention in regard to dealing with credit card processing. When dealing with customers' personal information and credit card number, security is of the utmost importance.

The first line of security is to encrypt important information that needs to be communicated between the user's browser and the store's server. This is typically done using Secure Hypertext Transfer Protocol (HTTPS), which uses Secure Sockets Layer (SSL) to encrypt all the data going between the browser and server. When data is not encrypted, malicious parties can easily read the information going back and forth between the browser and server.

Next, any data sources that store critical customer information should also be encrypted. If credit card numbers are stored in a database, the database should be encrypted. This will deter unauthorized access of this information. If data is stored in an XML file, the credit card numbers or the whole file should be encrypted. In addition, the data storage should be on a host that is not accessible from the Internet.

Firewalls must be used on all hosts. Properly configured firewall software can significantly reduce the risk of exposing information to unauthorized users. Not having a firewall allows all kinds of malicious attacks to occur, so this software is essential to any e-commerce Web site.

Test the system thoroughly. Errors in the system often expose security holes that are not present when the system is functioning smoothly. Testing the security of the system is very important. Setting up security in a system is dependent on the individual products used in implementing the system. To set up HTTPS, the Web server must be configured properly.

To encrypt the database, the individual database must also be configured properly. Because these products vary so much, we will not go into specifics about how to set up this security, but we cannot stress enough how important it is to do so.

Customer Confidence

Unless customers trust a Web site, they will not be willing to enter their credit card information. It is a major leap to get a customer from browsing a store to actually purchase a product from it. There are steps that can be taken to increase the customer's confidence in a Web site.

Site reliability affects the customer's perception of a site. If the customer encounters a lot of broken links or apparent system errors, they may not be willing to trust the Web site. These types of errors may be fine when browsing a site for information, but when it comes to giving the site personal information, having a reliable site is critical.

A privacy policy that is readily available is also important for building customer trust. If the customer has no idea what is going to be done with the information they enter, they are not going to be willing to do so. Provide clearly labeled links for a page that clearly explains exactly why information needs to be collected and what will be done with it.

Explaining the security measures that are in place to protect the customer's information is also a good idea. Explaining that all sensitive information will be encrypted before it is sent and saved in a secure, encrypted data store will also help the consumer understand that this site can be trusted.

The overall appearance of a site can help, too. The better the overall Web site looks, the more confidence you will instill in your customer. This means that the aesthetic of the site, ease of navigation, and any other features that affect the users' experience will also affect the users' confidence in the Web site. Seeing a site that contains spelling errors, looks shabby, and is hard to navigate will turn potential customers off.

Gathering Checkout Information

When the customer has selected the items they want to buy, the next stage is the checkout. Information about the customer, including name, address, and contact information, needs to be collected. The customer might also have a choice of shipping methods. Finally, and most importantly, credit card information used to make the purchase needs to be gathered. We will begin by examining the classes that will be used as JavaBeans by JSP. `CustomerInfo`,

`CreditInfo`, `Fulfillment`, `Authorization`, and `Order` are all classes that hold information that is gathered during the checkout process.

The next three classes we will examine, `TestPaymentAuthorizer`, `ShippingCalculator` and `Emailer`, are all classes that help with the checkout process. Finally, we will look at an HTML page, a servlet, and several JSPs that perform the interaction with the user to gather the needed information.

The *CustomerInfo* Class

The `CustomerInfo` class collects some standard information needed about a shopper at the store. Name and address information is necessary to know where to ship products, and the e-mail address and phone number are needed to contact the customer with updates or questions. The final item, `CreditInfo`, will be examined later. The class consists solely of `get` and `set` methods for its fields, as shown in Listing 5.1.

Listing 5.1 The *CustomerInfo* Class (*CustomerInfo.java*)

```
package com.XmlEcomBook.Chap05;

public class CustomerInfo {
  private String lastName;
  private String firstName;
  private String address1;
  private String address2;
  private String city;
  private String state;
  private String zip;
  private String email;
  private String phoneNumber;
  private CreditInfo creditInfo;

  public String getLastName() { return lastName; }

  public void setLastName( String newLastName ) {
    lastName = newLastName;
  }

  public String getFirstName() { return firstName; }

  public void setFirstName( String newFirstName ) {
```

```
      firstName = newFirstName;
  }

  public void setAddress1( String newAddress1 ) {
    address1 = newAddress1;
  }

  public String getAddress1() { return address1; }

  public void setAddress2( String newAddress2 ) {
    address2 = newAddress2;
  }

  public String getAddress2() { return address2; }

  public void setCity( String newCity ) { city = newCity; }

  public String getCity() { return city; }

  public void setState( String newState ) { state = newState; }

  public String getState() { return state; }

  public void setZip( String newZip ) { zip = newZip; }

  public String getZip() { return zip; }

  public void setEmail( String newEmail ) { email = newEmail; }

  public String getEmail() { return email; }

  public void setPhoneNumber( String newPhoneNumber ) {
    phoneNumber = newPhoneNumber;
  }

  public String getPhoneNumber() { return phoneNumber; }

  public CreditInfo getCreditInfo() { return creditInfo; }

  public void setCreditInfo( CreditInfo newCreditInfo ) {
    creditInfo = newCreditInfo;
  }
}
```

The *CreditInfo* Class

The CreditInfo class (see Listing 5.2) holds credit card data from the user. This includes the type of the credit card, such as Visa or MasterCard, the credit card number, and the expiration date of the card. All this is required information when communicating with the processing service provider.

Listing 5.2 The *CreditInfo* Class (*CreditInfo.java*)

```
package com.XmlEcomBook.Chap05;

public class CreditInfo {h

  private String creditCardType;
  private String creditCardNumber;
  private String expirationDate;

  public String getCreditCardType() {
    return creditCardType;
  }

  public void setCreditCardType( String newCreditCardType ) {
    creditCardType = newCreditCardType;
  }

  public String getCreditCardNumber() { return creditCardNumber; }

  public void setCreditCardNumber( String newCreditCardNumber) {
    creditCardNumber = newCreditCardNumber;
  }

  public String getExpirationDate() { return expirationDate; }

  public void setExpirationDate( String newExpirationDate ) {
    expirationDate = newExpirationDate;
  }
}
```

The *Fulfillment* Class

The order fulfillment process includes everything that must be done with an order to complete it once it has been received from the customer. This typically includes picking and packing the product at the warehouse, and shipping the product. We will take a fairly simple view of the fulfillment process and only include shipping information.

The Fulfillment class has fields for storing the shipper and the class of service. This enables the order be shipped with different carriers, such as Federal Express, UPS, or the U.S. Postal service, and services, such as overnight, second-day air, or regular. The amount that the customer is charged for the shipment must also be known. This amount is added to the price of the items to calculate the total cost of the order. Once an order has been shipped, a tracking number and shipping date should be generated, in case there are any inquiries from the customer.

The Fulfillment class (see Listing 5.3) has get and set methods for each of the fields. There is also one special set method, setShipperAndClass. This allows both the shipper and class of service to be set using one string. This method makes processing the user input easier, as you will see in the ShippingInfo.jsp section. The method uses a StringTokenizer object to split the two parts of the string, and sets the shipper field with the first part and the class field with the second part. This method is necessary to make the setting of these from the JSP easier. We will examine the JSP later to see how this method is used.

Listing 5.3 The *Fulfillment* Class (*Fulfillment.java*)

```
package com.XmlEcomBook.Chap05;

import java.util.StringTokenizer;
public class Fulfillment {

  String shipper;        //UPS, Fedex, USPS, etc.
  String shippingClass;  //Overnight, 2 Day, regular, freight, etc.
  double costToCustomer; //How much customer is charged for shipping
  String trackingNumber = "NO_TRACKING_NUMBER";
  String dateSent = "NOT_SENT_YET";

  public void setShipperAndClass( String shipperAndClass ) {
    StringTokenizer st = new StringTokenizer( shipperAndClass );
    if( st.hasMoreTokens() ) {
      shipper = st.nextToken();
      if( st.hasMoreTokens() ) {
```

```
        shippingClass = st.nextToken();
      }
    }
  }

  public void setShipper( String newShipper ) {
    shipper = newShipper;
  }

  public String getShipper() { return shipper; }

  public void setShippingClass( String newClass ) {
    shippingClass = newClass;
  }

  public String getShippingClass() { return shippingClass; }

  public void setTrackingNumber( String newNumber ) {
    trackingNumber = newNumber;
  }

  public String getTrackingNumber() { return trackingNumber; }

  public void setDateSent( String newDate ) { dateSent = newDate; }

  public String getDateSent() { return dateSent; }

  public double getCostToCustomer() { return costToCustomer; }

  public void setCostToCustomer( double newCost ) {
    costToCustomer = newCost;
  }
}
```

The *Authorization* Class

The Authorization class (see Listing 5.4) is used for keeping data returned by the processing service provider. There are three fields: first, a boolean field for knowing whether the authorization was approved or denied. Next, there is a string for storing the reason for any denials, and, finally, a string for keeping the authorization code returned for an approved transaction. All of these fields have get and set methods to access and modify the values.

Listing 5.4 The *Authorization* Class (*Authorization.java*)

```
package com.XmlEcomBook.Chap05;

public class Authorization {

  private boolean approved = false;
  private String  reason = "Unknown"; //reason for a denial
  private String  authorizationCode; // auth code from payment service

  public boolean isApproved() { return approved; }

  public void setApproved( boolean newApproved ) {
    approved = newApproved;
  }

  public String getReason() { return reason; }

  public void setReason( String newReason ) { reason = newReason; }

  public String getAuthorizationCode() { return authorizationCode; }

  public void setAuthorizationCode( String newAuthCode ) {
    authorizationCode = newAuthCode;
  }
}
```

The *Order* Class

The Order class is basically a container for all of the different parts that we need to gather while doing a checkout. This includes information on the customer, shipping, credit card, and authorization information from the processing service provider, and the items that the user has bought. We need a unique ID number for the order, so that it can be referenced. We also need a date so we know when the order took place. All of these can be seen in the fields of the Order class. The constructor is used to set the ID and the date. The method used to get a unique ID will be examined later. In Listing 5.5, we can see the set and get methods for the fields. The id and date fields do not have set methods because they are set in the constructor and can never be changed.

Listing 5.5 The Fields, Constructor, and Get and Set Methods of the *Order* Class (*Order.java*)

```java
package com.XmlEcomBook.Chap05;

import java.util.*;
import java.io.*;
import com.XmlEcomBook.catalog.CartItem;
public class Order {

  private int        id;              //unique id for this order
  private Date       date;            //date of order
  private Vector     items = new Vector();
  private CustomerInfo customerInfo;
  private Authorization authorization; //payment authorization
  private Fulfillment  fulfillment;

  public Order() {
    id = getUniqueId();
    date = new Date();
  }
  public int getId() { return id; }

  public Date getDate() { return date; }

  public void setItems( Vector newItems ) {
    if( newItems != null )
    items = newItems;
  }

  public Vector getItems() { return items; }

  public void setCustomerInfo( CustomerInfo newCustomer ) {
    if( newCustomer != null )
    customerInfo = newCustomer;
  }

  public CustomerInfo getCustomerInfo() { return customerInfo; }

  public void setAuthorization( Authorization newAuth ) {
    authorization = newAuth;
  }
```

```
public Authorization getAuthorization() { return authorization; }

public void setFulfillment( Fulfillment newFulfillment ) {
  fulfillment = newFulfillment;
}

public Fulfillment getFulfillment() { return fulfillment; }
```

Listing 5.6 shows several methods that operate on the items that are contained in the Order. The first, getTotalItemPrice, loops through all of the items. For each one, it gets the price of the item and multiplies it by the number of items that were ordered. These are totaled and returned. The getOrderTotal method adds the total of the items with the cost of shipping to get the final price of the order. Finally, the getTotalItemWeight is similar to the getTotalItemPrice method, except it totals the items' total weight instead of the price. The getPrice method is a helper function to strip the extraneous characters from the price string obtained from the CartItem, and then converts it to a double.

Listing 5.6 The *item total* Methods (*Order.java*)

```
public double getTotalItemPrice() {
  double total = 0;
  Enumeration enum = items.elements();
  while( enum.hasMoreElements() ) {
    CartItem item = (CartItem)enum.nextElement();
    total += getPrice( item ) * item.getNumberOrdered();
  }
  return total;
}

public double getOrderTotal() {
  return getTotalItemPrice() + fulfillment.getCostToCustomer();
}

public double getTotalItemWeight() {
  double total = 0;
  Enumeration enum = items.elements();
  while( enum.hasMoreElements() ) {
    CartItem cartItem = (CartItem)enum.nextElement();
    double d = Double.parseDouble(cartItem.getShippingValue());
    total += d * cartItem.getNumberOrdered();
  }
```

```
      return total;
  }

  private double getPrice( CartItem item ) {
    String s = item.getPrice();
    //remove dollar sign
    s = s.replace( '$', ' ' );
    //remove commas
    int i;
    while( (i = s.indexOf( ',' )) > 0 ) {
      s = s.substring( 0, i ) + s.substring( i + 1 );
    }
    return Double.parseDouble( s );
  }
```

There is also a method to write out the order in XML format. We need to be able to save this information for future use. We have created a DTD that is a straightforward translation of the Order class, and all the classes that it uses. Looking at order.dtd in Listing 5.7, we can see that each of the fields in the Order class is represented in the order element. The item, customerInfo, authorization and fulfillment fields are all represented by child elements of the order element. The id and date fields of the Order class are represented by attributes on the order element. We can see the same pattern in the rest of the elements in the DTD; each field in a class has a corresponding attribute or element in the DTD.

Listing 5.7 The *order* DTD (*order.dtd*)

```
<!ELEMENT order (item*, customer_info, authorization, fulfillment )>
<!ATTLIST order id    ID    #REQUIRED
                date CDATA #REQUIRED>

<!ELEMENT item (#PCDATA)>
<!ATTLIST item id       NMTOKEN #REQUIRED
               quantity NMTOKEN #REQUIRED
               price    CDATA   #REQUIRED>

<!ELEMENT customer_info (first_name, last_name, address1, address2,
                         city, state, zip, email, phone, credit_info )>
<!ELEMENT first_name (#PCDATA)>
<!ELEMENT last_name  (#PCDATA)>
<!ELEMENT address1   (#PCDATA)>
```

```
<!ELEMENT address2    (#PCDATA)>
<!ELEMENT city        (#PCDATA)>
<!ELEMENT state       (#PCDATA)>
<!ELEMENT zip         (#PCDATA)>
<!ELEMENT email       (#PCDATA)>
<!ELEMENT phone       (#PCDATA)>

<!ELEMENT credit_info (card_numer, card_type, expiration )>
<!ELEMENT card_number (#PCDATA)>
<!ELEMENT card_type   (#PCDATA)>
<!ELEMENT expiration_date (#PCDATA)>

<!ELEMENT authorization (reason?, auth_code?)>
<!ATTLIST authorization approved CDATA #IMPLIED>
<!ELEMENT reason  (#PCDATA)>
<!ELEMENT authorization_code (#PCDATA)>

<!ELEMENT fulfillment (backorder_date, shipper, shipping_class,
                       cost, tracking_number, date_sent)>
<!ELEMENT shipper         (#PCDATA)>
<!ELEMENT shipping_class  (#PCDATA)>
<!ELEMENT cost            (#PCDATA)>
<!ELEMENT tracking_number (#PCDATA)>
<!ELEMENT date_sent       (#PCDATA)>
```

Listing 5.8 shows a method to write an XML document that corresponds to the DTD. This is a very brute-force method that simply goes through each of the fields in the Order class and writes out the XML attributes or elements for it. This is not always the best approach, because changes to a class that Order depends on means changing this method, which does not take full advantage of the encapsulation that objects provide. These classes would be considered tightly coupled. We will look at a more robust approach to writing XML output in Chapter 6, "Online Catalog Upkeep."

Listing 5.8 The *writeXML* Method (*Order.java*)

```java
public void writeXML( Writer writer ) {
  try {
    writer.write( "<?xml version='1.0' ?>" );
    writer.write( "<!DOCTYPE order SYSTEM '.."
                   + File.separator + "order.dtd'>" );
    writer.write( "<order id='" + id + "' " );
```

```java
        writer.write( "date='" + date + "'>" );
        Enumeration enum = items.elements();
        while( enum.hasMoreElements() ) {
            CartItem item = (CartItem)enum.nextElement();
            writer.write( "<item id='" + item.getId() + "' " );
            writer.write( "quantity='" + item.getNumberOrdered() + "' ");
            writer.write( "price='" + item.getPrice() + "'>" );
            writer.write( item.getName() + "</item>" );
        }
        writer.write( "<customer_info>\n<first_name>" +
          customerInfo.getFirstName() + "</first_name>" +
          "\n<last_name>" + customerInfo.getLastName() + "</last_name>" +
          "\n<address1>" + customerInfo.getAddress1() + "</address1>" +
          "\n<address2>" + customerInfo.getAddress2() + "</address2>" +
          "\n<city>" + customerInfo.getCity() + "</city>" +
          "\n<state>" + customerInfo.getState() + "</state>" +
          "\n<zip>" + customerInfo.getZip() + "</zip>" +
          "\n<email>" + customerInfo.getEmail() + "</email>" +
          "\n<phone>" + customerInfo.getPhoneNumber() + "</phone>" );
        CreditInfo credit = customerInfo.getCreditInfo();
        writer.write( "\n<credit_info>\n<card_number>" +
          credit.getCreditCardNumber() + "</card_number>" +
          "\n<card_type>" + credit.getCreditCardType() + "</card_type>" +
          "\n<expiration_date>" + credit.getExpirationDate() +
          "</expiration_date>\n</credit_info>\n</customer_info>" );

        writer.write( "\n<authorization approved='" +
          authorization.isApproved() + "'>" +"\n<reason>" +
          authorization.getReason() + "</reason>\n<authorization_code>" +
          authorization.getAuthorizationCode() + "</authorization_code>" +
          "</authorization>" );
        writer.write( "\n<fulfillment>\n" +
          "\n<shipper>" + fulfillment.getShipper() + "</shipper>" +
          "\n<class>" + fulfillment.getShippingClass() + "</class>" +
          "\n<cost>" + fulfillment.getCostToCustomer() + "</cost>" +
          "\n<tracking_number>" + fulfillment.getTrackingNumber() +
          "</tracking_number>\n<date_sent>" +
          fulfillment.getDateSent() + "</date_sent>\n</fulfillment>" );
        writer.write( "\n</order>" );
    }
    catch( IOException e ) {}
}
```

The final method in the Order class is one to generate unique IDs, as shown in Listing 5.9. We do this by using a counter, which we increase every time we need a new ID. This counter needs to be stored persistently, so we can ensure a unique ID even between reboots of the system. Storing the counter in memory would not do, because every time we restarted the system, the ID would start repeating. We use a file as a persistent store for the counter.

Listing 5.9 The *getUniqueId* Method (*Order.java*)

```
synchronized private int getUniqueId() {
  int id;
  try {
    ObjectInputStream in
     = new ObjectInputStream( new FileInputStream( "orderID.txt" ) );
    id = in.readInt();
  }
  catch( IOException e ) {
    id = 1000;
  }
  try {
    ObjectOutputStream out
     = new ObjectOutputStream( new FileOutputStream( "orderID.txt" ) );
    out.writeInt( id + 1 );
    out.close();
  }
  catch( IOException e ) {}
  return id;
}
} - to end class
```

The *TestPaymentAuthorizer* Class

The next classes we will look at take part in processing an order at checkout time. The first, TestPaymentAuthorizer, takes care of getting authorization of the customer's credit card. Here, we will develop a simple class that returns an Authorization whose approval simply depends on the last digit of the credit card number included with the order. In a real store, this class would be substituted by one that is responsible for communication this information to the processing service provider that the store uses. The way this is done is highly dependent upon the service provider selected.

The first method in the class is getAuthorization. This method takes an Order object as a parameter and uses the credit information from it to do the authorization. In this case, we simply look at the last digit of the credit card, and if it is a "1," we decline the card. This is just an arbitrary decision to be able to test both types of return values.

The `capture` method is needed to finish the processing to the processing service provider. In our case, we do not need to do anything, but again, a real payment authorization class would need to communicate to the processing service provider to complete the payment. If we were to automate returns and void transactions, this would be a good place to have methods for those two transactions as well. Listing 5.10 shows the `TestPaymentAuthorizer` class.

Listing 5.10 The *TestPaymentAuthorizer* Class (*TestPaymentAuthorizer.java*)

```java
public class TestPaymentAuthorizer {

  static public Authorization getAuthorization( Order order ) {
    Authorization authorization = new Authorization();
    try {
      CustomerInfo custInfo = order.getCustomerInfo();
      CreditInfo creditInfo = custInfo.getCreditInfo();
      String num = creditInfo.getCreditCardNumber();
      if( num != null ) {
        if( num.endsWith( "1" ) ) {
          authorization.setApproved( false );
          authorization.setReason("Insufficent Funds");
        }
        else
        {
          authorization.setApproved( true );
          authorization.setReason( "Approved" );
          authorization.setAuthorizationCode( "Test" );
        }
      }
    }
    catch( Exception e ) {}
      return authorization;
  }

  static public void capture
    ( String authorizationCode, double amount ) {
  }

}
```

The *ShipperCalculator* Class

Now we need some way to calculate the cost of shipping the product to the customer. This depends on several variables: The shipping company chosen and the type of service are the main factors. The weight of the shipment and the destination could also play a role in the price. Here we simply use the shipping company, class of service, and the weight of the shipment to calculate the total. When creating a ShippingCalculator object, an Order object is passed as an argument. This is where the ShippingCalculator can get information, such as the weight of the order and the destination address, if needed.

The first method, getTypes, returns an array of all of the available service classes from each of the shipping companies. The second method, getPrice, returns a price based on the shipping class that was chosen. The input to this method needs to be one of the strings from the array returned by the getTypes method.

The getPrice method could be enhanced to calculate the price of the shipping based on more than just the service class and weight of the item (see Listing 5.11). In addition, it would be good to have the class read in information from a data source, such as an XML file or database, when calculating the price. This would allow the prices to change dynamically without changing the code.

Listing 5.11 The Start of *ShippingCalculator* Class and the Constructor (*ShippingCalculator.java*)

```java
public class ShippingCalculator {

  Order order;

  public ShippingCalculator( Order setOrder ) {
    order = setOrder;
  }

  public String[] getTypes() {
    String[] names = { "FedEx Overnight",
                       "FedEx 2-Day",
                       "UPS Overnight",
                       "UPS 3-Day",
                       "USPS 2-Day",
                       "USPS Regular" };
    return names;
  }
```

```
public String getPrice( String name ) {
  double weight = order.getTotalItemWeight();
  if( name.equals( "FedEx Overnight" ) )
    if( weight > 3.0 )
      return "$10.99";
    else
      return "$7.99";
  if( name.equals( "FedEx 2-Day" ) )
    if( weight > 3.0 )
      return "$5.99";
    else
      return "$3.49";
  if( name.equals( "UPS Overnight" ) )
    if( weight > 2.0 )
      return "$8.99";
    else
      return "$6.99";
  if( name.equals( "UPS 3-Day" ) )
    if( weight > 2.5 )
      return "$5.99";
    else
      return "$4.99";
  if( name.equals( "USPS 2-Day" ) )
    if( weight > 2.5 )
      return "$4.99";
    else
      return "$3.99";
  if( name.equals( "USPS Regular" ) )
    return "$2.99";
  return "0.00";
}
}
```

The *Emailer* Class

The Emailer class is used to send e-mail notices to the customer. These e-mails could be order confirmation or shipping notices. There are two static fields in this class to configure the Emailer. The first is the name of an SMTP host that is available to send e-mail. The second field is the e-mail address that should be used for the "from" field of the e-mail.

Here we have used a format that has a display name, XMLGifts, as well as the actual address, orders@xmlgifts.com. These need to be changed to values that will work on your system before the code is run. The name of an SMTP host that can be used to send messages can be found from the settings in an e-mail client, such as Microsoft Outlook, that has been configured properly. Listing 5.12 shows the start of the Emailer class.

Listing 5.12 The Start of the *Emailer* Class (*Emailer.java*)

```
package com.XmlEcomBook.Chap05;

import javax.mail.*;
import javax.mail.internet.*;
import java.util.*;
public class Emailer {

  static final String host = "SMTP-HOST-NAME";
  static final String from = "XMLGifts<orders@xmlgifts.com>";
```

The first method in the class is used to send order confirmation notices to the customer. Although this e-mail isn't absolutely necessary, it does give the customer a sense of security that the order has actually been processed, and gives them information in case they have any questions about the order. In the method, after getting the customer information from the order, we call a utility method named getMessage with the customer's e-mail address. The getMessage method creates a Message object from the JavaMail API that can be sent, and it will be examined later in this chapter. The subject and text of the message is filled in before it is sent. Sending the message is done using the JavaMail's Transport object's send method. This method (shown in Listing 5.13) creates a simple message that includes the order ID so the customer can refer to the order. This method could easily be extended to include information about more of the order.

Listing 5.13 The *sendConfirmation* Method (*Emailer.java*)

```
public static void sendConfirmation(Order order) {
  try {
    CustomerInfo cust = order.getCustomerInfo();
    Message msg = getMessage( cust.getEmail() );
    msg.setSubject("XMLGifts.com Order Confirmation");
    msg.setText("Your order is being processed");
    msg.setText("Your order number is:" + order.getId() );
```

```
      Transport.send(msg);
    }
    catch (MessagingException mex) {
    }
  }
```

The `sendShipped` method (see Listing 5.14) is similar to the `sendConfirmation` method, but the message text is a little different.

Listing 5.14 The *sendShipped* Method (*Emailer.java*)

```
public static void sendShipped(String email, String orderId ) {

  try {
    Message msg = getMessage( email );
    msg.setSubject("Your XMLGifts.com Order has shipped");
    msg.setText("Order number " + orderId + " has shipped" );
    Transport.send(msg);
  }
  catch (MessagingException mex) {
  }
}
```

The `getMessage` method is used by the other methods of the class to take care of most of the details of dealing with the JavaMail API. It takes the e-mail address of the recipient of the message as an argument. The first thing done in this method is creating a new `Session` object with the value of the SMTP host from the static field variable. A new `Message` object is then created, and the sender's and receiver's e-mail addresses, and the current date are all set.

The JavaMail API is a set of classes that model a mail system and is a Java standard extension. It can be used to send and receive mail using standard mail protocols. More information and a freely available implementation can be found at `http://java.sun.com/products/javamail`. The `getMessage` method (see Listing 5.15) uses this API to create a new `Message` object with the recipient and sender e-mails, and current date.

Listing 5.15 The *getMessage* Method (*Emailer.java*)

```
static Message getMessage( String toEmail ) throws MessagingException {
  Properties props = new Properties();
  props.put("mail.smtp.host", host);
```

```
      Session session = Session.getDefaultInstance(props, null);
      session.setDebug(false);

      Message msg = new MimeMessage(session);
      msg.setFrom(new InternetAddress(from));
      InternetAddress[] address = {new InternetAddress(toEmail)};
      msg.setRecipients(Message.RecipientType.TO, address);
      msg.setSentDate(new Date());
      return msg;
    }
}
```

The *CustomerInfo* Page

Next we will look at the classes that do the interaction with the customer to get all the information into the classes we have just seen. The first of these is an HTML page named `CustomerInfo.html`. This page has a form on it whose input fields match the fields of the `CustomerInfo` class (see Listing 5.16). As we will see from the `ShippingInfo` JSP, this makes the information easy to transfer from the form into the class.

Listing 5.16 The *CustomerInfo* Page (*CustomerInfo.html*)

```html
<html>
  <head>
    <title>Customer Info</title>
  </head>
<body>
  <form action="ShippingInfo.jsp">
    <p>
      First Name:<input name="firstName" />
      Last Name:<input name="lastName" />
    </p>
    <p>
      Address line 1:<input name="address1" /><br />
      Address line 2:<input name="address2" /><br />
      City:<input name="city" />
      State:<input size="2" name="state" />
      Zip:<input size="10" name="zip" />
    </p>
```

```
      <p>Email Address:<input name="email" /><br /></p>
      <p>Phone Number:<input size="13" name="phoneNumber" /><br /></p>
      <input type="submit" value="Submit Information" />
    </form>
  </body>
</html>
```

The *ShippingInfo* JSP

After importing the needed classes, a `jsp:useBean` element is used to get a new `Customer-Info` object that is bound to the current session. The properties of this bean are then set to the values entered into the `CustomerInfo.html` form by using the `jsp:setProperty` element. We then get an `Order` class that is bound to the current session, and the `Vector` that holds all of the items for the order. A JSP scriptlet is then used to call the `setCustomerInfo` and `setItems` methods to add the appropriate objects into the `Order` object, as shown in Listing 5.17.

Listing 5.17 The Start of the *ShippingInfo* JSP (*ShippingInfo.jsp*)

```
<%@ page import="com.XmlEcomBook.Chap05.*,java.util.*" %>

<jsp:useBean scope="session" id="custInfo" class="CustomerInfo" />
<jsp:setProperty name="custInfo" property="*" />
<jsp:useBean id="order" scope="session" class="Order" />
<jsp:useBean id="theorder" scope="session" class="Vector" />
<% order.setCustomerInfo( custInfo );
   order.setItems( theorder );
%>
```

Next, the JSP outputs HTML that allows the user to select the shipment choices for the order. This code uses the `ShippingCalculator` that we looked at earlier in the chapter. The scriptlet embedded in the HTML creates a `ShippingCalculator` object, and then gets the possible shipping types from it using the `getTypes` method. Here, we create a series of radio button inputs, one for each shipping type returned. This is done by using a `for` loop. For each type, we create an `input` element with a type of `radio`. The value attribute of the element is set by using the JSP expression "`<%=types[i]%>`". The same expression is then used to display the value of the type to the user. Another scriptlet is used to get the price of the shipping type from the `ShippingCalculator` using the `getPrice` method, as shown in Listing 5.18.

```html
<html>
<head>
    <title>Shipping Info</title>
</head>
<body>
    <form action="CreditInfo.jsp">
        Select a Shipper and Class:<br />
        <table>
        <% ShippingCalculator calc = new ShippingCalculator( order );
          String[] types = calc.getTypes();
          for( int i = 0; i < types.length; i++ ) {
        %>
        <tr><td><input type="radio" name="shipperAndClass"
                    value="<%=types[i] %>" /><%=types[i] %></td>
        <td><%=calc.getPrice(types[i]) %></td></tr>
        <% } %>
        </table>
    <input type="submit" value="Submit information">
    </form>
</body>
</html>
```

The *CreditInfo* JSP

A ShippingInfo object bound to the session is created in the CreditInfo JSP. The shipping information that was entered into the form of the ShippingInfo JSP is used in the Credit-Info JSP. The shipping type selected was put into a parameter named shipperAndClass, so the jsp:setProperty element calls the ShippingInfo object's setShipperAndClass method with the value of parameter. As we saw in the ShippingInfo class, this sets both the shipper and shippingClass fields (see Listing 5.19).

Listing 5.19 Setting the Shipper Information (*CreditInfo.jsp*)

```jsp
<%@ page import="com.XmlEcomBook.Chap05.*" %>

<jsp:useBean scope="session" id="shippingInfo" class="Fulfillment" />
<jsp:setProperty name="shippingInfo" property="*" />
```

The scriptlet in this JSP first sets the `Fulfillment` of the `Order` object that is bound to the session. A `ShippingCalculator` is created and used to get the price for the type of shipping being used. After the dollar sign is stripped from the price, `shippingInfo` is converted to a double and used to call the `setCostToCustomer` method of the `ShippingInfo` object (see Listing 5.20).

Listing 5.20 Setting the Cost of the Shipping (*CreditInfo.jsp*)

```
<jsp:useBean scope="session" id="order" class="Order" />
<% order.setFulfillment( shippingInfo );
   ShippingCalculator calc = new ShippingCalculator( order );
   String s = request.getParameter( "shipperAndClass" );
   String price = calc.getPrice( s );
   price = price.replace( '$', ' ' );
   shippingInfo.setCostToCustomer( Double.parseDouble( price ) );%>
```

The HTML on this JSP is used to gather information about the customer's credit card. First, we want to display in a table the total amount to be charged to the card. We display the total of the items, the shipping price, and then the total price of the order. Next, a form is displayed that will get information on the credit card type, number, and expiration date, as shown in Listing 5.21.

Listing 5.21 The HTML Output of the *CreditInfo* JSP (*CreditInfo.jsp*)

```
<html>
<head><title>Credit Card Information</title></head>
<body>
  Your order price<br />
  <table>
  <tr><td>Items</td><td><%=order.getTotalItemPrice()%></td></tr>
  <tr><td>Shipping</td><td><%=price%></td></tr>
  <trbgcolor="yellow">
      <td>Total</td><td><%=order.getOrderTotal()%></td></tr>
  </table>
  Please enter your credit card information:
    <form action="ConfirmInfo.jsp">
      <p>
      Credit Card Type:
      <input type="radio" name="creditCardType" value="Visa">
        Visa
```

```
      </input>
      <input type="radio" name="creditCardType" value="Master Card">
        Master Card
      </input>
      <input type="radio" name="creditCardType"
            value="American Express">
        American Express
      </input>
      <input type="radio" name="creditCardType" value="Discover">
        Discover
      </input>
    </p>
    <p>Credit Card Number:<input name="creditCardNumber" /></p>
    <p>Expiration Date:<input name="expirationDate" /></p>
    <input type="submit" value="Submit information">
    </form>
  </body>
</html>
```

The *ConfirmInfo* JSP

In the ConfirmInfo JSP, the first thing we do is put the information from the CreditInfo JSP from into a CreditInfo object. This is done using the jsp:useBean and jsp:setProperty elements, as we have seen in the last two JSPs. After the Order object is retrieved, a scriptlet gets the CustomerInformation from it, and then the setCreditInfo method is called to set the newly gathered information, as shown in Listing 5.22.

Listing 5.22 Setting the Credit Information (*ConfirmInfo.jsp*)

```
<%@ page import="com.XmlEcomBook.Chap05.*" %>

<jsp:useBean scope="session" id="creditInfo" class="CreditInfo" />
<jsp:setProperty name="creditInfo" property="*" />
<jsp:useBean scope="session" id="order" class="Order" />
<% CustomerInfo cust = order.getCustomerInfo();
   cust.setCreditInfo( creditInfo );
%>
```

The HTML on this page reprints all of the information entered by the customer. This presentation allows the customer to verify all of the information before the final submission for payment authorization. The `CustomerInfo` and `Fulfillment` objects that were previously associated with the session are retrieved, and then `jsp:GetProperty` elements are used to get individual properties from this object to populate the page. A button at the bottom of the screen allows the customer to proceed, if the information is correct. The customer can use the back button to correct any information that is incorrect. Listing 5.23 shows how to display information for user confirmation.

Listing 5.23 Displaying the Information for User Confirmation (*ConfirmInfo.jsp*)

```
<html>
<head><title>Confirm Info</title></head>
<body>
<jsp:useBean scope="session" id="custInfo" class="CustomerInfo" />
<jsp:useBean scope="session" id="shippingInfo" class="Fulfillment" />

<p>Verify the information you entered:</p>
<p>Name: <b><jsp:getProperty name="custInfo" property="firstName" />
        <jsp:getProperty name="custInfo" property="lastName" /></b>
</p>
<p>
Address:<br />
<b><jsp:getProperty name="custInfo" property="address1" /><br />
<jsp:getProperty name="custInfo" property="address2" /><br />
<jsp:getProperty name="custInfo" property="city" />,
<jsp:getProperty name="custInfo" property="state" />
<jsp:getProperty name="custInfo" property="zip" />
</b></p>
<p>Email: <b><jsp:getProperty name="custInfo"
                            property="email" /></b></p>
<p>Phone Number: <b><jsp:getProperty name="custInfo" property="phoneNumber" /></
b></p>
<p>
Credit Card Type  : <b><jsp:getProperty name="creditInfo"
property="creditCardType" /></b><br />
Credit Card Number: <b><jsp:getProperty name="creditInfo"
property="creditCardNumber" /></b><br />
Expiration Date   : <b><jsp:getProperty name="creditInfo"
property="expirationDate" /></b>
</p>
<p>
```

```
Shipper: <b><jsp:getProperty name="shippingInfo"
                             property="shipper" /></b><br />
Class  : <b><jsp:getProperty name="shippingInfo"
                             property="shippingClass" /></b>
</p>
<b><i>Press the back button on your browser to correct
      any information.</i></b>
<form action="servlet/SubmitOrder">
<input type="submit" value="Submit Order" />
</form>
</body>
</html>
```

The *SubmitOrder* Servlet

When the ConfirmOrder JSP is submitted, we need to send the payment information to the processing service provider. This is done by the SubmitOrder servlet. A servlet has been used here instead of a JSP because this is a fairly code-intensive procedure with relatively little output. Servlets are often easier to code and debug than JSPs are, but the tradeoff is that HTML output is harder to achieve.

The main entry point into the servlet, doGet, begins by getting the Session object that is active (see Listing 5.24). We then get the Order object that was set into the session by the previous JSPs. The TestPaymentAuthorizer is then used to get authorization for the order. If the authorization is approved, an e-mail is sent to the customer using the Emailer class, a method is called to write the order to a file, and a JSP named Approved.jsp is called to write the output. If the authorization is not approved, a JSP named Declined.jsp is called to write the output.

Listing 5.24 The *doGet* Method of the *SubmitOrder* Servlet (*SubmitOrder.java*)

```
import java.io.*;
import java.util.*;
import javax.servlet.*;
import javax.servlet.http.*;
import com.XmlEcomBook.Chap05.*;

public class SubmitOrder extends HttpServlet {
```

```
public void doGet(HttpServletRequest req,
                  HttpServletResponse res)
       throws IOException, ServletException {
  try {
    HttpSession session = req.getSession();
    Order order = (Order)session.getAttribute( "order" );
    Authorization auth
          = TestPaymentAuthorizer.getAuthorization( order );
    order.setAuthorization( auth );
    if( auth.isApproved() ) {
      Emailer.sendConfirmation( order );
      writeOrder( order );
      getServletContext()
          .getRequestDispatcher("/Approved.jsp").forward(req, res);
    }
    else {
      getServletContext()
          .getRequestDispatcher("/Declined.jsp").forward(req, res);
    }
  }
  catch( Exception e ) {
  }
}
```

The writeOrder method is used to save the order information to an XML file. The code saves each day's orders in a separate directory, so we create a GregorianCalendar object to get the current day, month, and year. The directory name is created using the date, and a file name is created using the order id. The mkdir method on the File is called to ensure that the directory exists, and then the Order object's writeXML method is used to write the order information to a file, as shown in Listing 5.25.

Listing 5.25 The *writeOrder* Method (*SubmitOrder.jsp*)

```
private void writeOrder( Order order ) {
  try
  {
    Calendar calendar = new GregorianCalendar();
    int day = calendar.get( Calendar.DAY_OF_MONTH );
    int month = calendar.get( Calendar.MONTH ) + 1;
    int year = calendar.get( Calendar.YEAR );
```

```
        String dir = "Orders_" + year + "-" + month + "-" + day;
        String filename = "Order_" + order.getId() + ".xml";
        File file = new File( dir );
        file.mkdir();
        FileWriter writer
            = new FileWriter( dir + File.separator + filename );
        order.writeXML(writer);
        writer.close();
    }
    catch( IOException e ) {
    }
}
```

The *Approved* JSP

This JSP is called from the SubmitOrder servlet when an order has been approved. It is a simple page that includes the order's ID. This page (see Listing 5.26) can also be used as a receipt that the user can save and print out, if necessary. Because the Order object is available, it is not difficult to iterate through the items and print them out, if that is desired.

Listing 5.26 The *Approved* JSP (*Approved.jsp*)

```
<%@ page import="com.XmlEcomBook.Chap05.*" %>

<html>
<head><title>Approved Order</title></head>
<body>

<jsp:useBean id="order" scope="session" class="Order" />
Your order has been approved.
Your order number is: <jsp:getProperty name="order" property="id" />
</body>
</html>
```

The *Declined* JSP

The DeclinedJSP (see Listing 5.27) gets outputted when the customer's credit card has been declined. The reason for the declined authorization is output here.

Listing 5.27 The *Declined* JSP (*Declined.jsp*)

```
<%@ page import="com.XmlEcomBook.Chap05.*" %>
<html>
<head><title>Credit Card Declined</title></head>
<body>

<jsp:useBean id="order" scope="session" class="Order" />
Your credit card was declined.<br />
The reason given was:
<% Authorization auth = order.getAuthorization();
   if( auth != null ) {
     out.println( auth.getReason() );
   }
%>
</body>
</html>
```

Updating Shipping Information

Once the customer has completed the order and it has been approved, you need to have some way of updated the shipping information associated with the order. The shipping department of the store needs a way to view the orders, and then update their tracking numbers and date-sent properties. We will provide a way of listing all of the orders for a day, and then select a specific order.

The *OrderDateSelector* JSP

OrderDateSelector (see Listing 5.28) is a simple JSP displays a form with single input field where the shipping department employee can enter a date. The field is pre-populated with the current date. This JSP is the entry point into the shipping information update process.

Listing 5.28 The *OrderDateSelector* JSP (*OutputDateSelector.jsp*)

```
<%@ page import="java.util.*" %>

<html>
<head><title>Order Date Selector</title></head>
<body>
```

```
<% Calendar calendar = new GregorianCalendar();
   int day = calendar.get( Calendar.DAY_OF_MONTH );
   int month = calendar.get( Calendar.MONTH ) + 1;
   int year = calendar.get( Calendar.YEAR ); %>
<form action="SelectOrder.jsp">
Select a date:<input name="date" value="
<%= new String( year + "-" + month + "-" + day ); %>">
<br /><input type="submit" value="Get Orders for Date">
</form>
</input>
</body>
</html>
```

The *SelectOrder* JSP

The SelectOrder JSP (see Listing 5.29) uses the predefined variable request to get the date entered by the employee in the OrderDateSelecor JSP. This date is then used to create a directory name. Because the filenames of the order's XML files contain the order ID, all we need to do to display the orders is parse the order ID from the file name. Using this order ID, we then create an HTML a element for each order that links to a JSP. Each link includes the directory and filename of the XML file selected. The user can just click on the link to see their order. For example, if order number 1014 was placed on Oct 16, 2000, then the link element would be: <a href="ShowOrder.jsp?dir=Orders_2000-10-16&file=Order_1014 .xml"> 1014 </a>.

Listing 5.29 The *SelectOrder* JSP (*SelectOrder.jsp*)

```
<%@ page import="java.io.*" %>

<html>
<head><title>Select Order</title></head>
<body>

<%
String date = request.getParameter( "date" );
File dir = new File( "Orders_" + date );
File[] files = dir.listFiles();
for( int i = 0; i < files.length; i++ ) {
  String name = files[i].getName();
  if( name.endsWith( ".xml" ) ) {
```

```
        int start = name.indexOf( '_' ) + 1;
        int end = name.indexOf( '.' );
        String orderNum =  name.substring( start, end );
%>
<a href="ShowOrder.jsp?dir=<%= dir %>&file=<%= name %> ">
<%= orderNum %>
</a><br />
<%  }
    }
%>
</body>
</html>
```

The *ShowOrder* JSP

This JSP displays the order that the user has selected. Using the directory and file selected in the previous JSP, a DOM Document object is constructed. Using scriptlets (code inside the <% ... %> tags), we parse the file using standard DOM calls. The results of the parsing are then written out inside JSP expressions (code inside the <%=! ... %> tags). There is a lot of code in Listing 5.30, but most of it is fairly repetitive.

Listing 5.30 The *ShowOrder* JSP (*ShowOrder.jsp*)

```
<%@ page
import="javax.xml.parsers.*,java.util.*,
        java.io.*,org.w3c.dom.*,org.xml.sax.*"
%>

<html>
<head><title>Order</title></head>
<body>
<%
    double price = 0.0;;
    String dir = request.getParameter( "dir" );
    String file = request.getParameter( "file" );
    Document document = null;
    DocumentBuilderFactory factory
      = DocumentBuilderFactory.newInstance();
    try {
      DocumentBuilder builder = factory.newDocumentBuilder();
      document = builder.parse( new File( dir, file ) );
```

```
    }
    catch( ParserConfigurationException pce ) {
      throw new IOException( "Parser Configuration Error" );
    }
    catch( SAXException se ) {
      throw new IOException( "Parsing Excpetion" );
    }

    Element order = document.getDocumentElement();
    String id = order.getAttribute( "id" );
%>
<h1>Order #<%=id%></h1>
<h2>Items</h2>
<table border="1">
<tr><th>Item</th>
    <th>Description</th><th>Quantity</th><th>Price</th></tr>
<% NodeList items = order.getElementsByTagName( "item" );
    int numItems = items.getLength();
    for( int i = 0;i < numItems; i++ ) {
      Element item = (Element)items.item( i );
%>
<tr><td><%=item.getAttribute( "id" )%></td>
    <td><%=item.getFirstChild().getNodeValue()%></td>
    <td><%=item.getAttribute( "quantity" )%></td>
    <td><%=item.getAttribute( "price" )%></td>
    <%String priceString = item.getAttribute( "price" );
      priceString = priceString.replace( '$', ' ' );
      price += Double.parseDouble( priceString ); %>
</tr>
<% }%>
</table>
<% NodeList n1 = order.getElementsByTagName( "customer_info" );
    Element cust = (Element)n1.item( 0 );
    Node firstName = cust.getElementsByTagName( "first_name").item(0);
    Node lastName = cust.getElementsByTagName( "last_name" ).item(0);
    Node address1 = cust.getElementsByTagName( "address1" ).item(0);
    Node address2 = cust.getElementsByTagName( "address2" ).item(0);
    Node city = cust.getElementsByTagName( "city" ).item(0);
    Node state = cust.getElementsByTagName( "state" ).item(0);
    Node zip = cust.getElementsByTagName( "zip" ).item(0);
    Node email = cust.getElementsByTagName( "email" ).item(0);
    Node phone = cust.getElementsByTagName( "phone" ).item(0);
```

```
%>
<h2>Customer Information</h2>
Name:
<%=firstName.getFirstChild().getNodeValue()%>
<%=lastName.getFirstChild().getNodeValue()%><br /><br />
Address:<br />
<%=address1.getFirstChild().getNodeValue()%><br/ >
<%=address2.getFirstChild().getNodeValue()%><br />
<%=city.getFirstChild().getNodeValue()%>
<%=state.getFirstChild().getNodeValue()%>
<%=zip.getFirstChild().getNodeValue()%><br /><br />
Email:<%=email.getFirstChild().getNodeValue()%><br />
Phone:<%=phone.getFirstChild().getNodeValue()%><br />

<%  NodeList n2 = order.getElementsByTagName( "credit_info" );
    Element credit = (Element)n2.item( 0 );
    Node number = credit.getElementsByTagName( "card_number").item(0);
    Node type = credit.getElementsByTagName( "card_type").item(0);
    Node exp = credit.getElementsByTagName( "expiration_date").item(0);
%>
<h2>Credit Card Information</h2>
Type:<%=type.getFirstChild().getNodeValue()%><br />
Number:<%=number.getFirstChild().getNodeValue()%><br />
Expiration Date:<%=exp.getFirstChild().getNodeValue()%><br />

<%  NodeList n3 = order.getElementsByTagName( "authorization" );
    Element auth = (Element)n3.item( 0 );
    String approved = auth.getAttribute( "approved");
    Node reason = auth.getElementsByTagName( "reason").item(0);
    Node auth_code = auth.getElementsByTagName( "authorization_code").item(0);
%>
<h2>Authorization Information</h2>
Auth Code:<%=auth_code.getFirstChild().getNodeValue()%><br />
Approved:<%=approved%><br />
Reason:<%=reason.getFirstChild().getNodeValue()%><br />
<% NodeList n4 = order.getElementsByTagName( "fulfillment" );
    Element fulfillment = (Element)n4.item(0);
    Node shipper = fulfillment.getElementsByTagName( "shipper" ).item(0);
    Node clas = fulfillment.getElementsByTagName( "class" ).item(0);
    Node cost = fulfillment.getElementsByTagName( "cost" ).item(0);
    Node tracking
        = fulfillment.getElementsByTagName( "tracking_number" ).item(0);
```

```
Node dateSent
    = fulfillment.getElementsByTagName( "date_sent" ).item(0);
String trackingString = tracking.getFirstChild().getNodeValue();
String dateSentString = dateSent.getFirstChild().getNodeValue();
%>
```

Near the bottom of this JSP is a form used for entering tracking number and shipment date information. The values will only be presented to the user as input fields if the value of the tracking number is currently NO_TRACKING_NUMBER. This special value is used to indicate that a value does not exist for this field, so an employee can enter a new one. If a value has already been set, the values will be simply displayed, and the employee will not be able to edit them. This form (see Listing 5.31) also has several hidden fields that contain information needed by the JSP that updates the XML file.

Listing 5.31 The Form for Entering Shipping Information (*ShowOrder.jsp*)

```
<form action="UpdateFulfillment.jsp">
<input type="hidden" name="dir" value="<%=dir%>" />
<input type="hidden" name="file" value="<%=file%>" />
<input type="hidden" name="email"
value="<%=email.getFirstChild().getNodeValue()%>" />
<input type="hidden" name="id" value="<%=id%>" />
<input type="hidden" name="auth_code"
value="<%=auth_code.getFirstChild().getNodeValue()%>" />
<input type="hidden" name="price" value="<%=price%>" />
<h2>Fulfillment Info</h2>
Shipper:<%=shipper.getFirstChild().getNodeValue()%><br />
Class:<%=clas.getFirstChild().getNodeValue()%><br />
Cost:$<%=cost.getFirstChild().getNodeValue()%><br />
Tracking #:
<%if( trackingString.equals( "NO_TRACKING_NUMBER" ) ) { %>
  <input name="tracking" value="<%=trackingString%>" />
  Date Sent:<input name="date_sent" value="<%=dateSentString%>" />
  <input type="submit" value="Submit New Fulfillment Data" />
<%} else {%>
  <%=trackingString%><br />
  Date Sent:<%=dateSentString%>
<%}%>
</form>
<br /><a href="OrderDateSelector.jsp">Back to date selection</a>
</body>
</html>
```

The *UpdateFulfillment* JSP

The last JSP we explore is responsible for updating the tracking number and shipment date entered in the ShowOrder JSP. In this JSP, we will use a different technique for processing an XML file. What needs to be done is fairly simple: Two values in the XML file need to be updated with new values. Instead of using the DOM to parse this file and then writing it back out as an XML file, we will use a simpler text processing approach. The elements that we are interested in—updating tracking_number and date_sent—were filled with the special values NO_TRACKING_NUMBER and NOT_SENT_YET when the XML file was created. Updating the XML is now as simple as searching for these special strings and replacing them with new values.

The JSP first gets the parameters that were passed to it, including the hidden fields that were in the form. A BufferedReader is created for reading in from the XML file and a FileWriter is used for outputting the newly updated XML. Each line read in from the XML is sent to the replace method to do any substitutions that are needed. The replace method is similar to the String's replace method, except it operates on Strings instead of chars.

This technique of using text processing to operate on XML file is useful if simple processing is needed. It saves the performance cost and code complexity associated with parsing the XML. However, this technique does not always work well with complex changes. Treating XML as raw text tends to produce brittle code that does not work if the XML is reformatted or small changes are made to the DTD. Using a parser is the best choice when doing more extensive processing of XML data.

After writing the XML, this JSP sends a confirmation notice to the customer using the Emailer class. It also informs the processing service provider that the order has been completed so that the funds can be transferred from the customer's account into the store's account, as shown in Listing 5.32.

Listing 5.32 The *UpdateFulfillment* JSP (*UpdateFulfillment.jsp*)

```
<%@ page import="java.io.*,com.XmlEcomBook.Chap05.*" %>

<html>
<head><title>Update Complete</title></head>
<body>

<% String tracking = request.getParameter( "tracking" );
   String dateSent = request.getParameter( "date_sent" );
   String dir = request.getParameter( "dir" );
```

```java
    String filename = request.getParameter( "file" );
    String email = request.getParameter( "email" );
    String id = request.getParameter( "id" );
    String auth_code = request.getParameter( "auth_code" );
    String priceString = request.getParameter( "price" );
    double price = Double.parseDouble( priceString );
    File inFile = new File( dir, filename );
    File outFile = new File( dir, filename + ".tmp" );
    BufferedReader reader = new BufferedReader(new FileReader(inFile));
    FileWriter writer = new FileWriter( outFile );
    String line;
    while( (line = reader.readLine()) != null ) {
      String newLine = replace( line, "NOT_SENT_YET", dateSent );
      newLine = replace( newLine, "NO_TRACKING_NUMBER", tracking );
      writer.write( newLine + "\n" );
    }
    reader.close();
    writer.close();
    inFile.renameTo( new File( dir, filename + ".old" ) );
    outFile.renameTo( inFile );
    Emailer.sendShipped( email, id );
    TestPaymentAuthorizer.capture( auth_code, price );
%>
<p>The fulfillment was updated with the new information.</p>
<a href="OrderDateSelector.jsp">Back to date selection</a>

</body>
</html>

<%!
String replace( String s, String oldString, String newString ) {
  int pos = s.indexOf( oldString );
  String newLine = s;
  if( pos != -1 ) {
    newLine = s.substring( 0, pos );
    newLine += newString;
    newLine += s.substring( pos + oldString.length() );
  }
  return newLine;
}
%>
```

The code discussed in this chapter shows an implementation of simple billing and order processing. To use this code in a real store, some changes would have to be made. The biggest changes required would be security related. The JSPs that the customer uses to enter information should use HTTPS instead of plain HTTP. Also, the customer's information has been stored in a non-encrypted file on the same file system on which the Web server is running. Ideally, this sensitive information should be stored in an encrypted, secure database running on an isolated server.

Another change would be to substitute the payment authorizer class with one that communicates with an actual payment service. The class presented here, however, can be useful for testing the system without needing to have these communications capabilities in place.

CHAPTER 6

Online Catalog Upkeep

- Change the price of a product in a catalog
- Edit the description of a product in a catalog
- Add a new product to a catalog
- Delete a product from a catalog

In Chapter 2, "A Catalog in XML," we created a DTD (Document Type Definition) for a product catalog for our fictional store, XMLGifts.com. In Chapter 3, "Presenting an XML Catalog Online," we created JSPs and servlets for viewing this catalog as well as presented a way to perform read operations. Now we need to be able to update product information as well as delete and add products to the XMLGifts.com catalog. These types of operations are commonly referred to as CRUD (Create, Read, Update, and Delete) operations.

Solution Overview

Because the data for our catalog is stored in an XML file, one way to make updates and changes is to use a text or XML editor. XML is a human readable format, so users can simply open up the XML file and edit the catalog directly. This technique has a couple of drawbacks. First, editing XML files with standard editors is not always easy. Tools may be error-prone, time-consuming, or may require some specialized training. Second, if the underlying data format is changed from XML files to, say, a database with a server that produces XML, text editors are no longer an option. To get around these drawbacks, you can create a custom catalog editor.

There are many ways that such an editor can be written. For example, you could use a Java application that reads the XML data and presents it in a standard Swing GUI for the user to edit. If you wanted a distributed solution, you could create an applet that runs in the browser. In this chapter, you will develop the editor using a Web server, HTML, and JSP, just as you did in Chapter 3 when you developed the catalog viewing system. Using similar techniques and tools on a project makes good sense as it allows for easier development and maintenance. The same developers can be used for all parts of the project, and there is a potential to be able to re-use ideas and code from different parts of the project.

Our solution to this editing-the-catalog problem is a browser-hosted application. Such an application will enable anyone with a browser and access to the site to edit the catalog. You can create JSPs that output HTML forms that the user will be able to fill in. The forms submit data back to the server to create, edit, and delete products contained in the catalog file.

There are four layers to the solution, starting from the XML data itself and ending with the browser that will display the information. The middle two layers are where code needs to be written. One middle layer is a set of data objects to do conversion between XML and Java, and the other is used to create and interpret HTML data displayed by the browser. Figure 6.1 shows a diagram of the different layers.

FIGURE 6.1
Overview of Solution

The first step in crafting the solution is to create a set of XML-aware objects to represent the catalog data. These objects will hold data about the product lines, individual products, and components of the individual products, such as images and clips. These objects can create themselves based on an XML data source, and can also write themselves out as XML. These objects translate between the XML world and the world of Java objects.

Next, you create servlets and JSPs that display information to the user and process information the user has entered. These take information from the data objects and create the forms that are displayed in the browser. Once the forms are completed, the information will be sent back to the server. There will also be code to take this information and update the data objects.

Data Objects

It can be difficult sometimes to deal with XML at the parser level. If an extensive document type is created, it can be a time-consuming, tedious, and error-prone process to deal with each element and attribute on its own. This is because the DOM or SAX parsers do not know the details of the schemas of individual documents. These general-purpose parsers need to be able to read any document, no matter what DTD it uses. It would be much easier if objects were available that were based on the structure of the XML document it was reading.

The process of creating a set of objects to convert XML data to easier-to-use Java objects is referred to as data binding. Data binding allows you to work with XML sources at the level of the document's structure, instead of dealing with elements and attributes directly. Once a set of data binding objects has been created, a programmer using them may not even realize that these objects use XML beneath the surface.

In this chapter, you manually create data binding objects for our catalog XML file, but it is also possible to have these classes generated automatically. There are many tools available to do this type of automatic code generation. These tools can read in a DTD, an XML Schema or a sample of an XML document to create code. Usually a new class is created for each element in the XML, and fields are used for attributes found in the XML.

As an example, the following DTD snippet represents a person:

```
<!ELEMENT person (address)>
<!ATTLIST person firstname CDATA #IMPLIED>
                 lastname  CDATA #IMPLIED>
<!ELEMENT address (Street, City, Zip)>
```

A data binding tool may create the following class for the person element:

```
class Person {
  private String lastname;
  private String firstname;
private Address address;

  public Address getAddress() {...}
  public void setAdress( Address a ) {...}
  public String getFirstname() {...}
  public void setFistname( String s ) {...}
  public String getLastname() {...}
  public void setLastname() {...}
}
```

An `Address` class would also be created that has methods to get and set the street, city, and zip code. As you can see, it would be much easier to code using these classes instead of using DOM or SAX classes.

NOTE   One such data binding tool is Castor by The ExoLab group. More information can be found at `http://castor.exolab.org`.

There are some advantages to hand coding these classes, aside from the great learning experience. The code can be written to be more efficient than a generic data binding tool. Most data binding tools use some kind of in-memory object model to load the data, and then create objects from the object model. This results in a large amount of memory being used when loading XML documents. Another advantage of hand coding classes is that the code can also be customized so it can be easier to use by a specific application. Extra flexibility can also be included when hand coding data binding classes.

To design the data binding classes, you need to look at the catalog DTD and decide which elements we need to create classes for, and which elements can be represented by standard classes, such as `Strings` or `Integers`. This decision depends the complexity of the element. Elements that have a PCDATA content type and no attributes can easily be represented by a `String` or `Integer`, depending on the contents of the element. For these simple elements, no new class needs to be created. However, if an element has a subelement or has attribute values, a simple `String` often does not suffice and you might need to create a new class to represent the element.

Looking at the DTD that was created in Chapter 2, you can pick out many elements that are not simple. The `catalog`, `product_line`, `product`, `image`, `clip`, and `onsale_date` elements all contain subelements so they are candidates for new classes. Some other elements are simple; they contain simple content, and no attributes. The `author`, `artist`, `quantity_in_stock` elements and all the onsale `date` subelements are simple, and can be represented by a `String` or `Integer`. This leaves a few elements, such as the `description` element and its subelements, and the `price` elements, which we will handle a bit differently. We will go into more details about how we will handle these elements later.

Figure 6.2 is a UML class diagram depicting the classes we will create. Utility classes that are used by these classes are not shown on this diagram in order not to overcomplicate it.

FIGURE 6.2
UML Class Diagram

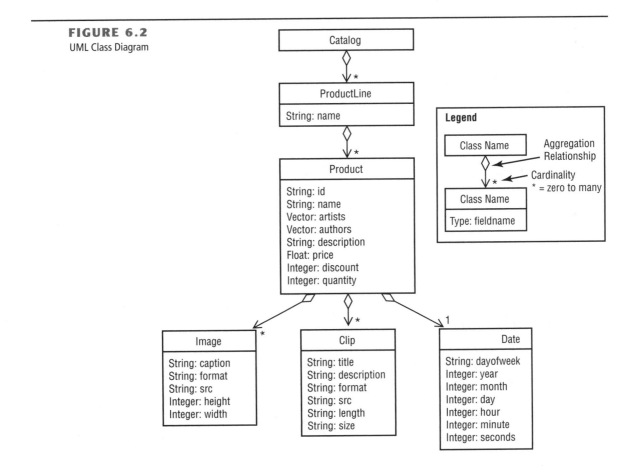

When you look at the code on the disk included in this book, you will see that each of the data object classes has `toString` methods. These methods are very useful when it comes to debugging the classes, but are not an integral part of the class. They have not been included in the descriptions of the code in this chapter so you can focus on the main parts of the code.

The *Catalog* Class

The `Catalog` class represents the root element of the catalog DTD, which is shown here:

```
<!ELEMENT catalog (product_line*) >
```

This element has no attributes and just a single repeatable subelement, called `product_line`. Listing 6.1 shows the code for declaring the beginning of the `Catalog` class.

Listing 6.1 The Start of the *Catalog* Class (*Catalog.java*)

```
package com.XmlEcomBook.Chap06;

import javax.xml.parsers.*;
import java.util.*;
import java.io.*;
import org.w3c.dom.*;
import org.xml.sax.*;
public class Catalog {
private Vector productLines = new Vector();
```

As you can see the names are changed from the format used in the XML, all lowercase with underscores, to a standard Java naming syntax. Classes begin with uppercase, and we use uppercase to separate words instead of underscores. The element named `catalog` becomes the class `Catalog`.

Because the `catalog` element allows any number of `product_line` elements to be child elements, a `Vector` is used to represent them. Any collection class that preserves the order of its elements could be used to represent repeatable elements. The best one depends on how the collection will be used, but `Vector` provides a good default collection, if you don't know the details of how it will be used right away.

Because the purpose of this class is to convert from XML to objects and back to XML again, you provide a constructor that can take the name of an XML file, which can be parsed to get data from. This is shown in Listing 6.2.

The first section of code in the constructor creates the needed JAXP objects to parse the XML file. A `DocumentBuilder` is created which is used to parse the document and get the DOM `Document` object.

The next section of code gets the root element from the document and extracts all of the elements named `product_line` from it. Loop through each of these elements and for each one, create a new `ProductLine` object and call a method that will add it to our catalog object. As you can see, the `Catalog` class is responsible only for finding its direct subelements and then hands off the decoding of these elements to the `ProductLine` class.

Listing 6.2 The *Catalog* Constructor (*Catalog.java*)

```java
public Catalog( String filename) throws IOException {
  Document document = null;
  DocumentBuilderFactory factory
    = DocumentBuilderFactory.newInstance();
  try {
    DocumentBuilder builder = factory.newDocumentBuilder();
    document = builder.parse( new File( filename ) );
  }
  catch( ParserConfigurationException pce ) {
    throw new IOException( "Parser Configuration Error" );
  }
  catch( SAXException se ) {
    throw new IOException( "Parsing Exception" );
  }

  Element root = document.getDocumentElement();
  NodeList nodes = root.getElementsByTagName( "product_line" );
  int num = nodes.getLength();
  for( int i = 0; i < num; i++ ) {
    Element e = (Element)nodes.item( i );
    ProductLine pl = new ProductLine( e );
    addProductLine( pl );
  }
}
```

The addProductLine method, seen in Listing 6.3 is straightforward. It takes a Product-Line object and adds it into the productLines Vector.

Listing 6.3 Adding New Product Lines (*Catalog.java*)

```java
public void addProductLine( ProductLine productLine ) {
  productLines.addElement( productLine );
}
```

Next, you need a way to access the ProductLine objects that a Catalog can contain. Because product lines are identified by name, you want to get product line based on the name. This is shown in Listing 6.4. The getProductLine method takes a product line name as a parameter and loops through all of the product lines it has until a match is found. If no match is found, a null is returned.

Listing 6.4 Accessing a Product Line (*Catalog.java*)

```java
public ProductLine getProductLine( String name ) {
  Enumeration enum = productLines.elements();
  while( enum.hasMoreElements() ) {
    ProductLine pl = (ProductLine)enum.nextElement();
    if( pl.getName().equals( name ) ) {
      return pl;
    }
  }
  return null;
}
```

Another useful operation to do on the Catalog is to get a specific product based on the product id. This allows for products to be displayed and edited. To do this, all of the product lines that a catalog has will be asked to look up the product. The details of how each product line finds a product does not need to be known, it is left up to the ProductLine object. This is a typical example of the encapsulation that object-oriented programming languages provide. Listing 6.5 shows the product lookup.

Listing 6.5 Getting a Product from the Catalog (*Catalog.java*)

```java
public Product getProduct( String id ) {
  Enumeration enum = productLines.elements();
  while( enum.hasMoreElements() ) {
```

```
      ProductLine pl = (ProductLine)enum.nextElement();
      Product p = pl.getProduct( id );
      if( p != null ) {
        return p;
      }
    }
    return null;
  }
```

Here again, a null object is returned if the product is not found. It is useful to have conventions, such as always returning a null or always throwing an exception if a search for something is unsuccessful. Throughout the code in this chapter, the decision was to always return a null when a search fails, and this will be done consistently.

Another operation that the `Catalog` object will allow is deleting Products. This method, shown in Listing 6.6 is similar to `getProduct` method, but when a product is found, it is deleted from the product line before it is returned. Again, if no product with the specified id is found, a null is returned.

Listing 6.6 Deleting a Product from the Catalog (*Catalog.java*)

```
  public Product deleteProduct( String id ) {
    Enumeration enum = productLines.elements();
    while( enum.hasMoreElements() ) {
      ProductLine pl = (ProductLine)enum.nextElement();
      Product p = pl.getProduct( id );
      if( p != null ) {
        pl.deleteProduct( id );
        return p;
      }
    }
    return null;
  }
```

You also need your `Catalog` class to be able to write out its data as XML. A method has been created that will write the data out using an `XMLWriter` object, shown in Listing 6.7. The `XMLWriter` class is a utility class to assist in outputting XML to an output stream. We will examine that class next. Much like the constructor of `Catalog`, where you only decoded enough of XML to be able to pass the rest of the parsing to `ProductLine` elements, you only write the actual catalog start and end tags. The writing of the product line elements is left up to the `ProductLine` class itself.

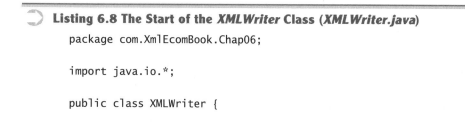

Listing 6.7 Write the Catalog as XML (*Catalog.java*)

```java
public void toXML( XMLWriter writer ) throws IOException {
  writer.writeln( "<catalog>" );
  writer.indent();
  Enumeration enum = productLines.elements();
  while( enum.hasMoreElements() ) {
    ProductLine pl = (ProductLine)enum.nextElement();
    pl.toXML( writer );
    writer.writeln( "" );
  }
  writer.unindent();
  writer.writeln( "</catalog>" );
}
```

The *XMLWriter* Class

The XMLWriter class is a utility class to help with the writing of XML output. This class writes to an OutputStream that is given to it in the constructor. The OutputStream is kept as a field of the object. The class also takes care of inserting the appropriate line separator. Different operating systems use different line separators; for example, Windows uses a carriage return and a line feed whereas UNIX uses only a line feed. You need some way to determine which one to use. Luckily, Java provides a System property that contains the correct line separator for the current operating system. The XMLWriter class defines a static byte array to hold this value.

The XMLWriter class also takes care of indenting the output. You define a byte array that contains the indenting string to use. You also need a Boolean field to keep track of whether we are currently writing a new line or continuing a current line. The start of the class with the fields is shown in Listing 6.8.

Listing 6.8 The Start of the *XMLWriter* Class (*XMLWriter.java*)

```java
package com.XmlEcomBook.Chap06;

import java.io.*;

public class XMLWriter {
```

```
static private final byte[] LINE_SEPARATOR
        = System.getProperty( "line.separator" ).getBytes();
static private final byte[] INDENT = "  ".getBytes();

private OutputStream    out;
private int             currentIndent;
private boolean         newLine = true;
```

The constructor for XMLWriter takes in the OutputStream that will be written to. By passing in a OutputStream you can have the XMLWriter output to a file, standard output or a HTTP response. This comes in handy when debugging the application. The constructor is shown in Listing 6.9.

Listing 6.9 *XMLWriter* Constructor (*XMLWriter.java*)

```
public XMLWriter( OutputStream newOut ) {
  out = newOut;
}
```

You need to be able to adjust the indent level of the output. This is done with two simple methods—one to increase the indent level and one to decrease it. These two method are shown in Listing 6.10.

Listing 6.10 Adjusting the Indent Level (*XMLWriter.java*)

```
public void indent() {
  currentIndent++;
}

public void unindent() {
  currentIndent--;
}
```

Finally, you need to be able to do the actual writing of output. You have two methods to do this—one to write output to be followed by a line separator and one just to add output to the current line. These two methods are called write and writeln. This is similar to the java .io.PrintStream classes print and println methods. Whenever you do an output, check to see if this is a new line we are writing. If it is, indent the output the appropriate number of times. The writeln method simply uses the write method to do the output and then outputs the line separator characters. This can be seen in Listing 6.11.

Listing 6.11 Writing Output (*XMLWriter.java*)

```java
public void write( String s ) throws IOException {
  if( newLine )
  {
      for( int i = 0; i < currentIndent; i++ ) {
        out.write( INDENT );
      }
  }
  out.write( s.getBytes() );
  newLine = false;
}

public void writeln( String s ) throws IOException {
  write( s );
  out.write( LINE_SEPARATOR );
  newLine = true;
}
}
```

The *ProductLine* Class

The next class is ProductLine, which is based on the DTD definition for the product_line element.

```
<!ELEMENT product_line (product*) >
<!ATTLIST product_line name CDATA #IMPLIED>
```

Like the catalog element, this element also contains a single, repeatable child element, so you represent this as a Vector of products, as shown in Listing 6.12. This element has an attribute, called name, which you also need to represent in the class. Add a field that has a type of String. String types are usually good defaults for a CDATA element.

Listing 6.12 The Start of the *ProductLine* Class (*ProductLine.java*)

```java
package com.XmlEcomBook.Chap06;

import java.util.*;
import java.io.*;
import org.w3c.dom.*;
```

```
public class ProductLine {
  private String name;
  private Vector products = new Vector();
```

You have two constructors for this class. The first one takes no argument and simply creates an empty product line with no name or products. The second constructor for this class will use a DOM Element to create itself. You have already seen that the Element is passed to the constructor by the Catalog class. This constructor needs to be able to get the name attribute from the element, and then find all of the product child elements and create new Product objects using them. These constructors are shown in Listing 6.13.

Listing 6.13 The *ProductLine* Constructors (*ProductLine.java*)

```
public ProductLine() {
}

public ProductLine( Element element ) {
  name = element.getAttribute( "name" );
  NodeList productNodes = element.getElementsByTagName( "product" );
  int num = productNodes.getLength();
  for( int i = 0; i < num; i++ ) {
    addProduct( new Product( (Element)productNodes.item( i ) ) );
  }
}
```

Next, look at the methods for accessing and modifying the products. These are similar to the methods in Catalog that were used for the product line Vector. One method, shown in Listing 6.14, is used for retrieving products by name, one method is used for deleting products and another method is used for adding products.

Listing 6.14 Accessing and Modifying Products (*ProductLine.java*)

```
public void addProduct( Product product ) {
  products.addElement( product );
}

public Product deleteProduct( String id ) {
  Enumeration enum = products.elements();
  while( enum.hasMoreElements() ) {
    Product p = (Product)enum.nextElement();
```

```
      if( p.getId().equals( id ) ) {
        products.remove( p );
        return p;
      }
    }
    return null;
  }

  public Product getProduct( String id ) {
    Enumeration enum = products.elements();
    while( enum.hasMoreElements() ) {
      Product p = (Product)enum.nextElement();
      if( p.getId().equals( id ) ) {
        return p;
      }
    }
    return null;
  }
```

You also need be able to access and modify the name field in the product, as shown in Listing 6.15.

Listing 6.15 Accessing and Modifying the Name (*ProductLine.java*)

```
  public String getName(){
    return name;
  }

  public void setName( String newName ) {
    name = newName;
  }
```

Finally, you need the method to write out the XML, as shown in Listing 6.16. Like the Catalog class, there is a method, called toXML, that writes the XML to a given XMLWriter. This time we also need to write out the name attribute. XML allows attribute values to be quoted with either the single quote character or double quote character. That is, you could write name='ABC' or name="ABC", and they are equivalent. To make it easier for you to output XML from Java, use the single quote character. To use a double quote character, you would need to escape it with a backslash, and this can make the code difficult to read.

Listing 6.16 Writing the XML for *ProductLine* (*ProductLine.java*)

```java
public void toXML( XMLWriter writer ) throws IOException {
  writer.write( "<product_line" );
  if( name != null )
    writer.write( " name='" + name );
  writer.writeln( "'>" );
  writer.indent();
  Enumeration enum = products.elements();
  while( enum.hasMoreElements() ) {
    Product p = (Product)enum.nextElement();
    p.toXML( writer );
    writer.writeln( "" );
  }
  writer.unindent();
  writer.writeln( "</product_line>" );
}
}
}
```

The *Product* Class

The product element is more complicated than the catalog and product_line elements you have already looked at. Here is the DTD for it:

```
<!ELEMENT product (name,author*,artist*,description,price,
quantity_in_stock,image*,onsale_date?,clip*)>
<!ATTLIST product  id       ID   #REQUIRED>
<!ATTLIST product  keywords CDATA #IMPLIED>
```

The product element can contain up to nine different types of child elements, many of which are optional or repeatable. It also has two attributes. Much like you did in the previous classes, Listing 6.17 defines fields for each of these elements and attributes. Again, Vectors are used for the repeatable elements. Most of the others are String types, but there are a few exceptions. Because you know that the price element will contain a number with dollars and cents, use a double to represent it. The quantity_in_stock is also a number, so you use an int type. The on_sale_date is represented by a Date class.

Listing 6.17 Start of *Product* Class (*Product.java*)

```java
package com.XmlEcomBook.Chap06;

import java.io.*;
import java.util.*;
import java.text.*;
import org.w3c.dom.*;

public class Product {
  private String    id;
  private String    keywords;
  private String    name;
  private Vector    authors = new Vector();
  private Vector    artists = new Vector();
  private String    description;
  private double    price;
  private Integer   discount;
  private int       quantityInStock;
  private Vector    images = new Vector();
  private DateTime  onSaleDate = new DateTime();
  private Vector    clips = new Vector();
```

If you look at the field definitions, you can see that there is one definition that does not look familiar from the DTD. The `discount` field does not have an equivalent attribute or element. This is because you took a shortcut when it came to the `price` element. The `price` element is fairly simple. It contains PCDATA content and a single attribute, `discount`, shown here:

```
<!ELEMENT price (#PCDATA)>
<!ATTLIST price discount CDATA #IMPLIED>
```

Instead of creating a new class for this, which has only two simple fields, include both of these fields directly into the `Product` class. The `discount` field is an `Integer` type. You could not use an `int` primitive type because the `discount` element is optional, so it can be nonexistent. Use a null `Integer` to represent this.

One other irregularity here is the `description` field. In the DTD this is represented by the following DTD:

```
<!ENTITY % running_text "(#PCDATA|bold|italics|quote|link|general)*">
<!ELEMENT description (paragraph|general)* >
<!ELEMENT paragraph %running_text;>
```

```
<!ELEMENT bold (#PCDATA)>
<!ELEMENT italics (#PCDATA)>
<!ELEMENT quote (#PCDATA)>
<!ATTLIST quote attrib CDATA #IMPLIED>
<!ELEMENT link (#PCDATA)>
<!ATTLIST link  href   CDATA #REQUIRED
                alt    CDATA #IMPLIED>
<!ELEMENT general (#PCDATA)>
<!ATTLIST general type CDATA #REQUIRED>
```

This is a complex content model involving many child elements, which can be repeated in any order. This causes two complexities. The first is being able to represent this in the Java code. You would need to create a `description` class, which can take `paragraph` and `general` objects in order and then access them again. The `Paragraph` class itself would be a complex type that would be able to contain any one of its five subelements and text items. The second complexity would be displaying all this data in an editable way. Trying to display this structure on an HTML form would be very difficult. We have decided to make a simplification to handle these elements.

If you look at the field definitions in the `Product` class, you see that the `description` field is a `String` type. Instead of trying to duplicate the structure of the description element, simply store it as a raw XML string. When you want to display the description information to the user, simply show the raw XML and allow the user to edit that.

There are two constructors for the `Product` class, as shown in Listing 6.18. The first one takes no arguments and is used for creating a new `Product`. The other one takes a DOM `Element` object so the `Product` object can be created from an XML source. This constructor first gets the two attributes, `id` and `name`, from the `product` element. For the rest of the fields, methods have been created to extract each of the child elements from the `product` elements.

Listing 6.18 *Product* Class Constructors (*Product.java*)

```
public Product() {
}

public Product( Element productElement ) {
  id = productElement.getAttribute( "id" );
  keywords = productElement.getAttribute( "keywords" );
  extractName( productElement );
  extractAuthors( productElement );
  extractArtists( productElement );
```

```
    extractDescription( productElement );
    extractPrice( productElement );
    extractQuantityInStock( productElement );
    extractImages( productElement );
    extractDate( productElement );
    extractClips( productElement );
}
```

The extractName method is straightforward. It is shown in Listing 6.19. It uses a utility method extractTextFrom to extract the text from the name element. The extractAuthors and extractArtists methods also use this utility method. Both of these methods get a list of child elements from the product elements, and then loops through all of them, extracting the text from each one, and calling the appropriate method to add the element to the object.

Listing 6.19 The *extractName*, *extractAuthors*, and *extractArtists* Methods (*Product.java*)

```
private void extractName( Element productElement ) {
  name = Util.extractTextFrom( "name", productElement );
}

private void extractAuthors( Element productElement ) {
  NodeList authorList = productElement.getElementsByTagName("author");
  for( int i = 0; i < authorList.getLength(); i++ ) {
    Element author = (Element)authorList.item(i);
    addAuthor( Util.extractTextFrom( "name", author ) );
  }
}

private void extractArtists( Element productElement ) {
  NodeList authorList = productElement.getElementsByTagName("artist");
  for( int i = 0; i < authorList.getLength(); i++ ) {
    Element author = (Element)authorList.item(i);
    addArtist( Util.extractTextFrom( "name", author ) );
  }
}
```

You will look at the extractDescription method next. This is shown in Listing 6.20. This method gets the description element from the product element. Because the DOM API does not have a way to specify to get just a single element with a certain name, you need to use the getElementsByTagName, which returns a collection of nodes. Then check the length of this collection. If the length is greater than zero, we know that there is a `description` element. If there is one, get the first match from the collection, because you know there will only be one `description` element. Finally, use another utility method `extractMarkupAs-Text` to set the description field.

Listing 6.20 The *extractDescription* Method (*Product.java*)

```
private void extractDescription( Element productElement ) {
  NodeList desc = productElement.getElementsByTagName( "description" );
  if( desc.getLength() > 0 ) {
    NodeList contents = desc.item(0).getChildNodes();
    description = Util.extractMarkupAsText( contents );
  }
}
```

The `extractPrice` method will need to extract both the contents of the `price` element for the actual price, and it also needs to get the `discount` attribute from the element. The first line of the method extracts the text content of the `price` element using a utility method. The string from the element is converted to a double using a `NumberFormat` object. This object knows how to parse a string representation of a dollar amount to extract a number. Next, you need to extract the discount information. Do this by getting the collection of `price` element, and then getting the discount attribute from this. An `Integer` is then created from the discount attribute string. The method is shown in Listing 6.21.

Listing 6.21 The *extractPrice* Method (*Product.java*)

```
private void extractPrice( Element productElement ) {
  String s = Util.extractTextFrom( "price", productElement );
  NumberFormat nf = NumberFormat.getCurrencyInstance();
  try {
    Number n = nf.parse( s );
    price = n.doubleValue();
  }
  catch( ParseException pe )
  {
    price = 0;
  }
  NodeList priceNodes = productElement.getElementsByTagName("price");
  if( priceNodes.getLength() > 0 ) {
```

```
        Element price = (Element)priceNodes.item(0);
        if( price != null ){
          String d = price.getAttribute( "discount" );
          if( d != null && !d.equals( "" ) ) {
            discount = new Integer( d );
          }
        }
      }
    }
```

To get the information from the `quantity_in_stock` element is fairly easy. Use the familiar `extractTextFrom` method to get the `String`, and then parse the `String` to create an `int` type, as shown in Listing 6.22.

Listing 6.22 The *extractQuantityInStock* Method (*Product.java*)

```
private void extractQuantityInStock( Element productElement ) {
  String s = Util.extractTextFrom("quantity_in_stock", productElement);
  quantityInStock = Integer.parseInt( s );
}
```

The `image` element is a repeatable one, so you need to get all of the children elements named "image" from the `product` element, and then use the `addImage` method to add them to the product object. The `extractClips` method is almost identical, except clips are extracted instead of images. These two methods are shown in Listing 6.23.

Listing 6.23 The *extractImages* and *extractClips* Method (*Product.java*)

```
private void extractImages( Element productElement ) {
  NodeList descNode = productElement.getElementsByTagName( "image" );
  for( int i = 0; i < descNode.getLength(); i++ ) {
    addImage( new Image( (Element)descNode.item(i) ) );
  }
}

private void extractClips( Element productElement ) {
  NodeList descNode = productElement.getElementsByTagName( "clip" );
  for( int i = 0; i < descNode.getLength(); i++ ) {
    addClip( new Clip( (Element)descNode.item(i) ) );
  }
}
```

As your final extraction method, use `extractDate`, shown in Listing 6.24. This uses the DOMs `getElementByTagName` method to extract the collection of nodes name "onsale_date", and then if it finds one, it knows it is the one and only `onsale_date` element that can exist, so it uses it to create a new `Date` object.

Listing 6.24 The *extractDate* Method (*Product.java*)

```
private void extractDate( Element productElement ) {
  NodeList date = productElement.getElementsByTagName( "onsale_date" );
  if( date.getLength() > 0 ) {
    onSaleDate = new Date( (Element)date.item( 0 ) );
  }
}
```

You need to create methods for getting and setting values of all the fields. Most of these are straightforward, much like the `getName` and `setName` shown in Listing 6.25. There are similar methods for the `id`, `keywords`, `description`, `price`, `discount`, `quantityInStock`, and `onSaleDate` fields. To save some space, we do not show these here, but they are included in the source code on the CD that comes with this book.

Listing 6.25 The *getName* and *setName* Methods (*Product.java*)

```
public String getName() {
  return name;
}

public void setName( String newName ) {
  name = newName;
}
```

The `author` field is a `Vector` so it will need to be handled differently than the above get and set methods. You have an `addAuthor` method that adds a `String` to the `authors` Vector using the `addElement` method. To be able to remove authors, have a method called `removeAllAuthors` that deletes every author from the Product. This allows you to change authors by removing all the authors and replacing them with new ones. There is also a `getAuthors` method that returns an enumeration of all the authors. The way you add, remove, and get `artists`, `images`, and `clips` is the same as what you did with `authors`, only you perform the operations on the appropriate `Vector` instead. These methods are shown in Listing 6.26.

Listing 6.26 Author and Artist Operations (*Product.java*)

```
public void addAuthor( String newAuthor ) {
  authors.addElement( newAuthor );
}

public void removeAllAuthors() {
  authors.removeAllElements();
}

public Enumeration getAuthors() {
  return authors.elements();
}
```

Like the other data binding objects, convert the `Product` objects into XML using the `toXML` method, shown in Listing 6.27. Begin by writing the start tag of the `product` element. The `id` attribute is required, so always write it out. Because the `keywords` attribute is optional, you need to check to see if it exists before it is written out. Next we write out child elements, so you need to add an indent. The `name` subelement is straightforward to write out because it is simply a `String`. You just need to write the start tag, the string, and then the end tag. The `author` and `artist` elements are repeatable ones, so loop through the `Vectors` and write each element individually. The `description`, `price`, and `quantity_in_stock` elements are all simple strings so the way you write them out is the same as you did for the `name` element. The image `Vector` contains instances of the `Image` class, so you need to loop through the `Vector` and call the `toXML` method on each of the images. The `onSaleDate` object also needs to have its `toXML` method called, as does each of the `Clip` objects in the `clips` Vector. Finally, set the indent back to the original level and then write out the end tag of the `product` element.

Listing 6.27 Converting the *Product* to XML (*Product.java*)

```
public void toXML( XMLWriter writer ) throws IOException {
  writer.write( "<product id='" + id + "'" );
  if( keywords != null )
    writer.write( " keywords='" + keywords + "'" );
  writer.writeln( ">" );
  writer.indent();
  writer.writeln( "<name>" + name + "</name>" );
  for( int i = 0; i < authors.size(); i++ ) {
    writer.writeln("<author>" + authors.elementAt( i ) +
                   "</author>");
  }
```

```
        for( int i = 0; i < artists.size(); i++ ) {
          writer.writeln("<artist>" + artists.elementAt( i ) + "</artist>");
        }
        writer.writeln( "<description>" + description + "</description>" );
        writer.writeln( "<price>" + price + "</price>" );
        writer.writeln( "<quantity_in_stock>" + quantityInStock +
                        "</quantity_in_stock>" );
      for( int i = 0; i < images.size(); i++ ) {
          Image image = (Image)images.elementAt( i );
          image.toXML( writer );
        }
        if( onSaleDate != null )
          onSaleDate.toXML( writer );
        for( int i = 0; i < clips.size(); i++ ) {
          Clip clip = (Clip)clips.elementAt( i );
          clip.toXML( writer );
        }
        writer.unindent();
        writer.writeln( "</product>" );
    }
}
```

The *Image* Class

The next data binding class you examine is the Image class. This is based on the follow-ing DTD:

```
<!ELEMENT image (caption?)>
<!ATTLIST image format (gif|png|jpg) #REQUIRED
           width  CDATA         #IMPLIED
           height CDATA         #IMPLIED
           src    CDATA         #REQUIRED>
<!ELEMENT caption (paragraph)* >
```

The caption element here is similar to the description element that you saw in the product element. Because the paragraph element has a complicated structure, we represent it as a string of raw XML that the user can edit directly. Both the format and src attributes can be repre-sented by String type fields. The height and width attributes are not required attributes, so you need to be able to account for occasions when these attributes don't exist. To do this, use an Integer class and a null value represents the lack of an attribute. This is shown in Listing 6.28.

Listing 6.28 The Start of the *Image* Class (*Image.java*)

```
package com.XmlEcomBook.Chap06;

import java.io.*;
import org.w3c.dom.*;

public class Image {
  private String  format;
  private Integer width;
  private Integer height;
  private String  src;
  private String  caption;
```

The Image constructors follow the same pattern as the previous data binding classes, a no-argument constructor creates a default Image object, and a second constructor is provided for creating an Image from a DOM Element object. The format and src attributes are extracted from the image element directly. The width and height attributes use a utility method called getInteger. Use this because it is possible to have null value for these two attributes. The getInteger method returns a null if a null is passed to it. Finally, if the caption element exists, its contents are extracted as text. The constructors are shown in Listing 6.29.

Listing 6.29 The *Image Class* Constructors (*Image.java*)

```
public Image() {
}

public Image( Element imgElement) {
  format = imgElement.getAttribute( "format" );
  width = Util.getInteger( imgElement.getAttribute( "width" ) );
  height = Util.getInteger( imgElement.getAttribute( "height" ) );
  src = imgElement.getAttribute( "src" );
  NodeList captionList = imgElement.getElementsByTagName( "caption" );
  if( captionList.getLength() > 0 ) {
    Element captionElement = (Element)captionList.item( 0 );
    caption = Util.extractMarkupAsText(captionElement.getChildNodes());
  }
}
```

Each of the fields for the Image has a get and a set method. These are simple methods that set or return the field. To save space, they won't be shown here, but the source on the CD includes them.

The toXML method that outputs the image element is shown in Listing 6.30. The start tag has four attributes—the format and src attributes are always output because they are required attributes, and the width and height attributes are checked to see if they do contain a value before they are output.

Listing 6.30 Converting the *Image* to XML (*Image.java*)

```java
public void toXML( XMLWriter writer ) throws IOException {
  writer.write( "<image " );
  writer.write( "format='" + format + "' " );
  if( width != null )
    writer.write( "width='" + width + "' " );
  if( height != null )
    writer.write( "height='" + height + "' " );
  writer.writeln( "src='" + src + "'>" );
  writer.indent();
  if( caption != null )
    writer.writeln( "<caption>" + caption + "</caption>" );
  writer.unindent();
  writer.writeln( "</image>" );
  }
}
```

The *Clip* Class

The clip element is similar to the image element, as you can see from the DTD for it:

```
<!ELEMENT clip (title,description?)>
<!ATTLIST clip format (mp3|mpeg|mov|rm) #REQUIRED
          length CDATA         #IMPLIED
          size   CDATA         #IMPLIED
          src    CDATA         #REQUIRED>
<!ELEMENT title (#PCDATA)>
```

All the attributes of the clip element will be string types, as shown in Listing 6.31. This is because the length and size attributes are free format string so units can be included. For example, the size element can contain a string like "1.1 Mb".

Listing 6.31 The Start of the *Clip* Class (*Clip.java*)

```java
package com.XmlEcomBook.Chap06;

import org.w3c.dom.*;
import java.io.*;

public class Clip extends Object {
  private String format ;
  private String length;
  private String size;
  private String src;
  private String title;
  private String description;
```

The constructors for Clip include one that takes no arguments for creating a default Clip, and another one for constructing a Clip from a DOM Element object. These can be seen in Listing 6.32. The first four lines of the second constructor get the attributes from the clip element. The description element will be handled the same way the description element of the product and the caption element of the image was handled. It will be gotten as text from the element and kept as a String. The last line of the constructor gets the title element as a String.

Listing 6.32 The *Clip* Constructors (*Clip.java*)

```java
public Clip() {
}

public Clip( Element clipElement ) {
  format = clipElement.getAttribute( "format" );
  length = clipElement.getAttribute( "length" );
  size = clipElement.getAttribute( "size" );
  src = clipElement.getAttribute( "src" );
  NodeList descList = clipElement.getElementsByTagName("description");
  if( descList.getLength() > 0 ) {
    Element descElement = (Element)descList.item( 0 );
    description=Util.extractMarkupAsText(descElement.getChildNodes());
  }
  title = Util.extractTextFrom( "title", clipElement );
}
```

The Clip class also contains standard get and set methods for each of the six fields it contains. They are included in the source on the CD, but are not shown here. The toXML class is similar to the others you have seen. Like the other data object, the Clip class has a method to convert the object into XML data, as shown in Listing 6.33.

Listing 6.33 Converting the *Clip* to XML (*Clip.java*)

```java
public void toXML( XMLWriter writer ) throws IOException {
  writer.write( "<clip " );
  writer.write( "format='" + format + "' " );
  if( length != null )
    writer.write( "length='" + length + "' " );
  if( size != null )
    writer.write( "size='" + size + "' " );
  writer.writeln( "src='" + src + "'>" );
  writer.indent();
  writer.writeln( "<title>" + title + "</title>" );
  if( description != null )
    writer.writeln("<description>" + description + "</description>");
  writer.unindent();
  writer.writeln( "</clip>" );
  }
}
```

DateTime Class

The DateTime class is used for represent a date in time. It is based on the following DTD snippet:

```
<!ENTITY % date_time
   "(day_of_week?,month?,day_of_month?,year?,(hour,minute,seconds?)?)">
<!ELEMENT day_of_week (#PCDATA)>
<!ELEMENT month (#PCDATA)>
<!ELEMENT day_of_month (#PCDATA)>
<!ELEMENT year (#PCDATA)>
<!ELEMENT hour (#PCDATA)>
<!ELEMENT minute (#PCDATA)>
<!ELEMENT seconds (#PCDATA)>
```

The date_time parameter entity can be used to represent any date and time. In the catalog DTD, it is only used for the in the onsale_date element, but it could be used elsewhere if the DTD was expanded. The DateTime class has a field for each of the elements in the DTD. It also has two constructors, one takes no arguments and the other takes an element that will be parsed. These can be seen in Listing 6.34.

Listing 6.34 The Start of the *DateTime* Class (*DateTime.java*)

```
package com.XmlEcomBook.Chap06;

import org.w3c.dom.Element;
import java.util.StringTokenizer;
import java.io.IOException;
import java.io.OutputStream;

public class DateTime extends Object {

  private String    dayOfWeek = null;
  private Integer   month = null;
  private Integer   dayOfMonth = null;
  private Integer   year = null;
  private Integer   hour = null;
  private Integer   minute = null;
  private Integer   seconds = null;

  public DateTime() {
  }

  public DateTime(Element dateElement) {
    dayOfWeek = Util.extractTextFrom( "day_of_week", dateElement );
    month = Util.extractIntFrom( "month", dateElement );
    dayOfMonth = Util.extractIntFrom( "day_of_month", dateElement );
    year = Util.extractIntFrom( "year", dateElement );
    hour = Util.extractIntFrom( "hour", dateElement );
    minute = Util.extractIntFrom( "minute", dateElement );
    seconds = Util.extractIntFrom( "seconds", dateElement );
  }
```

The date and time that is retrieved from the HTML forms needs to be parsed by the DateTime class. This is done by the fromString method, as shown in Listing 6.35. This method uses a StringTokenizer to break up the string into pieces. Each token retrieved by the StringTokenizer is checked. If the token has the string "day" in it, it is the day of the week, so it is saved. Because the date part of the string is separated by the "-" character, when this character is found, the month, day of the month and year is parsed from the string. If a ":" is found in the string, it is the time part of the string, so the hour, minute and second is parsed from the string.

Listing 6.35 The *fromString* Method (*DateTime.java*)

```java
public void fromString( String newDate ) {
  StringTokenizer tokenizer = new StringTokenizer( newDate, " " );
  while( tokenizer.hasMoreTokens() ) {
    String next = tokenizer.nextToken();
    if( next.indexOf( "day" ) > 0 ) {
      dayOfWeek = next;
    }
    if( next.indexOf( '-' ) > 0 ) {
      int first = next.indexOf( '-' );
      int second = next.indexOf( '-', first + 1 );
      month = new Integer( next.substring( 0, first  ) );
      dayOfMonth = new Integer( next.substring( first + 1, second ));
      year = new Integer(next.substring( second + 1, next.length()));
    }
    if( next.indexOf( ':' ) > 0 ) {
      int first = next.indexOf( ':' );
      int second = next.indexOf( ':', first + 1 );
      hour = new Integer( next.substring( 0, first ) );
      minute = new Integer( next.substring( first + 1, second ) );
      seconds =
              new Integer(next.substring(second + 1, next.length()));
    }
  }
}
```

The last method in the class is the **toXML** method, shown in Listing 6.36. This is similar to the other **toXML** methods, and writes each field out, along with the appropriate tags.

Listing 6.36 The *toXML* Method (DateTime.java)

```java
public void toXML( XMLWriter writer ) throws IOException {
  writer.writeln( "<onsale_date>" );
  writer.indent();
  if( dayOfWeek != null )
    writer.writeln( "<day_of_week>" + dayOfWeek + "</day_of_week>" );
```

```
      if( month != null )
        writer.writeln( "<month>" + month + "</month>" );
      if( dayOfMonth != null )
        writer.writeln( "<day_of_month>" + dayOfMonth + "</day_of_month>" );
      if( year != null )
        writer.writeln( "<year>" + year + "</year>" );
      if( hour != null )
        writer.writeln( "<hour>" + hour + "</hour>" );
      if( minute != null )
        writer.writeln( "<minute>" + minute + "</minute>" );
      if( seconds != null )
        writer.writeln( "<seconds>" + seconds + "</seconds>" );
      writer.unindent();
      writer.writeln( "</onsale_date>" );
    }
  }
```

The *Util* Class

The Util class contains several convenience methods that are called from both the data object and presentation classes. They are all public and static, so they can be called from anywhere. The first two methods in the class, shown in Listing 6.37, are used for getting information from XML input. The extractTextFrom method looks for a particular element, and if it finds it, gets the text content from it and returns it. The next method, extractIntFrom, uses the first method to extract the text from an element and then converts it into an Integer before it is sent back.

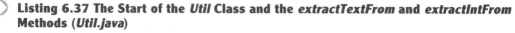

Listing 6.37 The Start of the *Util* Class and the *extractTextFrom* and *extractIntFrom* Methods (*Util.java*)

```
package com.XmlEcomBook.Chap06;

import org.w3c.dom.*;
import java.io.*;

public class Util {

    static public String extractTextFrom( String childElementName, Element element
) {
        NodeList nameList = element.getElementsByTagName(childElementName);
```

```
    if( nameList.getLength() < 1 ) {
      return null;
    }
    Text nameText = (Text)nameList.item(0).getFirstChild();
    return nameText.getData();
  }


  static public Integer extractIntFrom( String childElementName,
                                        Element element ) {
    String s = Util.extractTextFrom( childElementName, element );
    if( s == null || s.equals( "" ) ) {
      return null;
    }
    return new Integer( s );
  }
```

The next method also helps when dealing with XML data. This method, shown in Listing 6.38, takes a `NodeList` object and returns it as text. The main processing occurs in the `for` loop, where a string is constructed. For each element node in the node list, a "<" and then the tag name is added to the string. Each attribute for the node is then also added to the start tag, and the start tag is ended with a ">". A recursive call is then made to the `extractMarkupAsText` method to turn the children of the current node into text. If the node in the `for` loop was a text node, it is added to the string directly.

Listing 6.38. The *extractMarkupAsText* Method (*Util.java*)

```
static public String extractMarkupAsText( NodeList nodeList ) {
  //recursively extract
  String text = "";
  if( nodeList != null ) {
    for( int i = 0; i < nodeList.getLength(); i++ ) {
      Node node = nodeList.item(i);
      if( node instanceof Element ) {
        Element el = (Element)node;
        text += "<" + el.getTagName();
        NamedNodeMap attList = el.getAttributes();
        int length = attList.getLength();
        for( int j = 0; j < attList.getLength(); j++ ) {
          Attr att = (Attr)attList.item( j );
          text += " " + att.getName() + "='" + att.getValue() + "'";
        }
        text += ">";
```

```
          text += extractMarkupAsText( el.getChildNodes() );
          text += "</" + el.getTagName() + ">";
        }
        if( node instanceof Text ) {
          text += ((Text)node).getData();
        }
      }
    }
  }
  return text;
}
```

The next three methods, shown in Listing 6.39, are used for displaying different types of data. Because null `String`, `Integer`, and `Float` values are all displayed as "null," and we don't want the user to see that in forms, we have convenience methods that will return this data as an empty String instead of a null.

Listing 6.39 The *notNull* Methods (*Util.java*)

```
static public String notNull( String s ) {
  if( s == null ) {
    return "";
  }
  return s;
}

static public String notNull( Integer i ) {
  if( i == null ) {
    return "";
  }
  return i.toString();
}

static public String notNull( Float f ) {
  if( f == null ) {
    return "";
  }
  return f.toString();
}
```

The next set of methods, shown in Listing 6.40, are used for converting a String that has been input by the user into a value. We want to make sure that if the user left the input blank, we return a null value.

Listing 6.40 Converting *String* to Value (*Util.java*)

```java
static public int getInt( String s ) {
  if( s == null || s.equals( "" ) ) {
    return 0;
  }
  return Integer.parseInt( s );
}

static public Integer getInteger( String s ) {
  if( s == null || s.equals( "" ) ) {
    return null;
  }
  return new Integer( s );
}

static public float getFloat( String s ) {
  if( s == null || s.equals( "" ) ) {
    return 0.0f;
  }
  return Float.parseFloat( s );
}

static public double getDouble( String s ) {
  if( s == null || s.equals( "" ) ) {
    return 0.0;
  }
  return Double.parseDouble( s );
}

}
```

Presentation Code

Next, you need some code that will present all the information contained in the data classes to the user, and allow them to create, edit, and remove products in the catalog. This is done through HTML code, JSPs, and servlets. The JSPs and servlets generate HTML code that can be viewed on the user's browser. To start the process, the user selects an HTML page that presents options to edit, add, or delete products. This page has links to a servlet that can call a JSP to present an editable HTML form to the user to be filled in with new or changed product information.

The remainder of this chapter examines the HTML, JSPs, and servlets that provide this functionality.

The Main HTML Page

The main HTML page presents three main options to the user: Add Product, Delete Product, and Edit Product. There are also options to cancel all the changes that the user has made in a session, and to save all the changes that the user has done. All of the operation call the same servlet, but with different values in a hidden input field named operation. The start of the HTML page, seen in Listing 6.41, contains the title of this page and begins the body element.

Listing 6.41 The Start of the HTML Page (*main.html*)

```html
<html>
  <head><title>Catalog Upkeep</title></head>
  <body>
```

Each of the five options that the user has are presented as a different form on the page. The first of the options is the Add Product operation, seen in Listing 6.42. You need to get a new product id from the user, so check the existing set of products to make sure the id doesn't already exist. You also need to get the product line to which the product will belong. The form element's action attribute contains the name of the servlet that will be called when the form is submitted. Here you want the Main servlet to be called. The next line adds a heading to this form.

The first input element of the form is a hidden one. This means that the user won't see this element onscreen. It is simply passed to the servlet along with all the other inputs. This allows the servlet to identify what it was the user wants to do. The next two lines allow the user to specify what the product id for this new product should be and which product line to add the product to. The last line of the form element adds a button that the user clicks to submit this information.

Listing 6.42 The Add Product Form (*main.html*)

```
<form action="servlet/Main">
    <h3>Add Product:</h3>
    <input type="hidden" name="operation" value="add" />
    Product ID:<input name="productid" />
    Product Line:<input name="productline" />
    <input type="submit" value="Add"/>
</form>
```

The Delete Product and Edit Product forms are similar to the Add Product form, but for these you only need to ask the user for the product id. Add a horizontal line between each form to visually separate them. These are shown in Listing 6.43.

Listing 6.43 The Delete Product and Edit Product Forms (*main.html*)

```
<hr />
<form action="servlet/Main">
    <h3>Delete Product:</h3>
    <input type="hidden" name="operation" value="delete" />
    Product ID:<input name="productid" />
    <input type="submit" value="Delete"/>
</form>
<hr />
    <form action="servlet/Main">
    <h3>Edit Product:</h3>
    <input type="hidden" name="operation" value="edit" />
    Product ID:<input name="productid" />
    <input type="submit" value="Edit"/>
</form>
```

The last two operations for canceling and saving the changes that the user has done so far are shown in Listing 6.44. The servlet and JSP code loads in the XML from a file the first time the user starts an operation. The Cancel All Changes operation deletes all the changes that have been made since the file was loaded. The Save All Changes operation writes the XML file back out with all the changes that have been made by the user. The two forms for these operations visually just consist of a single button for the user to press. Each form has a hidden input element that sends information to the servlet about which operation the user selected.

Listing 6.44 The Cancel All Changes and Save All Changes Forms (*main.html*)

```html
<hr />
<form action="servlet/Main">
    <input type="hidden" name="operation" value="refresh" />
    <input type="submit" value="Cancel All Changes"/>
</form>
<form action="servlet/Main">
    <input type="hidden" name="operation" value="save" />
    <input type="submit" value="Save All Changes"/>
</form>
</body>
</html>
```

The *Main* Servlet Class

The Main servlet class that takes input from the forms in the main HTML file and processes it is shown in Listing 6.45. The main entry point of the servlet class is the doGet method. After setting up some initial variables, the method attempts to get a session from the request. If there is no Session object yet, a new one needs to be created. To do this, get a new Session object, and then create a new Catalog object from the catalog.xml file. This Catalog object gets put into the session using the setAttribute method. If a Session object is found, the catalog object is retrieved from the one already in the session.

Listing 6.45 The Start of the *Main* Class and the *doGet* Method (*Main.java*)

```java
import java.io.*;
import javax.servlet.*;
import javax.servlet.http.*;
import com.XmlEcomBook.Chap06.*;

public class Main extends HttpServlet {
  static private final String FILE_NAME = "catalog.xml";

  public void doGet(HttpServletRequest req,
                    HttpServletResponse res)
                            throws IOException, ServletException {
    PrintWriter out = res.getWriter();
    res.setContentType("text/html");
    Catalog catalog = null;
```

```
HttpSession session = req.getSession(false);
if( session == null ) {
  //There is no session, create a new one
  session = req.getSession( true );
  catalog = new Catalog(FILE_NAME);
  session.setAttribute( "catalog", catalog );
} else {
  catalog = (Catalog)session.getAttribute( "catalog" );
}
```

The next thing that is done in the doGet method is to retrieve all the values that the user had set in the HTML form, shown at the top of Listing 6.46. These values are retrieved from the HttpServletRequest object using the getParamter method. These parameters are then checked for errors. First, if one of the main operations—Delete Product, Edit Product, or Add Product—was chosen, make sure a product id was entered. The product that matches this id is then retrieved from the catalog. If an Edit Product or Delete Product operation was being done, ensure that this product does indeed exist, otherwise the error flag is set. If the operation is an Add Product, make sure that there is no product with the id that the user chose because the product id field must be unique. If the operation is Add Product, check that the product line that the user chose exists in the catalog. Check the status of the Boolean error flag; if it has been set to true, display an output page with the error message and return. The method that displays the output page will be examined later in the description of this class.

Listing 6.46 Checking for Errors in the Parameters (*Main.java*)

```
String operation = req.getParameter("operation");
String productID = req.getParameter("productid");
String productLine = req.getParameter("productline");

boolean error = false;
String errorMsg = "Unkown Error";
if( operation.equals( "delete" )
    || operation.equals( "edit" )
    || operation.equals( "add" ) ) {
  if( productID == null || productID.equals("") ) {
    error = true;
    errorMsg = "You must select a product ID with the "
                + operation + " operation.";
```

```
      } else {
  Product product = catalog.getProduct( productID );
  if( operation.equals("edit") || operation.equals("delete") ) {
    if( product == null ) {
      error = true;
      errorMsg = "Invalid product ID:" + productID;
    }
  }
  if( operation.equals( "add" ) ) {
    if( product != null ) {
      error = true;
      errorMsg = "Cannot add, product id " + productID +
                  " already exists.";
    }
    ProductLine pl = catalog.getProductLine( productLine );
    if( pl == null ) {
      error = true;
      errorMsg = "No product line " + productLine + " exists.";
    }
  }
}
}
if( error ) {
  outputPage( out, "Error", errorMsg );
  return;
}
```

Now that you know that the parameters are correct, you can actually process the parameters, shown in Listing 6.47. You have a series of "ifs" to determine which operation is to be called. Both the Add Product and Edit Product commands use the same JSP. To call a JSP from within a servlet, get the RequestDispatcher object from the ServletContext, and call the forward method on it passing the current request and response object. This allows all the current parameters to be passed along to the JSP. The Delete Product operation calls a separate JSP in a similar manner. The Refresh command is handled directly by this method. It simply calls invalidate on the session object. This deletes the current session and unbinds any objects that were associated with it. The final command, Save, is also handled directly in this method. Here you create a new XMLWriter object using the catalog.xml file. Write the needed XML declaration and DOCTYPE lines, and then use the toXML method of the catalog object to write the XML output to the file.

Listing 6.47 Handling the Various Operations (*Main.java*)

```java
if( operation.equals( "add" ) || operation.equals( "edit" ) ) {
  getServletContext().
      getRequestDispatcher("/Edit.jsp").forward(req, res);
}
if( operation.equals( "delete" ) ) {
  getServletContext().
      getRequestDispatcher("/Delete.jsp").forward(req, res);
}
if( operation.equals( "refresh" ) ) {
  session.invalidate();
  outputPage(out,"Session Cancelled", "Session has been canelled");
  return;
}
if( operation.equals( "save" ) ) {
  try {
    FileOutputStream outFile = new
FileOutputStream(FILE_NAME);
    XMLWriter writer = new XMLWriter( outFile );
    writer.writeln( "<?xml version='1.0' standalone='no' ?>" );
    writer.writeln( "<!DOCTYPE catalog SYSTEM 'catalog.dtd'>" );
    catalog.toXML( writer );
  }
  catch( IOException e ) {
    outputPage( out, "Error", "I/O Exception writing XML file" );
    return;
  }
  outputPage(out, "Changes saved", "The changes have been saved" );
}
}
```

You have a method in the Main servlet to output a simple HTML page, shown in Listing 6.48. Pass to it a PrintWriter, the title, and the text to be displayed on the page. The page will also include a link back to the main HTML page.

Listing 6.48 Output a Page (*Main.java*)

```java
private void outputPage( PrintWriter out, String title, String text ) {
  out.println("<html><head><title>" + title );
  out.println("</title></head><body>");
```

```
        out.println("<p>" + text + "</p>");
        out.println("<a href='/main.html'>Return to main page.</a>");
        out.println("</body></html>");
    }
}
```

The *Delete* JSP

The `Delete` JSP, shown in Listing 6.49, is a simple one. You retrieve the product id from the JSP's built in request object. This is the same object that was forwarded to the JSP by the Main servlet. You then get the catalog from the current session. Simply delete the product from the catalog, and output a simple HTML page indicating success.

Listing 6.49 The *Delete* JSP (*Delete.jsp*)

```
<%@ page import="com.XmlEcomBook.Chap06.*" %>
<%
String pid = request.getParameter( "productid" );
Catalog catalog = (Catalog)session.getValue( "catalog" );
catalog.deleteProduct( pid );
%>

<html>
<head>
<title>Delete</title>
</head>
<body>
<p><b>Product <%= pid %> deleted.<b></p>
<a href='/main.html'>Return to main page.<a>
</body>
</html>
```

The *Edit* JSP

The `Edit` JSP is much longer and more complex than the `Delete` JSP was. This JSP needs to output a form that contains all the data from a product in a user editable way. At the top of the JSP, you have some scripting elements. As you can see in Listing 6.50, after declaring the needed imports, get the parameters that you need from the **request** object. These are the same ones that were entered by the user and then forwarded to the JSP by the **Main** servlet.

This JSP handles both the Edit Product and Add Product commands from the Main servlet, so we check the operation parameter. If it is edit, you know that you need to get the product from the catalog. If the operation is not edit, you know that it is add, so for this you need to create a new product and set the id based on the one the user entered.

Listing 6.50 The Start of the *Edit* JSP (*Edit.jsp*)

```
<%@ page import="com.XmlEcomBook.Chap06.*" %>
<%@ page import="java.util.*" %>
<%
String pid = request.getParameter( "productid" );
String operation = request.getParameter( "operation" );
String productLine = request.getParameter( "productline" );
Catalog catalog = (Catalog)session.getValue( "catalog" );
Product product = null;
String name = "";
if( operation.equals( "edit" ) ) {
  product = catalog.getProduct( pid );
  name = "Edit";
}
else { //it's an "add" operation
  product = new Product();
  product.setId( pid );
  name = "Add";
}
%>
```

Next, you actually start the HTML output, as shown in Listing 6.51. First, set the title in the head, and in the main heading of the page, then start a form element that will contain the rest of the page. This form will call a servlet named UpdateProduct when it is submitted. The first two input elements of the form are hidden fields that contain information that will be needed by the UpdateProduct servlet: the product line and the product id that were entered by user. The title, product line, and product id are all inserted into the JSP output by an expression scripting element which start with "<%=".

Listing 6.51 Start of the HTML Elements (*Edit.jsp*)

```
<html>
<head><title><%= name %></title></head>
<body>
<h1><%= name %> Product</h1>
```

```
<form action="/servlet/UpdateProduct">
<input name="productline" type="hidden"
        value="<%= request.getParameter( "productline" ) %>" />
<input name="id" type="hidden" value="<%= product.getId() %>" />
```

Next, start a `table` element that will help align the information that you present in the form, this is seen in Listing 6.52. The first item you display will be the product id. This is simply outputted as data in the first row of the `table`. The name of the product is displayed in the same row as the product id, but it is presented to the user as a single line text input field, which is the default type for the input element. The utility method `notNull` is used because this method will return an empty string instead of return the `String` "null" if the name `getName` method returns a null value. The next row in the `table` displays the keywords of the product. The size of this `textfield` is set to 40 because it is expected that this string can get a bit longer.

Listing 6.52 Displaying the Product Name and Keywords (*Edit.jsp*)

```
<table>
  <tr>
    <td>Product ID</td>
    <td><%= product.getId() %></td>
    <td>Name</td>
    <td><input name="name"
                value="<%= Util.notNull(product.getName()) %>" /></td>
  </tr>
  <tr>
    <td>Keywords</td>
    <td colspan="3"><input size ="40" name="keywords"
                value="<%= Util.notNull(product.getKeywords()) %>"/>
    </td>
  </tr>
```

Next, you have two scriptlets, seen in Listing 6.53, that output the authors and the artists for this product. The first scriptlet loops through each author in the product and uses the `outputAuthor` method to display it. For the identifier that will be used for each author, turn the current loop iteration into a string by adding the value to an empty string, then output a blank artist with an identifier of "New." This will allow the user to add a new author to a product. The second scriptlet goes through this same process for artists. We will look at the `outputAuthor` and `outputArtist` code later in this section.

Listing 6.53 Displaying the Authors and Artists (*Edit.jsp*)

```
<% Enumeration authors = product.getAuthors();
   for( int i = 0; authors.hasMoreElements(); i++ ) {
       out.print(
           outputAuthor( "" + i, (String)authors.nextElement() ) );
   }
   out.print( outputAuthor( "New", "" ) );
%>
<% Enumeration artists = product.getArtists();
   for( int i = 0; artists.hasMoreElements(); i++ ) {
       out.print(outputArtist("" + i,(String)artists.nextElement()));
   }
   out.print( outputArtist( "New", "" ) );
%>
```

The next section of the JSP outputs the values for the price, quantity in stock and on sale price and description for the product, as shown in Listing 6.54. Each of these items will be on its own row in the table with each row having two data elements—one for an identifier for the input, and one for the input field itself. Because the description can contain a lot of text, a textarea element is used instead of a single line input element.

Listing 6.54 Displaying the Price, Quantity in Stock, On Sale Date, and Description (*Edit.jsp*)

```
<tr><td>Price</td>
    <td><input name="price" value="<%= product.getPrice() %>" /></td>
    <td>Discount</td>
    <td><input name="discount"
          value="<%= Util.notNull(product.getDiscount()) %>" /></td>
</tr>
<tr><td>Quantity in Stock</td>
    <td><input name="quantity" value="<%= product.getQuantityInStock() %>" /
></td>
</tr>
<tr><td>On Sale Date</td>
  <td colspan="3"><input name='onSaleDate' value='<%= product.getOnSaleDate()
%>' />
    (mm-dd-yyyy hh:mm:ss)</td>
</tr>
<tr><td>Description</td>
  <td colspan="3">
```

```
   <textarea rows="5" cols="40"
    name="description"><%= Util.notNull(product.getDescription()) %>
   </textarea>
  </td>
 </tr>
</table>
```

To display the images and clips associated with the product, you use a new table, shown in Listing 6.55 The scriptlets used to display these are similar to the scriptlets that were used for the authors and artists. After this table is written, a Submit button appears at the bottom of the page for the user to click when the editing is done.

Listing 6.55 Displaying Images, Clips, and the Submit Button (*Edit.jsp*)

```
<table>
  <tr><td><b>Images</b></tr></td>
  <% Enumeration images = product.getImages();
      for( int i = 0; images.hasMoreElements(); i++ ) {
          Image image = (Image)images.nextElement();
          out.print( outputImage( "" + (i + 1), image ) );
      }
      out.print( outputImage( "New", new Image() ) );
  %>
  <tr><td><b>Clips</b></tr></td>
  <% Enumeration clips = product.getClips();
      for( int i = 0; clips.hasMoreElements(); i++ ) {
          Clip clip = (Clip)clips.nextElement();
          out.print( outputClip( "" + (i + 1), clip ) );
      }
      out.print( outputClip( "New", new Clip() ) );
  %>
  </table>
  <input type="submit" value="Submit Changes" />
</form>
</body>
</html>
```

At the bottom of this JSP, you have several helper methods defined. The first one of these is outputImage. You have more than one place in the JSP that you need to output the form elements for an Image object, so you create a method to do this. This method is not in a regular Java class that is called from the JSP because it is very presentation oriented. It is useful to have a methods defined in a separate class if they handle some kind of non-presentation logic for the JSP, but here you are outputting HTML from the methods. If you put this method in a separate class, you would have two different places where we handled the presentation of one page, making the maintenance of the code harder. It is better to keep all the presentation code in one place.

The outputImage method, shown in Listing 6.56, takes a String identifier for the image, as well as the Image object itself. The name of the input field will be constructed by adding the String "image" to the passed in string. This way you can have each image uniquely named. The name is for both displaying to the user, and for the name attribute of the input object. Each of the attributes and elements of the Image object is displayed as a new text input field, which the user can fill in.

Listing 6.56 Outputting Image Objects (*Edit.jsp*)

```
<%!
private String outputImage(String i, Image image) {
    String s;
        s = "<tr><td>" + i + ")</td>";
        s += "<td>Format</td>";
        s += "<td><input name='img" + i + "-format' value='"
            + Util.notNull(image.getFormat()) + "' /></td>" ;
        s += "<td></td><td>Source File</td>";
        s += "<td><input name='img" + i + "-src' value='"
            + Util.notNull(image.getSrc()) + "' /></td>" ;
        s += "</tr>";
        s += "<tr>";
        s += "<td></td><td>Height</td>";
        s += "<td><input name='img" + i + "-height' value='"
            + Util.notNull(image.getHeight()) + "' /></td>";
        s += "<td></td><td>Width</td>";
        s += "<td><input name='img" + i + "-width' value='"
            + Util.notNull(image.getWidth()) + "' /></td>";
        s += "</tr>";
        s += "<tr>";
        s += "<td></td><td>Caption</td>";
        s += "<td colspan='4'><textarea rows='5' cols='40' name='img"
            + i + "-caption'>" + Util.notNull(image.getCaption())
            + "</textarea></td>";
        s += "</tr>\n";
        return s;
}
%>
```

The outputting of `Clip`, `Author`, and `Artist` objects is very similar to outputting `Images`. Each of the elements and attributes are displayed in the rows of a table. A string that identifies the item is also used in the output and in the name field of the input element. This is shown in Listing 6.57.

Listing 6.57 Outputting *Clip* Objects (*Edit.jsp*)

```
<%!
private String outputClip( String i, Clip clip )
{
    String s;
        s = "<tr><td>" + i + ")</td>";
        s += "<td>Format</td>";
        s += "<td><input name='clip" + i + "-format' value='" +
            Util.notNull(clip.getFormat()) + "' /></td>" ;
        s += "<td></td><td>Source File</td>";
        s += "<td><input name='clip" + i + "-src' value='" +
            Util.notNull(clip.getSrc()) + "' /></td>" ;
        s += "</tr>";
        s += "<tr>";
        s += "<td></td><td>Title</td>";
        s += "<td colspan='3'><input name='clip" + i + "-title'
            value='" + Util.notNull(clip.getTitle()) + "' /></td>";
        s += "</tr>";
        s += "<tr>";
        s += "<td></td><td>Length</td>";
        s += "<td><input name='clip" + i + "-length' value='" +
            Util.notNull(clip.getLength()) + "' /></td>" ;
        s += "<td></td><td>Size</td>";
        s += "<td><input name='clip" + i + "-size' value='" +
            Util.notNull(clip.getSize()) + "' /></td>";
        s += "</tr>";
        s += "<tr>";
        s += "<td></td><td>Description</td>";
        s += "<td colspan='4'><textarea rows='5' cols='40' name='clip"
            + i + "-description'>" +
            Util.notNull(clip.getDescription()) + "</textarea></td>" ;
        s += "</tr>";
    return s;
}
```

```
private String outputAuthor( String i, String author ) {
    String s = "<tr><td>Author</td>";
    s += "<td><input name='author" + i + "' value='" + author + "' /></td></tr>";
    return s;
}

private String outputArtist( String i, String artist ) {
    String s = "<tr><td>Artist</td>";
    s += "<td><input name='artist" + i + "' value='" + artist + "' /></td></tr>";
    return s;
}
%>
```

The *UpdateProduct* Servlet

The UpdateProduct servlet is called from the Edit JSP when the user has finished filling out
the form for product information. Its job is to collect the data from the input parameters on the
request object and update the Product data binding object. After some standard initialization in
the doGet method, the Session object is obtained from the current HttpServletRequest.
From the session you get the catalog object with which you are currently working. From the
session you can get the product with the correct product id. This can be seen in Listing 6.58.

Listing 6.58 The Start of the *UpdateProduct* Servlet (*UpdateProduct.java*)

```
import java.io.*;
import javax.servlet.*;
import javax.servlet.http.*;
import com.XmlEcomBook.Chap06.*;

public class UpdateProduct extends HttpServlet {

  public void doGet(HttpServletRequest req,
                    HttpServletResponse res)
             throws IOException, ServletException {
    res.setContentType("text/html");
    PrintWriter out = res.getWriter();

    HttpSession session = req.getSession();
    Catalog catalog = (Catalog)session.getValue( "catalog" );
    String id = req.getParameter( "id" );
    Product product = catalog.getProduct( id );
```

Next, as shown in Listing 6.59, the product is checked for null. If it is, you assume that an Add Product operation was being done, so you need to create a new product with the right product id and add it to the appropriate product line. Next, the keywords and name parameters get read from the request, and the product is updated with the values.

Listing 6.59 Creating a New Product, Updating Keywords and Name (*UpdateProduct.java*)

```java
if( product == null ) { //new product
    product = new Product();
    product.setId( id );
    String productLineString = req.getParameter( "productline" );
    ProductLine productLine
        = catalog.getProductLine( productLineString );
    productLine.addProduct( product );
}
String keywords = req.getParameter( "keywords" );
product.setKeywords( keywords );
String name = req.getParameter( "name" );
product.setName( name );
```

Next, the authors that were found in the form will be added to the product. Before you add in these new authors, you need to clear out any authors that already existed in the product. Use the removeAllAuthors method to do this. You are now ready to add in the new authors. To do this, use the getAuthor method, which is defined later in the section. The getAuthor method returns a Boolean true if it found an author with the given identifier, and returns a false if no author was found with the identifier. You also need to check for a new author by using the identifier of "New". This whole process is then repeated for artists, as shown in Listing 6.60.

Listing 6.60 Adding Authors and Artists (*UpdateProduct.java*)

```java
product.removeAllAuthors();
for( int i = 0; getAuthor( "" + i, req, product ); i++ )
    ;//do nothing
getAuthor( "New", req, product );

product.removeAllArtists();
for( int i = 0; getArtist( "New", req, product ); i++ )
    ;//do nothing
getArtist( "New", req, product );
```

The rest of the product's items are fairly similar to what was done in the preceding code. This is shown in Listing 6.61. Items are retrieved by using the getParameter method of the request object, and then the appropriate set method of Product is used. For the two collection fields, clips and images, a similar process to what you saw with artists and authors is used. Finally, HTML is written out, which indicates to the user that the update was successful, and a link back to the main page is provided.

Listing 6.61 Adding the Rest of the Product's Items (*UpdateProduct.java*)

```
String price = req.getParameter( "price" );
price = price.replace( '$', ' ' );
product.setPrice( Util.getDouble( price ) );
String quantity = req.getParameter( "quantity" );
product.setQuantityInStock( Util.getInt( quantity ) );
String dateString = req.getParameter( "onSaleDate" );
Date date = product.getOnSaleDate();
if( date == null ) {
  date = new Date();
  product.setOnSaleDate( date );
}
date.fromString( dateString );
String description = req.getParameter( "description" );
product.setDescription( description );

product.removeAllImages();
for( int i = 1; getImage( "" + i, req, product );  i++ )
  ;//do nothing
getImage( "New", req, product );

product.removeAllClips();
for( int i = 1; getClip( new String( "" + i ), req, product ); i++ )
  ;//do nothing

getClip( "New", req, product );
// Return HTML.
out.println( "<html><head><title>Update Successful</title></head>" );
out.println( "<body><h2>Update Succesful</h2>" );
out.println( "<a href='/main.html'>Return to main page</a></body></html>" );
}
```

The getAuthor method, shown in Listing 6.62. is called from the doPost method of the servlet to extract author information from the request and add it into the product. In the Edit JSP you varied the name field of each author input field by incrementing a counter and adding it to the string "author," and here you can get the information back by looking for the same string. If the string is not found, or the value has not been filled in, a false value is returned. If a value is found, the string is added to the product as an author name, and a true is returned.

Listing 6.62 The *getAuthor* Method (*UpdateProduct.java*)

```
boolean getAuthor( String i, HttpServletRequest req, Product product ){
  String author = req.getParameter( "author" + i );
  if( author == null || author.equals( "" ) ) {
    return false;
  }
  product.addAuthor( author );
  return true;
}
```

The getArtist, getImage, and getClip methods, shown in Listing 6.63, all use a similar technique as the getAuthor method. The getArtists method is almost identical and the getImage and getClip methods are a little longer because they have more parameters to get from the *request* and set onto the product's items.

Listing 6.63 The *getArtist*, *getImage*, and *getClip* Methods (*UpdateProduct.java*)

```
boolean getArtist(String i, HttpServletRequest req, Product product){
  String artist = req.getParameter( "artist" + i );
  if( artist == null || artist.equals( "" ) ) {
    return false;
  }
  product.addArtist( artist );
  return true;
}

boolean getImage( String i, HttpServletRequest req, Product product ) {
  String format = req.getParameter( "img" + i + "-format" );
  if( format == null || format.equals("") ) {
    return false;
  }
  Image img = new Image();
```

```
      img.setFormat( format );
      String src = req.getParameter( "img" + i + "-src" );
      img.setSrc( src );
      String height = req.getParameter( "img" + i + "-height" );
      img.setHeight( Util.getInteger( height ) );
      String width = req.getParameter( "img" + i + "-width" );
      img.setWidth( Util.getInteger( width ) );
      String caption = req.getParameter( "img" + i + "-caption" );
      img.setCaption( caption );
      product.addImage( img );
      return true;
    }

    boolean getClip( String i, HttpServletRequest req, Product product ) {
      String  format = req.getParameter( "clip" + i + "-format" );
      if( format == null || format.equals("") ) {
        return false;
      }
      Clip clip = new Clip();
      clip.setFormat( format );
      String src = req.getParameter( "clip" + i + "-src" );
      clip.setSrc( src );
      String title = req.getParameter( "clip" + i + "-title" );
      clip.setTitle( title );
      String length = req.getParameter( "clip" + i + "-length" );
      clip.setLength( length );
      String size = req.getParameter( "clip" + i + "-size" );
      clip.setSize( size );
      String description = req.getParameter( "clip" + i + "-description" );
      clip.setDescription( description );
      product.addClip( clip );
      return true;
    }
  }
```

The JSPs and servlets presented in this chapter show a how a browser hosted application can be used for adding, editing, and removing items that are located on the server. This allows the Web to move from presenting static data to become a full-fledged information processing system.

The solution presented here is missing some pieces that would be needed in a large, system-critical system. The error handling is not very robust and could be improved. There is no synchronization done on the XML file, so if two people were editing the file at the same time, one person's changes would be overwritten. But despite these shortcomings, this solution could handle the job of editing the XML catalog file for a small site.

CHAPTER 7

Using Surveys to Know Your Customer

- Privacy considerations

- The logic of surveys and XML

- A complete working survey system

To be successful, an Internet entrepreneur must be able to understand his or her customers. As that entrepreneur, your starting point will always be the records of sales and of user interactions with your Web site. However, in addition to these records, you have the possibility of getting information directly from the customer by means of online surveys. Most people love to provide their opinions if you can convince them that you won't invade their privacy.

The combination of XML and Java servlets is well suited to the creation of online surveys. In this chapter, we go beyond the simple linear survey and create a system that can alter the questions asked according to the user's input.

Customer Privacy Concerns

The general public and policy makers share a very widespread concern about privacy in this age, focusing on every organization that seems to have a computer database. On one hand, businesses are convinced that knowing as much as possible about their customers is the key to survival in a world of cutthroat competition. On the other hand, people view with dismay the possibility that every detail about their private lives could be open to review. You can make your customers feel more comfortable with using your site if you explicitly explain the privacy standards you follow.

Industry Standards

A desire to address the Internet commerce aspects of this issue without involving government led to the creation of an independent, nonprofit privacy initiative named TRUSTe (`www .truste.org`). The following is the premise of this group:

- Users have a right to informed consent.
- No single privacy principle is adequate for all situations.

TRUSTe operates as a privacy branding organization similar to the way the UL (United Laboratories) brand is used with electrical equipment.

Member organizations are entitled to display the TRUSTe logo if their published privacy policies meet the TRUSTe standards, they pay the membership fee, and they pass a privacy statement audit. The fees start at $299 for companies doing less than $1 million in revenue, so membership is really quite reasonable.

NOTE   Sites that may collect information from children under the age of 13 have an even more stringent privacy requirement standard. As this is written, Congress is considering new legislation in this area.

TRUSTe conducts monitoring of member sites to verify that they are adhering to their published privacy standards. This monitoring includes submitting user information for fake users and tracking resulting use of the information. Furthermore, TRUSTe aggressively pursues sites that use the TRUSTe logo without authorization.

For both member and non-member organizations, the `www.truste.org` site is an excellent location for catching up on the news affecting privacy considerations, particularly in the United States. TRUSTe also cooperates with other industry groups that are attempting to establish standard practices for ensuring user privacy.

Public Interest Organizations

Many people feel that there is as much danger from government data gathering as from corporate data gathering. Thus, it is no surprise that a number of public interest organizations exist and express their opinions on privacy issues. One such organization is the Electronic Privacy Information Center (EPIC) in Washington, D.C. (`www.epic.org/privacy`).

EPIC is concerned with civil rights and general privacy rights. It frequently testifies in hearings and actively uses the Freedom of Information Act to uncover government abuses of privacy in the United States.

EPIC is associated with Privacy International (`www.privacy.org/pi`), an international coalition of groups concerned with privacy issues. This group, founded in 1990, is based in London. Privacy International organizes international conferences on privacy issues. It also frequently gets in the news with its annual Big Brother awards to the government organizations and the corporations they deem to have the most invasive privacy records.

Knowing what your customer wants is essential to any online enterprise. But to avoid any semblance of privacy invasion, it is best to have a clearly stated privacy policy and to always allow your site visitors the chance to opt out of giving nonessential information. If your site caters to children, you also better make sure your information gathering is consistent with the latest legislation.

Creating Your Survey with XML Survey Script

A simple but effective form of information gathering is the online survey. Because XML is all about defining the structure of documents, and a survey is a highly structured document, XML is an ideal tool for our task. The XML-driven survey system discussed in the remainder of this chapter is very flexible. As written, it does not associate a particular user with his or her responses but simply aggregates the results. It could easily be modified to save user responses in a user database, but if you do that you should make sure the user understands what is being done with the data.

In this section, we will be developing a generalized XML structure for creating online surveys. Let's start with the following list of design criteria:

Control of Presentation   Ideally, we should be able to present questions within the context of our normal Web-page design.

Flexibility of Question Design   We need to be able to create a variety of survey methods, from simple yes-or-no questions to a list of multiple-choice options.

Branching Capability   A single script should be able to administer different questions to different users depending on their responses to specific questions. For example, if the response to one question indicates that the user never buys music CDs over the Internet, we need to branch away from questions related to music preferences.

Extensibility   If a new form of question presentation needs to be added to the system, it should be possible with minimum alteration to the code.

Recording Results   Results from each participant should be recorded completely and independently of other participants. This gives us maximum flexibility in analysis.

Determining the Flow of Questions

Figure 7.1 illustrates possible paths through a question script. Essentially, there are blocks of questions that are always presented without branching, ending in a question that provides branching to determine the next path. A branching question can lead all branches to the same block (blocks C and D in the figure both lead to block E, for example) or to different blocks (block A, for instance, leads to blocks B, C, and D, depending on the answers submitted). Blocks either end with a branching question or are "terminal" and end the questionnaire. On reaching a terminal, the system records all responses in a file. The designer has the option of using a unique file for each terminal.

Translating this diagram into XML entities, we have come up with the following structure. A `Questionnaire` document has an `Intro` (introduction) and one or more `Block` entities at the first level. Each `Block` has one or more `Ques` (question) entities and may end with a `Terminal` entity. A `Block` has a `name` attribute that is used to direct branching and a `type` attribute that has the value "terminal" if the block ends with a `Terminal` tag. This top-level structure is illustrated schematically in Listing 7.1.

FIGURE 7.1
Potential paths through
a script

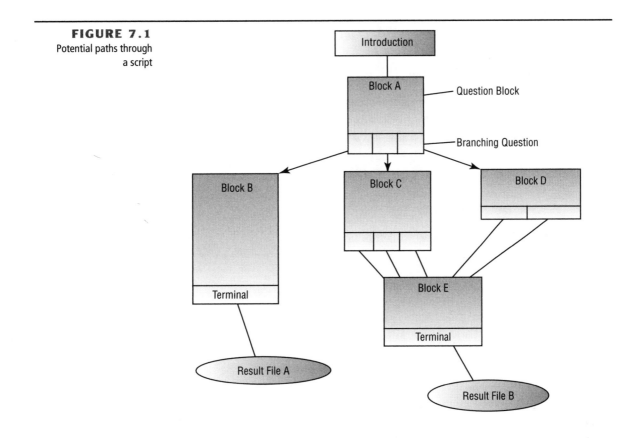

Listing 7.1: The First and Second Levels of a Questionnaire Hierarchy

```
<Questionnaire>
  <Intro>
  </Intro>
  <Block name="A">
  </Block>
  <Block name="B" type="terminal">
  </Block>
  <Block name="C">
  </Block>
  <Block name="D">
```

```
   </Block>
   <Block name="E" type="terminal">
   </Block>
</Questionnaire>
```

Each question in a block is created with the Ques tag, which encloses a text statement and two or more selectable options created with Qopt tags. Attributes in the Ques and Qopt tags provide control over branching and the way the question is presented. The easiest way to see this is to look at some example questions, which are shown in the sample survey in the next section.

A Sample Survey

Listing 7.2 presents the introduction and first question of an example survey that you might use to determine new products to stock in your catalog.

NOTE   The full example of this survey is on the CD that accompanies this book. The first question has the type attribute value of "QMC"; this style of question is presented so the user can only choose one of the options.

Listing 7.2: The Start of an XML Document Defining a Survey (*customersurvey.xml*)

```
<?xml version="1.0" standalone="yes" ?>
<Questionnaire title="Example Customer Survey"
   author="wbb" date="May 30, 2000"
   method="xml" file="e:\scripts\questionnaire\surveyresult.xml"
   >
<Intro><![CDATA[
<h1>Welcome Customers</h1><br>
<p>We here at <i>BuyStuff.com</i> want to meet your every desire
to buy <b>STUFF</b>. To that end, we are greatly expanding
our online catalog, and we want to concentrate on <b>STUFF</b>
you will want to buy as soon as you see it. Please help by
completing this simple survey.
</p>]]>
</Intro>
<Block name="intro" type="terminal" >
<Ques id="intro:1" type="QMC" >
  <Qtext>Which of the following are you most interested in buying online?
  </Qtext>
```

```
<Qopt val="a" branch="books" >Books</Qopt>
<Qopt val="b" branch="cds" >Cds</Qopt>
<Qopt val="c" branch="gadgets">Electronic goodies</Qopt>
<Qopt val="d" >I am not interested in buying stuff!</Qopt>
</Ques>
<!-- this terminates the block and the questionnaire -
     could substitute different file for recording -->
<Terminal><![CDATA[<h2>Thanks for looking anyway!</h2>
]]>
</Terminal>
</Block>
. . .
```

The Qopt options with val attributes of "a", "b", and "c" in the first question branch to other blocks, whereas option "d" leads to the terminal message. Only one of these options can be chosen, because the question type is "QMC". In this chapter, we use only two types of question, QMC (Question Multiple Choice) and QMCM (Question Multiple Choice Multiple answer). The results of the user response to this question are recorded using the question id attribute and the option val attribute values.

Listing 7.3 shows the block (from Listing 7.2) that the branch attribute in the Qopt tag with val="a" leads to. Question "books:1" uses the "QMCM" type, which allows multiple selections to be made. The "cds" and "gadgets" blocks have a similar organization.

Listing 7.3: The *"books"* Question Block (*customersurvey.xml*)

```
<Block name="books" type="terminal" >
<Ques id="books:1" type="QMCM" >
  <Qtext>Please select all of the book categories you
  would like to see in our catalog.
  </Qtext>
  <Qopt val="0">Best Sellers of All Types</Qopt>
  <Qopt val="1">Science Fiction</Qopt>
  <Qopt val="2">Fantasy Fiction</Qopt>
  <Qopt val="3">History and Biography</Qopt>
  <Qopt val="4">Computer Technology</Qopt>
  <Qopt val="5">Business Related</Qopt>
</Ques>
<Terminal><![CDATA[<h2>Thanks for answering the survey!</h2>]]>
</Terminal>
</Block>
```

The Survey Administering Servlet

This section describes the complete code for a Java servlet to administer a survey based on the XML script design we created in the preceding section and to record the results in a form suitable for analysis. We also describe a utility class to manage document objects in a servlet engine, and a servlet for tabulating and reporting survey results.

The Survey Servlet Code

Listing 7.4 shows the import statements, class declaration, and `init` method for the QuestionnaireServ servlet. The static variable `homedir`, which can be set from the ServletConfig, is used in the `init` method to read a properties file in which survey names are related to the system path to the source XML file. The properties file also can be used to set the `handler` String variable, which is the URL used by the Web server for this servlet.

Listing 7.4: The Start of the *QuestionnaireServ* Code (*QuestionnaireServ.java*)

```java
package com.XmlEcomBook.Chap07;

import com.XmlEcomBook.DOMlibrary ;
import org.w3c.dom.* ;
import java.io.*;
import java.util.* ;
import javax.servlet.*;
import javax.servlet.http.*;

public class QuestionnaireServ extends HttpServlet
{
  static String brcrlf = "<br>\r\n" ;
  static String homedir = "e:\\scripts\\questionnaire" ;
  static String handler = "http://localhost/servlet/Questionnaire" ;
  static String version = "v1.00";
  Properties qProp ;

  public void init(ServletConfig config) throws ServletException  {
    super.init(config);
    String tmp = config.getInitParameter("homedir");
    if( tmp != null ) homedir = tmp ;
    System.out.println("Start QuestionnaireServ using " + homedir );
    File f = new File( homedir, "questionnaire.properties");
```

```
try { qProp = new Properties();
  qProp.load( new FileInputStream(f) );
  tmp = qProp.getProperty("handler");
  if( tmp != null ) handler = tmp ;
  System.out.println("Loaded properties for Questionnaire handler: "
          + handler );
}catch(IOException e){
    System.out.println("Error loading " + e );
}
}
```

The `QuestionnaireServ` servlet uses sessions to keep track of individual users taking a survey. Initial entry is expected to be a GET from an HTML page with a simple form that sets a `qname` variable indicating which survey is to be administered. In customizing this servlet for your own application, you could also record a customer id at this point.

The `doGet` method, as shown in Listing 7.5, tries to get the document object corresponding to `qname`, using the file path from the properties file and the `DOMlibrary` utility. If it succeeds, it proceeds to get an `HttpSession` and to attach a new `Interpreter` object that holds the document to the session. A new `Recorder` object will also be initialized and attached to the session. Any error will use the `errorMsg` method (see Listing 7.7) to write an error message to the user.

The `Interpreter` object is responsible for creating the HTML forms that will administer the survey, whereas the `Recorder` object is responsible for recording the user's responses. These classes are discussed in the upcoming sections "The `Interpreter` Class" and "The `Recorder` Class."

Output from the `doGet` method is a page having the text from the `Intro` tag area of the XML document, which is written out by the `Interpreter` object `doIntro` method and includes a form with a button to start the first question.

Listing 7.5: The *doGet* Method Code (*QuestionnaireServ.java*)

```
public void doGet(HttpServletRequest req, HttpServletResponse resp)
   throws ServletException, IOException
{
  resp.setContentType("text/html");
  PrintWriter out = new PrintWriter(resp.getOutputStream());
  String qname = req.getParameter("qname") ;
  // System.out.println("Start doGet");
  if( qname == null || qname.length() == 0 ){
```

```
        errorMsg( out, "Bad QNAME data", null); return;
    }
      // MUST have qname = name of xml file
    String src = qProp.getProperty( qname );
    if( src == null ) {
        errorMsg( out, "Bad QNAME lookup", null ); return ;
    }
    String userid = "unknown" ; // customer or student id or unknown
    String tmp = req.getParameter("userid");
    if( tmp != null ) userid = tmp;
    String usertype = "unknown" ; // "student" "customer" etc etc
    tmp = req.getParameter("usertype");
    if(tmp != null ) usertype = tmp ;
    DOMlibrary lib = DOMlibrary.getLibrary();
    System.out.println("DOMlibrary initialized, try for " + src );
    Document doc = lib.getDOM( src );
    if( doc == null ){
        errorMsg( out, "DOM doc failed - unable to continue", null );
        return ;
    }
    HttpSession session = req.getSession( true );
    // if not new must be re-entering - could recover here
    Interpreter terpret = new Interpreter( doc, handler );
    // session.putValue( "xmldocument", terpret );
    session.setAttribute("xmldocument",terpret );
    // the putValue method was used in the 2.1 API but is now
    // a deprecated method, you might have to use it if you are
    // using an older servlet engine such as JRun 2.3
    //
    Recorder rb = new Recorder(userid, usertype,
        session.getId(), src );
    rb.setMethods( doc );
    //session.putValue("recorder", rb );
    session.setAttribute("recorder", rb );
    try { //
      terpret.doIntro( out ); // includes head and Form
      footer( out );
    }catch(Exception e){
        errorMsg( out, "doGet ", e );
    }
}
```

After the survey introduction, all requests and responses go through the doPost method, as seen in Listing 7.6. After recovering the Interpreter and Recorder objects from the HttpSession, data from the request is gathered and the response is generated by the Interpreter and Recorder objects.

Listing 7.6: The *doPost* Method of the *QuestionnaireServ* Class (*QuestionnaireServ.java*)

```
public void doPost(HttpServletRequest req, HttpServletResponse resp)
    throws ServletException, IOException
  {
    resp.setContentType("text/html");
    PrintWriter out = new PrintWriter(resp.getOutputStream());
    //System.out.println("Start doPost");
    HttpSession session = req.getSession(false);
    try {
      if( session == null ){ errorMsg(out, "No Session ", null );
        return ;
      }
      Interpreter terpret =
          (Interpreter)session.getAttribute("xmldocument");
       Recorder rb =
          (Recorder) session.getAttribute("recorder");
      if( terpret == null ||
          rb == null ){
            errorMsg( out, "Data not recovered from Session", null );
            return;
      }
      terpret.doPostQ( out, req, rb );
      footer( out );
    }catch(Exception e ){
        errorMsg( out, "doPost ", e );
    }
  }
```

Listing 7.7 shows some convenient utility methods in the QuestionnaireServ class. Using the footer method to write the end tags on each page lets you include the servlet version at the bottom. This is very handy during development and can easily be removed for the final version.

Debugging servlets can be very tricky, especially if the bugs only show up occasionally. It is especially hard if the users don't have any clear way of expressing the problem. We like to use the errorMsg method to report errors. If the error involves an exception, it will write a stack trace to the HTML output. It includes an e-mail address for the user to send a message and, hopefully, a copy of the stack trace. Naturally, you should plug in your own e-mail address here.

Listing 7.7: Utility Methods in the Servlet (*QuestionnaireServ.java*)

```java
public void footer( PrintWriter out ){
  out.println("<hr> Servlet version: " + version + "<br>");
  out.println("</BODY>");
  out.println("</HTML>");
  out.close();
}


    // assumes response has been set to text/html
private void errorMsg( PrintWriter out, String msg, Exception ex ){
  out.println("<html>");
  out.println("<head><title>QuestionnaireServ
  Output</title></head>");
  out.println("<body>");
  out.println("<h2>Error: " ); out.println( msg );
  out.println("</h2><br>");
  if( ex != null ){
     ex.printStackTrace( out );
  }
  out.println("<br>");
  out.println("<a href=\"mailto:wbrogden@bga.com\">" +
     "Please mail me the error message.</a><br>");
  footer( out );
}

public String getServletInfo()
{
  return "Administers a questionnaire";
}
}
```

The *Interpreter* Class

The work of creating survey form questions from the XML document is encapsulated in the Interpreter class. This class has been designed to be very flexible with respect to presentation of questions. Although only two styles of question are supported in this version, the mechanism can be expanded to provide additional styles.

The import statements and static methods for `Interpreter` are shown in Listing 7.9. The constants QMC and QMCM stand for the two styles that are provided, QMC meaning a question with multiple choices that allow only a single selection and QMCM a question with multiple choices that allow multiple selections. Consider the XML for an example question, as shown in Listing 7.8.

Listing 7.8: The Start of an Example Question Block in XML (*customersurvey.xml*)

```
<Block name="cds" type="terminal" >
<Ques type="QMCM" id="palm:1">
  <Qtext>Please select all of the CD categories
  that you would like to see in our catalog.
  </Qtext>
  <Qopt val="0">Classical</Qopt>
  <Qopt val="1">Country and Western</Qopt>
  <Qopt val="2">The Latest Pop Groups</Qopt>
  <Qopt val="3">Current Rock</Qopt>
  <Qopt val="4">Golden Oldies Rock</Qopt>
  <Qopt val="5">Environmental</Qopt>
  <Qopt val="6">Novelty and Humor</Qopt>
</Ques>
```

The opening `Ques` tag uses the `type` attribute to establish that this is a "QMCM" style question. The `id` attribute is a unique value for this question.

Instead of comparing the type attribute `String` with the various possible question styles, we use a `Hashtable` to look up an `int` value that can be used in a `switch` statement to select proper handling for the question. The `Hashtable` is named `typeHash` and the lookup is performed by the `lookUpType` method as shown in Listing 7.9.

To add a new type, you would simply define a new `String` and `int` constant in the static variables and in the `typeHash Hashtable`.

Listing 7.9: Imports and Constants at the Start of the *Interpreter* Source Code (*Interpreter.java*)

```
package com.XmlEcomBook.Chap07;
//
import org.w3c.dom.* ;
import com.sun.xml.tree.* ;
import java.io.*;
import java.util.* ;
```

```
import javax.servlet.*;
import javax.servlet.http.*;

public class Interpreter
{
   static final String brcrlf = "<br>\r\n";
   static final int QMC = 1 ;
   static final int QMCM = 2 ;

   static Hashtable typeHash = new Hashtable();
   static { // static initialization block
     typeHash.put("QMC", new Integer( QMC ));
     typeHash.put("QMCM", new Integer( QMCM ));
   }

   static int lookUpType( String type ){
      Integer N = (Integer)typeHash.get( type );
      if( N == null ) return 0 ;
      return N.intValue();
   }
```

Listing 7.10 continues with the instance variables and constructor method of the `Interpreter` class. Each user session has an instance of `Interpreter` that stores the document and information about the user's current position in the survey. The `nowBlock` and `nowNode` variables are references of the `org.w3c.dom.Node` interface type.

Listing 7.10: Instance Variables and the *Interpreter* Class Constructor (*Interpreter.java*)

```
// instance variables below this
Document theDom ;
Node nowBlock, nowNode ; // nowNode should be quest type
boolean terminal = false ; // true if the block is terminal
String title ;
String css = "" ; // may change from block to block
String actionStr ;

NodeList blockNodeList ; // Nodes that are <Block> type

// the constructor - doc is the XML script document
public Interpreter( Document doc, String handler ){
   theDom = doc ; actionStr = handler ;
   Element E = theDom.getDocumentElement(); // the root
```

```
        blockNodeList = E.getElementsByTagName("Block");
        // note that in contrast to other get methods, getAttributes
        // returns "" if the attribute does not exist
        title = E.getAttribute("title");
        css = E.getAttribute("css");   // used for <Intro>
    }
```

To provide some flexibility in formatting the questions, there is a provision for specifying a Cascading Style Sheet for the overall document and for overriding that default in each block. The writeHead method shown in Listing 7.11 handles the output of the start of an HTML page and includes a style sheet reference if it exists. This listing also shows the startForm and endForm methods. Note that the quesid variable is written into the form as a hidden variable that is later recovered in the doPostQ method (see Listing 7.16).

Listing 7.11: Methods that Write Various Parts of the HTML Page (*Interpreter.java*)

```
// output title and <head> tag area, using css if present
void writeHead( PrintWriter out ){
    out.println("<html>");
    out.println("<head><title>" + title + "</title></head>");
     if( css.length() > 0 ){
       out.println("<link href=\"" + css +
           "\" type=\"text/css\" rel=\"stylesheet\">" );
    }
    out.println("<body>");
}


// assumes nowNode is set to the first question
// output form start and question text
public void startForm(PrintWriter out ){
  out.print("<form method=\"POST\" action=\"" );
  out.print( actionStr ); out.println("\" >");
}


// fills in hidden variable and button
public void endForm( PrintWriter out, String id ){
    out.print("<input type=\"hidden\" name=\"quesid\" value=\""
       + id + "\" ><br>" );
    out.print("<input type=\"submit\" value=\"" );
    out.print("Next" );
    out.println("\" name=\"action\" ><br>");
    out.println("</form><br>");
}
```

Creating the Question Display

The genQuest method in Listing 7.12 is called after the nowNode variable has been set to the Ques element to be displayed. Note the use of the question type to select the prompt that is displayed. After printing the question text, and the prompt, genQuest creates a form containing the options.

Listing 7.12: The *genQuest* Method (*Interpreter.java*)

```java
// nowNode known to be a <Quest>
  public void genQuest( PrintWriter out ){
    Element E = (Element) nowNode ;
    String qid = E.getAttribute("id") ;
    String type = E.getAttribute("type");
    String lim  = E.getAttribute("limit");
    // out.print("Question id: " + qid + " type: " + type + brcrlf );
    writeHead( out );
    NodeList nm = E.getElementsByTagName("Qtext");
    out.print( nm.item(0).getFirstChild().getNodeValue() );
    out.println(brcrlf );
    NodeList opm = E.getElementsByTagName("Qopt");
    int optCt = opm.getLength();
    int typeN = lookUpType( type );
    switch( typeN ){
      case QMC :
        out.print("Choose one"); break ;
      case QMCM :
        if( lim.length() == 0 ){
            out.print("Choose any number");
        }
        else { out.print("Choose up to " + lim );
        }
        break ;
      default :
        out.print("Unknown type");
    }
    out.print( brcrlf );
    startForm( out ); // creates <form...
    for( int i = 0 ; i < optCt ; i++ ){
      doOption(out, opm.item(i), typeN );
    }
    endForm( out, qid );
  }
```

The genQuest method in the preceding listing calls the doOption method (Listing 7.13) for each <Qopt> element. If you want to add additional option types, such as a text entry field, this is the method that would have to be modified. This listing also shows the checkBlock-Type method that is used to locate attributes in a Block element.

Listing 7.13: The *doOption* Method (*Interpreter.java*)

```
// opN is from node list of <Qopt> - create output
// <Qopt val="a" branch="" >Option a.</Qopt>
private void doOption(PrintWriter out, Node opN, int typeN ){
  Element E = (Element) opN;
  String val = E.getAttribute("val") ;
  String branch = E.getAttribute("branch");
  String content = E.getFirstChild().getNodeValue();
  // what else? type of option display?
  switch( typeN ){ // known valid
    case QMC :
      out.print("<input name=\"opt\" value=\"" + val +
        "\" type=\"RADIO\" >" );
        break ;
    case QMCM :
      out.print("<input name=\"opt\" value=\"" + val +
        "\" type=\"CHECKBOX\" >" );
        break ;
  } // now for the text
  out.println( content );
  out.println( brcrlf );
}

// look at the type and css attributes in <Block>
private void checkBlockType( ){
  Element E = (Element)nowBlock ;
  String tmp = E.getAttribute("type");
  terminal = tmp.equals("terminal");
  tmp = E.getAttribute("css");
  if( tmp.length() > 0 ) css = tmp ;
  System.out.println("checkBlockType - css:" + css );
}
```

Creating the Introduction Display

Listing 7.14 presents the doIntro method, which sets up the starting Block element by looking at the first element in the blockNodeList. With the nowBlock variable set, a call to setQnodeInBlock sets the nowNode variable to the first Ques element. Assuming this is accomplished correctly, the Intro text is output with a simple form that will call up the first question.

Listing 7.14: The *doIntro* Method that Outputs Text from the *<Intro>* Tag (*Interpreter.java*)

```
// <head> has been set, we are in <body>
public void doIntro(PrintWriter out ){
  writeHead( out );
  nowBlock = blockNodeList.item(0);
  if( nowBlock == null ){
     out.println("Error 1 setting up first question.<br>");
     return ;
  }
  if( setQnodeInBlock( 0 )== null ){
     out.println("Error 2 setting up first question.<br>");
     return ;
  }
  checkBlockType( ); // sets the terminal flag
  out.println( getIntro() );
  out.print("<form method=\"POST\" action=\"" );
  out.print( actionStr ); out.println("\" >");
  endForm( out, "intro" );
}
```

Handling a Questionnaire Branch

Listing 7.15 shows the setBranch method that is called by doPostQ when a user response that selects a branch has been found in a question response. This method simply looks through all of the Block elements for a matching name and sets the nowBlock and nowNode variables accordingly.

Listing 7.15: The *setBranch* Method (*Interpreter.java*)

```
// jump to another block has been detected
private void setBranch(String block ){
   int ct = blockNodeList.getLength();
```

```
    for( int i = 1 ; i < ct ; i++ ){ // block 0 was the start
      nowBlock = blockNodeList.item(i);
      String name = ((Element)nowBlock).getAttribute("name");
      if( name.equals( block )){
        checkBlockType() ; // to set terminal flag
        setQnodeInBlock( 0 ) ; // set nowNode
        return ;
      }
    }
    System.err.println("Interpreter.setBranch failed to find " + block );
    nowBlock = nowNode = null ;
  }
```

The doPostQ method starting in Listing 7.16 is called from the servlet doPost method and manages the creation of a new HTML page. Note that the first thing this method does is check to see if the associated Recorder object has recorded the fact that the survey has previously been terminated. This prevents a user from using the browser Back function to return to an earlier page and input data once the end of the survey has been reached and the data recorded.

The next section of code takes care of the special case of the first question by detecting the fact that the quesid equals "intro". In all other cases, the user input must be recorded by comparing the select "opt" values from the form with the <Qopt> tag attributes, using the associated Recorder object.

Listing 7.16: The Start of the *doPostQ* Method (*Interpreter.java*)

```
    // req contains user response
  public void doPostQ( PrintWriter out, HttpServletRequest req,
        Recorder recordB ){
    if( recordB.terminated ){
      writeHead( out );
      out.println("<b>This questionnaire has been terminated.</b>");
      return ;
    }
    String action =  req.getParameter("action");
    String quesid =  req.getParameter("quesid");
    if( !action.equals("Next") ){
      out.println("Unexpected state in Interpreter.doPost<br>");
      return ;
    }
    if( quesid.equals("intro") ){
```

```
    // this calls for generating first question
    // doIntro already set nowNode to first <Ques> node
    genQuest( out );
    return ;
}
// if here, not generating first question, examine request
Element E = (Element) nowNode ;
NodeList oplist = E.getElementsByTagName("Qopt");
int type = lookUpType( E.getAttribute("type"));
String lim  = E.getAttribute("limit"); // ?
String[] optS = req.getParameterValues("opt");
recordB.record( quesid, type, optS );
```

The next step in the doPostQ method, as seen in Listing 7.17, is to determine whether or not one of the user's responses just recorded causes a branch to be taken. Naturally, a new branch will start at the first question in a block as set by the setBranch method. If a branch is not taken, we have to locate the present question in the current Block element and pick the next question to be displayed. We also have to account for the situation in which the element following the current question is a Terminal, in which case we call genTerminal to handle the output.

Listing 7.17: The *doPostQ* Method, Continued (*Interpreter.java*)

```
String branch = branchLookUp( oplist, optS );
if( branch != null ){
  //System.out.println("Taking Branch:" + branch );
  setBranch( branch ); // sets nowBlock and nowNode to new value
  if( nowNode == null ) genTerminal( out, recordB );
  else genQuest( out );
  return ;
}

// branch is null, nowBlock has 1 or more <Ques
NodeList qlist = ((Element)nowBlock).getElementsByTagName("Ques");
int n = 0 ;
int nct = qlist.getLength();
while( qlist.item(n) != nowNode &&
        n < nct ) n++ ;
// n = nowNode
Node nxtN = qlist.item(n+1);
if( nxtN != null ){
```

```
            nowNode = nxtN ;
            genQuest( out );
            // System.out.println("Found nextQ");
            return ;
        }
        if( terminal ) genTerminal( out, recordB );
        else out.println("nextQ NULL, not terminal<br>" );
    } // end doPostQ
```

Handling a *Terminal* Element

As shown in Listing 7.18, the genTerminal method has two main tasks. First, it has to output the final page of the survey, using either the text associated with the Terminal element or a stock phrase. Next, it has to look for an "altfile" attribute attached to the Terminal. If present, this value is used by the Recorder object to save the results to a file; otherwise, the Recorder uses the default file established at the start of the XML document.

Listing 7.18: The *genTerminal* Method (*Interpreter.java*)

```
// we have reached the end of a terminal block
// note that a <Terminal> tag may have an altfile="filepathandname"
// that replaces the default established in the file attribute of
// the <Questionnaire> tag for this particular branch
private void genTerminal( PrintWriter out, Recorder recordB ){
    NodeList nl = ((Element)nowBlock).getElementsByTagName("Terminal");
    int ct = nl.getLength();
    String altfile = "" ;
    writeHead( out );
    if( ct == 0 ){
        out.println("Thank you for participating.<br>");
    }
    else { // use text from <Terminal>...</Terminal>
        Element E = (Element)nl.item(0); // only one <Terminal> tag
        out.println( E.getFirstChild().getNodeValue() );
        altfile = E.getAttribute("altfile");
    }
    try {
        recordB.terminal( altfile );
    }catch(IOException e ){
        out.println("Problem recording results; please notify Webmaster.");
    }
}
```

Utility Methods in the *Interpreter* Class

Listing 7.19 finishes the `Interpreter` class listing with various utility methods.

Listing 7.19: The Last of the *Interpreter* Code (*Interpreter.java*)

```java
private Node setQnodeInBlock( int n ){
  Element E = (Element) nowBlock ;
  NodeList nl = E.getElementsByTagName("Ques");
  nowNode = nl.item( n );
  return nowNode ;
}

public String getIntro() {
  Element E = theDom.getDocumentElement(); // the root
  NodeList nl = E.getElementsByTagName("Intro");
  Element I = (Element)nl.item(0);
  nl = I.getChildNodes();
  int ct = nl.getLength();
  if( ct == 0 ) return "Bad Intro Data<br>" ;
  return nl.item(0).getNodeValue();
}

// return String if any chosen opt has a branch="", else null
private String branchLookUp( NodeList oplist,String[] optS ){
  if( optS == null ||
      optS.length == 0 ) return null ;
  Hashtable opHash = new Hashtable();
  int i, ct = oplist.getLength();
  String val, branch ;
  for( i = 0 ; i < ct ;i++ ){
    val = ((Element)oplist.item(i)).getAttribute("val");
    branch = ((Element)oplist.item(i)).getAttribute("branch");
    opHash.put( val, branch ); // branch = "" if no attribute
  }
  if( opHash.size() == 0 ) return null ; // branch not possible
  for( i = 0 ; i < optS.length ; i++ ){
    branch = (String)opHash.get( optS[i] );
    if( branch != null &&
        branch.length() > 0 ) return branch ;
  }
  return null ;
}
```

```
   public String toString()
   {
     StringBuffer sb = new StringBuffer("Interpreter ");
     return sb.toString() ;
   }
}
```

The *Recorder* Class

The `Recorder` class is responsible for storing the user responses to each question and for writing them to a file for later analysis. Each user gets an instance of `Recorder` that is stored in a session and records only that user's responses.

The root element of the XML document is the `Questionnaire` tag, which has several attributes used by the `Recorder` class. As shown in the following example tag, these attributes are named `title`, `author`, `date`, `method`, and `file`:

```
<Questionnaire title="Survey 1" author="WBB" date="May 19, 2000"
method="xml" file="e:\scripts\questionnaire\testresult.xml" >
```

The `title`, `author`, and `date` are simply held by the `Recorder` for later output, but `method` and `file` control the `Recorder` operation. We have provided the `method` attribute in case you want to save the data in some format besides XML. For example, if you like to use a spreadsheet analysis program, you could add methods to write a comma-delimited line of text. The output filename established is a default that can be replaced by a filename in a `Terminal` tag.

In the XML format we are using here, each user's responses are stored within a `Qresults` tag, with a `Ques` tag for each question and a `Qopt` tag for each selected response. This is certainly more bulky than a comma-delimited file, but it is very flexible. The file that is written is not a complete XML document because it does not have a root element. Later, in the "Survey Analysis Options" section, we show how this is handled.

Listing 7.20 shows the import statements, the instance variables, and the single static variable in the `Recorder` class. The static variable is a `String` object that is used in a `synchronized` statement to ensure that only one instance of `Recorder` is actually writing to a file at any one time.

Listing 7.20: The Start of the *Recorder* Class Source Code (*Recorder.java*)

```
package com.XmlEcomBook.Chap07;

import org.w3c.dom.* ;
```

```
import com.sun.xml.tree.* ;
import java.io.*;
import java.util.* ;
import javax.servlet.*;
import javax.servlet.http.*;

public class Recorder
{ // this String is used to prevent more than one Recorder from
  // writing anywhere at the "same time"
  static String filelock = "RecorderLock" ;

  // these are instance variables
  String userid, usertype, sessionid ;
  String qresultStr ;
  String source ; // the xml file
  String method, output ; // how and where we save
  Hashtable record ; // one string per response
  public boolean terminated = false ;
```

The `Recorder` constructor method, shown in Listing 7.21, is called from the `doGet` method of the servlet. It sets several variables that characterize a particular user. It also creates the `Hashtable` that will be used to record responses to questions.

Listing 7.21 also shows the `setMethods` method, which uses the XML document to locate the method and file attributes. It also creates the starting `Qresults` tag and stores it in the `qresultStr` variable for later use.

Listing 7.21: The *Recorder* constructor and *setMethods* Methods (*Recorder.java*)

```
public Recorder(String id, String typ, String ses,String src ){
  userid = id ; usertype = typ ; sessionid = ses ;
  source = src ;
  record = new Hashtable();
}

  // locate method information in the document
public void setMethods( Document doc  ){
  NamedNodeMap nnm = doc.getDocumentElement().getAttributes();
  method = nnm.getNamedItem("method").getNodeValue();
  output = nnm.getNamedItem("file").getNodeValue();
```

```
    // for xml method
    StringBuffer sb = new StringBuffer( 50 );
    sb.append("<Qresults source=\"");
    sb.append( source ); sb.append( "\" date=\"" );
    sb.append( new Date().toString() );
    sb.append( "\" userid=\""); sb.append(userid);
    sb.append( "\" usertype=\"" ) ; sb.append( usertype );
    sb.append( "\" sessionid=\""); sb.append( sessionid );
    sb.append("\">\r\n");
    qresultStr = sb.toString();
  }
```

Listing 7.22 shows the `terminal`, `record`, and `toString` methods. The `terminal` method is responsible for writing the collected results from this user to the designated file. The `toString` method is provided to aid in debugging.

The `record` method is called from the `Interpreter doPostQ` method after each question response is received. Note that the `record` method provides for switching on the question type in case you want to create another question type that requires specialized recording. For example, if you want to accept a text input, it should be saved embedded in a CDATA section so that the user's accidental entry of characters having XML meanings will not cause problems.

Each call to `record` creates a `String` containing a `Ques` tag that is stored in the `record` `Hashtable`, using the `quesid` as a key. Because a `Hashtable` does not retain the order of the addition of items, the order in which `Ques` tags are later written is not predictable. However, this does not matter because we can use the XML survey document to determine the order of questions.

Listing 7.22: The *Recorder* Class Source, Continued (*Recorder.java*)

```
    // called when a <Terminal> block is reached
    // if altdest is not "" this changes the default output
    public void terminal(String altdest ) throws IOException {
      if( altdest != null &&
          altdest.length() > 4 ) output = altdest ;
      if( output == null || output.length() < 5 ){
        System.out.println("QARG output is: " + output );
        return ;
      }
      terminated = true ;
      // write in append mode
      synchronized( filelock ){
```

```java
        FileWriter fw = new FileWriter( output,true );
        PrintWriter pw = new PrintWriter( fw );
        pw.print( qresultStr ); // string constant
        Enumeration e = record.elements();
        while( e.hasMoreElements() ){
          pw.print( (String)e.nextElement() ) ;
        }
        pw.print("</Qresults>\r\n");
        pw.close();
      } // end synchronized block
  }

  public void record( String quesid, int type, String[] optS ){
    if( terminated ) return ; // prevent backing up from terminal Q
    // System.out.println("Start record: " + quesid );
    StringBuffer sb = new StringBuffer( 100 );
    sb.append("<Ques id=\"" ); sb.append( quesid ); sb.append("\" >");
    switch( type ){
      case Interpreter.QMC :
      case Interpreter.QMCM :
        if( optS == null || optS.length == 0 ) break ;
        for(int i =0 ; i < optS.length ; i++ ){
          sb.append("<Qopt val=\""); sb.append( optS[i] );
          sb.append("\"></Qopt>");
        }
        break ;
      default :
        sb.append("UNKNOWN TYPE");
    }
    sb.append("\r\n</Ques>\r\n");
    String tmp = sb.toString();
    // note this will replace answer if user backed up with browser back
    record.put( quesid, tmp );
    return ;
  }

  public String toString() // for debugging
  { StringBuffer sb = new StringBuffer( "Recorder user: " );
    sb.append( userid ); sb.append(" type: " );
    sb.append( usertype ); sb.append(" session: " );
```

```
    sb.append( sessionid );sb.append(" method: ");
    sb.append( method ); sb.append( " output: " );
    sb.append( output ); // how and where we save
    return sb.toString() ;
  }
}
```

Listing 7.23 shows the lines of text written for a single user taking a simple survey. The source attribute records the XML file used to create the survey. The date attribute records the date and time for the user's initial entry and presentation of the introduction. We have recorded the sessionid as an attribute to aid in debugging, but this could probably be eliminated.

Listing 7.23: A Single Survey Results Record in XML

```
<Qresults source="e:\scripts\javatest.xml" date="Mon May 22 22:30:20 CDT 2000"
    userid="unknown" usertype="passed" sessionid="9590526208594804">
<Ques id="studying:4" >
    <Qopt val="a"></Qopt><Qopt val="b"></Qopt>
    <Qopt val="d"></Qopt><Qopt val="e"></Qopt>
    <Qopt val="k"></Qopt><Qopt val="l"></Qopt>
    <Qopt val="m"></Qopt>
</Ques>
<Ques id="studying:3" ><Qopt val="1"></Qopt>
</Ques>
<Ques id="studying:2" ><Qopt val="2"></Qopt>
</Ques>
<Ques id="studying:1" ><Qopt val="a"></Qopt><Qopt val="f"></Qopt>
</Ques>
</Qresults>
```

Survey Analysis Options

Because the recording format keeps each individual user's input as a single record, there are many options for analysis. For the purposes of this chapter, we present one of the simplest, a simple tabulation that shows a breakdown by question of the number of users selecting each of the options. The tabulation classes are separated from the presentation servlet and could be used to create HTML pages offline.

The first problem we have to solve is converting all of the output files that the `Question-naireServ` servlet writes into a form suitable for analysis. Recall that the `Recorder` class simply writes `<Qresults>` tags that accumulate in the output file (or files). We need to create a file that has a root element. This file will essentially be a snapshot of the accumulated questionnaire results. To do this, the analysis program will take these steps:

1. Get the `org.w3c.dom.Document` object containing the survey script.

2. Locate the output-file names.

3. Create a new file for each by combining root elements with the current output-file contents.

The advantages of working with this snapshot of the survey results include the fact that users can continue to take the survey while we are working with analysis.

A Snapshot-File-Creating Class

Creating snapshot files is done by the `PrepQxml` class, as shown in Listing 7.24 and following listings. The constructor takes an XML `Document` object and locates the output-file attributes in the `Questionnaire` and `Terminal` tags. This class is used in the analysis servlet that we present later in this chapter, but it could also be part of other processes.

Listing 7.24: The *PrepQxml* Class Source Code (*PrepQxml.java*)

```
package com.XmlEcomBook.Chap07;

import com.XmlEcomBook.DOMlibrary ;
import org.w3c.dom.* ;
import com.sun.xml.tree.* ;
import java.io.*;
import java.util.* ;

public class PrepQxml
{
  public int state = 1 ;
  Document doc ;
  public String primaryfile ;
  public String title ;
  public String author ;
  public String date ;
  String[] files ;
  Vector allfiles = new Vector() ;
```

```
Hashtable prepHash = new Hashtable() ;

PrepQxml( Document d ){
  doc = d ;
  Element E = doc.getDocumentElement();
  primaryfile = E.getAttribute("file");
  allfiles.addElement( primaryfile );
  title = E.getAttribute("title");
  author = E.getAttribute("author");
  date = E.getAttribute("date");
  NodeList terminals = E.getElementsByTagName("Terminal");
  int ct = terminals.getLength();
  // this locates any output files created by <Terminal> tags
  for( int i = 0 ; i < ct ; i++ ){
    E = (Element)terminals.item(i);
    String tmp = E.getAttribute("file");
    if( tmp.length() > 0 ) allfiles.addElement( tmp );
  }
}
public String[] getFiles(){ return files ; }
```

For each output file from the survey, the `createFiles` method shown in Listing 7.25 calls `makeXML` to create a file that has beginning and ending `<QResultSet>` tags to create a root element. The name of this file is created by appending `"FMT"` to the name of the record file.

Listing 7.25: The *createFiles* and *makeXML* Methods (*PrepQxml.java*)

```
// for every file in allfiles, create a temporary with xml root
// return array of file path/names
public String[] createFiles() throws IOException {
  files = new String[ allfiles.size() ];
  int n = 0 ;
  Enumeration e = allfiles.elements();
  while( e.hasMoreElements() ){
    String tmp = (String)e.nextElement();
    files[n++] = tmp ;
    System.out.println("Create temporary for " + tmp );
    prepHash.put( tmp, makeXML( tmp ) );
  }
  return files ;
}
```

```java
// fn is the name of the answers file, return the name of
// the formatted file with root for creation of DOM
public String getAnsXml( String fn ){
  return (String) prepHash.get( fn );
}
// this creates a complete XML document by adding a root
// element to the Questionnaire output file contents
private String makeXML(String fn )throws IOException {
  File inf = new File( fn );
  BufferedReader read = new BufferedReader( new FileReader( inf ));
  int p = fn.lastIndexOf('.');
  String outFN = fn.substring( 0,p ) + "FMT" + fn.substring(p);
  File outf = new File( outFN );
  BufferedWriter bw = new BufferedWriter( new FileWriter( outf ), 4096);
  PrintWriter write = new PrintWriter( bw );
  write.println( "<?xml version=\"1.0\" standalone=\"yes\" ?>");
  write.println( "<!-- formatted Questionnaire results -->");
  write.println( "<QresultSet title=\"" + title + "\" >");
  String tmp = read.readLine();
  int ct = 1 ;
  while( tmp != null ){
      write.println( tmp );
      tmp = read.readLine();
  }
  read.close();
  write.println("</QresultSet>");
  write.close();
  System.out.println("Created " + outFN );
  return outFN ;
}

public String toString()
{ StringBuffer sb = new StringBuffer("PrepQxml title: ");
  sb.append( title ); sb.append(" author: ");
  sb.append( author ); sb.append(" date: " );
  sb.append( date ); sb.append(" primary output: ");
  sb.append( primaryfile ); sb.append(" other files: " );
  sb.append( "none");
  return sb.toString();
}
}
```

A Survey-Tabulating Class

The TallyQues class uses SAX-style processing to tabulate the response occurrences in a QResultSet document. SAX processing is the obvious choice because the amount of memory used is independent of the number of total responses in the data.

Listing 7.26 shows the import statements, class declaration, variables, and constructor for the TallyQues class. Note that we base the class on the HandlerBase class in the org.xml.sax package, because it provides default handlers as required by the SAX interfaces. All we have to do is override these handler methods for the events we find interesting.

The operation of TallyQues uses a Hashtable with an entry for each option that appears in the complete set of questions. The entries are instances of the inner class, Counter (Listing 7.30). The key for each entry is the Ques tag id attribute plus the Qopt tag val attribute.

We also keep a Vector named ordered (which holds question information in the order it is presented in the survey) and a Hashtable named qtext (which stores the question Qtext text strings, keyed by the Ques id attribute). The constructor uses the survey Document to create all of these objects.

Listing 7.26: The Start of the _TallyQues_ Source Code (_TallyQues.java_)

```
package com.XmlEcomBook.Chap07;

import java.io.* ;
import java.util.* ;
import org.w3c.dom.* ;
import org.xml.sax.* ;
import org.xml.sax.helpers.ParserFactory ;
import com.sun.xml.parser.Resolver ;

/* org.xml.sax.HandlerBase is a convenience class that
   extends java.lang.Object and implements the SAX interfaces
   implements EntityResolver, DTDHandler, DocumentHandler, ErrorHandler */
public class TallyQues extends HandlerBase
{
  static public String parserClass = "com.sun.xml.parser.Parser" ;
 static int counterTextLen = 40 ; // see Counter

  private Hashtable tally = new Hashtable();  // Counters keyed by unique
    // ordered has a Vector of Counters per question
```

```
private Vector ordered  = new Vector();
private Hashtable qtext = new Hashtable(); // <Qtext> by id

public String tableStyle = "align=\"center\" border=\"3\" " ;
public String lastErr = null ;
public int resultCt = 0 ;
String id ; // <Ques> attribute "id" as detected during parse

// constructor creates the vectors and hashtables to store results
// qd is the questionnaire source XML doc
public TallyQues( Document qd ){
  Element E = qd.getDocumentElement();
  NodeList qnl = E.getElementsByTagName("Ques");
  int ct = qnl.getLength();
  for( int i = 0; i < ct ; i++ ){
    Vector quesv = new Vector(); // for this <Ques>
    ordered.addElement( quesv );
    E = (Element)qnl.item(i);  // Element is a <Ques>
    NodeList txn = E.getElementsByTagName("Qtext");
    String tx = txn.item(0).getFirstChild().getNodeValue(); // question text
    String id = E.getAttribute( "id" );
    qtext.put( id, tx );
    quesv.addElement( id ); // first element of quesv is the id
    NodeList opt = E.getElementsByTagName("Qopt");
    int opct =opt.getLength();
    for( int n = 0 ; n < opct ; n++ ){
      Element opE = (Element) opt.item(n);
      String val = opE.getAttribute("val");
      String text = opE.getFirstChild().getNodeValue();
      Counter cntr = new Counter( id, val, text );
      quesv.addElement( cntr );
      tally.put( cntr.unique, cntr );
    }
  }
}
```

Processing the Survey Snapshot

Actual processing of the survey-results snapshot file is started by the `tallyAns` method, as shown in Listing 7.27, using the following steps:

1. Open the file as an `org.xml.sax.InputSource` object.

2. Create a parser as specified by the `parserClass String`. (We use the parser from the Sun package, but you can substitute any compliant parser.)

3. Attach the `TallyQues` object to the parser so that it will get the event method calls.

4. Call the `parse` method to start parsing.

If no error occurs, when the `parse` method returns, all the tabulating has been done. The `tallyAns` method returns `null` to indicate that an error has occurred or returns the `ordered` variable if all went well.

Listing 7.27: The *tallyAns* Method (*TallyQues.java*)

```
// srcdoc is complete path to a formatted answer set file
public Vector tallyAns(String srcdoc ){
  Parser parser ;
  InputSource input ;
  try {
    File f = new File( srcdoc );
    input = Resolver.createInputSource( f );
    parser = ParserFactory.makeParser( parserClass );
    parser.setDocumentHandler( this );
    System.out.println("Start parse");
    parser.parse( input );
  }catch(SAXParseException spe){
    StringBuffer sb = new StringBuffer( spe.toString() );
    sb.append("\n  Line number: " + spe.getLineNumber());
    sb.append("\nColumn number: " + spe.getColumnNumber() );
    sb.append("\n Public ID: " + spe.getPublicId() );
    sb.append("\n System ID: " + spe.getSystemId() + "\n");
    lastErr = sb.toString();
    ordered = null ;
  }catch(Exception e){
    lastErr = e.toString();
    ordered = null ;
  }
  return ordered ;
```

SAX Event Processing

Now let's look at the method that processes the SAX events, as shown in Listing 7.28. Out of all of the SAX interface methods, the only one we need to pay attention to is the `startElement` method. For every Ques tag, we get the value of the id attribute for use with the Qopt tags that follow in the question. For every Qopt, we create a String that combines the question id value with the option val value, and we use this as a key to get the matching Counter object from the tally Hashtable and to count the occurrence of this user selection.

Listing 7.28: The SAX Event Processing Methods (*TallyQues.java*)

```
// this is the SAX specified "callback" called when the
// parser detects an element
public void startElement( String name, AttributeList attrib)
      throws SAXException  {
  if( name.equals("Ques") ){
      id = attrib.getValue("id");
  }
  else {
    if( name.equals("Qopt") ){
      String unique = id + ":" + attrib.getValue("val");
      Counter cntr = (Counter)tally.get( unique );
      if( cntr != null ) cntr.countIt();
    }
    else {
      if( name.equals("Qresults"))resultCt++ ;
    }
  }
}
```

To recap the collections that the TallyQues class creates, the Vector named ordered has one element for each question in the order of the original XML script. This element is itself a Vector that contains the question id (a String), followed by a Counter object for each of the question options. In the Hashtable named qtext, we have the text for each question keyed by the question id.

Creating the Formatted Tally

Keeping these collections in mind, you can see how the formatTally method shown in Listing 7.29 outputs an HTML table for each question using the original order. Figure 7.2 shows one of these tables from a questionnaire we recently ran at a Web site related to the Java programmer certification exam.

FIGURE 7.2
A browser display of a table
output by formatTally

FIGURE 7.2
A browser display of a table
output by formatTally

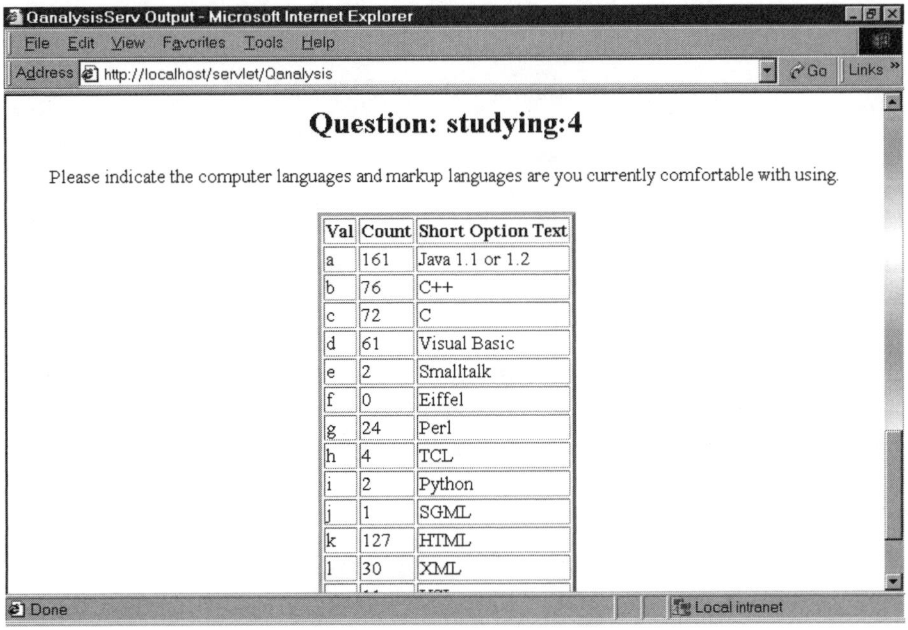

Listing 7.29: The *formatTally* Method Creates HTML Output (*TallyQues.java*)

```java
// assumes that tallyAns was just run
public void formatTally(PrintWriter out ){
  out.println("<center><h2>" + ordered.size() + " Questions "
    + resultCt + " Responses</h2></center>");
  Enumeration e = ordered.elements();
  while( e.hasMoreElements() ){
    Vector v = (Vector) e.nextElement();
    String id = (String)v.firstElement();
    out.println("<center><h2>Question: " + id + "</h2>");
    out.println("<p>" + qtext.get(id) + "</p>" ) ;
    out.println("<table cols=\"3\"" + tableStyle + " >");
    out.print("<tr>");
    out.print("<th>Val</th><th>Count</th><th>Short Option Text</th>");
    out.println("</tr>");
    for( int i = 1 ; i < v.size(); i++ ){
      Counter c = (Counter) v.elementAt(i);
      out.print("<tr><td>" + c.val + "</td>");
```

```
            out.print("<td>" + c.count + "</td>" );
            out.println("<td>" + c.text + "</td></tr>");
        }
        out.println("</table></center><br><hr>");
    }
}


public String toString()
{ StringBuffer sb = new StringBuffer("TallyQues ");
  return sb.toString() ;
}
```

The remaining component of the TallyQues class is the inner class named Counter. As shown in Listing 7.30, a Counter object is created with the question id, option val, and option text. The text is limited in length to keep the table compact, but you could easily remove this limitation.

Listing 7.30: The *Counter* Inner Class (*TallyQues.java*)

```
// counter objects represent a single question/option combo
class Counter {
    public String val ;
    public String unique ; // <Ques id plus ":" plus <Qopt val
    public String text ; // the first counterTextLen chars
    public int count = 0 ;

    Counter( String id, String v, String tx ){
        val = v ;
        unique = id + ":" + val ;
        if( tx.length() > counterTextLen ) {
            text = tx.substring(0, counterTextLen);
        }
        else { text = tx ;
        }
    }
    public void countIt(){ count++ ; }

    public String toString(){
        return "ID: " + unique + " " + count + " " + text ;
    }
  }
}
```

The PrepQxml and TallyQues classes discussed in the preceding sections can be used in a variety of ways to create HTML-formatted tabulations. For this chapter, however, we use a servlet described in the next section.

A Reporting-Servlet Example

This section's servlet, QanalysisServ, allows online access to a snapshot of ongoing survey results; this can be called a *reporting servlet*. It uses the questionnaire.properties file to locate all surveys currently being conducted and lets you choose one. It then determines the output files this survey generates and lets you choose one of them for report generation.

Listing 7.31 shows the start of the servlet code with the import statements, variables, and init method.

Listing 7.31: The *QanalysisServ* Servlet (*QanalysisServ.java*)

```java
package com.XmlEcomBook.Chap07;

import com.XmlEcomBook.DOMlibrary ;
import org.w3c.dom.* ;
import com.sun.xml.tree.* ;
import java.io.*;
import java.util.* ;
import javax.servlet.*;
import javax.servlet.http.*;

public class QanalysisServ extends HttpServlet
{
  static String brcrlf = "<br>\r\n" ;
  static String homedir = "e:\\scripts\\questionnaire" ;
  static String handler = "http://www.lanw.com/servlet/Qanalysis" ;
  static String passwd = "lovexml" ;
  static String version = "v1.0 May 28";
  Properties qProp ;

  // note we share properties file with QuestionnaireServ
  public void init(ServletConfig config) throws ServletException
  {
    super.init(config);
    System.out.println("Start QanalysisServ ");
    homedir = config.getInitParameter("homedir") ;
```

```
File f = new File( homedir, "questionnaire.properties");
try { qProp = new Properties();
  qProp.load( new FileInputStream(f) );
  String tmp = qProp.getProperty("analysis");
  if( tmp != null ) handler = tmp ;
  System.out.println("Loaded properties for Qanalysis: "
         + handler );
}catch(IOException e){
    System.out.println("QanalysisServ Error loading " + e );
}
}
```

Initial entry to the servlet is through the **doGet** method, as shown in Listing 7.32. This would typically be done through a form that requires a user password, just to reduce the chance of a casual user accidentally accessing the servlet. Assuming all goes well, the method generates a page with a form providing for selection among all available surveys. The selected file is passed to the **doPost** method.

Listing 7.32: The *doGet* Method of the *QanalysisServ* Class (*QanalysisServ.java*)

```
// entry with password
public void doGet(HttpServletRequest req, HttpServletResponse resp)
throws ServletException, IOException
{ System.out.println("Qanalysis doGet");
  resp.setContentType("text/html");
  PrintWriter out = new PrintWriter(resp.getOutputStream());
  String user = req.getParameter("username");
  String tmp = req.getParameter("userpw");
  // Obviously this could be a lot more complex
  if( !passwd.equals( tmp )){
      errorMsg( out, "404 page not found", null );
      return ;
  }
  if( qProp == null ||
      qProp.size() == 0 ){
      errorMsg( out, "Bad Initialization", null ); return ;
  }
  HttpSession session = req.getSession( true );
  // session.putValue( "username", user );
  // with older servlet engines you will have to use putValue
```

```
        session.setAttribute( "username", user );
//
    Enumeration e = qProp.keys();
    Vector v = new Vector();
    while( e.hasMoreElements()){
      String key = (String)e.nextElement();
      // everything not "handler" or "analysis" is a XML file path name
      if( !( key.equals("handler") || key.equals("analysis"))){
        v.addElement( key );
      }
    }
    if( v.size() == 0 ){
        errorMsg( out, "No Questionnaire files found", null );
        return ;
    }
    out.println("<HTML>");
    out.println("<HEAD><TITLE>QanalysisServ Output</TITLE></HEAD>");
    out.println("<BODY>");
    out.println("<h2>Select The Questionnaire XML File</h2>");
    out.println("Found " + v.size() + " XML files" + brcrlf );
    out.println("<form method=\"POST\"" +
     "action=\"http://localhost/servlet/Qanalysis\" >");
    out.println("<select name=\"source\" >");
    for( int i = 0 ; i < v.size() ; i++){
      tmp = (String) v.elementAt( i );
      out.println("<option value=\"" + tmp + "\" >" + tmp );
    }
    out.println("</select>");
    out.println("<input type=\"hidden\" name=\"username\" value=\""
        + user + "\"><br>" );
    out.println("<input type=\"hidden\" name=\"action\" " +
        "value=\"select\" ><br>");
    out.println("<input type=\"submit\" value=\"Start\" ><br>" );
    out.println("</form>");
    footer( out );
  }
```

The first POST submission will have the value "select" for the `action` variable. As shown in Listing 7.33, this causes output of a selection form with all of the possible results files using the `createQList` method.

Listing 7.33: The First Part of the *doPost* Method (*QanalysisServ.java*)

```
public void doPost(HttpServletRequest req, HttpServletResponse resp)
throws ServletException, IOException
{
  resp.setContentType("text/html");
  PrintWriter out = new PrintWriter(resp.getOutputStream());
  String source = req.getParameter( "source");
  String action = req.getParameter( "action");
  String ansfile = req.getParameter("ansfile");
  // select when choosing questionnaire XML file
  // analyze when choosing reformatted result file
  String[] files = null ;
  if( action == null ||
      source == null || source.length() == 0 ){
      errorMsg(out,"Bad source selection", null );return ;
  } // source is short name from properties
  String srcfile = qProp.getProperty( source );
  if( srcfile == null ) {
      errorMsg( out, "Bad Source lookup", null ); return ;
  }
  HttpSession session = req.getSession(false);
  try {
    if( session == null ){ errorMsg(out, "No Session ", null );
      return ;
    }
    DOMlibrary lib = DOMlibrary.getLibrary();
    System.out.println("DOMlibrary ok, try for " + srcfile );
    Document doc = lib.getDOM( srcfile );
    if( doc == null ){
      errorMsg( out, "DOM doc failed - unable to continue", null );
      return ;
    }
    //PrepQxml pQ = (PrepQxml)session.getValue("prepqxml");
    // you will have to use getValue with older servlet engines
    PrepQxml pQ = (PrepQxml)session.getAttribute("prepqxml");
    header( out );
    if( pQ == null ){  // first pass
      pQ = new PrepQxml( doc );
      files = pQ.createFiles();
```

```
        // session.putValue("prepqxml",pQ);
        session.setAttribute("prepqxml",pQ);
    }
    else {
      files = pQ.getFiles();
    }
    if( action.equals("select") ){
      out.println("<h1>Test: " + pQ.title +"</h1>" );
      out.println("<p>XML questionnaire file: <i>" + source + "</i></p>");
      out.println("<p>Author: " + pQ.author + " Dated: "
        + pQ.date + "</p>");
      out.println("<p>The primary answer file is: " +
         pQ.primaryfile + "</p>" );
      out.println("<p>There " );
      if( files.length < 2 ) out.println("are no other ");
      if( files.length == 2 ) out.println("is one other ");
      if( files.length > 2 ) out.println( (files.length - 1) + " other ");
      out.println(
         "answer file(s). Select a file and click <b>Start</b></p>");
      createQList( out, source, files );
    }
```

When the user selects one of the answer files, the value of the `action` variable will be `"analyze"`. As shown in Listing 7.34, this action causes the creation of a new `TallyQues` object that is used to create formatted output.

Listing 7.34: The *doPost* Method, Continued (*QanalysisServ.java*)

```
    if( action.equals("analyze") ){
      out.println("<h1>Analysis</h1>");
      out.println("<p>XML questionnaire file: <i>" + source + "</i></p>");
      String ansXml = pQ.getAnsXml( ansfile );
      out.println("<p>Answer file: " + ansfile + "</p>");
      out.println("<p>Processing file: " + ansXml + "</p>");
      TallyQues tQ = new TallyQues( doc ); // build with questions
      if( tQ.tallyAns( ansXml )== null ){
        out.println("<h2>Error " + tQ.lastErr + "</h2>") ;
      }
      else {
        tQ.formatTally( out );
      }
```

```
        }
        footer( out );
    }catch( Exception ex ){
        errorMsg( out, "QanalysisServ.doPost ", ex );
    }
}
```

The `createQList` method, as shown in Listing 7.35, creates the HTML form used to present the possible answer files.

Listing 7.35: The *createQList* Method (*QanalysisServ.java*)

```
// the PrepQxml has located all of the answer files - only one
// can be analyzed at at time
void createQList( PrintWriter out, String source, String[] files ){
    out.println( "<form method=\"POST\"" +
        "action=\"http://localhost/servlet/Qanalysis\" >");
    out.println("<input type=\"hidden\" name=\"action\"" +
        "value=\"analyze\" ><br>");
    out.println("<input type=\"hidden\" name=\"source\" value=\""
        + source + "\" ><br>");
    out.println("<select name=\"ansfile\" >");
    for( int i = 0 ; i < files.length ; i++){
        String tmp = files[i];
        out.println("<option value=\"" + tmp + "\" >" + tmp );
    }
    out.println("</select>");
    out.println("<input type=\"submit\" value=\"Start\" ><br>" );
    out.println("</form><br>");
}
```

We are almost at the end of the `QanalysisServ` class! Listing 7.36 shows some utility methods required to format the output pages or report errors.

Listing 7.36: Utility Methods in the *QanalysisServ* Class (*QanalysisServ.java*)

```
public void header( PrintWriter out ){
    out.println("<HTML>");
    out.println("<HEAD><TITLE>QanalysisServ Output</TITLE></HEAD>");
    out.println("<BODY>");
}
```

```
   public void footer( PrintWriter out ){
     out.println("<hr>" + version + "<br>");
     out.println("</BODY>");
     out.println("</HTML>");
     out.close();
   }
// assumes response has been set to text/html
   private void errorMsg( PrintWriter out, String msg, Exception ex ){
     out.println("<html>");
     out.println("<head><title>QanalysisServ Output</title></head>");
     out.println("<body>");
     out.println("<h2>" ); out.println( msg );
     out.println("</h2><br>");
     if( ex != null ){
        ex.printStackTrace( out );
     }
     out.println("<br>");
     footer( out );
   }
}
```

XML Document Library Utility

An alternate approach to having each servlet manage its own XML document storage is to use a library utility. That way, the servlet just requests the document from the library and does not have to know where the XML file lives on the disk or whether it is already in memory due to a request in some other transaction.

The DOMlibrary class we have created has the following characteristics:

- It uses the *Singleton* design pattern to ensure that only one instance is created. In this pattern there is no public constructor, instead, a static method controls creation of and access to a single instance of a class.

- When XML documents are requested, the DOMlibrary instance checks the timestamp on the document file to ensure that it never serves up an out-of-date document.

- It implements the Runnable interface so that it can have a Thread that periodically performs maintenance tasks. A typical task is discarding Document objects that have not been used recently. This way, documents that tend to be used a lot will generally be found in memory, while infrequently used documents will not waste memory capacity.

An alternative to using the Singleton approach would be to implement everything in static methods. However, using the Singleton pattern, we gain considerable flexibility, including the ability to implement `Runnable` and to use the `run` method to manage the life cycle of documents in memory. The Singleton design pattern is used in a number of places in the standard Java library.

Listing 7.37 shows the static method, `getLibrary`, which creates a new `DOMlibrary` object if necessary. All servlets needing access to an XML document call `getLibrary` to get a reference to the single library instance, and then they use that reference to request a document. The variable `maxAge` is used in the run method to determine when a document should be discarded.

Listing 7.37: The *DOMlibrary* Class Import Statements and Static Method (*DOMlibrary.java*)

```
package com.XmlEcomBook;

import java.io.* ;
import java.util.* ;
import com.sun.xml.tree.* ;
import com.sun.xml.parser.Resolver ;
import org.xml.sax.* ;
import org.w3c.dom.* ;

public class DOMlibrary implements  Runnable {
  private static DOMlibrary theLib ;
  private static int maxAge = 6000 ; // age in seconds
  public synchronized static DOMlibrary getLibrary(){
    if( theLib == null ) theLib = new DOMlibrary();
    return theLib ;
  }
  public static void setMaxAge(int t) { maxAge = t ;}
```

As shown in Listing 7.38, the only constructor is private to ensure that only the static `getLibrary` method can create a new object. Resident XML document objects are stored in the `domHash Hashtable`, using the complete file path as a key. The `Hashtable` named `trackerHash` keeps a `DomTracker` object for each XML document object, using the same key. The `DomTracker` class is an inner class in `DOMlibrary`; the code is shown in Listing 7.43. Note that the `Thread` that executes the `run` method is given the lowest possible priority.

Listing 7.38: **Listing 7.38: The *DOMlibrary* Constructor and Instance Variables (*DOMlibrary.java*)**

```
private Hashtable domHash, trackerHash ;
boolean running ;
private String lastErr = "none" ;

  // private constructor to ensure singleton
private DOMlibrary(){
  domHash = new Hashtable();
  trackerHash = new Hashtable();
  Thread upkeep = new Thread(this,"DOMlibrary upkeep");
  upkeep.setPriority( Thread.MIN_PRIORITY );
  running = true ;
  upkeep.start();
}
```

Parsing an XML document in DOMlibrary is done in the loadXML method, as shown in Listing 7.39. In order to avoid repeated attempts to load a document with an incorrect src path, or a document that causes a parse error on loading, this method puts a String containing an error report in the domHash table if any error is encountered. If document parsing succeeds, a matching DomTracker object is saved in the trackerHash table. This is the only method in which parser-specific methods are called; if you were using something besides the Sun parser, some modification of this method would be required.

Listing 7.39: The *loadXML* Method Handles Parsing (*DOMlibrary.java*)

```
private synchronized void loadXML(File xmlFile, String src ) {
    //File xmlFile = new File( src ) ;
    try {
      long timestamp = xmlFile.lastModified();
      InputSource input = Resolver.createInputSource( xmlFile );
// ... the "false" flag says not to validate
// XmlDocument is in the com.sun.xml.tree package
      Document doc = XmlDocument.createXmlDocument (input, false);
      domHash.put( src, doc );
      trackerHash.put( src, new DomTracker( timestamp ) );
    }catch(SAXParseException spe ){
        StringBuffer sb = new StringBuffer( spe.toString() );
        sb.append("\n  Line number: " + spe.getLineNumber());
        sb.append("\nColumn number: " + spe.getColumnNumber() );
        sb.append("\n Public ID: " + spe.getPublicId() );
```

```
            sb.append("\n System ID: " + spe.getSystemId() + "\n");
            lastErr = sb.toString();
            System.out.print( lastErr );
        }catch( SAXException se ){
            lastErr = se.toString();
            System.out.println("loadXML threw " + lastErr );
            domHash.put( src, lastErr );
            se.printStackTrace( System.out );
        }catch( IOException ie ){
            lastErr = ie.toString();
            System.out.println("loadXML threw " + lastErr +
                " trying to read " + src );
            domHash.put( src, lastErr );
        }
    } // end loadXML
```

Servlets call the `getDOM` method, shown in Listing 7.40, when a document is needed. Any problem with creating the document causes a `null` to be returned instead of the document reference. Every time a document is found in the `Hashtable`, the associated `DomTracker` object is updated with the current time. Note that there are several places where a message is written to `System.out` for debugging purposes. We suggest you comment these out after you get your system running.

Listing 7.40: The *getDOM* Method (*DOMlibrary.java*)

```
    // either return the doc or null if a problem
    public synchronized Document getDOM( String src ){
        Object doc = domHash.get( src );
        DomTracker dt = (DomTracker) trackerHash.get( src );
        boolean newflag = false ;
        File f = null ;
        if( doc == null ){
            System.out.println("DOMlibrary.getDOM new " + src );
            f = new File( src );
            loadXML( f, src ); // sets trackerHash
            doc = domHash.get( src );
            dt = (DomTracker) trackerHash.get( src );
            newflag = true ;
            System.out.println("DOMlibrary load OK");
        }
        else { // found a document - is it up to date?
```

```
    f = new File( src );
    if( dt.changed( f )){
      System.out.println("DOMlibrary reloads " + src );
      loadXML( f, src ); // sets trackerHash
      newflag = true ;
      doc = domHash.get( src );
      dt = (DomTracker)trackerHash.get( src );
    }
  }
  // if not a document, must be a string due to error
  if( ! (doc instanceof Document )){
      System.out.println("DOMlibrary: " + doc );
      // could try for re-read here
  }
  if( doc instanceof Document ) {
    if( ! newflag ){
      dt = (DomTracker)trackerHash.get( src );
      dt.setLastUse( System.currentTimeMillis());
    }
    return (Document) doc ;
  }
  return null ;
}
```

Listing 7.41 presents a couple of utility methods that remove or force a reload of a document.

Listing 7.41: Some Utility Methods (*DOMlibrary.java*)

```
// use this to force removal of a dom. it
// returns last copy of dom or null if dom not in hash
public Document removeDOM( String src ){
  Document dom = (Document)domHash.get( src );
  if( dom != null ){
    domHash.remove( src );
    trackerHash.remove( src );
  }
  return dom ;
}

// call this to force a reload after src is modified
public Document reloadDOM( String src ){
```

```
    if( domHash.get( src ) != null ){
      domHash.remove( src );
      trackerHash.remove( src );
    }
    return getDOM( src );
  }
```

The reason for making the DOMlibrary class implement the Runnable interface is so we can have a background Thread that runs at a low priority and can do upkeep chores. The example provided in Listing 7.42 is pretty simpleminded: It just removes any document that has not been recently used. Listing 7.42 also shows the utility methods toString and getLastErr.

Listing 7.42: The *run* Method and More Utilities (*DOMlibrary.java*)

```java
// run is used for upkeep, not reading XML
public void run()
{ while( running ){
    try{ Thread.sleep( 60000 );
           // example management code
      Enumeration keys = trackerHash.keys();
      long time = System.currentTimeMillis();
      while( keys.hasMoreElements() ){
          String key = (String) keys.nextElement();
        if(((DomTracker)trackerHash.get(key)).getAge(time) > maxAge ){
            removeDOM( key );
        }
      }
    }catch(InterruptedException e){
    }
  }// end while
}

public String getLastErr(){ return lastErr ; }

public String toString()
{ StringBuffer sb = new StringBuffer("DOMlibrary contains ");
  int ct = domHash.size();
  if( ct > 0 ){
      sb.append(Integer.toString( ct ) );
      sb.append( " DOM objects ");
      Enumeration e = domHash.keys();
```

```
        while( e.hasMoreElements() ){
          String key = (String)e.nextElement();
          sb.append( key );
          sb.append("  " );
        }
    }
    else { sb.append("no DOM objects");
    }
    sb.append(" Last error: " );
    sb.append( lastErr );
    return sb.toString();
}
```

An instance of the inner class DomTracker is created every time an XML document is loaded. This instance is managed in parallel with the document object. In the present version, it records two things of interest: the timestamp on the XML file that created the document object and the timestamp of the last request for the document. As shown in Listing 7.43, the getAge method returns the number of seconds since the last use, and the changed method checks the timestamp on the source file.

Listing 7.43: The *DomTracker* Definition As a Member of *DOMlibrary* (*DOMlibrary.java*)

```
// utility class to aid in tracking memory resident DOM
class DomTracker {
  private long lastMod ;
  private long lastUse ;
  DomTracker( long timestamp ){
     lastMod = timestamp ; // from File.lastModified();
     lastUse = System.currentTimeMillis();
  }

  void setLastUse( long ts ){ lastUse = ts ; }
  int getAge( long now ){ // return value in seconds
    return (int)(( now - lastUse)/ 1000) ;
  }

  boolean changed( File f ){
    long n = f.lastModified();
    return !( n == lastMod );
  }
} // end DomTracker class
} // end DOMlibrary class
```

With the tools described in this chapter, you have a flexible system for gathering information from your current customers and potential customers. Because it uses an XML-driven script that can be changed without restarting the server, you can modify the way you track your customer's interest and opinions on the fly.

CHAPTER 8

And Now for the News

- Company news items to attract site visitors

- Design criteria for an XML-based news system

- Flexible presentation by servlet

- Presentation by JavaServer Pages technology

- A simple system for adding news items

Have you ever visited Web sites of small organizations where their most recent news bulletin was six months old? These enterprises are missing a great opportunity for grabbing the attention of the casual visitor. It may be that the people doing the newsworthy things are not communicating with their respective Webmasters, or maybe it is just too darn much trouble to edit those pages again. Naturally, we have an XML solution in mind, which we detail in this chapter.

Designing a News System

We want users who visit our Web site to see the latest company news in a compact and easy to scan format. Remember, you only have a few seconds to entice the typical Web surfer to stick around. We want it to be obvious to the user how to find out more information about an item, and then hopefully enter the catalog system to purchase something.

Consider a news system's desired characteristics and your list will likely include the following:

- Flexibility of output
- Ease of data entry
- Minimum server load

Along with accounting for these characteristics, your primary design decisions are to select the XML elements and attributes to represent the data first, to choose between the SAX and DOM styles of Java processing (the mechanisms for displaying the data to users) next, and to then determine the mechanism for adding new news items.

Flexibility of Output

Because we have already decided to use XML for the primary storage medium, the way to ensure output flexibility is by storing all the data required for the different output formats. Looking around at various commercial Web sites, you see that company news is typically presented to the user in the following three different lengths:

- Headlines linked to the full story
- Short teasers linked to the full story
- Complete news releases

Other news formats include e-mail newsletters, hard copy newsletters, and corporate reports. The three different lengths (headline, short, and full length) appear to be suitable for these other formats, too. Our first design task is to come up with an XML format that will support all of these formats.

News Text Elements

Although artificial intelligence and computer understanding of language have made great progress, nobody expects a computer to write a great headline by scanning a story, so you have to conclude that news items will need separate headline text created by a human for each presentation length. News items also usually have a date attached that can be a simple date or a dateline, such as "Austin, TX, 1 Jan 2000" that will have to be generated by a human.

Some news items are greatly enhanced by graphics, sound clips, or off-site links , so consider how the XML format might be designed to accommodate various additional enhancements. For our example in this chapter, we concluded that designing in all possible embellishments would just be too complicated and restrictive. So we decided to store the text for the short and full-length news stories using the XML <[[CDATA ..]]> tag.

Because XML parsers do not attempt to parse text inside a CDATA section, you can store any kind of HTML markup inside the CDATA section without confusing the XML parser.

The elements for holding the date, the headline, and the short and full-length text are illustrated in Listing 8.1.

Listing 8.1: A News Item, Date, and Three Sizes of Text (*thenews.xml*)

```
<date>Austin, TX, Jun 14 2000</date>
<head>Best Seller at a Great Price</head>
<short><![CDATA[Due to a special deal with the publisher, we can now
offer <i>Dryer Lint Art</i> at 50% off the retail price.]]></short>
<long><![CDATA[This books starts with simple Dryer Lint projects
suitable for the novice and advances through easy stages to the
(literally) <b>monumental</b> recreation of famous monuments in that
most flexible of craft materials, dryer lint. Even though you may
never attempt major constructions like the Statue of Liberty project
documented in the final chapter, your projects will benefit by a study
of this famous creation. Includes UML diagrams.]]></long>
```

Another aspect of flexibility is the capability to selectively present news items according to topic. Given the wide variety of expected interests of visitors to XMLGifts.com, we want to show each customer the news affecting his or her favorite topic in the spot where they are most likely to look. There is bound to be overlap; for example, a book about a musical group would be of interest to both book purchasers and CD purchasers. Therefore, each news item should be tagged with one or more topic categories, and presentation should allow for selecting topics.

We could tag an item with topic information using either an attribute or an element. Following the suggestions discussed in the "Elements versus Attributes" section of Chapter 2, it appears that topic information is best stored as an attribute because it is data about content and we expect to restrict the number of topic terms.

News Item Age Representation

The most current news should always be presented first. Because an XML document automatically preserves the order of items, new items must go to the start of the document. Furthermore, it's a good idea to allow the presentation software to select only the most recent items. Therefore, we need a representation of the age of a news item.

After dithering over the many different ways to represent a date so that we can select for recent items, we ended up using a simple integer representing the days since Java's basic timekeeping start. The `long` value returned by `System.currentTimeMillis()` is divided by the number of milliseconds per day to get a `timestamp` attribute value stored in the `Newsitem` tag. Alternatives using the Java `Date DateFormat` or `Calendar` classes were rejected because lots of object creation would be involved and we want the news function to have a low load on the server.

News Item Management Information

Because you or your employees will update the news file online, it seems to be a good idea to keep track of who has created a particular item. For instance, you need to know who to blame for a particular error. This is accomplished with an `author` attribute in the `<Newsitem>` element. The news updating servlet discussed in the "Adding The Latest News" section of this chapter has a simple access control mechanism using an author name and password; it is this author name that becomes the `author` attribute.

To create HTML markup in which headline text is linked to the full-length text of a news item, there must be a unique identifier. For our example, we have taken the simplest approach: a serial number that is attached as the `id` attribute to each `<Newsitem>` as it is added.

The Document Root

We keep track of some parameters used in the entire file in attributes in the document root element, `Newsfile`. The next `id` attribute is simply `nextid`. It is the responsibility of the item-adding software or, in the case of offline editing, the Newsitem author to update the nextid attribute.

The root element is also a good place to store attributes related to various display default values. The present example only uses one, called longtemplate, which names an HTML template file as a default value used to format news items.

Listing 8.2 shows an example of all of the XML tags in use.

Listing 8.2: The *<Newsfile>* Element and One *<Newsitem>* (*thenews.xml*)

```
<?xml version="1.0" standalone="yes" ?>
<!-- output by NewsUpkeep -->
<Newsfile longtemplate="tmlong.html" nextid="1010"  >
<Newsitem timestamp="11045" topic="CDs" author="wbrogden" id="1008" >
<head>Your Favorite Music Now Available</head>
<date>Austin, Feb 1, 2000</date>
<short><![CDATA[XMLGifts proudly announces the availability of the CD
 that has all the geeks singing, <i>It's Dot Com Enough for
Me.</i>]]></short>
<long><![CDATA[<p><i>It's Dot Com Enough For Me.</i> now in stock!</p>
<p>All those great songs created during breaks in all-night coding
sessions - now recorded by top Silicon Valley garage bands on our
private label. <i>It's Dot Com Enough for Me</i> will have you singing
along - or maybe laughing till the Jolt cola spurts out your nose.
Seventeen songs from geeks at Sun, Microsoft, Apple, Cisco, and other
top tech outfits. </p>]]></long>
</Newsitem>
</Newsfile>
```

Ease of Data Entry

Because we have opted to use a simple news format as seen in Listing 8.2, data entry can also be very simple. The HTML form- and servlet-based system described in the upcoming "Adding the Latest News" section allows updating with new items over the Internet.

However, making it so easy to enter news items does nothing to control the quality of the writing. To get the best results, management must ensure that both the topics used to classify news items and the styles of writing remain consistent. Management should create guidelines and ensure that they are available to all employees authorized to post news items.

Minimum Server Load

Because we hope to have a lot of traffic on this Web site, we want to make the display of the main pages as simple as possible. We want a page that loads quickly and does not take a lot of server processor power to generate. Consider the following alternatives for displaying news items:

Static News Pages   Static pages are fast to serve, and the main pages can be rebuilt from XML sources every time a change is made, but that prevents a custom appearance to each returning customer.

Servlet-Generated News Pages   Everything can be generated with Java servlets, presumably making use of HTML template files to control many aspects of the site appearance.

JavaServer Pages (JSP)   The advantage of JSP over servlets is that the Web designer does not need to know how to program Java to change the appearance.

The choices to be made in selecting Java processing methods include choosing between SAX and DOM models and validating versus non-validating parsers. The SAX approach would require running a parser for every news-page access. The DOM approach gives rapid access at the expense of keeping the data in memory. Given that the number of news items will probably be in the hundreds, the memory used by keeping a DOM in memory will not have a significant impact on total memory resources, so DOM is the obvious choice.

We can't see any reason to use a validating parser in the online functions. Because we use automated methods to create new entries, there is little chance for a formatting error. Besides, showing the user an error page with validation errors would cause nothing but confusion.

The News System

The final design for the news system is summarized in the block diagram shown in Figure 8.1. Data flow that takes place on the server is shown on the right, whereas offline processing is on the left side of the diagram. The master XML news file can be updated online or offline, but for normal operation, online is preferred because it automatically maintains the `id` and `timestamp` attributes.

The Document Object Model in memory is maintained by the `DOMlibrary` class that was described in Chapter 7, "Using Surveys to Know Your Customer." Online updating of the master XML file is accomplished by the `CompanyNewsServ` servlet and `NewsUpkeep` classes, which are discussed later in this chapter. The formatting of news items into Web-page output by servlets or JavaServer Pages (JSP) depends on the `NewsFormatter` class, which is discussed in the next section. Other types of formatting for newsletters and print formats should be easy to write, based on the following examples.

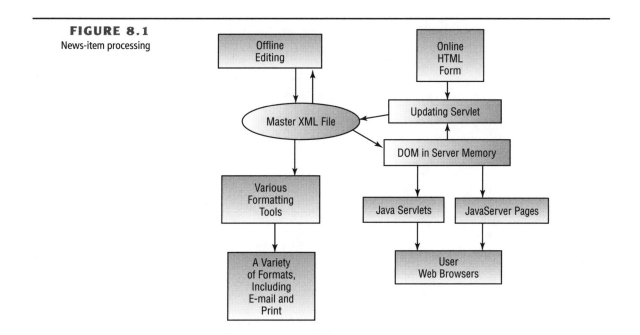

FIGURE 8.1
News-item processing

Web Page Presentation

Before we dive into the code needed for our news system, let's look at an example of the final product. Figure 8.2 shows the framework of a page for news presentation in the context of a larger site. We have left out the various site navigation tools and other content that a real site would use.

JSP, making use of the `NewsFormatter` class, which is detailed in the following section, generated this Web-browser display from an XML news file. On the left side of the screen, headlines summarize the most recent news items in all topics. The full news item for the most recent news in the CDs topic appears in the center. And short-format news items in the CDs topic are listed on the right but skip the item that is displayed in full. The headlines and short-format items can be clicked to display the associated full-length news item.

FIGURE 8.2
A news-item Web page
generated with JSP

FIGURE 8.2
A news-item Web page
generated with JSP

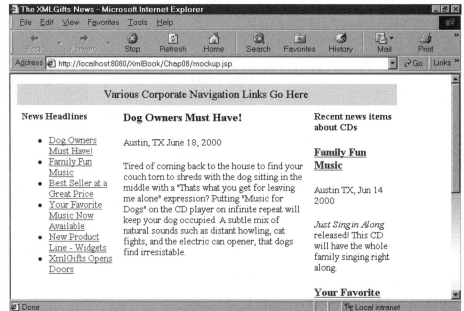

The *NewsFormatter* Class

The key Java class for presentation is the NewsFormatter class. As shown in Listing 8.3 and following listings, a NewsFormatter is created with a File object that points to an XML file. The NewsFormatter class uses the DOMlibrary class that was described in Chapter 7 to get a Document object that holds all the data in a news-item file. The constructor gets a NodeList containing all of the Newsitem nodes and uses this to create an array called itemNodes. This array is used by the various formatting methods.

Listing 8.3: The Start of the *NewsFormatter* Class (*NewsFormatter.java*)

```
package com.XmlEcomBook.Chap08;

import com.XmlEcomBook.DOMlibrary ;
import java.io.*;
import java.util.* ;
import javax.servlet.*;
```

```java
import javax.servlet.http.*;
import org.w3c.dom.* ;

public class NewsFormatter
{
  static String handler ; // the servlet for single item presentation
  public static void setHandler(String s){handler=s; }

    // instance variables
  File newsFile ;
  String newsFileName ;
  String newsFilePath ;
  String headStr, footStr ;

  Node[] itemNodes ;
  Element docRoot ;
  Hashtable nodeHash ; // <Newsitem Elements keyed by tag name

  int maxNitems, skipNitems;
  int itemsCount = 0 ;

  public NewsFormatter( File f ) throws IOException {
    newsFile = f ;
    newsFileName = f.getAbsolutePath() ;
    int p = newsFileName.lastIndexOf( File.separatorChar );
    if( p > 0 ){ newsFilePath = newsFileName.substring(0,p);
    }
    else { System.out.println("NewsFormatter path problem");
    }
    DOMlibrary library = DOMlibrary.getLibrary();
    Document doc = library.getDOM( newsFileName );
    if( doc == null ){
        throw new FileNotFoundException( newsFileName );
    }
    docRoot = doc.getDocumentElement();
    NodeList newsItemNodes = doc.getElementsByTagName("Newsitem");
    int ct = newsItemNodes.getLength();
    itemNodes = new Node[ ct ];
    for( int i = 0 ; i < ct ; i++ ){
      itemNodes[i] = newsItemNodes.item( i );
    }
  }
```

You will recall from Chapter 7 that the DOMlibrary class reloads an XML file when the timestamp has changed. Because the Document object is not changed by the operation of NewsFormatter, it can be shared by any number of servlets and access to it doesn't have to be synchronized.

There are two versions of the doNews method. The version in Listing 8.4 is used to output multiple news items in headline, short, and long formats. It provides the capability of selecting items by topic and age, and it also can control skipping over items and limiting the total number of items displayed. The hs and fs strings are optional inputs that provide limited additional formatting capabilities.

The doNews method checks for the input of topic- or age-limiting String parameters. If a topstr parameter is not null and not empty, the selectNodes method is called to reduce the full list of news items to those matching the specified topics. Similarly, if an age string is specified, the limitAge method is called. If either call reduces the list of qualifying items to zero, the doNews method exits immediately. Other parameters control the maximum number of items to show and the relative item number to start showing.

Listing 8.4: The *doNews* Method Selects the Output Method Used (*NewsFormatter.java*)

```
// hs and fs are head and foot used in short and long display
// you can also specify templates in the <Newsfile element
// PrintWriter, hs, fs, topics, H,S or L, age, mx#
// skpN is used to skip the first N items that qualify
// presumably printed elsewhere on the page, use 0 to see all
// returns number of news items printed
  public int doNews( PrintWriter out, String hs, String fs,
      String topstr, String sz, String age, int skpN, int mxN ){
    headStr = hs ; footStr = fs ;
    skipNitems = skpN ; maxNitems = mxN ;
    itemsCount = 0 ;
    if( topstr != null && topstr.length() > 0 ){
       if( selectNodes(topstr, out )== 0 ) return 0 ;
    }
    if( age != null && age.length() > 0 ){
       if( limitAge( age, out ) == 0 ) return 0 ;
    }
    char szch ;
    if( sz == null || sz.length() == 0 ) szch = 'L' ; // default to long form
```

```
    else szch = sz.toUpperCase().charAt(0);
    switch( szch ) {
      case 'H' :
        doHeadlineNews( out ); break ;
      case 'S' :
        doShortNews( out ); break ;
      case 'L' :
      default :
        doLongNews(out );
    }
    return itemsCount ;
}
```

The doNews method shown in Listing 8.5 locates a single news item by the id attribute and formats the long form of the text output. The remaining method in the NewsFormatter class exists to support the two doNews methods.

> **Listing 8.5: The Version of *doNews* for a Selected Item (*NewsFormatter.java*)**

```
// version to do a single item by id - always full length
public int doNews( PrintWriter out, String hs, String fs, String id ){
  headStr = hs ; footStr = fs ;
  itemsCount = 0 ;
  Node n = null ; //
  for( int i = 0 ; i < itemNodes.length ; i++ ){
    n = itemNodes[i];  // <Newsitem nodes
    String nid = ((Element)n).getAttribute("id");
    if( id.equals( nid )){
      break ;
    }
  } // if not located by id, will be oldest item
  findNodes((Element) n ); // locates the parts of <Newsitem
  doNewsItemLong( out ); // with the single id
  return itemsCount ;
}
```

We have assumed that news-item headlines will always be formatted as HTML "unordered list" lists. This makes the doHeadlineNews method shown in Listing 8.6 very simple.

Listing 8.6: The Method That Formats Headlines (*NewsFormatter.java*)

```java
// Headline always formatted as <UL> with link
public void doHeadlineNews(PrintWriter out){
  out.println( "<ul>" );
  for( int i = skipNitems ; i < itemNodes.length ; i++ ){
    if( i >= maxNitems ) break ;
    Node n = itemNodes[i];  // <Newsitem nodes
    String id = ((Element)n).getAttribute("id");
    findNodes((Element) n ); // locates the parts of <Newsitem
    out.print("<li><a href=" + handler + "?id=" + id + "&size=L >" );
    out.print( nodeHash.get("head") );
    out.println("</a></li>");
  }
  out.println("</ul>");
}
```

The doShortNews method, as shown in Listing 8.7, checks for the presence of default formatting information and then outputs the short form of news items. Note that the id attribute is extracted from each news item before the doNewsItemShort method is called. This id will be attached to each item as a link to the presentation of the full-length news item.

Listing 8.7: The *doShortNews* Method (*NewsFormatter.java*)

```java
public void doShortNews(PrintWriter out){
  NamedNodeMap attrib = docRoot.getAttributes();
  Node n = attrib.getNamedItem( "shorttemplate") ;
  String template = null ;
  if( n != null ) template = n.getNodeValue();
  if( headStr == null &&
      template != null &&
      template.length() > 2 ){
    try {
      setFromTemplate( template );
    }catch(IOException ie ){
      System.out.println("Unable to read " + template );
    }
  }
  out.println( headStr );
  for( int i = skipNitems ; i < itemNodes.length ; i++ ){
    if( i >= maxNitems ) break ;
```

```
      n = itemNodes[i];  // <Newsitem nodes
      String id = ((Element)n).getAttribute("id");
      findNodes((Element) n ); // locates the parts of <Newsitem
      doNewsItemShort( out, id );
   }
   out.println( footStr );
}
```

As shown in Listing 8.8, the **doLongNews** method checks for the availability of default formatting information before cycling through the news items in the **itemNodes** array.

Listing 8.8: The *doLongNews* Method Outputs the Full-Length News Item (*NewsFormatter.java*)

```
public void doLongNews(PrintWriter out){
   NamedNodeMap attrib = docRoot.getAttributes();
   Node n = attrib.getNamedItem( "longtemplate");
   String template = null ;
   if( n != null ) template = n.getNodeValue();
   if( headStr == null &&
       template != null &&
       template.length() > 2 ){
     try {
       setFromTemplate( template );
       System.out.println("Template set ok " + headStr + footStr );
     }catch(IOException ie ){
       System.out.println("Unable to read " + template );
     }
   }
   out.println( headStr );
   for( int i = skipNitems ; i < itemNodes.length ; i++ ){
     if( i >= maxNitems ) break ;
     n = itemNodes[i];
     findNodes((Element) n );
     doNewsItemLong( out );
   }
   out.println( footStr );
}
```

Listing 8.9 shows the **limitAge** method that is called whenever a **String** giving an age limit is supplied to the **doNews** method. After checking for a valid integer number in the **age String**, it rebuilds the **itemNodes** array with the selected news items.

Listing 8.9: The Method That Selects Items by Age (*NewsFormatter.java*)

```
// limit to only most recent entries - return number, may be zero
  private int limitAge(String age, PrintWriter out ){
    int days = 100 ;
    try {
      days = Integer.parseInt( age );
      if( days <= 0 ) days = 1 ;
    }catch(NumberFormatException nfe){
       return itemNodes.length ; // no change
    }
    int today =(int)( System.currentTimeMillis() /( 24 * 60 * 60 * 1000));
    int oldest = today - days ;
    Vector v = new Vector( itemNodes.length );
    int nidate = today ; // in case of parse problem
    int i ;
    for( i = 0 ; i < itemNodes.length ; i++ ){
      Node n = itemNodes[i];  // <Newsitem nodes
      String t = ((Element)n).getAttribute("timestamp");
      try { nidate = Integer.parseInt( t );
      }catch(Exception nfe){ // number format or null pointer
         System.out.println( "NewsFormatter.limitAge " + nfe );
      }
    if( nidate >= oldest ){
        v.addElement( n );
    }
  }
  itemNodes = new Node[ v.size() ]; // may be zero
  for( i = 0 ; i < v.size(); i++ ){
    itemNodes[i] = (Node) v.elementAt(i);
  }
  return itemNodes.length ;
}
```

The reason the selectNodes method is so complex is that both the topics parameter selecting the output and the topic attribute in the news items can have a single topic or multiple topics separated by commas. As shown in Listing 8.10, we build a java.util .Hashtable to speed up recognition of topics.

Listing 8.10: The Method That Selects Items by Matching Topics (*NewsFormatter.java*)

```java
// topics string has topics separated by commas
// as does the attribute topics="general,books,java"
// output capability only used for debugging
private int selectNodes(String topics, PrintWriter out ){
   Hashtable recognize = new Hashtable();
   StringTokenizer st = new StringTokenizer( topics.toUpperCase(), ",");
   while( st.hasMoreTokens()){
      String tmp = st.nextToken().trim();
      recognize.put( tmp,tmp );
   }
   // hashtable can now be used to recognize selected topics
   Vector v = new Vector( itemNodes.length );
   int i ;
   for( i = 0 ; i < itemNodes.length ; i++ ){
     Node n = itemNodes[i];  // <Newsitem nodes
     String t = ((Element)n).getAttribute("topic");
     st = new StringTokenizer(t.toUpperCase(),",");
     while( st.hasMoreElements()){
       // We just use hashtable get to see if topic is present]
       if( recognize.get( st.nextToken().trim() ) != null ){
          v.addElement(n);
          break;
       }
     } // end while over topic list
   } // end loop over all nodes
   // build new array from selected nodes
   itemNodes = new Node[ v.size() ];
   for( i = 0 ; i < v.size(); i++ ){
      itemNodes[i] = (Node) v.elementAt(i);
   }
   return itemNodes.length ;
}
```

The findNodes method shown in Listing 8.11 is called for each news item to be output. The input Element is a Newsitem node of the XML document. This method creates the nodeHash variable that enables other methods to recover text elements, such as short, from the nodeHash collection by name.

Listing 8.11: The *findNodes* Method of the *NewsFormatter* Class (*NewsFormatter.java*)

```
// locate the nodes that are Elements for text data
private void findNodes( Element ne ){
  NodeList nl = ne.getChildNodes(); // all nodes
  int ct = nl.getLength();
  nodeHash = new Hashtable( 2 * ct );
  for( int i = 0 ; i < ct ; i++ ){
    Node n = nl.item(i);
    if( n instanceof Element ){
      nodeHash.put( n.getNodeName(), n );
    }
  }
}
```

Headline and short-form news item output is always formatted with a link that enables display of the full-length item. This link is built into the HTML page by the doNewsItemHead and doNewsItemShort methods, as shown in Listing 8.12.

Listing 8.12: The *doNewsItemHead* and *doNewsItemShort* Methods (*NewsFormatter.java*)

```
//   <Newsitem >has been hashed, id is attribute
  private void doNewsItemHead( PrintWriter out, String id ){
    out.print("<a href=" + handler + "?id=" + id + "&size=L >" );
    out.print("<h3>"); out.print( nodeHash.get("head") );
    out.println("</h3></a>");
    out.println();
  }

//   <Newsitem has been hashed, id is attribute
//   output with <p>..</p> formatting
  private void doNewsItemShort( PrintWriter out, String id ){
    // note anchor to full item display
    out.print("<a href=" + handler + "?id=" + id + "&size=L >" );
    out.print("<h3>"); out.print( nodeHash.get("head") );
    out.println("</h3></a>");
    Element de = (Element)nodeHash.get("date");
    out.print( de.getFirstChild() );
    out.println("</p>");
    Element ne = (Element)nodeHash.get("short");
    String wrk = ne.getFirstChild().getNodeValue().trim() ;
```

```
    if( !(wrk.startsWith("<P") || wrk.startsWith("<p")) ){
        out.print("<p>");
    }
    out.print( wrk );
    if( !(wrk.endsWith("/p>") || wrk.endsWith("/P>"))){
        out.print("</p>");
    }
    itemsCount++ ;
    out.println();
}
```

As shown in Listing 8.13, the doNewsItemLong method formats the headline text with an
<h3> tag. A nice improvement for this code would be to allow customizing this sort of format-
ting. The main long text is formatted as a paragraph using the <p> tag. The item can have any
desired HTML formatting tags inside the long text, but the <p> tags will always be used for
the entire text.

**Listing 8.13: The *doNewsItemLong* Method Outputs Long-Form News Items
(*NewsFormatter.java*)**

```
// <Newsitem >elements have been hashed
// output long form with <p>...</p> formatting
private void doNewsItemLong( PrintWriter out ){
  out.print("<h3>"); out.print( nodeHash.get("head") );
  out.println("</h3>");
  Element de = (Element)nodeHash.get("date");
  out.print( de.getFirstChild() );
  out.println("</p>");
  Element ne = (Element)nodeHash.get("long");
  String wrk = ne.getFirstChild().getNodeValue().trim() ;
  if( !(wrk.startsWith("<P") || wrk.startsWith("<p")) ){
      out.print("<p>");
  }
  out.print( wrk );
  if( !(wrk.endsWith("/p>") || wrk.endsWith("/P>"))){
      out.print("</p>");
  }
  itemsCount++ ;
  out.println();
}
```

Finally, two utility methods are presented in Listing 8.14. The setFromTemplate method locates a file and reads it line by line. It assumes there will be a line starting with the text "<!--INSERT" that separates the HTML markup into two sections that become the headStr and footStr variables. The toString method is provided to assist in debugging.

Listing 8.14: The End of the *NewsFormatter* Source Code (*NewsFormatter.java*)

```java
    private void setFromTemplate(String template ) throws IOException {
        File f = new File( newsFilePath, template );
        FileReader fr = new FileReader( f );
        BufferedReader br = new BufferedReader( fr );
        StringBuffer hsb = new StringBuffer( 100 );
        StringBuffer fsb = new StringBuffer( 100 );
        String tmp = br.readLine(); // strips line terminators
        while( !tmp.startsWith("<!--INSERT" )){
            hsb.append( tmp ); fsb.append("\r\n");
            tmp = br.readLine();
        }
        tmp = br.readLine();
        while( tmp != null ){
            fsb.append( tmp ); fsb.append("\r\n");
            tmp = br.readLine();
        }
        headStr = hsb.toString();
        footStr = fsb.toString();
    }


    public String toString(){
        StringBuffer sb = new StringBuffer("NewsFormatter item ct= ");
        sb.append( Integer.toString( itemNodes.length ));
        return sb.toString() ;
    }

}
```

Using *NewsFormatter*

This section presents two ways to use the NewsFormatter class: with the general-purpose servlet TheNewsServ and with JavaServer Pages.

The Code for *TheNewsServ*

This servlet can be used to show a single news item with an `id` parameter or to present selected items using `topic` and `age` parameters. Listing 8.15 shows the import statements and static variables. We have set the static variables to default values for our systems; obviously, you should change these to reflect your own setup.

Listing 8.15: The Start of *TheNewsServ* Source Code (*TheNewsServ.java*)

```java
package com.XmlEcomBook.Chap08 ;

import java.io.*;
import java.util.* ;
import javax.servlet.*;
import javax.servlet.http.*;

public class TheNewsServ extends HttpServlet
{
  static String workDir = "E:\\scripts\\CompanyNews" ;
  static String newsFile = "thenews.xml" ;
  static String handler = "http://localhost/servlet/thenews" ;
  static String propfile = "conewserv.properties";
  static String version = "v1.0";
  static String pversion = "" ;
  static Properties cnProp ;
  static String brcrlf = "<br />\r\n" ;
  static String defaultHead = "<html>\r\n" +
    "<head><title>Company News Servlet</title></head>\r\n" +
    "<body>\r\n" +
    "<h2>Here is the news</h2>\r\n" ;
  static String defaultFoot = "</body></html>\r\n";
```

The `init` method, as shown in Listing 8.16, reads a properties file whose values can be used to replace the default values in the static variables.

Listing 8.16: The *init* Method of the *TheNewsServ* Class (*TheNewsServ.java*)

```java
public void init(ServletConfig config) throws ServletException
  super.init(config);
  String tmp = config.getInitParameter("workdir");
  if( tmp != null ) workDir = tmp ;
```

```
tmp = config.getInitParameter("propfile");
if( tmp != null ) propfile = tmp;
System.out.println("Start TheNewsServ using " + workDir );
File f = new File( workDir, propfile );
try { cnProp = new Properties();
  cnProp.load( new FileInputStream(f) );
  tmp = cnProp.getProperty("thenewshandler");
  if( tmp != null ) handler = tmp ;
  pversion = cnProp.getProperty("version");
  if( pversion != null ){
    defaultFoot = "<hr><br>News Servlet " + version +
        " properties: " + pversion + "<br>\r\n" +
        "</body>\r\n</html>\r\n" ;
  }
  NewsFormatter.setHandler( handler );
  System.out.println( new Date().toString() +
    " Loaded properties for TheNewsServ: "
        + handler );
}catch(IOException e){
    System.out.println("Error loading " + e );
}
}
```

The work of the servlet is performed in the **doGet** method, as shown in Listing 8.17. Parameter values for topics, the maximum age of news items, the desired size of output, and the news-item **id** can be passed in the request. Note that a **File** object that refers to the XML news file is created and passed to the **NewsFormatter** constructor. Using a **File** object ensures that the conventions for path separators for the particular system are adhered to; the **NewsFormatter** does not open this file but uses the name to get a DOM for the file from the **DOMlibrary**.

Listing 8.17: The *doGet* Method (*TheNewsServ.java*)

```
public void doGet(HttpServletRequest req, HttpServletResponse resp)
throws ServletException, IOException
{
  resp.setContentType("text/html");
  PrintWriter out = new PrintWriter(resp.getOutputStream());
  String topics = req.getParameter("topic");
  String ageStr = req.getParameter("days");
  String len = req.getParameter("size" ); // "S","H" or "L"
```

```
  String id  = req.getParameter("id"); // a single item is requested
  try {
    File f = new File( workDir, newsFile );
    NewsFormatter nf = new NewsFormatter( f );
    if( id != null ){
      nf.doNews( out, defaultHead,defaultFoot, id );
    }
    else {
      // PrintWriter, head, foot, topics, H,S or L, age, skip#, mx#
      nf.doNews( out, defaultHead, defaultFoot, topics, len, ageStr,0, 10 );
    }
    out.close();
  }catch(Exception e){
    System.err.println("TheNewsServ.doGet " + e );
    errorMsg( out, "TheNewsServ.doGet", e );
  }
}
```

Note that a try-catch structure in doGet directs all exceptions to the errorMsg method shown in Listing 8.18. Obviously, you should insert your own e-mail address in place of the one here or the message could be a String variable set from the properties file. The header and footer methods simply write standard HTML tags.

Listing 8.18: The *errorMsg*, Header, and Footer Methods (*TheNewsServ.java*)

```
// assumes response has been set to text/html
  private void errorMsg( PrintWriter out, String msg, Exception ex ){
    header( out );
    out.println("<h2>Error: " ); out.println( msg );
    out.println("</h2><br>");
    if( ex != null ){
       ex.printStackTrace( out );
    }
    out.println("<br>");
    out.println("<a href=\"mailto:wbrogden@bga.com\">Please mail me"
  + " the error message.</a><br>");
    footer( out );
  }

  private void header(PrintWriter out ){
    out.println("<html>");
```

```
        out.println("<head><title>Company News Servlet</title></head>");
        out.println("<body>");
    }

    private void footer(PrintWriter out ){
        out.println("<hr><br>Company News Servlet " + version + " properties: <br>"
);
        out.println("</body>");
        out.println("</html>");
        out.close();
    }
}
```

A JavaServer Pages Example

The basic form of the example page is a table having three columns. In order to save space in this listing, we cut the example down as much as possible; a real page would, of course, have much more company-related material.

It is the ease of incorporating Java output into HTML markup that makes JavaServer Pages so attractive. Listing 8.19 shows the page source up through the creation of the first row of the table.

Listing 8.19: The First Part of a Simplified JSP News Presentation Page (*mockup.jsp*)

```
<!DOCTYPE HTML PUBLIC "-//W3C//DTD HTML 4.0 Transitional//EN">
<html>
<head>
<title>The XMLGifts News </title>
</head>

<body bgcolor="#FFFFFF">
<%@ page language="java"
    import="com.XmlEcomBook.Chap08.NewsFormatter,java.io.*" %>
<%!
    String newsFilePath = "e:\\scripts\\CompanyNews" ;
    String newsFileName = "thenews.xml" ;
    String newsHandler  = "http://localhost:8080/XMLbook/Chap08/thenews.jsp" ;
    File newsFile = new File( newsFilePath, newsFileName );
    public void jspInit(){
        super.jspInit();
```

```
          NewsFormatter.setHandler( newsHandler );
    }
%>
<table width="89%" border="0" align="left" cellpadding="8">
  <tr align="center" bgcolor="cyan">
    <td colspan="3"><font size="4">
 Various Corporate Navigation Links Go Here</font>
    </td>
  </tr>
```

For the purposes of this example, we hard coded a topic value of `"CDs"`, as shown in Listing 8.20. The first use of the `NewsFormatter` object is to create the left-hand column of headlines. This is done first because, after the topic selection has been done, the `NewsFormatter` object will only contain data for news items that match the topics.

Listing 8.20: The JSP Page Continues, with *NewsFormatter* Output (*mockup.jsp*)

```
    <!-- the nf and pw objects will be used for all three td -->
    <tr valign="TOP" ><font size="3">
        <td><b>News Headlines</b><br>
<%
    // topic could be set from customer records or the previous form
    String topic = "CDs" ;
    NewsFormatter nf = new NewsFormatter( newsFile );
     PrintWriter pw = new PrintWriter( out );

/*  Note the doNews signature
    doNews( PrintWriter out, String hs, String fs,
        String topstr, String sz, String age, int skpN, int mxN ) */
    // headlines - all topics
    nf.doNews( pw, "","", "", "H", null, 0, 8 );
%>
    </td>
    <td width="50%">
<%
    nf.doNews( pw, "","", topic, "L", null, 0, 1 );
%>
    </td>
    <!-- the short form column -->
    <td width="23%">
```

```
<%= "<b>Recent news items about " + topic + "</b><br>" %>
<%
 /*  Note the doNews signature
    doNews( PrintWriter out, String hs, String fs,
       String topstr, String sz, String age, int skpN, int mxN ) */

    nf.doNews( pw, "","", topic, "S", null, 1, 8 );
%>
    </td>
    </font>
  </tr>
  <tr align="center" bgcolor="cyan">
    <td colspan="3"><font size="4" >
    Repeat the Navigation links here for convenience<br></font>
    </td>
  </tr>
  <tr>
    <td colspan="3" align='center'><font face='arial, helvetica' size='3'>
       &copy;2000 XMLGifts.com<sup>SM</sup>
    <br /></font>
    </td>
  </tr>
</table>
</body>
</html>
```

Adding the Latest News

An important feature of this application is the capability to add new news items without disturbing the normal operation of the Web site. This is the function that appears on the upper-right corner of Figure 8.1. Instead of modifying the DOM in server memory, the CompanyNewsServ servlet writes a modified version of the master XML file to disk storage. This revised news item file will automatically be loaded the next time the DOM is requested from the DOMlibrary.

The *CompanyNewsServ* Servlet

The HTML form for updating is created and managed by the CompanyNewsServ servlet. Initial entry to the servlet is through an HTML page that has an ordinary HTML form for inputting an author's name and a password. We have included an example of such a page in the CoNewsUpdate.html file on the CD. The servlet looks up the author's name in the properties file to verify that that person is authorized to input news items.

Listing 8.21 shows our properties file for working on the localhost server. Note that the author's name is the property name and the value is the password.

Listing 8.21: The Properties File Used by *CompanyNewsServ* (*conewserv.properties*)

```
# properties for CompanyNewsServ
handler=http://localhost/servlet/conewserv
thenewshandler=http://localhost/servlet/thenews
newsfile=thenews.xml
version=June 15, 2000
wbrogden=xmlrules
```

Listing 8.22 shows the import statements, static variables, and init method for the CompanyNewsServ servlet.

Listing 8.22: The Start of the *CompanyNewsServ* Servlet Code (*CompanyNewsServ.java*)

```
package com.XmlEcomBook.Chap08 ;

import com.XmlEcomBook.DOMlibrary ;
import java.io.*;
import java.util.* ;
import javax.servlet.*;
import javax.servlet.http.*;
import org.w3c.dom.* ;

public class CompanyNewsServ extends HttpServlet
{
  static String workDir = "E:\\scripts\\CompanyNews" ;
  static String propfile = "conewserv.properties" ;
  static String newsFile = "thenews.xml" ;
  static String handler = "http://localhost/servlet/conewserv" ;
  static String version = "v0.12";
  static String pversion = "" ;
  static Properties cnProp ;
  static String brcrlf = "<br />\r\n" ;
```

```
public void init(ServletConfig config) throws ServletException
{
  super.init(config);
  String tmp = config.getInitParameter("workdir");
  if( tmp != null ) workDir = tmp ;
  tmp = config.getInitParameter("propfile");
  if( tmp != null ) propfile = tmp ;
  System.out.println("Start CompanyNewsServ using " + workDir );
  File f = new File( workDir, propfile );
  try { cnProp = new Properties();
    cnProp.load( new FileInputStream(f) );
    tmp = cnProp.getProperty("handler");
    if( tmp != null ) handler = tmp ;
    tmp = cnProp.getProperty("newsfile");
    if( tmp != null ) newsFile = tmp ;
    pversion = cnProp.getProperty("version");
    System.out.println("Loaded properties for CompanyNewsServ: "
            + handler + " file:" + newsFile );
  }catch(IOException e){
      System.out.println("Error loading " + e );
  }
}
```

The **doGet** method, as shown in Listing 8.23, checks the input username and password against the properties file loaded when the servlet is initialized. If a name and password match is found, it calls the **generateForm** method to create the HTML form for entering a news item.

Listing 8.23: The *doGet* Method Creates the News Entry Form (*CompanyNewsServ.java*)

```
public void doGet(HttpServletRequest req, HttpServletResponse resp)
throws ServletException, IOException
{
  resp.setContentType("text/html");
  PrintWriter out = new PrintWriter(resp.getOutputStream());
  String username = req.getParameter("username");
  String password = req.getParameter("password");
  String action   = req.getParameter("action");
  String tmp = cnProp.getProperty(username);
  boolean userok = false ;
  if( tmp != null ){
```

```
      userok = tmp.equals( password );
    }
    header( out );
    if( userok ){
      generateForm( out, username, password );
    }
    else {
      out.println("<p>User: " + username + "  password: " + password +
        " not found.</p>" );
    }
    footer( out );
```

A filled-out form is sent to the **doPost** method. As shown in Listing 8.24, you extract the various text items and pass them to a new **NewsUpkeep** object with the **addItem** method.

Listing 8.24: The *doPost* Method Captures Data from the Form (*CompanyNewsServ.java*)

```
public void doPost(HttpServletRequest req, HttpServletResponse resp)
throws ServletException, IOException
{
  resp.setContentType("text/html");
  PrintWriter out = new PrintWriter(resp.getOutputStream());
  String username = req.getParameter("username");
  String password = req.getParameter("password");
  String action   = req.getParameter("action");
  String head = req.getParameter("head");
  String date = req.getParameter("date");
  String topics = req.getParameter("topics");
  String shrtStr = req.getParameter("short").trim();
  String longStr = req.getParameter("long").trim();
  DOMlibrary library = DOMlibrary.getLibrary();
  File f = new File( workDir, newsFile );
  try {
   NewsUpkeep nup = new NewsUpkeep( f );
   nup.addItem( head, date, topics, username, shrtStr, longStr );
   header( out );
   out.println("NewsUpkeep is " + nup + "<br />");
   footer( out );
  } catch( Exception e ){
      errorMsg( out, "CompanyNewsServ.doPost ", e );
  }
}
```

The HTML form for news-item input is created by the generateForm method, as shown in Listing 8.25. Note that the username and password are inserted as hidden values in the form.

Listing 8.25: The *generateForm* Method Creates an Entry Form (*CompanyNewsServ.java*)

```java
private void generateForm( PrintWriter out, String name, String pw ){
    out.println("<h2>Enter Company News Item Data</h2>");
    out.println("<form method=\"POST\" action=\"" + handler + "\" >");
    out.println("Headline - 80 char max<br />");
    out.println("<input type=\"text\" maxlength=\"80\" size=\"60\"" +
        " name=\"head\" ><br />" );
    out.println("Dated <br />");
    out.println("<input type=\"text\" maxlength=\"50\" size=\"40\"" +
        " name=\"date\" value=\"" + new Date().toString() + "\" ><br />" );
    out.println(
    "Topics separated by commas - please stick to the official list.<br />");
    out.println("<input type=\"text\" maxlength=\"80\" size=\"60\"" +
        " name=\"topics\" ><br />" );
    out.println("Short version <br />");
    out.println("<textarea cols=\"60\" rows=\"3\" name=\"short\" >");
    out.println("</textarea><br />");
    out.println("Long version <br />");
    out.println("<textarea cols=\"60\" rows=\"10\" name=\"long\" >");
    out.println("</textarea><br />");
    out.println("<input type=\"hidden\" name=\"username\" value=\""
        + name + "\"><br>" );
    out.println("<input type=\"hidden\" name=\"password\" value=\""
        + pw + "\" ><br>");
    out.println(
    "<input type=\"submit\" name=\"action\" value=\"Submit\" ><br />" );
    out.println("</form></center>");
}
```

Finally, we have the typical servlet utility methods, as shown in Listing 8.26. Naturally, you should replace the message with your own address or provide a String variable initialized from the properties file.

Listing 8.26: The Utility Methods in *CompanyNewsServ* (*CompanyNewsServ.java*)

```
// assumes response has been set to text/html
  private void errorMsg( PrintWriter out, String msg, Exception ex ){
    header( out );
    out.println("<h2>Error: " ); out.println( msg );
    out.println("</h2><br>");
    if( ex != null ){
       ex.printStackTrace( out );
    }
    out.println("<br>");
    out.println("<a href=\"mailto:wbrogden@bga.com\">" +
      "Please mail me the error message.</a><br>");
    footer( out );
  }

  private void header(PrintWriter out ){
    out.println("<html>");
    out.println("<head><title>Company News Servlet</title></head>");
    out.println("<body>");
  }

  private void footer(PrintWriter out ){
    out.println("<hr><br>Company News Servlet " + version +
       " properties: <br>" );
    out.println("</body>");
    out.println("</html>");
    out.close();
  }
}
```

The *NewsUpkeep* Class

The NewsUpkeep class takes an existing <Newsfile> DOM object and the various text strings that make up a new <Newsitem> and rewrites the XML news file. This method is simpler than creating and inserting the <Newsitem> in the memory-resident DOM and ensures that the news file is updated correctly. It also avoids the possibility of one of the display methods encountering a partially changed DOM.

Listing 8.27 shows the start of the NewsUpkeep class source code. The constructor uses the complete filename to get the DOM from the DOMlibrary. Because this DOM is not modified during the rewrite of the XML file, you don't have to worry about interfering with the possibly simultaneous access to this object by NewsFormatter.

Note the creation of the NamedNodeMap variable, rootNNM, which holds the attribute names and values found in the document root, the <Newsfile> tag. The constructor also puts all of the <Newsitem> nodes in the itemNodes array.

Listing 8.27: The Start of the *NewsUpkeep* Class (*NewsUpkeep.java*)

```java
package com.XmlEcomBook.Chap08;

import com.XmlEcomBook.DOMlibrary ;
import java.io.*;
import java.util.* ;
import javax.servlet.*;
import javax.servlet.http.*;
import org.w3c.dom.* ;

public class NewsUpkeep
{
  File newsFile ;
  String newsFileName ;
  Node[] itemNodes ;
  NamedNodeMap rootNNM ; // for root attributes

  public NewsUpkeep( File f) throws IOException {
    newsFile = f ;
    newsFileName = f.getAbsolutePath() ;
    DOMlibrary library = DOMlibrary.getLibrary();
    Document doc = library.getDOM( newsFileName );
    if( doc == null ){
        throw new FileNotFoundException( newsFileName );
    }
    Element re = doc.getDocumentElement();
    rootNNM = re.getAttributes();
    System.out.println("Root has " + rootNNM.getLength() + " attributes");
    NodeList newsItemNodes = doc.getElementsByTagName("Newsitem");
    int ct = newsItemNodes.getLength();
    itemNodes = new Node[ ct ];
```

```
    for( int i = 0 ; i < ct ; i++ ){
      itemNodes[i] = newsItemNodes.item( i );
    }
  }
```

Listing 8.28 shows some of the support methods required by NewsUpkeep. The format-Topics method ensures that the text that will be written as the topic attribute is correctly formatted.

Listing 8.28: Various Support Functions in *NewsUpkeep* (*NewsUpkeep.java*)

```
//ensure there are no leading or trailing spaces on the
// individual topics, comma separated, general, food, etc
private String formatTopics(String s ){
  if( s.indexOf(',') < 0 ) return s.trim();
  // only separator is comma
  StringTokenizer st = new StringTokenizer( s, "," );
  StringBuffer sb = new StringBuffer( s.length() );
  while( st.hasMoreTokens() ){
    sb.append( st.nextToken().trim() );
    if( st.hasMoreTokens() ) sb.append(',');
  }
  return sb.toString();
}
 // convert system millisecs to days since epoch
private String timeInDays(){
  long t = System.currentTimeMillis() ;
  int tid = (int)(t / ( 1000 * 60 * 60 * 24 ));
  return Integer.toString( tid );
}

// s expected to be decimal number used in <Newsitem id=
private String incrementID(String s ){
  try{
    int n = Integer.parseInt( s );
    return Integer.toString( n + 2 );
  }catch(NumberFormatException e){
    return s + "a" ;
  }
}
```

```
public String toString(){
  StringBuffer sb = new StringBuffer("NewsUpkeep ");
  sb.append(" Newsitem count: " );
  sb.append( Integer.toString( itemNodes.length ));
  return sb.toString();
}
```

Now we come to the main working method, addItem. The first thing this method does is creates a new file with a temporary name and write the standard XML declaration and a comment. Next, the <Newsfile> tag is created by writing the attributes from the rootNNM collection.

As shown in Listing 8.29, the nextid attribute is specially treated. The current value, which becomes the id attribute of the new <Newsitem>, is saved, and the incremented value is written into the <Newsfile> tag.

Listing 8.29: The Start of the *addItem* Method (*NewsUpkeep.java*)

```
// items are always added at the top of the file
// so you have to rebuild the start of the root element
public void addItem(
    String head, String date, String topics, String author,
    String shrtStr,
    String longStr ) throws IOException {
  String idVal = "" ;
  String tmpfile = newsFileName + "$$" ;
  File f = new File( tmpfile );
  FileWriter fw = new FileWriter(f);
  PrintWriter out = new PrintWriter( new BufferedWriter( fw ) );
  out.println("<?xml version=\"1.0\" standalone=\"yes\" ?>");
  out.println("<!-- output by NewsUpkeep -->");
  int ct = rootNNM.getLength();
  if( ct == 0 ){
    out.println("<Newsfile>");
  }
  else {
    out.print("<Newsfile ");
    for( int i = 0 ; i < ct ; i++ ){
      Node an = rootNNM.item(i);
      String name = an.getNodeName();
```

```
        String val  = an.getNodeValue();
        out.print( name + "=\"" );
        if( name.equals("nextid") ){
            idVal = val ;
            val = incrementID( val );
        }
        out.print( val + "\" " );
    }
    out.println(" >");
}
```

Next, the new `<Newsitem>` tag is written out, as shown in Listing 8.30, followed by the head, the date, and the short and long text elements. The old `<Newsitem>` elements are written out by calls to the `writeNewsNode` method. After closing the temporary file, the old XML file is deleted and the temporary file is renamed. The next time this file is requested, the `DOMlibrary` class will see the changed timestamp and read in the new file.

Listing 8.30: The *addItem* Method, Continued (*NewsUpkeep.java*)

```
out.print("<Newsitem timestamp=\"");
out.print( timeInDays() + "\" topic=\"");
out.print( formatTopics( topics ) );
out.println( "\" author=\"" + author + "\" id=\"" + idVal + "\" >");
// end of <Newsitem .. >
out.println("<head>" + head.trim() + "</head>" );
out.println("<date>" + date.trim() + "</date>" );
out.println("<short><![CDATA[");
out.println( shrtStr.trim() );
out.println("]]></short>");
out.println("<long><![CDATA[");
out.println( longStr ); out.println("]]></long>");
out.println("</Newsitem>");
for( int i = 0 ; i < itemNodes.length ; i++ ){
    writeNewsNode(out, (Element)itemNodes[i] );
}
out.println("</Newsfile>");
out.flush(); out.close();
File forig = new File( newsFileName );
DOMlibrary library = DOMlibrary.getLibrary();
// to prevent overlapping XML file operations
```

```
      synchronized( library ){
        forig.delete();
        if( !f.renameTo( forig )){
          System.out.println("NewsUpkeep.addItem rename failed") ;
        }
      }
    }
```

The writeNewsNode method, which writes a single <Newsitem> element, is shown in Listing 8.31.

Listing 8.31: The Method That Writes a Single News Item from the DOM (*NewsUpkeep.java*)

```
// write a <Newsitem Element duplicating the attributes
public void writeNewsNode(PrintWriter out, Element e) {
  NamedNodeMap nnm = e.getAttributes();
  out.print("<Newsitem " ) ; //timestamp=\"");
  int i ;    for( i = 0 ; i < nnm.getLength() ; i++ ){
    Attr na = (Attr) nnm.item(i); //  Attr extends Node
    String atr = na.getName();
    String val = na.getValue();
    out.print( atr ); out.print("=\"");
    out.print( val ); out.print("\" ");
  }
  out.println(">");
  NodeList nl = e.getChildNodes();
  int ct = nl.getLength();
  for( i = 0 ; i < ct ; i++ ){
    Node nde = nl.item( i );
    if( nde instanceof Element ){
      Element ce = (Element)nde;
      String name = ce.getTagName();
      out.print("<" + name + ">");
      NodeList chnl = ce.getChildNodes() ;
      if( chnl.getLength() == 0 ) continue ;
      Node chn = chnl.item(0);
      if(  name.equals("long") || name.equals("short") ){
          out.print("<![CDATA[");
          out.println( chn.getNodeValue().trim() );
```

```
            out.print("]]>");
        }
        else { out.print( chn.getNodeValue() );
        }
        out.println("</" + name + ">");
      }
    } // loop over <Newsitem> child nodes
    out.println("</Newsitem>");
  }

}
```

Based on our experience with adding news items using the CompanyNewsServ servlet, you should write out a complete news item in a text editor first. Then, when working with the input form, you can just cut and paste into the form.

CHAPTER 9

Keep Them Coming Back

- Finding news sources on the Internet
- How to download XML headline files
- Keeping headlines in memory
- How to select and present headlines

Aside from offering great products at competitive prices, what can you, as a commercial-site operator, do to keep customers coming back? Ideally, your front page would be so interesting that people would return to it just to see what is going on.

You have probably noticed over the last year or so that many sites are now including news headline items on their front page to keep users interested. These sites don't create this material but "grab" it from various Web services set up for the purpose of sharing or syndicating information; in this chapter, we demonstrate how you can do it, too.

In this chapter, we will look at the kinds of news sources available on the Internet. We will also present example code for downloading XML formatted news headlines from one of the largest sources. When the XML files have been downloaded, the next step is creating a Java class to organize the headlines for efficient searching and selection. Finally, we provide examples of HTML generation of headline data.

News Sources and Standards

You are probably familiar with the idea of syndication in the world of print media. Syndicated columnists, editorial writers, and cartoonists are published outside of their "home" newspaper in newspapers that are contracted to print their work. Syndication allows a newspaper to draw on tremendous resources for news items to print without a big investment.

In the world of print, the actual content is moved around to various newspapers; the reader expects to find the entire column or comic strip in her own paper. The payoff for the content creator is a small payment, which is managed by the syndicating organization.

However, in the world of the Internet, where the user moves from site to site with great ease, only the fact that a certain resource exists has to be syndicated. By syndicating headline information with links to the complete story, the content creator gets visits to his site so his ads will be viewed or his products ordered.

Understanding the Rich Site Summary

Netscape pioneered the idea of creating personalized news pages on the Netscape Netcenter site (`www.netscape.com`), developing what is now known as the Rich Site Summary (RSS) format to make the process simpler. The idea was that cooperating Web sites would summarize their available content in a common format that could be picked up automatically and made available on the Netscape site. This approach made the Netscape site one of the most visited portals on the Web.

Defined in XML, the Rich Site Summary format (alternatively, RDF Site Summary) is still one of the dominant formats for distributing news items on the Web. A content-producing site creates an RSS *feed* file, defining a news *channel*. This file has to be placed on a publicly accessible Web site so it can be picked up automatically. Instructions for creating your own channel can be found at the following site:

```
http://my.netscape.com/publish/help/quickstart.html
```

A major Web site that picks up RSS channels on an hourly basis and organizes the material can be really fascinating. For example, try the `http://my.userland.com/` site. (But watch out: It can really eat up your time.)

A technically oriented site that picks up RSS channels is the Meerkat system (`www.oreillynet.com/meerkat/`).

NewsML and Future Standardization

The International Press Telecommunications Council (`www.iptc.org`) is attempting to create an XML encoding standard to simplify the delivery, creation, and retrieval of news items. As of the writing of this book, this standard, called NewsML, has just been released as version 1.0.

This project has a much more ambitious scope than the RSS standard. For example, it provides for many different media types and provides for explicit connections between news items.

Because so many organizations are involved in the council, and because many of these organizations earn income by creating news items, many conflicting interests must still be resolved. If NewsML does take over as the standard for syndicating news items, the techniques outlined in this chapter will still be applicable.

The Moreover.com Newsfeed

For purposes of this chapter, we have chosen to use the data format of the news feed from the Moreover.com organization (`www.moreover.com`). We have chosen Moreover.com for this demonstration because of the simplicity of their format and the large number of available categories. Of course, the fact that it is free helps too.

Although Moreover.com was only established in December 1999, by July 2000 it was harvesting headlines from about 1,500 sites. Their news-headline-harvesting software automatically places items into over 250 categories. All headline URLs go indirectly through the

Moreover.com site. The company intends to earn money by providing custom services and from information generated by the click-though traffic.

The format used by Moreover.com is simpler than RSS and only provides headline information. Setting up a customized newsfeed involves registering with the system by using your e-mail address and a password and then selecting the categories and the number of headline items you want to see. Figure 9.1 shows a small portion of the category-selection screen.

FIGURE 9.1
Selecting headline categories at Moreover.com

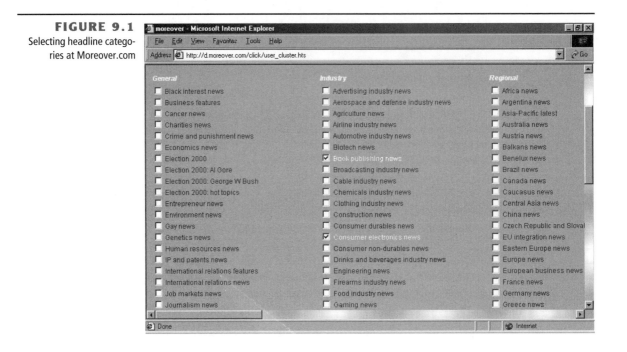

An XML File Grabber

The first step in the process of setting up your Web site to draw from Web information syndicators is to get the XML source file from the supplier. In this example, we access the `www.moreover.com` site with a search parameter that generates data for our preselected news categories. The following is the complete URL:

```
www.moreover.com/cgi-local/page?wbrogden@bga.com+xml
```

When this URL is accessed, a process at the Moreover.com server returns a text stream in XML format with the selected headline topics. Listing 9.1 shows the header and first item as originally retrieved in a download. Note that the DOCTYPE line refers to the DTD using a URL on the Moreover.com site. In order to enable interpretation of the XML file during testing, without accessing the Moreover.com Web site, the XMLgrabber class modifies the DOCTYPE line so that it refers to the DTD as a local file.

Listing 9.1: The Header and First Article from an Original Download (*xmldump.xml*)

```
<?xml version="1.0" encoding="iso-8859-1"?>
<!DOCTYPE moreovernews SYSTEM
        "http://p.moreover.com/xml_dtds/moreovernews.dtd">
 <moreovernews>
<article id="_8510757">
<url>http://c.moreover.com/click/here.pl?x8510756</url>
<headline_text>Cyclone Commerce Poised to Fulfill Promise of E-Signature
Legislation</headline_text>
<source>Java Industry Connection</source>
<media_type>text</media_type>
<cluster>Java news</cluster>
<tagline> </tagline>
<document_url>http://industry.java.sun.com/javanews/more/hotnews/
</document_url>
<harvest_time>Jul 25 2000  8:34AM</harvest_time>
<access_registration> </access_registration>
<access_status> </access_status>
</article>
```

Note that the element that Moreover.com calls cluster is the basic classification of the article. In the example servlet, we only use the url, headline_text, source, and cluster elements. The moreovernews DTD, as shown in Listing 9.2, is relatively simple.

Listing 9.2: The *moreovernews.dtd* File (*moreovernews.dtd*)

```
<!ELEMENT moreovernews (article*)>
<!ELEMENT article (url,headline_text,source,media_type,cluster,tagline,
    document_url,harvest_time,access_registration,access_status)>
<!ATTLIST article id ID #IMPLIED>
<!ELEMENT url (#PCDATA)>
<!ELEMENT headline_text (#PCDATA)>
<!ELEMENT source (#PCDATA)>
<!ELEMENT media_type (#PCDATA)>
<!ELEMENT cluster (#PCDATA)>
```

```
<!ELEMENT tagline (#PCDATA)>
<!ELEMENT document_url (#PCDATA)>
<!ELEMENT harvest_time (#PCDATA)>
<!ELEMENT access_registration (#PCDATA)>
<!ELEMENT access_status (#PCDATA)>
```

The servlet application we describe in this chapter includes a class, NetNewsSuper, that
runs a Thread, which creates an XMLgrabber object to download the most recent headlines
file and the current DTD file as well. Listing 9.3 shows the start of this class, including the
constructor. Note that the constructor is supplied with the URL to be accessed and the path
and filename to be used for the local copy.

Listing 9.3: The Start of the *XMLgrabber* Class (*XMLgrabber.java*)

```
package com.XmlEcomBook.Chap09;

import java.net.* ;
import java.io.* ;
import java.util.*;

public class XMLgrabber
{
  String source ; // complete URL to run std query
// example
//"http://www.moreover.com/cgi-local/page?wbrogden@bga.com+xml";
  String saveDir  ; // for both temp and final xml file
  String tfnxml ; // temp file name - see createTempXmlWriter
  String tfndtd ; // temp file name for dtd
  String saveName ; // for xml
  String dtdURL ; // complete  DTD url from <!DOCTYPE line
  String dtdFname ; // for dtd

  PrintWriter pw ;
  URL theURL ;
  Thread queryT ;

  // all files from a given source will go to dest directory
  XMLgrabber( String src, String dest, String fname ){
    source = src ;
    saveDir = dest ;
    saveName = fname ;
  // System.out.println("XMLgrabber initialized for " + src );
  }
```

Because we can't rely on a rapid connection to the Moreover.com site, and because, in some cases, the attempt to retrieve new data may fail, retrieval of the XML is executed by a Thread that is separate from servlet functions. Furthermore, the old data file is not over-written; instead, the retrieved data is written to a temporary file. Only when we are sure that the XML file is complete is the old data file discarded and the temporary file renamed. As shown in Listing 9.4, the doQueryNow method provides the framework for retrieving the latest information. In addition to retrieving the XML article file, we also attempt to retrieve the latest DTD.

Listing 9.4: The *doQueryNow* Method (*XMLgrabber.java*)

```
// run by external Thread to get file resident
// return true if succeeds
  public boolean doQueryNow() throws IOException {
    theURL = new URL( source );
    createTempXmlWriter();
    grabXml();
    if( !renameTemp( tfnxml, saveName )) return false ;
    tfnxml = null ;
    // now for the dtd
    if( dtdURL == null ) return true ;
    // System.out.println("Start DTD retrieval");
    theURL = new URL( dtdURL );
    createTempDtdWriter();
    grabDtd();
    boolean ret = renameTemp( tfndtd,dtdFname );
    tfndtd = null ;
    return ret ;
}
```

There are several ways for doQueryNow to fail, either by encountering an IOException when trying to access the source URL or by encountering problems with the local file system. In order to avoid cluttering the local disk with temporary files that were created but not cor-rectly processed, the tfnxml and tfndtd filenames get special handling.

The tfnxml file is created in the call to createTempXmlWriter. Note that if an exception does not occur and renaming the tfnxml file to saveName succeeds, the tfnxml variable is set to null. Otherwise the finalize method (Listing 9.9) will attempt to delete the temporary file. The temporary file for the DTD download gets the same treatment.

Listing 9.5 shows the methods in XMLgrabber that are used to create and manage temporary files.

Listing 9.5: Methods Used to Manage Temporary Files (*XMLgrabber.java*)

```
// saveDir used for all
private boolean renameTemp(String tmp, String saveN ) {
  File src = new File( saveDir, tmp );
  File dest = new File( saveDir, saveN);
  dest.delete();
  return src.renameTo( dest );
}


private void createTempXmlWriter() throws IOException {
  tfnxml = "$" + Integer.toString((int) System.currentTimeMillis())
              + ".xml";
  File tfile = new File( saveDir, tfnxml );
  while( tfile.exists() ){ // hunt for unique name
     tfnxml = tfnxml + "X" ;
     tfile = new File( saveDir, tfnxml );
  }
  // ok, unique file name in tfnxml, File tfile set up
  FileWriter fw = new FileWriter( tfile.getAbsolutePath() );
  pw = new PrintWriter( fw );
}


private void createTempDtdWriter() throws IOException {
  tfndtd = "$" + Integer.toString((int) System.currentTimeMillis())
              + ".dtd";
  File tfile = new File( saveDir, tfndtd );
  while( tfile.exists() ){ // hunt for unique name
     tfndtd = tfndtd + "X" ;
     tfile = new File( saveDir, tfndtd );
  }
  // ok, unique file name in tfndtd, File tfile set up
  FileWriter fw = new FileWriter( tfile.getAbsolutePath() );
  pw = new PrintWriter( fw );
}
```

As shown in Listing 9.6, the grabXml method reads lines of text from the source-URL input stream. The XML header line containing the reference to the DTD file is reformatted by the reformDoctype method to change the reference from a URL to a local filename. This is to ensure that parsing the XML file will be independent of an Internet connection.

Listing 9.6: The *grabXml* Method Reads from the URL (*XMLgrabber.java*)

```
// at this point pw is open to a temp file
private void grabXml() throws IOException {
  URLConnection urlC = theURL.openConnection();
  urlC.setUseCaches( false );
  urlC.setAllowUserInteraction(false);
  urlC.connect();
  InputStream is = urlC.getInputStream();
  InputStreamReader isr = new InputStreamReader(is);
  BufferedReader br = new BufferedReader( isr );
  String tmp = br.readLine() ;
  while( tmp != null ){
     tmp = tmp.trim();
     if( tmp.startsWith("<!DOCTYPE") ) { // change to use local copy
        tmp = reformDoctype( tmp );
     }
     pw.println( tmp );
     tmp = br.readLine();
  }
  pw.close(); // does a flush()
}
```

Assuming that the reformDoctype method correctly set up the dtdURL variable, the grabDtd method, as shown in Listing 9.7, downloads it to a local temporary file. This listing also shows the utility method, createURL, that sets the theURL instance variable.

Listing 9.7: The *grabDtd* Method Gets the Current *moreovernews.dtd* (*XMLgrabber.java*)

```
// at this point pw is open to a temp file for dtd
private void grabDtd() throws IOException {
  System.out.println("grabDtd:" + dtdURL );
  URLConnection urlC = theURL.openConnection();
  urlC.setUseCaches( false );
  urlC.setAllowUserInteraction(false);
  urlC.connect();
  InputStream is = urlC.getInputStream();
  InputStreamReader isr = new InputStreamReader(is);
```

```
    BufferedReader br = new BufferedReader( isr );
    String tmp = br.readLine() ;
    while( tmp != null ){
       pw.println( tmp.trim() );
       tmp = br.readLine();
    }
    pw.close(); // does a flush()
    //System.out.println("grabDtd OK");
}

private boolean createURL(String str){
  try {
    theURL = new URL( str );
    return true ;
  }catch(MalformedURLException e){
    return false ;
  }
}
```

As shown in Listing 9.8, the `reformDoctype` method extracts the DTD file reference from the DOCTYPE line, then sets the `dtdURL` and `dtdFname` variables.

Listing 9.8: The *reformDoctype* Method Modifies the DTD Reference (*XMLgrabber.java*)

```
// string has doctype declaration, revise to point to local version
private String reformDoctype( String dts ){
  int p1 = dts.indexOf( "http:"); // points at h
  if( p1 < 0 ) return dts ;
  //
  int p2 = dts.indexOf( '"', p1 );
  int p3 = dts.lastIndexOf('/', p2);
  if( p3 < 0 ) return dts ;
  dtdURL = dts.substring( p1 , p2 );
  dtdFname = dts.substring( p3 + 1, p2 );
  // System.out.println("DTD url:" + dtdURL + "<");
  // System.out.println("DTD fname:" + dtdFname + "<");
  String tmp = dts.substring(0,p1); // includes "
  return tmp + dts.substring( p3 + 1 );
}
```

Because the downloading process can be interrupted at several points, there is a danger of accumulating empty or partially written temporary files. The `finalize` method, as shown in Listing 9.9, tries to delete these files if they exist. Under normal conditions, both the `tfnxml` and `tfndtd` variables will contain `null`, and no attempt to delete files will occur.

Listing 9.9: The Finalize Method Can Clean Up Temporary Files (*XMLgrabber.java*)

```
// last chance to clean up temp files if something failed
public void finalize(){
  if( tfnxml != null ){
    new File( saveDir, tfnxml ).delete();
  }
  if( tfndtd != null ){
    new File( saveDir, tfndtd ).delete();
  }
}
}
```

Introducing the *NewsModel* Class

Now that an XML file and a matching DTD file reside on the local hard disk, we need a class to parse the XML file and create a DOM. The class we have created for this purpose is called `NewsModel`, which also creates collections of the items according to the content type, or the cluster in the Moreover.com nomenclature. The `NewsModel` class provides methods for retrieving and formatting items as well.

Creating the DOM

Listing 9.10 shows the start of the `NewsModel` class, including the instance variables and the constructor. Note that there are two collections, a `Hashtable` and a `Nodelist`, that will be populated by article elements when the DOM is created. The constructor simply takes parameters for the path and filename of the XML file. Depending on the XML parser you are using, you may have to adjust the import statements and the `loadXML` method shown in Listing 9.11, but the remaining methods should work with any parser because they use the `org.w3c.dom` interfaces.

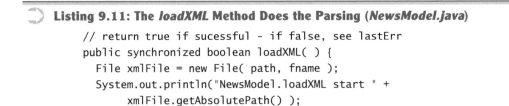

Listing 9.10: The Start of the *NewsModel* Class (*NewsModel.java*)

```
package com.XmlEcomBook.Chap09;

import java.io.* ;
import java.util.* ;
import com.sun.xml.tree.* ;
import com.sun.xml.parser.Resolver ;
import org.xml.sax.* ;
import org.w3c.dom.* ;

public class NewsModel {
  long timestamp ;
  public String dateStr ;
  Document doc ;
  String path, fname ;
  public boolean usable ;
  public String lastErr ="no error";
  // see locateCategories for creation of following
  Hashtable clusterHash ;
  NodeList articleNodeList ;

  public NewsModel( String pth, String fn ) {
    path = pth ; fname = fn ;
  }
```

The parsing process is controlled by the loadXML method, as shown in Listing 9.11. Note that, in order to keep the maximum debugging information, SAXParseException exceptions are caught separately, and detailed information on the cause is extracted and saved as the lastErr variable. Although the XML from the Moreover.com site is usually well formed, we had one instance of badly formed XML due to an illegal character. In that instance, the detailed information from the parse exception was very valuable.

Listing 9.11: The *loadXML* Method Does the Parsing (*NewsModel.java*)

```
// return true if sucessful - if false, see lastErr
public synchronized boolean loadXML( ) {
  File xmlFile = new File( path, fname );
  System.out.println("NewsModel.loadXML start " +
      xmlFile.getAbsolutePath() );
```

```
     try {
       timestamp = xmlFile.lastModified();
       dateStr = new Date( timestamp ).toString();
       InputSource input = Resolver.createInputSource( xmlFile );
     // the "false" flag says not to validate (faster)
     // XmlDocument is in the com.sun.xml.tree package
       doc = XmlDocument.createXmlDocument (input, false);
       System.out.println("Created document");
       usable = true ;
       return true ;
     }catch(SAXParseException spe ){
         StringBuffer sb = new StringBuffer( spe.toString() );
         sb.append("\n  Line number: " + spe.getLineNumber());
         sb.append("\nColumn number: " + spe.getColumnNumber() );
         sb.append("\n Public ID: " + spe.getPublicId() );
         sb.append("\n System ID: " + spe.getSystemId() + "\n");
         lastErr = sb.toString();
         System.out.print( lastErr );
         return false ;
     }catch( SAXException se ){
         lastErr = se.toString();
         System.out.println("loadXML threw " + lastErr );
         se.printStackTrace( System.out );
         return false ;
     }catch( IOException ie ){
         lastErr = ie.toString();
         System.out.println("loadXML threw " + lastErr +
           " trying to read " + xmlFile.getAbsolutePath() );
         return false ;
     }
   } // end loadXML
```

If parsing the XML succeeds in creating a DOM, the locateCategories method is
called. As shown in Listing 9.12, this method gets a NodeList of all article elements for the
articleNodeList variable and then calls the processArticle method for each element.
The processArticle method builds a Vector of elements for each value of the cluster
element. It is this Vector that will supply the articles when the user requests a specific content type.

```java
public void locateCategories(){
  Element dE = doc.getDocumentElement(); // the root element
  clusterHash = new Hashtable();
  articleNodeList = dE.getElementsByTagName("article");
  int act = articleNodeList.getLength();
  //System.out.println("Article count: " + act );
  for( int i = 0 ; i < act ; i++ ){
    Element aE = (Element) articleNodeList.item( i ) ;
    processArticle( aE );
  }
}

private void processArticle( Element artE ){
  NodeList clusterNL = artE.getElementsByTagName("cluster");
  if( clusterNL.getLength() == 0 ) return ;
  Element clE = (Element)clusterNL.item(0);
  String clusterStr = clE.getFirstChild().getNodeValue().trim() ;
  Object obj = clusterHash.get( clusterStr );
  Vector v = null ;
  if( obj == null ){
        v = new Vector();
        clusterHash.put( clusterStr, v );
  }
  else {v = (Vector)obj ;
  }
  v.addElement( artE );
}
```

Selecting Headline Elements

Now we come to the methods that respond to requests for articles from a servlet. For this example, we provide two selection methods: You can search the entire collection for all articles that have specific character sequences in the headline text element, or you can retrieve all articles in a particular category.

The articlesByKeyWord method, as shown in Listing 9.13, is called with a String that contains one or more character sequences, separated by commas. The first step is turning the keystring variable into an array of type String. This step is performed by the prepKeys method, which also converts the characters to uppercase. Next, a search of each article is performed by the `searchArticle` method, and the hits are returned as an array of `Element` references.

Listing 9.13: The *articlesByKeyWord* Is Called by the Servlet (*NewsModel.java*)

```
// articles by keyword appearance in headline
// keys may be word or phrase, one or more, sep by comma
// just use original order
public Element[] articlesByKeyWord( String keystring ){
  String[] keys = prepKeys( keystring ); // uppercase and separated
  Vector v = new Vector();
  int i ;
  int ct = articleNodeList.getLength();
  for( i = 0 ; i < ct ; i++ ){
    Element aE = (Element) articleNodeList.item( i ) ;
    if( searchArticle( aE, keys )){
      v.addElement(aE);
    }
  }
  Element[] ret = new Element[ v.size() ];
   for( i = 0 ; i < ret.length ; i++ ){
    ret[i] = (Element) v.elementAt(i);
  }     return ret ;
}
// convert to uppercase and separate at commas
private String[] prepKeys( String s ){
  StringTokenizer st = new StringTokenizer( s.toUpperCase(), ",");
  String[] ret = new String[ st.countTokens() ];
  int i = 0 ;
  while( st.hasMoreTokens() ){
    ret[i++] = st.nextToken().trim();
  }
  return ret ;
}
```

The `searchArticle` method, as shown in Listing 9.14, is more complex than you might expect, because of a peculiarity of the XML parser. Consider the content of an element that contains an entity such as the & in the following headline:

```
<headline_text>Q&amp;A: Will Sony Rule the Digital World</headline_text>
```

This will be parsed into three Node objects: two text nodes separated by an EntityReference node. Because we want to search the entire headline text, a call to the getFullText method is used to get a String with the complete text.

The getFullText method, which is also shown in Listing 9.14, concatenates the text representing all parts of the headline. The text representing an EntityReference node has to be built from the name of the node plus the '&' and ';' characters.

Listing 9.14: The Methods That Support Searching Headlines for Keywords (*NewsModel.java*)

```
// return true if one of the keys appears in the headline_text element
   private boolean searchArticle( Element aE, String[] keys ){
     NodeList htNL = aE.getElementsByTagName("headline_text");
     if( htNL.getLength() == 0 ) return false ;
     // there is only one headline_text
     Element htE = (Element)htNL.item(0);
     String str = getFullText( htE ).toUpperCase() ;
     for( int i = 0 ; i < keys.length ; i++ ){
       if( str.indexOf( keys[i] ) >= 0 ) return true ;
     }
     return false ;
   }
   // this is needed to cope with headline text that has entities
   private String getFullText( Node nd ){
     NodeList nl = nd.getChildNodes();
     int ct = nl.getLength();
     if( ct == 0 ) return "";
     if( ct == 1 ) return nd.getFirstChild().getNodeValue();
     StringBuffer sb = new StringBuffer();
     for( int i = 0 ; i < ct ; i++ ){
       Node n = nl.item(i);
       if( n instanceof EntityReference ){ // reconstruct &amp; notation
         sb.append( '&' ); sb.append( n.getNodeName());
         sb.append( ';' );
       }
       else {
         sb.append( n.getNodeValue() );
       }
     }
     return sb.toString();
   }
```

The `locateCategories` method (Listing 9.12) created the `clusterHash` collection, in which headline elements are stored according to the `cluster` tag. We're not sure why Moreover.com calls that element `cluster`; it seems more like a topic to us, so that's why the method shown in Listing 9.15 is called `articlesByTopic`. This listing also shows the `getAllTopics` method, which simply turns the full `articleNodeList` into an array of type `Element`.

Listing 9.15: This Method Returns All Items with a Given Cluster (*NewsModel.jav*)

```
// return array of Element for this topic
// or null if none available
public Element[] articlesByTopic( String topic ){
  Vector v = (Vector) clusterHash.get( topic );
  if( v == null ) return null ;
  Element[] ret = new Element[ v.size() ];
  for( int i = 0 ; i < ret.length ; i++ ){
    ret[i] = (Element) v.elementAt( i );
  }    return ret ;
}

public Element[] getAllTopics(){
  int ct = articleNodeList.getLength();
  Element[] ret = new Element[ ct ];
  for( int i = 0 ; i < ct ; i++ ){
     ret[i] = (Element)articleNodeList.item( i );
  }
  return ret ;
}
```

To let a user choose which topic is to be displayed, we need to have a list of topics in the current DOM. The `String` array provided by the `getTopics` method, as shown in Listing 9.16, will be used in the `NetNewsBean` class, which we look at toward the end of the chapter, to create a list of available topics. Note that the `shellSort` utility method is needed to sort the `String` objects in the array because the order of keys in a `Hashtable` is unpredictable.

Listing 9.16: The *getTopics* Method (*NewsModel.java*)

```
// return exact names of all topics available
public String[] getTopics(){
  Enumeration keys = clusterHash.keys();
  String[] ret = new String[ clusterHash.size() ];
```

```
      int i = 0;
      while( keys.hasMoreElements() ){
        ret[i++] = (String)keys.nextElement();
      }
      shellSort( ret );
      return ret ;
    }
```

The `formatElement` method, as shown in Listing 9.17, provides a simple method for inserting text from an article, represented by the `art Element`, into a `String` that would typically include HTML formatting information. Here is an example of a formatting string that has tags showing where the `url`, `headline_text`, and `source` element text should be inserted:

```
<tr><td><a href="<%url>" ><%headline_text></a> "  
from <%source></td></tr>
```

This method works by locating "<%" characters, isolating the element name, and calling the `getContent` method to get the text of the element from the article `Element` object. Note that `getContent` calls `getFullText` to get the complete text for the selected element.

⊃ **Listing 9.17: The *formatElement* Method (*NewsModel.java*)**

```
    // Element known to be an article, formatting string
    public String formatElement( Element art, String fmt ){
      StringBuffer sb = new StringBuffer( 3 * fmt.length() );
      int p0 = 0 ;
      int p1 = fmt.indexOf("<%");
      int p2 = fmt.indexOf('>', p1);
      while( p1 > p0 && p2 > p1 ){
        sb.append( fmt.substring( p0, p1 ));
        sb.append( getContent( art, fmt.substring(p1 + 2, p2) ));
        p0 = p2 + 1 ;
        p1 = fmt.indexOf("<%", p0);
        if( p1 > p0 ){
            p2 = fmt.indexOf('>', p1);
        }
      }
      sb.append( fmt.substring( p0 ));
      return sb.toString();
    }
    // element known to be an article
```

```
private String getContent( Element art, String key ){
  NodeList nl = art.getElementsByTagName( key );
  if( nl.getLength() == 0 ) return "";
  Element kE = (Element)nl.item(0);
  return getFullText( kE ) ;
}
```

The last part of the NewsModel class listing, shown in Listing 9.18, contains shellSort and some other utility methods.

Listing 9.18: The Sorting and Other Utility Methods (*NewsModel.java*)

```
public  void shellSort (String[] srted ) {
    // h is the separation between items we compare.
    int h = 1;
    while ( h < srted.length ) {
       h = 3 * h + 1;
    }
    // now h is optimum
    while ( h > 0 ) {
       h = (h - 1)/3;
       for ( int i = h; i < srted.length; ++i ) {
          String item = srted[i];
          int j=0;
          for ( j = i - h;
               j >= 0 && compare( srted[j], item ) < 0;
               j -= h ) {
             srted[j+h] = srted[j];
          } // end inner for
          srted[j+h] = item;
       } // end outer for
    } // end while
} // end sort

 // return -1 if a < b , 0 if equal, +1 if a > b
int compare(String a, String b ){
   String aa = a.toUpperCase() ;
   String bb = b.toUpperCase() ;
   return bb.compareTo( aa ) ;
}
```

```
public String toString() {
  StringBuffer sb = new StringBuffer( "NewsModel " );
  if( !usable ){
    sb.append("is not usable due to ");
    sb.append( lastErr );
    return sb.toString();
  }
  sb.append("count of articles ");
  sb.append( Integer.toString( articleNodeList.getLength()) );
  sb.append("Unique clusters " + clusterHash.size() );
  sb.append("\n");
  Enumeration keys = clusterHash.keys();
  while( keys.hasMoreElements() ){
    String key = (String)keys.nextElement();
    Vector v = (Vector)clusterHash.get( key );
    sb.append(" Topic: " ); sb.append( key ) ;
    sb.append(" has " ) ; sb.append(Integer.toString( v.size()));
    sb.append("\n");
  }
  return sb.toString();
}
}
```

A Supervising Class

Now let's look at the class that handles acquisition of a new set of headlines at predetermined intervals and makes them available to servlets. The NetNewsSuper class follows a typical singleton pattern. It has static variables and methods that ensure that only one NetNewsSuper instance is created for each XML source. As shown in Listing 9.19, the source URL is used as a key to retrieve a NetNewsSuper instance from the nnsHash Hashtable or to create one if it doesn't already exist.

Listing 9.19: The Start of the *NetNewsSuper* Class (*NetNewsSuper.java*)

```
package com.XmlEcomBook.Chap09;

import java.util.*;
import java.io.* ;
```

```
public class NetNewsSuper extends java.lang.Thread {
  static Hashtable nnsHash = new Hashtable() ;
  static long classLoaded = System.currentTimeMillis();
  static long longTime = 1000 * 60 * 60 * 2 ;// two hours
  static int maxErrCt = 10 ;
  // source is URL + query, dest is abs file path, destFname = name
  // hash stored by complete source string as key
  static synchronized NetNewsSuper getNetNewsSuper(String source,
      String destPth, String destFname ){
    NetNewsSuper nns = (NetNewsSuper)nnsHash.get( source );
    if( nns == null ){
      nns = new NetNewsSuper( source, destPth, destFname ) ;
      nnsHash.put( source, nns );
    }
    return nns ;
  }

  static synchronized void removeNetNewsSuper( NetNewsSuper nns ){
    Object obj = nnsHash.remove( nns.sourceURL );
    if( obj == null ){
      System.out.println("Remove of " + nns.sourceURL + " failed." );
    }
  }
}
```

The reason we have the NetNewsSuper class extend Thread instead of implementing Runnable has to do with the ease of debugging and the management of a set of servlets. It is straightforward to write a servlet that lists all running Threads in the JVM of a servlet engine. You can display both the name of the instance and the result of calling the toString method.

As you see in the class constructor shown in Listing 9.20, the name of the Thread is set to include the name of the file it retrieves. The constructor is called with the source URL and with the directory and filename to be used for the XML file. Because acquiring a new set of headlines is intended to be a background process, the Thread is assigned minimum priority.

Listing 9.20: The Instance Variables and Constructor of *NetNewsSuper* (*NetNewsSuper.java*)

```
// instance variables and methods follow
String sourceURL ;
String destPath, destFname ;
public String errStr ;
public boolean usable ;
```

```
int errCt = 0 ;
boolean running ;

NewsModel newsM ;
private NetNewsSuper(String source, String dest, String fname ){
  sourceURL = source ; destPath = dest ; destFname = fname ;
  setName("NetNewsSuper " + fname );
  setPriority( Thread.MIN_PRIORITY );
  start();
  System.out.println("NetNewsSuper Thread started");
}
```

As shown in Listing 9.21, the initial operation of the run method calls the checkSrc method to see if the required XML file already exists. If not, it creates an XMLgrabber and executes the doQueryNow method to get the initial XML file. With an XML file resident, it executes the createModel method, which creates a new NewsModel object.

Listing 9.21: The *run* Method of the *NetNewsSuper* Class (*NetNewsSuper.java*)

```
// low priority - check for need to update xml
public void run(){
  running = true ;
  try { // runs when first started
   if( !checkSrc() ){
     XMLgrabber grab = new XMLgrabber( sourceURL, destPath, destFname );
     System.out.println("NetNewsSuper runs doQueryNow");
     if( !grab.doQueryNow() ){
       errCt++ ;
       System.out.println("NetNewsSuper.run - bad return from grab");
     }
   }
   createModel();
  }catch(Exception e1){
    errCt++ ;
  }
  while( running ){
    try {
      sleep( longTime );
      XMLgrabber grab = new XMLgrabber( sourceURL, destPath, destFname );
      System.out.println("NetNewsSuper.run runs doQueryNow");
      if( grab.doQueryNow() ){
```

```
        if( errCt > 0 ) errCt-- ;
        createModel();
      }
      else {
       errCt++ ;
       System.out.println("NetNewsSuper.run - bad return from grab");
      }
    }catch(InterruptedException ie){
      errCt++ ;
      System.err.println("NetNewsSuper.run " + ie );
    }catch(Exception ee ){
      errCt++ ;
      System.err.println("NetNewsSuper.run " + ee );
    }
    if( errCt > maxErrCt ){
      System.out.println("NetNewsSuper.run too many errors: " + errCt +
          " run exiting.");
      running = false ;
    }
  }
  System.out.println("Leaving NetNewsSuper.run method");
}

  // return true if XML source file is found
private boolean checkSrc(){
  File f = new File( destPath, destFname );
  return (f.exists() && f.canRead());
}
```

Listing 9.22 shows the method that creates a new NewsModel instance and then calls the loadXML and locateCategories methods of that instance. In the event of an error, the usable variable is set to false.

Listing 9.22: This Method Creates a New *NewsModel* Object (*NetNewsSuper.java*)

```
// xml source known to exist, go for it
private synchronized void createModel(){
    newsM = new NewsModel( destPath, destFname );
    if( !newsM.loadXML()){ // error in getting data
      errStr = newsM.lastErr ;
      usable = false ;
    }
```

```
      else {
        newsM.locateCategories();
        usable = true ;
      }
    }
```

As we will see in the upcoming discussion of the NetNewsBean and NetNewsServ classes, a servlet requests the current NewsModel via the getNewsModel method, as shown in Listing 9.23. If none exists, which might happen in the event of a network error that interrupts the normal run method, the getNewsModel method attempts to get a new one.

Listing 9.23: The *getNewsModel* Method Returns a *NewsModel* (*NetNewsSuper.java*)

```
// Note that there are two steps to getting a news model resident:
// 1. grabbing the current XML to local file if not there already
// 2. creating the NewsModel from the local XML
public NewsModel getNewsModel() throws Exception {
  if( newsM != null ) return newsM ;
  // must be newly created NetNewsSuper
  if( !checkSrc() ){
    XMLgrabber grab = new XMLgrabber( sourceURL, destPath, destFname );
    //System.out.println("getNewsModel runs doQueryNow");
    if( !grab.doQueryNow() ){
      // System.out.println(" bad return from grab");
      return null ;
    }
  }
  // source exists, create model
  createModel();
  return newsM ; // may or may not be usable
}
```

The toString method, as shown in Listing 9.24, provides a useful summary of the current state of the NetNewsSuper object.

Listing 9.24: The *toString* Method (*NetNewsSuper.java*)

```
public String toString()
{
  StringBuffer sb = new StringBuffer( "NetNewsSuper for ");
  sb.append( sourceURL );
```

```
        if( newsM == null ){
            sb.append(" No NewsModel resident ");
        }
        else {
            sb.append(" NewsModel resident, status: " + usable );
        }
        sb.append(" class loaded: " );
        sb.append( new Date( classLoaded ).toString() );
        return sb.toString() ;
    }
}
```

Classes to Display Headlines

We use two classes, a servlet named NetNewsServ and a formatting class named NetNews-Bean, to display the headline items. There are many ways the functionality we have created so far could be used in a Web site. For example, you could record each customer's preferences for news items in a database and create a customized start page automatically. For the purposes of this chapter, we use a simple approach.

The *NetNewsServ* Servlet

The servlet has two essential functions: The doGet method creates a form that lets a user select topics and/or keywords, and the doPost method handles displaying the selected headlines. Listing 9.25 shows the start of the servlet code. In order to keep the example simple, we have hard-coded the queryStr variable that contains the search URL, the path and filename used for the XML file, and the alias variable that contains the servlet URL. In a working installation, these variables would be read in from a properties file in the init method.

Listing 9.25: The Start of the *NetNewsServ* Source Code (*NetNewsServ.java*)

```
package com.XmlEcomBook.Chap09;

import java.io.*;
import javax.servlet.*;
import javax.servlet.http.*;

public class NetNewsServ extends HttpServlet
{
```

```
static String version = "1.00 July 20, 2000";
static String queryStr = "http://www.moreover.com/cgi-local/page" +
  "?wbrogden@bga.com+xml";
static String destDir = "e:\\scripts\\netnews" ;
static String queryFile = "xmldump.xml" ;
static String alias = "http://localhost/servlet/netnews" ;

String keywords = "";
String fmt = "<tr><td><a href=\"<%url>\" ><%headline_text></a>" +
  "   from <%source></td></tr>" ;
public void init(ServletConfig config) throws ServletException
{
  super.init(config);
}
```

The **doGet** method generates a simple form that provides for selection of one or more categories and/or the input of keywords. As shown in Listing 9.26, it gets a **NetNewsBean** object for the specific news source. The **getTopicsAsSelect** method in **NetNewsBean** creates the code for a selection list. The resulting HTML page is shown in Figure 9.2.

Listing 9.26: The *doGet* Method Creates a Simple Form (*NetNewsServ.java*)

```
public void doGet(HttpServletRequest req, HttpServletResponse resp)
throws ServletException, IOException
{
  resp.setContentType("text/html");
  PrintWriter out = new PrintWriter(resp.getOutputStream());
  out.println("<HTML>");
  out.println("<HEAD><TITLE>NetNewsServ Output</TITLE></HEAD>");
  out.println("<BODY>");
  try {
    NetNewsBean nnb = new NetNewsBean( queryStr, destDir, queryFile );

    out.println("<h1>The News</h1>");
    out.println("<p>Select the general categories you would like to see. "+
    "You can also enter a list of key words or phrases separated by " +
    "commas and the system will locate any headlines containing them.</p>"
    );
    out.println("<center><form method=\"POST\" action=\"" + alias
       + "\" >" );
```

```
out.println("Key Words: <input type=\"TEXT\" size=\"60\"" +
    " maxlength=\"120\" name=\"keywords\" ><br>");
out.println("Select one or more topics (use &lt;ctrl&gt;click.<br>");
out.println( nnb.getTopicsAsSelect() );
out.println("<br><input type=\"SUBMIT\" value=\"Continue\" >");
out.println("</form></center><br>");
footer( out );
}catch(Exception e){
    errorMsg( out, "NetNewsServ.doGet ", e );
}
}
```

FIGURE 9.2
The headline selection form

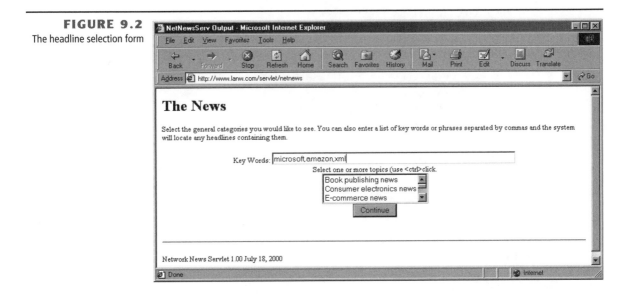

When the user clicks the Continue button on the form, the request goes to the doPost method shown in Listing 9.27. If the user has not entered any keywords or made any selections from the list, the form is regenerated by calling doGet. Otherwise, a page is generated based on an HTML table, where the table rows are created by calling doNetNews. Of course, this is a very simplified version of how this capability would be used on a commercial Web site.

Listing 9.27: The *doPost* Method (*NetNewsServ.java*)

```java
public void doPost(HttpServletRequest req, HttpServletResponse resp)
throws ServletException, IOException
{
  String[] topics = req.getParameterValues("topics");
  String keywords = req.getParameter("keywords").trim();
  System.out.println("topics " + topics + " keywords " + keywords );
  // topics may not be present, keywords may be empty
  if( topics == null && keywords.length() == 0 ){
     doGet( req, resp ); return ;
  }
   //
  resp.setContentType("text/html");
  PrintWriter out = new PrintWriter(resp.getOutputStream());
  try {
    header( out );
    out.println("<center><table width=\"45%\" cellpadding=\"2\"" +
          " cellspacing=\"6\" cols=\"1\" >");
    doNetNews( out, keywords, topics );
    out.println("</table></center>");
    footer( out );
  }catch(Exception e){
     errorMsg( out, "NetNewsServ.doPost ", e );
  }
}
```

As shown in Listing 9.28, the doNetNews method gets a NetNewsBean and formats the output as rows of a table.

Listing 9.28: This Method Formats the Retrieved Headline Items (*NetNewsServ.java*)

```java
// assumes a table has been started
// topics[] are tags from list, ie 0, 1 etc.
private void doNetNews( PrintWriter out,String keywords, String[] topics ){
  int i =0 ;
  try {
    NetNewsBean nnb = new NetNewsBean( queryStr, destDir, queryFile );
    out.println("Update " + nnb.getDocDate());
    String[] tstr = nnb.getTopicsAsArray();
    if( keywords.length() > 0 ) {
```

```
        out.println("<tr><td>Selected by keywords: " + keywords
            + "</td></tr>");
        out.println( nnb.getContentByKeyWord( keywords, fmt )) ;
      }
      out.println("<hr>") ;
      if( topics == null ){ // none selected
        for( i = 0 ; i < tstr.length ; i++ ){
          out.println("<tr><td>topic: " + tstr[i] + "</td></tr>" );
          out.println( nnb.getContentByTopic( tstr[i], fmt ) );
        }
      }
      else {
        for( i = 0 ; i < topics.length ; i++ ){
          int tn = Integer.parseInt( topics[i] );
          out.println("<tr><td>topic: " + tstr[tn] + "</td></tr>" );
          out.println(nnb.getContentByTopic(tstr[ tn ], fmt));
        }
      }
    }catch(Exception e){
        out.println( "<tr><td>" );
        e.printStackTrace(out );
        out.println("</td></tr>");
    }
  }
```

The only other methods in the NetNewsServ class are utility methods, as shown in Listing 9.29.

Listing 9.29: Some Utility Methods (*NetNewsServ.java*)

```
    // assumes response has been set to text/html
  private void errorMsg( PrintWriter out, String msg, Exception ex ){
    header( out );
    out.println("<h2>Error: " ); out.println( msg );
    out.println("</h2><br>");
    if( ex != null ){
       ex.printStackTrace( out );
    }
    out.println("<br>");
    out.println("<a href=\"mailto:wbrogden@bga.com\">"
      + "Please mail me the error message.</a><br>");
```

```
    footer( out );
  }
  private void header(PrintWriter out ){
    out.println("<html>");
    out.println("<head><title>Network News Servlet</title></head>");
    out.println("<body>");
  }

  private void footer(PrintWriter out ){
    out.println("<hr><br>Network News Servlet " + version + " <br>" );
    out.println("</body>");
    out.println("</html>");
    out.close();
  }

}
```

The *NetNewsBean* Class

This class provides the interface between the servlet and the memory-resident `NewsModel`
object for a particular news source. As shown in Listing 9.30, the constructor uses the
`NetNewsSuper` class to get the current `NewsModel` for the given source.

Listing 9.30: The Start of the *NetNewsBean* Class (*NetNewsBean.java*)

```
package com.XmlEcomBook.Chap09;

import java.util.* ;
import org.w3c.dom.* ;

public class NetNewsBean
{
  static String noDataStr ="No Data is available";
  static String dataSourceErr = "Error when loading data " ;
  NewsModel newsM ; // has public  boolean usable  and errStr

  // create with source url string, dest file path, dest fname
  NetNewsBean( String source, String pth, String fn )
        throws Exception {
    NetNewsSuper nns = NetNewsSuper.getNetNewsSuper( source,pth,fn );
    newsM = nns.getNewsModel() ; // throws exception
  }
```

```
public String getDocDate(){
   if( newsM == null ) return noDataStr ;
   if( newsM.usable ) return newsM.dateStr ;
   return dataSourceErr ;
}
```

Listing 9.31 shows the methods that provide access to the list of topics in a particular NewsModel. The getTopicsAsArray method simply returns a String array, whereas the getTopicsAsSelect returns formatted HTML.

Listing 9.31: Methods that Return Topics as an Array or as Formatted HTML (*NetNewsBean.java*)

```
public String[] getTopicsAsArray(){
   if( newsM == null || !newsM.usable ) return null;
   return newsM.getTopics();
}
// return available topics as a Select control with values
// matching the index of the topics array
public String getTopicsAsSelect(){
   if( newsM == null ) return noDataStr ;
   StringBuffer sb = new StringBuffer(1000);
   if( newsM.usable ){
      String[] topics = newsM.getTopics();
      sb.append("<select name=\"topics\" MULTIPLE size=\"3\">\r\n");
      for( int i = 0 ; i < topics.length ; i++ ){
         sb.append("<option value=\"");
         sb.append( Integer.toString( i ));
         sb.append("\" > ");
         sb.append( topics[i] );
      }
      sb.append("</select>\r\n");
   }
   else {
      sb.append( dataSourceErr );
      sb.append( newsM.lastErr );
   }
   return sb.toString();
}
```

The getContentByKeyWord method shown in Listing 9.32 controls the selection and the formatting of headlines that are selected by one or more keywords.

Listing 9.32: The Method That Controls the Headline Keyword Search (*NetNewsBean.java*)

```java
public String getContentByKeyWord( String kwds, String fmt ){
  if( newsM == null ) return noDataStr ;
  StringBuffer sb = new StringBuffer(1000);
  if( newsM.usable ){
    Element[] art = newsM.articlesByKeyWord( kwds );
    for( int i = 0 ; i < art.length ; i++ ){
      sb.append( newsM.formatElement( art[i], fmt ));
      sb.append("\n");
    }
  }
  else {
      sb.append( dataSourceErr );
      sb.append( newsM.lastErr );
  }
  return sb.toString();
}
```

The alternative of simply showing all headlines is supported by the `getAllTopics` method. As shown in Listing 9.33, it creates a String containing a formatted headline for every headline item.

Listing 9.33: The *getAllTopics* Method Formats All Available Headlines (*NetNewsBean.java*)

```java
public String getAllTopics( String fmt ){
  if( newsM == null ) return noDataStr ;
  StringBuffer sb = new StringBuffer(1000);
  if( newsM.usable ){
  Element[] art = newsM.getAllTopics();
    for( int i = 0 ; i < art.length ; i++ ){
      sb.append( newsM.formatElement( art[i], fmt ));
      sb.append("\n");
    }
  }
  else {
      sb.append( dataSourceErr );
      sb.append( newsM.lastErr );
  }
  return sb.toString();
}
```

Figure 9.3 shows a page of recent headlines selected by keywords as formatted by the getContentByTopic method, which is shown in Listing 9.34.

FIGURE 9.3
Presentation of headlines

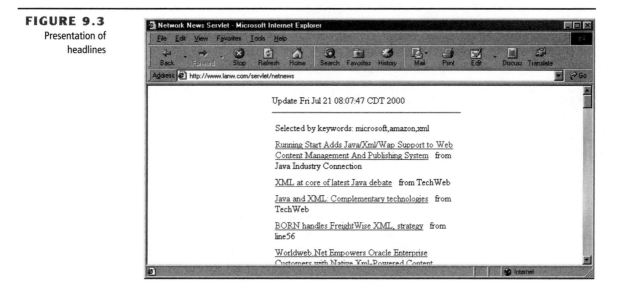

Listing 9.34: The *getContentByTopic* Method (*NetNewsBean.java*)

```java
public String getContentByTopic( String content, String fmt ){
  if( newsM == null ) return noDataStr ;
  StringBuffer sb = new StringBuffer(1000);
  if( newsM.usable ){
    Element[] art = newsM.articlesByTopic( content );
    if( art == null ) return dataSourceErr ;
    for( int i = 0 ; i < art.length ; i++ ){
      sb.append( newsM.formatElement( art[i], fmt ));
      sb.append("\n");
    }
  }
  else {
      sb.append("getContentByTopic " + dataSourceErr );
      sb.append("getContentByTopic " + newsM.lastErr );
  }
  return sb.toString();
}
```

```
  public String toString()
  {
    StringBuffer sb = new StringBuffer("NetNewsBean ");
    return sb.toString() ;
  }
}
```

Possible Improvements

Although the DOM-based approach presented in this chapter is reasonable for systems with a small load, it is rather inefficient because the same computations are repeated for every page access. The worst case occurs when headline text is interrupted by entity references.

A reasonable alternative to keeping a DOM in memory is to use a Java class to represent a headline item and create a collection of these classes by catching SAX parser events. If this class also has access to the desired HTML formatting for headline items, the constructor can preformat the entire item and save only a single `String` representing the item plus a `String` of the headline text for searching.

It would not take much coding to create a custom JavaServer Pages tab library for headlines. Having such a library would make it easy for a Web page designer to add news headline capability to any page without requiring modification of the Java code.

CHAPTER 10

Java Web Applications

- The API for Web applications

- Application deployment descriptors

- Directory organization for servlets and JSP

- Scaling up to multiple servers

This final chapter gives you the requirements for setting up Java Web applications according to Sun's latest APIs for Java servlets and JavaServer Pages. In addition, this chapter helps you explore some of the complexities involved in scaling up applications as the load on a Web site increases.

Specifications In The Servlet API

Getting a Java servlet or JSP application running on a Web server involves coordination of a number of resources:

- HTML pages
- Multimedia resources
- Java servlet class files
- Shared Java library files
- JSP files
- Initialization parameters for servlets
- Security settings
- Database access

Early implementations of the Java servlet API did not specify how to organize these resources, so vendors created their own systems. As the complexity of Web applications grew, the user interfaces for setting up and controlling applications got (let's face it) very confusing and prone to error. For example, the older JRun servlet engine installation that I (Bill) have been using, which is the generation before the 2.2 API compliant release, has 259 files with a file type of `.properties` scattered through a maze of directories that is difficult to understand.

Sun had to confront this problem when working on the J2EE (Java 2 Enterprise Edition) and EJB (Enterprise JavaBean) user and programmer interfaces. The first releases of these technologies involved creation of a serialized Deployment Descriptor object for each EJB. This mechanism proved to be clumsy and difficult to understand.

For the next release of EJB, Sun made a complete change. In the 1.1 version of EJB for deployment, an XML document is responsible for communicating the setup parameters of EJBs. The fact that Sun was willing to completely scrap an existing API for an XML solution shows the value of the XML approach.

Web Application Deployment

The Java Servlet Specification version 2.2 develops the concept of a Web application in considerable detail. A Web application is the collection of servlets, Java classes, JSP pages,

HTML pages, and other resources that can be bundled together as a unit and moved to any compliant Web server. For this to be possible, Web servers can no longer make up their own directory and initialization schemes; rather, they must comply with certain deployment conventions laid down by Sun.

It is clear from the changes in the servlet API that the Java developers have been thinking seriously about security, both in terms of external access and erecting walls between and within Web applications. For example, in earlier versions of the API, the `getServletNames` method in the `ServletContext` class would enable one servlet to determine the names of all of the other servlets running from a particular application directory. The `getServlet` method could then get a reference to the actual servlet object. There was also a `getServlets` method that returned an enumeration over all servlet instances.

All of these methods are deprecated in the 2.2 API and no longer return usable information. The programmers of all servlets involved must now specifically provide for cooperation between servlets. For example, an object that is to be shared between all servlets in an application can be attached to the `ServletContext` with the `setAttribute` method. The same `ServletContext` object is shared among all servlets in an application.

If you are accustomed to using static class methods and variables for sharing certain resources, you should be aware that in the 2.2 API each Web application on a server has its own class loader. This means that nothing can be shared between Web applications by means of static class methods and variables.

Defining A Web Application

The servlet API does not lay down the law on this phase of Web application definition, individual vendors are free to create their own system for defining the context of an application to the server. The Tomcat server uses the `server.xml` file to define a `ContextManager` element that contains numerous `Context` elements. Many of the basic server functions are defined in `Context` elements, and they are also used to define Web applications. For example, here is the `Context` we have been using for this book:

```
<Context path="/XMLbook" docBase="webapps/XMLbook" debug="0"
    reloadable="true" >
</Context>
```

This establishes the document root in the physical file directory structure that the Web server uses for the `XMLbook` application, relative to the server home directory. Directories descending from this root are used by the server for serving HTML pages, JSP pages, and other resources associated with this application, as you will see in the next section.

You can also define parameters that will be available through the `ServletContext` for all servlets or JSP in the application. Here is an example use of a `Parameter` element:

```
<Context path="/XMLbook" docBase="webapps/XMLbook" debug="0"
    reloadable="true" >
  <Parameter name="workdir" value="e:\\scripts\\XMLgifts" />
</Context>
```

Tomcat uses the convention that a `ROOT` subdirectory holds the default Web application as defined by the following `Context` declaration:

```
<Context path="" docBase="webapps/ROOT" debug="0" reloadable="true" >
</Context>
```

The `ROOT` directory holds the `index.html` file you would see with a URL, such as: `http://localhost:8080/`.

Directory Structure

The `docBase` attribute defines a base location for the application files relative to the installed Tomcat location. Assuming that location is `c:\tomcat`, the server supplies the default base of Web applications `webapps` and the complete path to the application files becomes:

```
c:\tomcat\webapps\XMLbook
```

Web server requests using the URL `http://localhost/XMLbook` will be served from the physical disk directory from this path. Therefore, if the user requests a file using this URL

```
http://localhost/XMLbook/catalog/index.html
```

the Web server will map this request to the following physical file:

```
c:\tomcat\webapps\XMLbook\catalog\index.html
```

Naturally, any requests for style sheets, images, or other resources will also be served from this directory path. This brings up the subject of class files used by Java applets, a frequent cause for confusion. Because class files must be served to the user's Web browser like any other resource, applet class or `.jar` files must be kept with the plain HTML files, NOT with the class files used by servlets.

To separate the class files and class libraries used by this application from plain HTML pages, images, applet class files, and other resources, the servlet 2.2 API requires that the application directory have a subdirectory named `WEB-INF`. The Web server is forbidden to serve any resources from this subdirectory to user requests.

If an application is being distributed as a WAR file (more about this later), then a directory named `META-INF` must be present. The intent is that this directory will contain additional information about the application. As with the WEB-INF directory, the Web server may not serve any of the contents to users.

The *WEB-INF* Directory Contents

The WEB-INF directory for a Web application must have a deployment descriptor in the form of a file named web.xml. This file is required to conform to Sun's published DTD for Web application deployment descriptors.

Any Java servlet class files unique to this application, including classes used by JSP, are required to be deployed under a subdirectory named classes if they are supplied as individual class files. The normal package hierarchy continues under this directory, so the QanalysisServ servlet in the com.XmlEcomBook.Chap07 package will have a class file at the following subdirectory of the application directory:

```
WEB-INF/classes/com/XmlEcomBook/QanalysisServ.class
```

The alternative to keeping individual class files under the classes subdirectory is to create an all .jar files library. .jar files placed in WEB-INF/lib are available to the JVM when loading classes and other resources for the Web application. Note that .zip files in this directory will be ignored; the .jar file type must be used.

General classes and toolkits that are to be made available to the entire Web site may be deployed in the usual Java fashion using standard locations or a classpath setting. There is no way to share classes between only certain applications; access is either restricted to a single Web application or available to all.

Web Application Deployment Descriptor

Specifications are laid down in the servlet API for the types of information required in an application deployment descriptor, based on a Sun specified DTD. Listing 10.1 shows part of the Web-app XML used for some servlets described in this book.

Listing 10.1 Part of the *web.xml* File for a Web Application (*web.xml*)

```
<?xml version="1.0" encoding="ISO-8859-1"?>

<!DOCTYPE web-app
    PUBLIC "-//Sun Microsystems, Inc.//DTD Web Application 2.2//EN"
    "http://java.sun.com/j2ee/dtds/web-app_2.2.dtd">

<web-app>
  <servlet><servlet-name>catalog</servlet-name>
```

```
    <servlet-class>com.XmlEcomBook.catalog.CatalogServ</servlet-class>
        <init-param>
        <param-name>workdir</param-name>
        <param-value>e:\\scripts\\XMLgifts</param-value>
        </init-param>
    </servlet>
    <servlet><servlet-name>Questionnaire</servlet-name>
        <servlet-class>com.XmlEcomBook.Chap07.QuestionnaireServ</servlet-class>
            <init-param>
                <param-name>homedir</param-name>
                <param-value>e:\\scripts\\questionnaire</param-value>
            </init-param>
    </servlet>
```

Listing 10.2 shows the initial part of the web.dtd file from the servlet 2.2 API. A copy of the complete file, which is over 400 lines, is on the companion CD.

Listing 10.2 Part of the DTD for Web Applications Showing the First Level Elements (*web.dtd*)

```
<?xml version="1.0" encoding="ISO-8859-1"?>

<!-- The web-app element is the root of the deployment descriptor for
a web application -->

<!ELEMENT web-app (icon?, display-name?, description?, distributable?,
context-param*, servlet*, servlet-mapping*, session-config?,
mime-mapping*, welcome-file-list?, error-page*, taglib*,
resource-ref*, security-constraint*, login-config?, security-role*,
env-entry*, ejb-ref*)>
```

Configuration Parameters

As you can see from the element names in Listing 10.2, there are a large number of configuration parameters for Web applications that can be set from the web.xml file. It is convenient to divide these into the following categories:

- ServletContext initialization parameters
- HttpSession configuration
- Servlet and JSP definition and mapping

- MIME Type mapping
- Welcome default files
- Error pages
- Security settings

The usage of each of these is described in great detail in the official servlet API, so we won't cover all of them here. The configuration parameters you are most likely to be using are the Servlet and JSP definition and mapping parameters. For example, in Listing 10.1, the section

```
<servlet><servlet-name>catalog</servlet-name>
    <servlet-class>com.XmlEcomBook.catalog.CatalogServ</servlet-class>
    <init-param>
      <param-name>workdir</param-name>
      <param-value>e:\\scripts\\XMLgifts</param-value>
    </init-param>
</servlet>
```

maps the servlet class to the name catalog and creates a single initialization parameter named workdir that has the value e:\\scripts\\XMLgifts. The "\\" is used because a single "\" is the escape character for Java strings.

Web Application Archive Files

With the rules for application file directories laid down by the servlet API, it is possible to define a file format that can package all resources needed by an application into a single file. Sun calls this the WAR, or Web Application Archive format. The actual file format is the same as the familiar .jar file. The idea is that a vendor's application WAR file can be placed on the file system of any compliant server and automatically expanded into the application directory structure.

Automatic expansion occurs when the server starts up and discovers that a new WAR file has been installed. The Web server is responsible for conducting this expansion.

The Next Generation

As of this writing, the next revision of the servlet API, version 2.3, is in public review. It will probably become official about the time this book reaches you. The Apache organization is working on version 4 of the Tomcat server that will implement both the servlet 2.3 and Java-Server Pages 1.2 APIs. This new version will require the support of JDK 1.2 or later.

The new capabilities being added include *filters* and *event listeners*. Filters are Java classes that can modify the contents of a request before it is passed to a servlet or the contents of a response generated by a servlet. As an example, a filter could decrypt the request and encrypt the response. Another potential use would be applying an XSLT transform to XML data generated by a servlet.

Event listeners are intended to give a programmer greater control over an application as a whole. For example, a listener object could be notified whenever a servlet changed an attribute in the `ServletContext`.

The next generation of the JavaServer Pages specification offers some exciting changes for users of XML. The standard will define how the JSP compiler will create an exact equivalent XML document for every JSP document. Furthermore, the JSP compiler will accept input in either the JSP markup style or as an XML document. It is anticipated that this change will encourage the development of advanced tools for JSP creation and maintenance.

Another improvement has to do with security. The implementation of security in the 2.3 servlet API is based on the Java 2 platform architecture so it will be capable of a very fine-grained distinction of security roles.

In the proposed 2.3 servlet API, support for the HTTP 1.1 specification is strongly suggested but not required. This requires new servlet methods to support PUT, DELETE, OPTIONS, and TRACE requests. However, these additions in the new servlet and JSP APIs are not expected to break any applications written to the 2.2 servlet and 1.1 JSP API standards.

The Next Generation of XML

The Tomcat 3.1 version we have been using works with Sun's JAXP 1.0 parser, which implements only the DOM level 1 and SAX 1.0 APIs. The JAXP 1.1 version parser will support DOM level 2 and SAX version 2.0. Many of the changes will simply make customizing the parser capabilities easier, but some will add major new capabilities.

JAXP 1.1 will include a new package, `javax.xml.transform`, to define interfaces that will support style sheet transformation of XML data. Other features include namespace handling, more generalized parser creation, and support for easily setting many parser options.

If you want to experiment with the latest XML support in Java, the Xerces parser project from the Apache organization is continuing to experiment with the latest proposals. Many of these proposed additions are in different stages of development so the Xerces parser is very much an ongoing development rather than a finished product. Go to the following site for more information:

```
http://xml.apache.org/xerces-j/
```

The SOAP Initiative

A protocol that is relevant to Web applications and of great interest to XML fans is the Simple Object Access Protocol (SOAP). SOAP defines standards for encoding various data types and conventions for representing calling methods in remote objects. This is a "lightweight" protocol for message exchange between objects in a distributed environment. By using XML and plain-text transmission through the standard HTTP port, SOAP messages can be passed through firewalls.

SOAP has widespread industry support and is said to be a major part of Microsoft's .NET framework for distributed computing. Maintenance of the standard has been turned over to the W3C.

Problems Of Scaling Up

Every application we have demonstrated in this book has assumed that there is only a single computer running a single instance of a Java servlet engine. Given that the typical CPU speed and memory capacity of severs has grown about as fast as the Internet itself, this is a reasonable assumption for servers handling up to several thousand requests per minute—especially because Java works well in server configurations with multiple CPUs.

In the event of overwhelming success, however, you may have to consider the possibility of your request load outstripping a single server's capacity. In addition to just plain load handling, another reason to use more than one Web server for a site is for fault tolerance.

Using two or more distinct machines on a network to handle one site is frequently referred to as clustering. A single front-end processor redirects requests to one of the servers, depending on some criteria.

Preserving Session Information

The biggest problem with sharing the load between multiple machines has to do with applications that track the user's state. In the shopping cart project, we used an `HttpSession` object managed by the servlet container to hang onto a `ShoppingCart` object from one request/response cycle to the next. Unfortunately, `HttpSession` management is handled entirely inside a single `ServletContext` in a single JVM. To keep the shopping cart data usable for the user's entire visit, a system using clustering must use one of the following techniques.

- Direct a returning user to the same machine every time by watching user's requests for characteristic data, such as a session id cookie in the header lines or user's IP address. This has the disadvantage of not being fault tolerant in that only one machine keeps the session information.

- Direct user requests to the same machine as above, but create a backup copy of every session so that if one machine fails, the session can be restored to another.

- Provide for transparently distributing session information to any system in the cluster on demand so that it doesn't matter which system gets the request.

The other consideration in server clusters is balancing the request load so that all machines have roughly the same utilization of resources. The individual machines must be able to tell the request distributor how busy they are.

J2EE And Enterprise JavaBeans

The Java 2 Enterprise Edition (J2EE) packaging of libraries, toolkits, and APIs is the edition of Java for creating multi-tiered Web applications on a large scale. As shown in Figure 10.1, in this vision of multi-tier applications, Java servlets, and JavaServer Pages act to create the interface to users while the "back-end" processes of business logic and database access are managed through Enterprise JavaBeans (EJB).

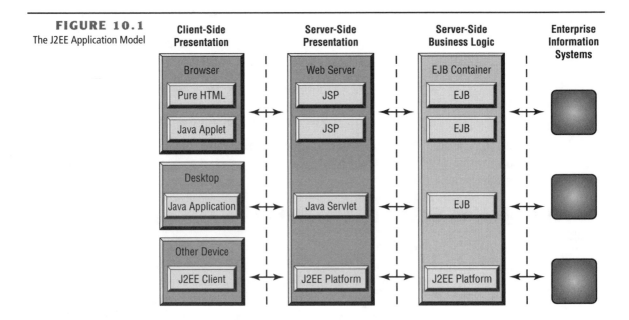

FIGURE 10.1
The J2EE Application Model

EJB operates within the context of a specialized EJB container, similar to how servlets operate in the context of the servlet container. However, the EJB container is capable of providing many more functions for your application. These functions include preserving session data and conducting database transactions. In theory, the EJB container takes care of all scaling considerations.

The Spaces Alternative

In contrast to the highly structured environment of J2EE, it is possible to create a Web application as a loosely coupled system through the "Spaces" concept. Discussed in academic circles for a number of years, the idea has recently found new utility. Sun's JINI initiative for communication between distributed processes makes use of a new JavaSpaces API. IBM also has the similar TSpaces initiative.

Processes communicating through JavaSpaces exchange messages indirectly through a separate process that manages a message space. Messages contain data (Java objects) plus identifying labels that are used to match up jobs with processes that are available to perform them. A process that submits a message to the message space can be notified when the object has been processed. Contrasting this situation with jobs being assigned to processes by a supervisor program, we can see that space-based communication tends to automatically balance the load between available systems.

As an example, a shopping cart program could place a message representing the cart contents with a label requesting the calculation of shipping charges into a JavaSpace. A shipping charge calculating program looking for work would grab the object, fill in the charge calculation, and return the filled out object to the space.

For more information on space-based programming with JavaSpaces, a good starting point is:

```
http://java.sun.com/products/javaspaces/
```

For an example in Java but not using JavaSpaces, see "Using Space Based Programming for Loosely Coupled Distributed Systems," *Java Developer's Journal*, volume 5, number 10, pages 8-12.

The Servlet and JSP APIs

While working with the servlet and JSP APIs, we have found the JDK documentation to be very thorough from a class documentation standpoint, but not very useful from a functional standpoint. The formal Servlet 2.2 and JSP 1.1 APIs also seem to be hard to integrate into real practices. The purpose of this appendix is to present the most frequently used APIs from a functional point of view, along with hints on usage.

Just to review, we are concerned with the following packages:

javax.servlet   The basic generalized servlet package

javax.servlet.http   Specialized extensions for Web pages

javax.servlet.jsp   Classes for creating JavaServer Pages

javax.servlet.jsp.tagext   Specialized extensions to JSP classes that permit creation of custom tag libraries

Setting Parameters for Applications

The servlet and JSP APIs treat parameters as having a scope that reflects the parts of the system in which the parameter has validity. The different scopes in order of decreasing extent are Server, Application, Session, Request, and Page. Each is described here:

Server Scope   Parameters visible to all applications.

Application Scope   Sun uses the "Web application" term to refer to the collection of servlets, JSP, and other resources installed in a particular server address space. The `Servlet-Context` class is intended to let all these resources share information by means of mutually accessible stored objects in "application scope." The application scope affects the interpretation of relative URL specifications.

Session Scope   As you learned in Chapter 3, servlets and JSP pages can save information specific to a user in an `HttpSession` object managed by the servlet engine. Objects stored this way are said to have "session" scope.

Request Scope   A request can actually be processed by several pages because of the forwarding mechanism. The request object (either a `ServletRequest` or `HttpServletRequest`) can carry additional objects with it.

Page Scope   In JSP engine-created servlets, this is the scope of a single page. If the request is processed by forwards or includes, a variable with page scope is only available in the page where it is created.

Servlet Creation

Because servlet methods are defined in an interface and interfaces cannot define constructors, all initialization of a servlet is carried out in the `init` method. The servlet engine is guaranteed to call `init` after the servlet object is constructed and before any request is handled. The `init` method as specified in the `Servlet` interface is handed a `ServletConfig` object that can be used to obtain initialization parameters. Remember this distinction:

- `ServletConfig`—Objects using this interface hold information used during servlet initialization. A frequent source of mysterious runtime errors in servlets occurs when the programmer forgets to include a call to `super.init()` in an `init()` method.

- `ServletContext`—Objects using this interface let a servlet locate information about the servlet engine it is running in and its environment. You can get a `ServletContext` from the `ServletConfig` object.

All servlet engines provide for defining initialization parameters to be passed to a given servlet. The conventions by which the server administrator can set these parameters vary between servlet engines, but the basic idea remains the same. Hopefully, more vendors will be moving to Sun's standard approach using XML.

A parameter name is associated with a text value. Programmers familiar with Java applets will note the parallel with the way in which an applet container (the browser) provides named parameters to an applet. The three most commonly used methods that `ServletConfig` provides are shown in Table A.1.

TABLE A.1: The *ServletConfig* Methods

Returns	Method	Usage
String	getInitParameter(String name)	This method returns a `String` corresponding to the name or returns `null` if no such parameter exists.
Enumeration	getInitParameterNames()	This method returns an `Enumeration` over all the names in the set of parameters.
ServletContext	getServletContext()	This method gets the `ServletContext` the servlet is operating in.

Table A.2 lists the methods your custom servlet must provide for when implementing the `Servlet` interface. The `javax.servlet` package also includes the `GenericServlet` class that implements the `Servlet` interface. This class includes some convenience methods, such as a no-arguments version of the `init` method, which you can override instead of using the version of `init` that takes a `ServletConfig` argument.

TABLE A.2: The *Servlet* Interface Methods

Returns	Method	Usage
void	init(ServletConfig config)	Called by the servlet container before any user requests are submitted. Remember to call `super.init(config)`.
void	destroy()	Called by the servlet container to indicate to a servlet that the servlet is being taken out of service.
ServletConfig	getServletConfig()	Returns a `ServletConfig` object, which contains initialization and startup parameters for this servlet. Note: This reference will be `null` if you forget to have your `init` method call `super.init(config)`.
String	getServletInfo()	Optional method to return information about the servlet, such as author, version, and copyright.
void	service(ServletRequest req, ServletResponse res)	Called by the servlet container to allow the servlet to respond to a request.

HttpServlet Methods

The `HttpServlet` class adds methods to support HTTP protocol requests. Your custom servlet class should override at least one of these methods, as shown in Table A.3.

TABLE A.3: The *HttpServlet* Methods That Are Commonly Overridden

Override this method	To support this request
doGet(HttpServletRequest req, HttpServletResponse resp)	HTTP GET
doPost(HttpServletRequest req, HttpServletResponse resp)	HTTP POST
doPut(HttpServletRequest req, HttpServletResponse resp)	HTTP PUT
doDelete(HttpServletRequest req, HttpServletResponse resp)	HTTP DELETE

The *ServletContext* Interface

The servlet engine creates an object implementing this interface and makes it available to servlets. This is the primary path for communication between a servlet and the enclosing servlet container. Each Web application, which may contain many servlets and JSP, shares a `ServletContext`. Table A.4 summarizes the methods by which objects and parameter settings are shared through `ServletContext`. The remaining methods are summarized in Table A.5.

TABLE A.4: *ServletContext* Methods Related to Parameters and Attributes

Returns	Method	Usage
Object	getAttribute(String name)	Returns the servlet container attribute with the given name, or **null** if there is no attribute by that name.
Enumeration	getAttributeNames()	An **Enumeration** containing the attribute names (**Strings**) in this servlet context.
void	removeAttribute(String name)	Removes the attribute with the given name from the servlet context.
void	setAttribute(String name, Object object)	Binds an object to a given attribute name in this servlet context.
String	getInitParameter(String name)	Returns a **String** containing the value of the named context-wide initialization parameter, or **null** if the parameter does not exist.
Enumeration	getInitParameterNames()	Returns the names of the context's initialization parameters as an **Enumeration** of **String** objects, or an empty **Enumeration** if the context has no initialization parameters.

TABLE A.5: More *ServletContext* Methods

Returns	Method	Usage
ServletContext	getContext(String uripath)	Returns a **ServletContext** object that corresponds to a specified URL on the server.
String	getMimeType(String file)	Returns the MIME type of the specified file, or **null** if the MIME type is not known.
RequestDispatcher	getNamedDispatcher(String name)	Returns a **RequestDispatcher** object that acts as a wrapper for the named servlet.
RequestDispatcher	getRequestDispatcher(String path)	Returns a **RequestDispatcher** object that acts as a wrapper for the resource located at the given path.
String	getRealPath(String path)	Returns a **String** containing the real path for a given virtual path.
URL	getResource(String path)	Returns a **URL** to the resource that is mapped to a specified path.
InputStream	getResourceAsStream(String path)	Returns the resource located at the named path as an **InputStream** object.
String	getServerInfo()	Returns the name and version of the servlet container on which the servlet is running.

TABLE A.5: More *ServletContext* Methods *(continued)*

Returns	Method	Usage
int	getMajorVersion()	Returns the major version of the Java Servlet API that this servlet container supports (i.e., 2 for version 2.2).
int	getMinorVersion()	Returns the minor version of the Servlet API that this servlet container supports.

Getting Request Information

User request information comes to your servlet as an object implementing the `javax.servlet.ServletRequest` or the `javax.servlet.http.HttpServletRequest` interface created by the servlet engine. Servlets that extend `javax.servlet.GenericServlet` or implement the `javax.servlet.Servlet` interface get a `ServletRequest` object (typically named `req`). JSP pages always get an `HttpServletRequest` object named `request` because JSP pages are used only in an HTTP context.

The basic methods for getting request information are all in the `ServletRequest` interface (see Table A.6), whereas `HttpServletRequest` adds some methods for getting protocol information.

TABLE A.6: Getting User Request Parameters from *ServletRequest*

Returns	Method	Usage
Enumeration	getParameterNames()	The names of parameters parsed out of the request are made available as an Enumeration rather than a String array because the name-value pairs are stored in a Hashtable, and Hashtable objects return the list of all keys as an Enumeration.
String	getParameter(String name)	This method returns the String value corresponding to a parameter name or returns null if the name does not appear in the request. It is a wise precaution to always check the returned value versus null. If there may be more than one parameter with the same name, this method returns only the first one in the request.
String[]	getParameterValues(String name)	If there may be more than one value associated with a particular name, this method should be used. The String array that is returned preserves the original order of the parameters. If no parameter with this name exists, null is returned.

Methods Added by *HttpServletRequest*

This interface extends `ServletRequest` and adds a number of useful methods as shown in Table A.7. Most of these methods are related to getting at information in the HTTP header or characterizing the way the request has come to the servlet. None of the `get` methods that access the header information by the header name is sensitive to case.

TABLE A.7: *HttpServletRequest* Methods Characterizing the Request

Returns	Method	Return value
String	getContextPath()	The portion of the request URI that indicates the context of the request.
long	getDateHeader(String name)	The value of the specified request header as a long value that represents a `Date` object.
String	getHeader(String name)	The value of the specified request header. The name is not case sensitive.
Enumeration	getHeaderNames()	An enumeration of all the header names this request contains.
Enumeration	getHeaders(String name)	All the values of the specified request header as an `Enumeration` of `String` objects.
int	getIntHeader(String name)	A convenience method that tries to convert the specified request header into an `int` value. Returns minus 1 if the header does not exist. Throws `NumberFormatException` if the header value can't be converted, so use cautiously.
String	getMethod()	The name of the HTTP method with which this request was made (for example, GET, POST, or PUT).
String	getPathInfo()	Any extra path information associated with the URL the client sent when it made this request.
String	getPathTranslated()	Translates any extra path information after the servlet name but before the query string into a real path.
String	getQueryString()	The query string that is contained in the request URL after the path.
String	getRequestURI()	The part of this request's URL from the protocol name up to the query string in the first line of the HTTP request.
String	getServletPath()	The part of this request's URL that calls the servlet.

HttpServletRequest Methods Related to Security

The security methods listed in Table A.8 may not be supported in older servlet engines.

TABLE A.8: Security-related Methods in *HttpServletRequest*

Returns	Method	Return value
String	getAuthType()	Returns the name of the authentication scheme used to protect the servlet, for example, "BASIC" or "SSL," or null if the servlet was not protected.
String	getRemoteUser()	In sessions using authentication, returns the login of the user or null if the user has not been authenticated.
Principal	getUserPrincipal( )	Returns a java.security.Principal object containing the name of the current authenticated user.
boolean	isUserInRole(String role)	Returns true if the authenticated user is included in the specified logical "role."

Methods Related to Sessions and Cookies

Because a cookie is a concept tied to the HTTP protocol, all cookie and session methods related to requests are in the HttpServletRequest class as shown in Table A.9. Methods such as getRequestedSessionId refer to the session id that was attached to the request, as either a cookie or a rewritten URL. They all return null if there was no session attached to the request.

TABLE A.9: *HttpServletRequest* Methods Related to Sessions and Cookies

Returns	Method	Return value/use
Cookie[]	getCookies()	Returns an array containing all the Cookie objects the client sent with this request.
String	getRequestedSessionId()	Returns the session id specified by the client.
HttpSession	getSession()	Returns the current session associated with this request, or if the request does not have a session, creates one.
HttpSession	getSession(boolean create)	Returns the current HttpSession associated with this request or, if there is no current session and create is true, returns a new session.
boolean	isRequestedSessionIdFromCookie( )	Returns true if the requested session id came in as a cookie (as opposed to a rewritten URL).
boolean	isRequestedSessionIdFromURL( )	Checks whether the requested session id came in as part of the request URL.
boolean	isRequestedSessionIdValid()	Checks whether the requested session id is still valid.

Other Methods in *ServletRequest*

We have tried to group the methods shown in Table A.10 by functional area instead of alphabetic order. If you want alphabetic order, use the standard JDK documentation files provided with Tomcat or the JSDK.

TABLE A.10: Some More *ServletRequest* Methods

Returns	Method	Return value/use
void	setAttribute(String name, Object obj)	This method is used when you want to store an object in a ServletRequest object that will be handed to another servlet for processing.
Object	getAttribute(String name)	This method retrieves a stored object or returns null if no such object exists.
Enumeration	getAttributeNames()	Returns an Enumeration over all the names of available attributes.
void	removeAttribute(String name)	Removes an attribute by name.
ServletInputStream	getInputStream()	An object for reading a stream of binary data from the request using the InputStream methods.
BufferedReader	getReader()	A BufferedReader would be used to read and parse the request body text line by line instead of using the parsed parameters.

HttpSession and *Cookie*-Related Classes

In this section, we discuss the HttpSession and Cookie-related classes and methods. An HttpSession object is used to maintain state information between transactions with a particular user.

HttpSession   Objects implementing this interface allow the programmer to store information about a user between individual page visits or transactions. Servlet engines provide methods for keeping track of HttpSession objects using unique IDs. See Chapter 3 for examples.

HttpSessionBindingListener   This interface is analogous to the many listener interfaces in Java GUI design. A programmer would implement this interface in an object that needed to be notified when it was attached to or detached from an HttpSession object.

Cookie These objects are used to manipulate cookie information that is sent by the server to a browser and returned on subsequent requests. Cookie information in a request is turned into Cookie objects by the HttpServletRequest.

HttpUtils Static methods in this class are useful occasionally.

HttpSessionBindingEvent Objects of this type are used to communicate information to HttpSessionBindingListener objects when it is attached to or detached from an HttpSession object.

HttpSession Methods

Notice the similarity between the *attribute*-related method names listed in Table A.11 and those used in ServletRequest. An earlier API included HttpSession methods using *value* rather than *attribute* (for example, getValue), but these are deprecated in the interest of more consistent method naming.

TABLE A.11: Methods in *HttpSession*

Returns	Method	Return value/use
Object	getAttribute(String name)	Returns the object attached with the specified name or returns null if no object has the name.
void	setAttribute(String name, Object obj)	Attaches the object to this session with this name. Any previous reference with this name is lost.
Enumeration	getAttributeNames()	An Enumeration of String objects containing the names of all the objects attached to this session.
void	removeAttribute(String name)	Removes the object with this name from the session.
long	getCreationTime()	The system time when this session was created, as in System.currentTimeMillis().
long	getLastAccessedTime()	The last time the client sent a request associated with this session; same scale as get-CreationTime.
int	getMaxInactiveInterval()	The maximum time interval, in seconds, that the servlet container will keep this session open between client accesses.
void	setMaxInactiveInterval(int interval)	Sets the time, in seconds, between client requests before the servlet container will invalidate this session.
void	invalidate()	Invalidates this session and unbinds any objects bound to it.

TABLE A.11: Methods in *HttpSession (continued)*

Returns	Method	Return value/use
boolean	isNew()	Returns true if the client does not yet know about the session or if the client chooses not to join the session. This is usually called right after calling the getSession method of an HttpServletRequest object.
String	getId()	Returns the unique identifier assigned to this session.

HttpSessionListener Interface Methods

If an object is being stored in a session and needs to "know" when it has been attached to a session or when it is being dropped from a session, you can have that class implement the HttpSessionListener interface. It will have to implement these two methods:

valueBound(HttpSessionBindingEvent event) The object that it is being bound to a session. The event carries the session ID and the name the object is bound with.

valueUnbound(HttpSessionBindingEvent event) The object that is being unbound from a session, possibly because the session is expiring.

Cookie Methods

The Cookie constructor uses a String name and a String value. Note that the name cannot use arbitrary characters, but must conform to RFC 2109. Names are not case sensitive. Table A.12 shows useful methods in the Cookie class.

TABLE A.12: Methods in the *Cookie* Class

Returns	Method	Return value/use
Object	clone()	Overrides the standard Object.clone method to return a copy of this cookie. Note, however, that you still have to cast the reference to Cookie.
String	getValue()	Returns the value of the cookie.
void	setValue(String newValue)	Assigns a new value to a cookie after the cookie is created.
String	getComment()	The comment describing the purpose of this cookie, or null if no comment was attached.
void	setComment(String purpose)	Attach a comment that describes a cookie's purpose.
String	getDomain()	Returns the domain name set for this cookie.
void	setDomain(String pattern)	Set the domain within which this cookie should be presented.
void	setPath(String uri)	Set the path to which the client should return the cookie.

TABLE A.12: Methods in the *Cookie* Class *(continued)*

Returns	Method	Return value/use
int	getMaxAge()	Returns the maximum age of the cookie, specified in seconds. The default, minus 1, indicates the cookie should persist until the browser shuts down.
void	setMaxAge(int expiry)	Sets the maximum age of the cookie in seconds. A value of zero means discard immediately.
String	getName()	The name of the cookie.
String	getPath()	The path on the server to which the browser returns this cookie.
boolean	getSecure()	Returns true if the browser is sending cookies only over a secure protocol; returns false if the browser can send cookies using any protocol.
void	setSecure(boolean flag)	Indicates to the browser whether the cookie should only be sent using a secure protocol, such as HTTPS or SSL.
int	getVersion()	Returns the version of the protocol this cookie complies with.
void	setVersion(int v)	Sets the version of the cookie protocol this cookie complies with.

Specialty Objects Associated with *Request*

The RequestDispatcher interface defines two methods that enable one servlet or JSP to forward to or include the output of another servlet or file resource on the server. You obtain a RequestDispatcher object from the ServletRequest object with a constructor that specifies the resource to be attached. The object is created by the servlet engine as in this example:

```
RequestDispatcher rd = req.getRequestDispatcher(String path);
```

Using this object, you call either of these methods:

```
forward(ServletRequest req, ServletResponse resp)
include(ServletRequest req, ServletResponse resp)
```

Setting Response Information

In this section, we consider the classes and methods involved in sending response data to a user.

ServletResponse An object implementing this interface must be created by the servlet engine and passed to the servlet's service method to be used for output of the MIME body to the client.

HttpServletResponse   An extension of the `ServletResponse` interface, which adds methods specific to HTTP transactions.

ServletOutputStream   A class for writing a stream of binary data as part of a response.

Methods in *ServletResponse*

The servlet engine creates an object implementing the `ServletResponse` interface before your servlet or JSP is called. The methods in this class are shown in Table A.13.

TABLE A.13: Methods in the *ServletResponse* Interface

Returns	Method	Return value/use
void	setBufferSize (int size)	Sets the preferred buffer size for the body of the response.
void	flushBuffer()	Forces any content in the buffer to be written to the client.
void	reset()	Clears any data that exists in the buffer as well as the status code and headers.
int	getBufferSize()	The actual buffer size used for the response.
boolean	isCommitted()	Returns true if the response has been committed.
String	getCharacterEncoding()	Returns the name of the charset used for the MIME body sent in this response.
Locale	getLocale()	Returns the locale assigned to the response.
ServletOutputStream	getOutputStream()	This is the output stream to use for writing binary data in the response. Note that you cannot change output stream types after one is selected. It is an extension of `java.io.OutputStream` and can be used to create specialized output streams such as `ObjectOutputStream` or `ZipOutputStream.`
PrintWriter	getWriter()	This is the output stream to use for writing character text. Because it does a character conversion according to the content type and locale, you should set those parameters before writing any data. You can call the `flush()` method to force the data out. The `close()` method must be called when your servlet has finished writing output, or the client may never receive anything.
void	setContentLength (int len)	Sets the length of the content body in the response. In HTTP servlets, this method sets the HTTP Content-Length header. This must be called before any content is actually sent. Although a content length is not required for all content types, in general it is required for binary types.

TABLE A.13: Methods in the *ServletResponse* Interface *(continued)*

Returns	Method	Return value/use
void	setContentType (String type)	Sets the content type of the response. The response type will be one of the MIME types and may optionally include character encoding information. An example of the type for HTML in the "Latin-4" character set for Northern European languages would be "text/html; charset=ISO-8859-4". If the character set is not specified, the default of ISO-8859-1 (ASCII) will be used.
void	setLocale(java.util .Locale loc)	Sets the locale of the response, setting the headers (including the Content-Type's charset) as appropriate.

Methods Added by *HttpServletResponse*

The HttpServletResponse interface extends ServletResponse and adds some useful methods specific to HTTP output as shown in Table A.14. It also defines a bunch of constants corresponding to the response status codes, such as the infamous "404—page not found" message.

Note that the header methods using add can add values to an existing header creating a comma-separated list, whereas the methods using set replace any existing header.

TABLE A.14: Methods in the *HttpServletResponse* Interface

Returns	Method	Return value/use
void	addCookie(Cookie cookie)	Adds the cookie to the response. This method can be called multiple times, but note that browsers might only accept 20 cookies from a given source or might be set to refuse all cookies.
void	addDateHeader(String name, long date)	Adds a response header with the given name and date-value. The date parameter is of course in the System.currentTimeMillis() style, but the header value will be text in the specific HTTP format as in Tue, 15 Nov 1994 08:12:31 GMT.
void	setDateHeader(String name, long date)	Sets a response header with this name and date-value. Any previously set header with this name is lost, so watch it.

TABLE A.14: Methods in the *HttpServletResponse* Interface *(continued)*

Returns	Method	Return value/use
void	addHeader(String name, String value)	Adds a response header with the given name and value. If the header already exists, adds the value to the existing value with comma separation between values.
void	setHeader(String name, String value)	Sets a response header with the given name and value. If the header already exists, replaces it.
void	addIntHeader(String name, int value)	Adds a response header with the given name and integer value. Naturally, the value is converted to a **String** when attached to the header.
void	setIntHeader(String name, int value)	Sets a response header with the given name and integer value.
boolean	containsHeader(String name)	Returns true if the named response header has already been set.
void	sendRedirect(String location)	Sends a temporary redirect response to the client using the specified redirect location URL.
String	encodeRedirectURL(String url)	Encodes the specified URL for use in the **send-Redirect** method or, if encoding is not needed, returns the URL unchanged.
String	encodeURL(String url)	Encodes the specified URL by including the session ID in it, or if encoding is not needed, returns the URL unchanged.
void	sendError(int sc)	Sends an HTTP error code to the client.
void	sendError(int sc, String msg)	Sends an error code with a descriptive message.
void	setStatus(int sc)	Sets the status code for this response.

JSP Output to *Response*

An instance of the JspWriter class, called out, is created automatically in the _jspService method from a PageContext. A JspWriter object is similar to a java.io.PrintWriter object in that it writes a character stream with a specific encoding. However, a significant difference is that JspWriter output methods can throw an IOException. In the PrintWriter class, an IOException is handled internally, and the programmer has to call checkError() to determine if an exception was thrown.

The capability of throwing an IOException is essential for managing the buffering behavior of the JspWriter.

Errors and Exceptions

The servlet API provides the specialized exception classes ServletException and UnavailableException, which are described here:

ServletException   A general-purpose exception used throughout the servlet API. The various constructors shown in Table A.15 provide various ways to incorporate another Exception or Error with or without an explanation. Use the method getRootCause() to extract the incorporated Exception or Error from a ServletException.

UnavailableException   This exception is to be thrown when a servlet needs to indicate that it is temporarily or permanently unavailable. The cause might be lack of availability of a database server or system maintenance. Table A.16 explains the usefulness of this exception.

TABLE A.15: *ServletException* Constructors

Constructor	Usage
ServletException()	Constructs a new servlet exception.
ServletException(java.lang.String message)	Constructs a new servlet exception with the specified message.
ServletException(java.lang.Throwable rootCause)	Constructs a new servlet exception when the servlet needs to throw an exception and includes a message about the "root cause" exception that interfered with its normal operation.
ServletException(java.lang.String message, java.lang.Throwable rootCause)	Constructs a new servlet exception when the servlet needs to throw an exception and includes a message about the "root cause" exception that interfered with its normal operation, including a description message.

TABLE A.16: *UnavailableException* Constructors

Constructor	Usage
UnavailableException(java.lang .String msg)	Constructs a new exception with a descriptive message indicating that the servlet is permanently unavailable.
UnavailableException(java.lang .String msg, int seconds)	Constructs a new exception with a descriptive message indicating that the servlet is temporarily unavailable and giving an estimate of how long it will be unavailable.

The capability of throwing an IOException is essential for managing the buffering behavior of the JspWriter.

JSP Errors and Exceptions

Remember that the JSP API provides for special designation of a JSP error-handling page as discussed in Chapter 5. This is accomplished with a page directive such as the following:

```
<%@ page language="java" errorPage="/JSPbook/Chapt02/whoops.jsp" %>
```

Any JSP page that is designated as the error page must include a tag similar to the following

```
<%@ page language="java" isErrorPage="true" %>
```

that sets the isErrorPage parameter. This ensures that the page will have a default variable named exception that will refer to the actual error or exception. This variable will refer to one of the two error-related classes, JspException and JspError. These classes have no particular extra methods beyond those in the parent class, java.lang.Exception. Table A.17 shows the constructors for JspException and JspError.

TABLE A.17: Constructors for *JspException* and *JspError*

Constructor	Usage
JspException()	Construct a JspException.
JspException(String msg)	An exception with a message.
JspError()	Note that JspError descends from JspException.
JspError(String msg)	Adds a message to the error.

HTTP Status and Error Codes

The HttpServletResponse interface includes constants for all the HTTP status and error codes, shown in Table A.18. This is essentially the same information as in the HTTP 1.1 standard, RFC 2616. The general classification of codes can be summarized as follows:

- 100 series—Informational, process continues.
- 200 series—Success.
- 300 series—Redirection, further action required to complete the request.
- 400 series—Client error, the request contains bad syntax or cannot be fulfilled.
- 500 series—Server error, the server failed to fulfill an apparently valid request.

Now for the error codes! Table A.19 lists those.

TABLE A.18: HTTP Constants for Status Codes

Constant name	Value	Meaning
SC_CONTINUE	100	The client can continue.
SC_SWITCHING_PROTOCOLS	101	The server is switching protocols according to Upgrade header.
SC_OK	200	The request succeeded normally.
SC_CREATED	201	The request succeeded and created a new resource on the server.
SC_ACCEPTED	202	A request was accepted for processing but was not completed.
SC_NON_AUTHORITATIVE_ INFORMATION	203	The meta information presented by the client did not originate from the server.
SC_NO_CONTENT	204	The request succeeded, but there was no new information to return.
SC_RESET_CONTENT	205	The agent should reset the document view that caused the request to be sent.
SC_PARTIAL_CONTENT	206	The server has fulfilled the partial GET request for the resource.
SC_MULTIPLE_CHOICES	300	The requested resource corresponds to any one of a set of representations, each with its own specific location.
SC_MOVED_PERMANENTLY	301	The resource has permanently moved to a new location, and future references should use a new URI with their requests.
SC_MOVED_TEMPORARILY	302	The resource has temporarily moved to another location, but future references should still use the original URI to access the resource.
SC_SEE_OTHER	303	The response to the request can be found under a different URI.
SC_NOT_MODIFIED	304	A conditional GET operation found that the resource was available and not modified.
SC_USE_PROXY	305	The requested resource must be accessed through the proxy given by the Location field.

TABLE A.19: HTTP Error Code Constants

Constant name	Value	Meaning
SC_BAD_REQUEST	400	The request sent by the client was syntactically incorrect.
SC_UNAUTHORIZED	401	The request requires HTTP authentication.
SC_PAYMENT_REQUIRED	402	Reserved for future use.
SC_FORBIDDEN	403	The server understood the request but refused to fulfill it.
SC_NOT_FOUND	404	The requested resource is not available.
SC_METHOD_NOT_ALLOWED	405	The method specified in the Request-Line is not allowed for the resource identified by the Request-URI.

TABLE A.19: HTTP Error Code Constants *(continued)*

Constant name	Value	Meaning
SC_NOT_ACCEPTABLE	406	The resource identified by the request is capable of generating only response entities that have content characteristics not acceptable according to the accept headers sent in the request.
SC_PROXY_AUTHENTICATION_ REQUIRED	407	The client must first authenticate itself with the proxy.
SC_REQUEST_TIMEOUT	408	The client did not produce a request within the time the server was prepared to wait.
SC_CONFLICT	409	The request could not be completed due to a conflict with the current state of the resource.
SC_GONE	410	The resource is no longer available at the server and no forwarding address is known.
SC_LENGTH_REQUIRED	411	The request cannot be handled without a defined Content-Length.
SC_PRECONDITION_FAILED	412	The precondition given in one or more of the request-header fields evaluated to false when it was tested on the server.
SC_REQUEST_ENTITY_TOO_ LARGE	413	The server refuses to process the request because the request entity is larger than the server is willing or able to process.
SC_REQUEST_URI_TOO_LONG	414	The server refuses to service the request because the Request-URI is too long for the server to interpret.
SC_UNSUPPORTED_MEDIA_ TYPE	415	The server refuses to service the request because the entity of the request is in a format not supported by the requested resource for the requested method.
SC_REQUESTED_RANGE_NOT_ SATISFIABLE	416	The server cannot serve the requested byte range.
SC_EXPECTATION_FAILED	417	The server could not meet the expectation given in the Expect request header.
SC_INTERNAL_SERVER_ERROR	500	An error inside the HTTP server prevented it from fulfilling the request.
SC_NOT_IMPLEMENTED	501	The HTTP server does not support the functionality needed to fulfill the request.
SC_BAD_GATEWAY	502	The HTTP server received an invalid response from a server it consulted when acting as a proxy or gateway.
SC_SERVICE_UNAVAILABLE	503	The HTTP server is temporarily overloaded and unable to handle the request.
SC_GATEWAY_TIMEOUT	504	The server did not receive a timely response from the upstream server while acting as a gateway or proxy.
SC_HTTP_VERSION_NOT_SUP PORTED	505	The server does not support or refuses to support the HTTP protocol version that was used in the request message.

NOTE On diagnosing error codes: Microsoft's Internet Explorer has a "friendly" mode that will prevent you from seeing actual error messages from a servlet or JSP. To turn it off, start at the Tools menu and follow this command sequence: Tools ➤ Internet Options ➤ Advanced ➤ Show Friendly Http Error Messages.

The JavaServer Pages API

The variables shown in Table A.20 are always created in a JSP page with the exception of session and exception. The session variable is not available if the page directive includes session="false". The exception variable is available only when the page directive includes the isErrorPage attribute with a value of true as in this example:

```
<%@ page language="java" isErrorPage="true" %>
```

TABLE A.20: The Implicit JSP Page Variables

Variable name	Type	Usage
request	A descendent of javax.servlet.ServletRequest	Represents the user's request.
response	A descendent of javax.servlet.ServletResponse	Creates the output response.
pageContext	A javax.servlet.jsp.PageContext object	Contains attributes of this page.
session	A javax.servlet.http.HttpSession	Contains arbitrary variables attached to this user's session.
application	A javax.servlet.ServletContext object	Contains attributes for the entire application; affects the interpretation of several other tags.
out	A javax.servlet.jsp.JspWriter object	The output stream for the response
config	A javax.servlet.ServletConfig object	Contains servlet initialization parameter name—value pairs, and the ServletContext object.
page	An object reference pointing to this	The current servlet object.
exception	A throwable object	Only pages designated as error pages in the page directive have this object.

The `JspPage` and `HttpJspPage` interfaces are very simple, as shown in Table A.21. Because the JSP engine is responsible for creating the `_jspService` method, you only need to worry about defining the `jspInit` and `jspDestroy` methods.

TABLE A.21: Methods in the *JspPage* and *HttpJspPage* Interfaces

Method	Interface	Usage
void jspDestroy()	JspPage	The method called when the JspPage is about to be destroyed. Use this to clean up any resources.
void jspInit()	JspPage	The method invoked when the JspPage is initialized. Use this to set up parameters.
void _jspService(HttpServletRequest request, HttpServletResponse response)	HttpJspPage	The method created by the JSP engine to write the body of the JSP page.

The *PageContext* Class

`PageContext` is an abstract class. The JSP engine will provide a class extending `PageContext` for a particular server. A `PageContext` object manages all the resources used by the servlet that the JSP engine writes. It is important to note that resource management recognizes several different scopes.

Access to the Standard Variables

The `PageContext` class provides methods to get references to the standard (implicit) JSP variables listed in Table A.20. Because these variables are automatically defined in your JSP page (in its `_jspService()` method), the `PageContext` methods shown in Table A.22 are mainly of use in other classes.

TABLE A.22: *PageContext* Methods for Getting Implicit Variables

Implicit variable	Type	PageContext method
exception	Exception	getException()
out	JspWriter	getOut()
page	Object	getPage()
request	ServletRequest	getRequest()

TABLE A.22: *PageContext* Methods for Getting Implicit Variables *(continued)*

Implicit variable	Type	PageContext method
response	ServletResponse	getResponse()
config	ServletConfig	getServletConfig()
application	ServletContext	getServletContext()
session	HttpSession	getSession()

Table A.23 shows the PageContext methods used for recovery of various objects. Note that the scope variables refer to constants in the PageContext class (see Table A.25).

TABLE A.23: *PageContext* Methods Related to Attribute Storage and Recovery

Returns	Method	Usage
Object	getAttribute(String name)	The object associated with the name in the page scope. Returns **null** if the object does not exist.
void	removeAttribute(String name)	The named object, in any scope, is removed.
void	setAttribute(String name, Object attribute)	Attach this object to the **PageContext** in page scope.
Object	getAttribute(String name, int scope)	The object associated with the name in the specified scope. Returns **null** if there is no such object.
void	removeAttribute(String name, int scope)	Removes the object reference associated with this name.
void	setAttribute(String name, Object obj, int scope)	Attach the object with this name and the specified scope.
Enumeration	getAttributeNamesInScope(int scope)	Returns an **Enumeration** of **String** objects over all named attributes in this scope.
int	getAttributesScope(String name)	Returns the scope of the named attribute.
Object	findAttribute(String name)	Searches for this name in page, request, session (if valid), and application scope(s) in order and returns the value associated or **null**.

Table A.24 summarizes the `PageContext` methods that didn't fall into any of the previous categories.

TABLE A.24: The Remaining *PageContext* Methods

Returns	Method	Usage
void	forward(String relativeUrlPath)	Redirects, or "forwards," the current `ServletRequest` and `ServletResponse` to another active component in the application.
void	handlePageException(Exception e)	This method is called from the `try-catch` clause that includes your JSP page code. As such, it redirects the exception to the specified error page for this JSP, or if none was specified, it performs custom action.
void	include(String relativeUrlPath)	The resource specified is processed as part of the current `ServletRequest` and `ServletResponse`.
void	initialize(Servlet servlet, Servlet-Request request, ServletResponse response, String errorPageURL, boolean needsSession,int bufferSize, boolean autoFlush)	The initialize method is called to initialize an uninitialized `PageContext` so that it can be used by a JSP implementation class to service an incoming request and response in a `_jspService()` method. Creating this call is handled by the JSP engine.
JspWriter	popBody()	Return the previous `JspWriter` "out" saved by the matching `pushBody()` and then update the value of the "out" attribute in the page scope attribute namespace of the `PageContext`. See Chapter 11 for examples.
BodyContent	pushBody()	Return a new `BodyContent` object, save the current "out" `JspWriter`, and update the value of the "out" attribute in the page scope attribute namespace of the `Page-Context`.
void	release()	Reset the internal state of a `PageContext` object so it can be reused. Calling this method is handled by the JSP engine.

The `PageContext` class defines a number of static constants mostly related to scope definition. Table A.25 summarizes these constants.

TABLE A.25: Constants in the *PageContext* Class

Type	Name	Usage
String	APPLICATION	Name used to store ServletContext in PageContext name table.
int	APPLICATION_SCOPE	Application scope: Named reference remains available in the ServletContext until it is reclaimed.
String	CONFIG	Name used to store ServletConfig in PageContext name table.
String	EXCEPTION	Name used to store uncaught exception in ServletRequest attribute list and PageContext name table.
String	OUT	Name used to store current JspWriter in PageContext name table.
String	PAGE	Name used to store the Servlet in this PageContext's name tables.
int	PAGE_SCOPE	Page scope (default): The named reference remains available in this Page-Context until the return from the current servlet service() invocation.
String	PAGECONTEXT	Name used to store this PageContext in its own name tables.
String	REQUEST	Name used to store ServletRequest in PageContext name table.
int	REQUEST_SCOPE	Request scope: The named reference remains available from the ServletRequest associated with the servlet until the current request is completed.
String	RESPONSE	Name used to store ServletResponse in PageContext name table.
String	SESSION	Name used to store HttpSession in PageContext name table.
int	SESSION_SCOPE	Session scope (valid only if this page participates in a session): The named reference remains available from the HttpSession (if any) associated with the servlet until the HttpSession is invalidated.

The *JspWriter* Class

The JspWriter class extends the java.io.Writer abstract class. The purpose of this class is to provide output functionality similar to the BufferedWriter and PrintWriter classes in JSP context, as shown in Table A.26. An important difference is that JspWriter methods can throw an IOException whereas PrintWriter does not.

TABLE A.26: *JspWriter* Buffer Management Method Summary

Returns	Method	Usage
void	clear()	Clear the contents of the buffer. Throws an IOException if any contents have been flushed to the output stream to warn your application that some output has already been sent.
void	clearBuffer()	Clear the current contents of the buffer but does not throw an exception if some data has already been sent.

TABLE A.26: *JspWriter* Buffer Management Method Summary *(continued)*

Returns	Method	Usage
void	close()	Close the stream, flushing it first.
void	flush()	Flush the stream.
int	getBufferSize()	The current buffer size.
int	getRemaining()	The unused space in the buffer.
boolean	isAutoFlush()	The state of the auto-flush flag.

The output methods in Table A.27 parallel those of the `java.io.PrintWriter` class, but they can throw an `IOException` if there is a problem with the output stream.

TABLE A.27: The *JspWriter* Output Methods

Returns	Method	Usage
void	newLine()	Write a line separator.
void	print(boolean b)	Print a boolean value.
void	print(char c)	Print a character.
void	print(char[] s)	Print an array of characters.
void	print(double d)	Print a double-precision floating-point number.
void	print(float f)	Print a floating-point number.
void	print(int i)	Print an integer.
void	print(long l)	Print a long integer.
void	print(java.lang.Object obj)	Print an object.
void	print(java.lang.String s)	Print a String.
void	println()	Terminate the current line by writing the line separator string.
void	println(boolean x)	Print a boolean value and then terminate the line.
void	println(char x)	Print a character and then terminate the line.
void	println(char[] x)	Print an array of characters and then terminate the line.
void	println(double x)	Print a double-precision floating-point number and then terminate the line.
void	println(float x)	Print a floating-point number and then terminate the line.
void	println(int x)	Print an integer and then terminate the line.
void	println(long x)	Print a long integer and then terminate the line.
void	println(java.lang.Object x)	Print an Object and then terminate the line.
void	println(java.lang.String x)	Print a String and then terminate the line.

The *javax.servlet.jsp.tagext* Package

When writing custom JSP tags, you will be concerned with only a few of the classes in this package. Your custom tag must extend either the Tag or BodyTag interface. The Tag methods are shown in Table A.28.

TABLE A.28: The *Tag* Interface Methods

Returns	Method	Usage
int	doEndTag()	Process the end tag.
int	doStartTag()	Process the start tag for this instance.
Tag	getParent()	For nested tags, returns the parent.
void	release()	Called on a Tag handler to release state.
void	setPageContext(PageContext pc)	Set the current page context.
void	setParent(Tag t)	Set the current nesting Tag of this Tag.

The Tag interface is for custom tags that do not process a body. You have to add the methods shown in Table A.29 to be able to handle body content.

TABLE A.29: The *BodyTag* Interface Adds These Methods

Returns	Method	Usage
int	doAfterBody()	Perform actions after some body has been evaluated.
void	doInitBody()	Prepare for evaluation of the body.
void	setBodyContent(BodyContent b)	Setter method for the bodyContent property.

The *BodyContent* Class

This class inherits from JspWriter (Tables A.26 and A.27), adding methods that provide for buffering character information and manipulating it, as shown in Table A.30. Also note that the flush method has to be redefined because a BodyContent object is not attached to an output stream but only to an internal buffer.

TABLE A.30: Methods in the *BodyContent* Class

Returns	Method	Usage
void	clearBody()	Clear the body buffer, typically in preparation for re-reading the body into it.
void	flush()	Redefine the flush() method of JspWriter because you can't flush a BodyContent. Throws an IOException if called.
JspWriter	getEnclosingWriter()	Get the enclosing JspWriter.
Reader	getReader()	Return the value of this BodyContent as a Reader.
String	getString()	Return the value of the BodyContent as a String.
void	writeOut(java.io.Writer out)	Write the contents of this BodyContent into a Writer output stream.

GLOSSARY

100% Pure Java   Designation for classes and applications that comply with Sun's criteria for total independence from the underlying operating system.

A

absolute positioning   Placing and sizing `Component` objects with reference to pixel coordinates; useable only when a `Container` has a `null` layout manager.

abstract   Java keyword describing classes or methods that define a runtime behavior but that don't provide a complete implementation. You can't create an object from an `abstract` class, but an object created from a class extending the `abstract` class can be referred to with the `abstract` class name.

abstract pathname   Internal path designation inside a `File` object that is independent of the underlying operating system.

Abstract Window Toolkit (AWT)
Package of Java interfaces, classes, exceptions, and errors that create a Java GUI using the GUI components of the underlying platform. The AWT is simpler than the "Swing" GUI package.

accessibility   `javax.accessibility` package stipulates interfaces that provide ease-of-use Java application features for users with disabilities.

Active Server Pages (ASP)   Microsoft's technology for embedding code inside HTML pages to create dynamic Web pages.

adapter   Design pattern for converting or adapting one class interface to another. For example, there are classes in the `java.awt` `.event` package that support the creation of event listeners.

Adjustable (interface)   Java interface (`java.awt.Adjustable`) that stipulates methods for handling changeable control, such as a scrollbar.

algorithm   Problem-solving operation that proceeds one step at a time to accomplish a specific program task.

alpha   Typical designation given a program or application that is undergoing initial (internal) testing before being released for testing outside the company that developed it. *See also* beta.

alpha value   Computer graphics term indicating degree of opacity. Together with the more familiar RGB (red, green, and blue) intensity values, alpha is part of Java color representation. When Java represents a graphics pixel as an `int` value, the alpha value is in the high byte range.

American Standard Code for Information Interchange (ASCII)   Ubiquitous computer industry standard for encoding text and control characters.

anonymous   Unnamed Java local class declared and instantiated in a single statement.

API   *See* application programming interface.

applet   Java program that operates within a Java Virtual Machine (JVM), supplied by the user's Web browser. You can think of the browser as providing an applet container that lets it run on the client machine more or less independently of the underlying operating system.

application   Java program that runs on a client machine and that can access all the client system's resources. *See also* applet.

application programming interface (API)   Calling conventions or instruction set used by an application to access operating system and library services.

Application Service Provider (ASP) Internet server that provides more than simple Web pages.

Application Services   Sun's classification of a collection of interface improvements that are included in the Java Foundation Classes (JFC).

argument   Java method call data item that can designate a Java primitive or object.

ArithmeticException   Java runtime exception that indicates integer division by zero.

array   Group of data items that share the same type, in which a 32-bit integer index addresses each data item uniquely.

Arrays (class)   Java class (`java.util .Arrays`) that includes `static` methods for searching, sorting, and other utility operations on arrays of primitives and object references.

ASCII   *See* American Standard Code for Information Interchange.

ASP   *See* Active Server Pages; *see* Application Service Provider.

assignable   Relationship between an object reference and a reference variable when both are the same type or the variable is an ancestor of the object reference in the class hierarchy.

assignment   Java operators that assign a value to a variable; for example, = and +=.

atomic   Program step that cannot be interrupted by another `Thread` is said to be atomic. All Java assignment operations with 32-bit variables are atomic, but 64-bit variable (`long` and `double`) operations are not.

attribute   In XML tags, a name-value pair within the start tag of an element.

automatic (local) variable   Variable declared inside a method, to which memory is automatically allocated when the method is called.

AWT   *See* Abstract Window Toolkit (sometimes called the Annoying Windowing Toolkit by frustrated programmers).

B

bean   *See* Java bean.

beta   Typical designation given a program or application that is under development and is released for testing outside the company that developed it; usually the step just prior to commercial release. *See also* alpha.

bitwise   Operator that works on individual bits; an operator that manipulates Java integer primitive types on an individual-bit basis.

block   Section of Java code that is contained within matching { and } characters.

break   Java keyword governing two programmatic actions. Used alone, it prompts continuation of program execution after the present code block; used with a statement label, it prompts continuation of program execution after the code block tagged by that label. *See also* continue.

byte   An eight-bit Java integer-type primitive that is treated as a signed integer.

Byte (class)   Java wrapper class for values of eight-bit byte primitives.

bytecode   Java Virtual Machine (JVM) instruction in platform-independent format, such as that used with Java applets.

C

CAB (cabinet)   Microsoft's format for compressed class and other resource files and for distributing installation files.

case-insensitive   Programming language naming convention that does not distinguish between upper- and lowercase letters.

case-sensitive   Programming language naming convention that distinguishes between upper- and lowercase letters; in other words, "Text" and "text" are read differently. Java is case sensitive.

cast   Java expression that changes the type of an expression by the new type in parentheses.

catch   Java keyword that declares specific exception type and creates a block of code or clause that executes when that exception contained in code with a try statement is thrown.

CGI   *See* Common Gateway Interface.

char   Java integer primitive variable that represents Unicode characters as 16-bit unsigned integers.

Character (class)   Java wrapper class for char values.

character data   Text contents of an element or attribute.

checked exceptions   Java programmatic exceptions that require explicit handling code.

child   In context of object-oriented programming, any object that inherits from and obtains information from another object; a Java class that inherits from another class (parent of superclass).

class   In general context of object-oriented programming, a method for grouping objects that share some characteristic or characteristics; all Java classes descend from the `Object` class.

Class (class)   Java class (`java.lang.Class`) that indicates the runtime type of any object.

class file   Outcome of compiling a Java class.

class method   Java method declared `static` and attached to an entire class, rather than to instances of the class.

class modifiers   Java keywords (`public`, `abstract`, and `final`) that establish class properties or characteristics.

class variable   Variable (`static`) that belongs to a Java class rather than to an instance of the class.

ClassCastException   Exception that is thrown whenever the JVM identifies an attempt to cast an object reference to an incompatible type.

clone method   Java method in the `Object` class that can generate a copy of an object.

Collection (interface)   Java interface (`java.util.Collection`) that defines basic behavior for Collections API objects.

Collections API   Java 2 set of classes and interfaces that provide a number of methods for handling collections of objects.

Collections (class)   Java class (`java.util.Collections`) containing `static` methods applicable to collections.

Color (class)   Java class (`java.awt.Color`) that encompasses red, green, and blue intensities of screen color. *See also* alpha.

Common Gateway Interface (CGI)
Conventions governing communication between Web servers and auxiliary programs, such as search engines. Scripts or executables that support interaction between users (via browsers) and Web servers.

Comparator (interface)   Java interface (`java.util.Comparator`) that provides the methods used to permit custom classes to use the `Arrays` class sorting and searching methods.

completeness   Object-oriented programming term denoting whether a class behavior is fully developed or requires further development by subclasses.

Component (class) Java abstract class (`java.awt.Component`) that is the parent of all screen components in the AWT graphics package except those related to menus.

constraints Java object that is passed to a layout manager that implements the `Layout-Manager2` interface and that defines the way in which a component is handled.

constructor Special kind of member function called on the creation of a class instance using `new`; initializes the object. Java classes can declare none, one, or many constructor methods.

constructor chaining A Java constructor that calls another constructor, according to a specific set of Java-enforced rules.

container In Sun's terminology, the environment a Java applet, servlet, or EJB operates in is a specialized container that is required to provide specific services.

Container (class) Java class (`java.awt.Container`) that is the ancestor for all AWT GUI objects that contain and manage interface components.

content pane In Swing primary container classes, such as `JFrame`, the container to which all interface components are added.

continue Java keyword used in two contexts: Inside a looping construct, it causes continuation of execution with the next innermost loop activity; when used with a statement label, it moves control to the next labeled loop. *See also* break.

controller In the Model-View-Controller design pattern, the controller provides functions or services for communicating user input to the model and view(s).

cookie Small chunk of text data stored by a Web browser as a consequence of visiting a Web site. This data is returned to the Web server on subsequent visits to the site and may be used to identify a user.

D

data binding Java object with accessor and mutator methods that affect the underlying data store.

daemon Thread Daemon is a UNIX term for programs that operate in the background and handle requests for network services. Java threads can be tagged daemon by the `setDaemon` method as a way of distinguishing them from user threads, and they are generally JVM utilities, such as the garbage collection `Thread`. A Java application stops when the only threads left running are `daemon threads`.

deadlock Situation in which two or more Java `Threads` need the same resource and consequently come to a stop.

decorator Java design pattern in which an attached object adds functions to a core class.

decrement   Operator (--) attached to a primitive numeric variable and that subtracts one from the variable.

deep copy   Programming term for a method of cloning objects that copies both the object and all objects to which that object refers. The `clone` method in the `Object` class does not make a deep copy.

delegate   Object that handles a component's look and feel (Swing convention) or that combines view and controller functions (Model-View-Controller design pattern).

delegation (model)   Java 1.1 event model in which event-generating components transfer event handling to specific event listeners.

deprecated   JDK (Java Developers' Kit) term that indicates a method whose use is no longer recommended.

deserialize   To reconstruct a Java object stored by serialization, usually by use of `ObjectInputStream`.

destructor   C++ method that cleans up for a user-defined object type, reclaiming designated memory and other resources. Java uses automatic garbage collection rather than destructors. *See also* finalizer.

Dimension (class)   Java class (`java .awt.Dimension`) objects typically used for reading and setting a component's width and height.

directives   In JavaServer Pages, directives are tags that define general policies or conditions for a page or part of a page.

distributed computing   In general, an architecture in which programs running on different physical computers cooperate to solve a problem by communicating over a network.

DLL   *See* dynamic link library.

doclet   Java program developed with classes in `sun.tools.javadoc` package for customizing javadoc output.

Document Object Model (DOM)
An approach to processing an XML document in which the entire document is stored in memory as a parsed hierarchy of elements. Also, in Web browsers, the hierarchical structure of the HTML document.

document type declaration   A structure within an XML document that points to or contains markup declarations that describe a class of XML documents.

Document Type Definition (DTD)
Markup declarations that describe a class of XML documents.

DOM   *See* Document Object Model.

double (double precision)   Java 64-bit floating-point primitive type.

Double (class)   Java wrapper class for `double` primitive values.

drag & drop JFC (Java Foundation Classes; in the `java.awt.dnd` package) capability that supports moving data between Java applications and between Java and native applications.

DTD *See* Document Type Definition.

dynamic link library (DLL) Executable packages or modules that a programmer can bring into memory and link to as needed by an application.

dynamic method lookup The manner in which the JVM (Java Virtual Machine) locates and calls the appropriate method at runtime based on an object's actual (rather than reference) type.

E

editable A property of `TextArea` and `TextField` components that is true if the contents can be changed by a user.

element An XML structural construct consisting of a start tag, an end tag, and information between the tags (contents).

enabling events Java method (`enable-Events`) in `java.awt.Component` called to enable creation of user interface events. The exact events enabled are determined by an event mask.

encapsulation Term used in object-oriented programming for enclosing information and behavior within an object, hiding its structure and implementation from other objects. Encapsulation allows programmers to modify the object's internal functions, without affecting any other code using the object.

entity An XML structural construct that associates character data, or well-formed XML, with a name. An entity can be referred to using an *entity reference*.

entity reference An XML structural construct that is used to refer to an entity. An entity reference is delimited by an ampersand and a semicolon.

Enumeration (interface) Java 1.0 interface (`java.util.Enumeration`) that stipulates the manner in which a collection generates a series of the collection's elements, using `nextElement` and `hasMoreElements` methods. Sun intends that `Enumeration` be replaced by the Java 2 `Iterator` interface but it is still widely used.

equals Java method that compares two object references and returns `true` when the objects' content is identical. The `Object` class default `equals` method returns `true` when both are references to the same object.

Error (class) Java class (`java.lang .Error`) that is the parent class of all Java error classes and a subclass of `Throwable`. Errors are typically conditions that a program cannot recover from, such as running out of memory.

escape sequence   Character string for encoding a character that is not a normal keyboard character or would cause trouble for the Java compiler.

event listener   Java object that is registered with a particular control associated with user activity and that is notified when a specific event takes place.

event mask   `java.awt.Component` class feature that dictates the types of GUI events the object generates.

Exception (class   Java class (`java.lang .Exception`) that is the parent class of all Java exceptions and a subclass of `Throwable`. Exceptions generally signal conditions that the program may be able to recover from.

extends   Java keyword used to define a new class that indicates the base class from which the new class will inherit.

Extensible Markup Language (XML)
A simplified form of SGML proposed as a standard for creating custom markup languages. The purpose of this is to permit the tags in a document to exactly describe the contents.

Extensible Stylesheet Language (XSL)
A proposed specification for transforming and presenting documents created with XML.

F

field   Java variable that defines a particular class characteristic.

File (class)   Java class (`java.io.File`) that manages file and directory pathnames instead of actual data files.

file separator   Character that indicates the division of path and file name components.

filter (file I/O sense)   Package of interfaces (`java.io`) that specify filtering methods for input and output streams, and file names.

filter (image sense)   Java `java.awt .image` package that provides so-called filter classes for transforming image information.

final   Java keyword that stipulates that a class cannot have subclasses. Applied to a member method, this stipulates that the method cannot be overridden by subclasses. Applied to a member variable, it stipulates that the variable is a constant whose value cannot be changed once it is set.

finalize   Object method executed by the Java garbage collection process when the memory that object occupies is to be reclaimed. Typically used to ensure that system resources are recovered when an object is discarded.

finally   Java keyword for attaching a code block that always has to be executed to a `try` block.

float   Java 32-bit floating-point primitive type.

Float (class)   Java wrapper class for `float` primitive values.

Font (class)   Java class (`java.awt.Font`) that holds specific font information.

font family   Class or group of fonts with common design or font family characteristics.

FontMetrics (class)   Java class (`java.awt.FontMetrics`) whose objects are required for all positioning calculations for a particular font.

form   Structure used in HTML pages to create elements that can accept user input and transmit it to a Web server using CGI conventions.

G

garbage collection   JVM (Java Virtual Machine) process of locating and recovering memory that is allocated to objects the program can no longer use.

GIF   *See* Graphics Interchange Format.

graphical user interface (GUI)
Computer user interface that uses graphical elements, windows, and a pointing device; Mac OS, Windows, and X11 are examples of GUIs; supported by JVM.

Graphics   Java class (`java.awt.Graphics`) that supplies the context for drawing components and screen images.

graphics context   Hardware-specific information used by an operating system in allowing applications to draw on a graphics device, such as the computer screen.

Graphics Interchange Format (GIF)
Ubiquitous HTML-compressed graphics file format (`.gif` file extension) for inline graphic elements. Unisys owns the format's patent. *See also* Joint Photographic Experts Group (JPEG).

Graphics2D (class)   Java 2 class (`java.awt.Graphics2D`) that extends `Graphics`.

GUI   *See* graphical user interface.

H

hashcode   In computing context, a characteristic number derived from a data item's contents that allows a program or application to locate the item quickly by operating on the number.

hashCode   Method in every Java object that generates an `int` primitive hashcode value characteristic of the object.

Hashtable (class)   Java class (`java.util.Hashtable`) object that stores `Object` references denoted by "key" objects using the key's hashcode.

heavyweight components   Java GUI interface components that use a corresponding operating system peer. In contrast to "lightweight" components in the "Swing" GUI toolkit.

hex (hexadecimal)   Mathematical base 16 system used in computer programming that uses alphanumeric characters 0 through 9 and A through F or a through f.

hidden variable   In an HTML form, a hidden variable holds information that cannot be seen or modified by the user but which will be transmitted to the Web server.

hierarchical   Logical arrangement of elements, also called a tree structure, in which every element with the exception of the root object has parents and might or might not have child objects (children). Examples of this structure can be found in the Java class library, XML documents, and computer file systems.

HTML   *See* Hypertext Markup Language.

HttpServlet (class)   Base class in the `javax.servlet.http` package extended by servlets that need to respond to GET and POST operations.

Hypertext Markup Language (HTML)
Document markup language used to create Web pages and standardized by the W3C.

Hypertext Transfer Protocol (HTTP)
Set of rules (protocols) based on TCP/IP that provides the foundation for communication between Web clients and servers.

I

IDE   *See* Integrated Development Environment.

identifier   Name given an item in a Java program or application.

IEEE   *See* Institute of Electrical and Electronics Engineers.

Image (class)   Java abstract class (`java.awt.Image`) that defines how graphics representation information is held.

implements   Java keyword in class declarations that precedes a list of one or more interfaces for which the class supplies methods.

implicit variables   In a JavaServer Page, these variables are automatically created.

import   Java source code file statement that informs the Java compiler as to which package holds classes used in the code.

increment   Operator (++) attached to a primitive numeric variable that adds one to that variable to which it is attached.

IndexOutOfBoundsException
Java exception thrown when an attempt is made to address a nonexistent array element; `ArrayIndexOutOfBoundsException` and `StringIndexOutOfBoundsException` are subclasses of `IndexOutOfBoundsException`.

inheritance In object-oriented programming, relationship among hierarchically arranged objects by which some objects (children) are granted attributes of another object (parent).

init (applet method) By convention, a method that belongs to a Java applet's initial class and that is called by a Web browser's JVM after the applet object is created, but before it is displayed.

init (servlet method) Method that belongs to a Java servlet class and that is called by the servlet engine after the servlet object is created, but before it services any user requests.

initialize; initialization Setting a variable's starting value.

inner class Nested class or interface with access to all member fields and methods of the class in which it is nested, including any declared `private`.

InputStream (class) Java abstract base class (`java.io.InputStream`) for various Java classes that read data as a byte stream.

Insets (class) Java class (`java.awt.Insets`) used in graphic interfaces containing an object that delineates border widths on all sides of a container.

instance Object created from a specific class is said to be an instance of that class.

instance fields Set of distinct member variables for each class instance.

instance methods Member methods that are executable only through a reference to a class instance.

instance variable Java variable that is part of a class instance instead of the class itself (class or `static` variable).

instanceof Logical operator used to determine the type of a reference in an expression.

Institute of Electrical and Electronics Engineers (IEEE) Professional organization that develops computer hardware and software standards, as well as standards for the electronics industry.

int Java 32-bit integer primitive type that is always treated as a signed integer.

Integer (class) Java wrapper class for `int` values.

Integrated Development Environment (IDE) Application development system that incorporates in one package programming tools, such as a source code editor, compiler, debugger, and project tracking functions.

interface Similar to a Java class definition, but this provides only method declarations, not implementations. A Java class is free to implement as many interfaces as needed.

International Organization for Standardization (ISO) Group composed of national standards organizations from 89 countries that establishes international standards for telecommunications and technology.

interrupt   Java Thread class instance method; if Thread is in sleep or wait state, calling interrupt wakes the Thread and generates an InterruptedException; otherwise, the interrupted flag is set.

interrupted (Thread static method) Java static method that a running Thread uses to determine whether it has been interrupted.

InterruptedException   Exception that can be generated when a Thread that is sleeping or waiting is interrupted. The Thread cannot continue with what it was doing, but must instead handle the exception.

IOException (class)   Java class (java.io .Exception) that is the parent class of all exceptions related to I/O processes; e.g., opening and reading a file.

isInterrupted   Java Thread class instance method by which a Thread can be queried to determine whether or not it has been interrupted.

ISO   *See* International Organization for Standardization.

Iterator (interface)   Java interface (java.util.Iterator) intended to replace Enumeration as the preferred method of examining elements in a collection.

J

J2EE   *See* Java 2 Enterprise Edition.

J2ME   *See* Java 2 Micro Edition.

J2SE   *See* Java 2 Standard Edition.

JAR (Java ARchive)   File format similar to Zip for collecting multiple resources (such as class files and Java class libraries) in a single file.

Java 2 Enterprise Edition (J2EE) Largest of Sun's collection of Java utilities and libraries, designed for creation of core business applications that are Internet friendly.

Java 2 Micro Edition (J2ME)   Sun's collection of Java utilities and libraries that have been reduced in size and complexity to fit small computing environments such as the Pilot from Palm.

Java 2 Standard Edition (J2SE)   Sun's collection of Java utilities and libraries designed to fit most developer's needs, designed for creation of Internet applications.

Java 2D   Group of Java classes that provide a number of advanced graphics methods.

JavaBean   Reusable software component written for a specific function or use and that meets the specific JavaBeans standard for getting and setting instance variable values.

Java Communications API   Group of Java classes and operating-system-specific code that supports direct interaction with serial and parallel I/O ports.

Java Database Connectivity (JDBC)   Collection of Java classes in the `java.sql` package that enables Java programs to connect to SQL-style databases.

Java Development Kit (JDK)   Java package of development tools, utilities, a class library, and documentation that is downloadable from the `java.sun.com` Web site.

Java Foundation Classes (JFC)   Sun's name for the collection of five Java toolkits (Swing, Java 2D, Accessibility, Drag & Drop, and Application Services) for creating advanced GUIs in Java 2.

Java Native Interface (JNI)   Java interface (API) that gives programmers access to a host system's language and determines Java's interaction with native code modules.

Java Runtime Environment (JRE) Collection of programs and libraries for a particular operating system that enables execution of Java programs, but doesn't include the compiler or classes used in the compiler.

Java Virtual Machine (JVM)   Nonphysical (virtual) computer that is part of the Java runtime environment and interprets Java bytecodes, providing the foundation for the cross-platform features of Java programs.

JavaBeans   Java programming standard for components that comply with a standard interface.

javac   Java application that starts the compiler.

javadoc   Java utility that allows automatic documentation by processing source code and producing reference pages in HTML format.

JavaScript   Web page scripting language developed by Netscape (originally called LiveScript) that controls the way in which Web pages appear in browsers. Provides limited support for embedded Java applets.

JavaServer Pages (JSP)   Java API that allows a programmer to combine HTML and Java code in a single document to create a dynamic Web page.

JComponent (class)   Java class (`javax.swing.Jcomponent`) that is base class for the Swing visual components.

JDBC   *See* Java Database Connectivity.

JDK   *See* Java Development Kit.

JFC   *See* Java Foundation Classes.

JIT   *See* Just In Time.

join   `Thread` class instance method for coordinating `thread` communication.

Joint Photographic Experts Group (JPEG)   Compressed graphics file format (`.jpg` file extension) supported by JVM and often found in Web pages. *See also* Graphics Interchange Format (GIF).

JNI   *See* Java Native Interface.

JPEG   *See* Joint Photographic Experts Group.

JRE   *See* Java Runtime Environment.

JSP   See JavaServer Pages.

jspDestroy (JSP method)   Method that is always called just before a Web server removes JSP code from memory.

jspInit (JSP method)   Method that is always created in a JSP page and is always called before a user request is processed.

_jspService (JSP method)   Method that is always created in a JSP page to process a user's HTTP request.

Just In Time (JIT)   Technology that speeds up the execution of Java programs by dynamically replacing the Java bytecode with machine language on-the-fly as methods are called.

JVM   *See* Java Virtual Machine.

L

label   Name of an identifier followed by a colon appended to a Java statement; used only with `break` and `continue` statements.

layout manager   Object for controlling screen component position and size within a `java.awt.Container` object.

lightweight components   Java interface components that lack an operating system peer and for which the JVM carries out all screen drawing and event processing.

List (interface)   Java interface (`java.util.List`) that supplies an ordered collection of object references.

listener   Java 1.1 event model object registered with a generating component that is informed about a particular class of events.

local class   Java inner class defined within a member method that can access all class members and all local `final` variables.

local variable   *See* automatic variable.

lock   Equivalent of a variable associated with every object that controls access to the object by threads. Locks can be manipulated only by the JVM in the process of synchronizing access to the object.

long   Java 64-bit integer primitive type; always treated as signed integer. *See also* `double` (double precision).

Long (class)   Java wrapper class for `long` values.

low-level event   Java events that are close to operating system raw events; for example, mouse movements.

M

main (application method)   Java `static` method required by a Java application's initial class and that is executed by the JVM after loading the class, to start the application.

manifest   File in all JAR files that provides supplementary information about other files in the JAR (such as digital signatures and encryption information). Manifest information is accessed via the `java.util.jar` `.Manifest` class.

Map (interface)   Java interface (`java.util` `.Map`) that requires the class implementing it to associate unique key objects with value objects. Classes implementing `Map` include `Hashtable` and `SortedMap`.

marshalling   In distributed computing techniques, the process of assembling objects and variables for transmission to a remote process.

maximumSize   Parameter that applies to graphic interface objects descended from `JComponent`; set with `setMaximumSize` method.

MAX_PRIORITY   Java `Thread` class constant that is used in the `setPriority` method to give a `Thread` the highest priority possible for a user `Thread`.

member   Java variables, methods, and inner classes declared as part of a class are called members of the class.

member class   Java inner class not declared as `static`, nor within a member method.

MenuComponent (class)   Java class (`java` `.awt.MenuComponent`) that is the parent class of all `java.awt` classes that are used in displaying screen menus.

method   Java class function that is named and for which specific input parameters and return types are declared.

method signature   Combination of name and parameters that distinguishes one method from others.

minimumSize   Parameter applicable to Java components that descend from `JComponent` (set with the `setMinimumSize` method) that stipulates the smallest amount of space a layout manager will give the component.

MIME   *See* Multipurpose Internet Mail Extensions.

MIN_PRIORITY   Java `Thread` class constant that is used with the `setPriority` method to give a `Thread` the lowest priority.

model   In the Model-View-Controller design pattern, the Java object that contains data.

Model 1   Refers to a JSP application architecture in which the JSP code does both the primary decision making and formatting. In Model-View-Controller terminology, the JSP page is both controller and view while JavaBean objects handle the model function.

Model 2 Refers to a JSP application architecture in which the primary decision making is handled by a servlet that delegates display to JSP pages using a `RequestDispatcher`. In Model-View-Controller terminology, the controller is a servlet while JSP handles only the view.

Model-View-Controller Design pattern in which data is held by the *model* object and displayed by the *view* object, and a *controller* object informs both model and view objects of user input.

modulus (modulo) Java operator (%) used with either integer and floating-point types that divides the left operand by the right operand and returns the result.

monitor JVM mechanism that uses object locks in controlling `Thread` access to objects.

multiple inheritance In object-oriented programming, inheriting variables and methods from more than one class. Java does not provide for multiple inheritance.

Multipurpose Internet Mail Extensions (MIME) Standard way of denoting content type in a resource; originated for use with e-mail but now widely used in network applications.

multitasking Process by which an operating system runs or appears to be running more than one program simultaneously.

multithreading Characteristic of a runtime environment that executes multiple independent paths (threads) within a program, allowing each thread access to the entire program's main memory and resources.

N

namespace 1. Complete set of class and method names and other program items that the Java compiler tracks to identify an item uniquely. 2. Way to resolve naming conflicts between elements from different vocabularies in an XML document.

NaN *See* Not a Number.

narrowing conversion (primitives) Java process of converting one primitive type to another primitive type that might lose information; for example, the conversion of `int` to `byte` eliminates extra bits.

narrowing conversion (reference type) Java process of converting a reference type to a subclass; for example, a conversion from `Object` to `String`.

NEGATIVE_INFINITY Java constant defined in the `Float` and `Double` classes that results from the floating-point division of a negative floating-point primitive by zero.

nested top-level inner class or interface Java inner class that's declared `static` and handled in the same way as any other Java outer class.

new Java keyword indicating the creation of a new object or array.

NORM_PRIORITY Java Thread class constant that is used with the setPriority method to give a Thread the normal application priority.

Not a Number (NaN) Java special floating-point constant that denotes results of arithmetical operations, such as taking the square root of a negative number, that don't have a correct numerical representation; defined in the Float and Double classes.

notify Java Object class method that causes a Thread on the object's wait list to become runnable; Thread does not run until allowed to do so by the JVM scheduling mechanism.

notifyAll Similar to notify, but causes all Threads on the object's wait list to become runnable.

null Java special literal value that is used for the value of an uninitialized reference variable.

O

object A class instance.

Observable (class) Java class (java.util .Observable) that supplies basic methods or procedures for adding and notifying objects that implement the Observer interface; in Observer-Observable design pattern, object whose change in state is of interest to an Observer.

Observer (interface) Java interface (java.util.Observer) that designates the update method used by Observable objects in notifying Observer objects.

OutputStream (class) Java abstract base class (java.io.OutputStream) for classes that write data as a stream of bytes.

overloading Refers to a Java class containing multiple methods with the same name, but different parameter lists; called *overloading the method name.*

overriding Subclass method supercedes (overrides) a superclass method with the same return type and signature as a method.

P

package Collection of associated Java classes and interfaces organized into distinct namespaces.

parent In a hierarchical system, any class that is the ancestor of another class.

path separator Character that separates paths in a list; as in the Windows environment variable PATH. The File class supplies the pathSeparator String appropriate to a given environment.

peer Operating system GUI object that corresponds to some Java AWT object.

pixel (picture element)   Smallest visible, addressable unit on a monitor or other output device and used in Java to define size and location of screen and image operations.

pointer   C programming language mechanism that provides indirect access to objects and variables; not available in Java.

polymorphic   Object's capacity to have multiple identities, based on the object's interfaces, inheritance, and overloaded methods.

port address   On computer networks based on TCP/IP, the socket identifier at a given network address for which a program or a service looks.

POSITIVE_INFINITY   Java constant defined in the `Float` and `Double` classes that results from floating-point division of a positive floating-point primitive by zero.

preferredSize   Parameter assigned to components descended from `Jcomponent`; set with the `setPreferredSize` method.

primary container   Swing object that has an operating system peer and that can support an independent window.

primitive   Java types (`boolean`, `char`, `byte`, `short`, `int`, `long`, `float`, and `double`) that are stored and accessed directly in binary form.

priority   Value from one to 10 that is assigned to `Threads` and that the JVM uses in determining which `Thread` is to run next.

private   Java keyword used to tag variables and methods that can be accessed only by methods declared within the same class.

promotion   Compiler process that uses widening conversion of a number to a type a particular operation requires.

protected   Keyword used to tag variables and methods that can be accessed only by methods of classes in the same package or by methods of classes for which that class is the superclass.

protocol   Rules that govern a transaction or data transmission between devices.

public   Java keyword for modifying visibility of classes and members, making them accessible by all objects, regardless of package boundaries.

R

random access   Ability of a programmer to move a file pointer to any point in a file and begin reading or writing at that point.

Reader (class)   Java `abstract` base class (`java.io.Reader`) for classes that read data as a stream of 16-bit Unicode characters.

reference   In Java, the process handled by the JVM by which a programmer works a "pointer" to an object (object reference) rather than directly with an object's physical memory address.

reference variable   All Java variables with the exception of primitives.

Reflection API Java API composed of classes that enable a program to ascertain the constructors, methods, and variables available in any class, as well as the interface the class implements.

Remote Method Invocation (RMI) Java communications standard for distributed computing that allows a Java program to execute a method on an object that resides on another system or JVM as if it were a local object.

resume Java `Thread` instance method (deprecated) that allows continuation of a suspended `Thread`. Use of this method is not recommended.

RMI *See* Remote Method Invocation.

root The one item or object from which all others descend in a hierarchical system.

Runnable Java interface (`java.lang.Runnable`) that defines the `Threads run` method.

RuntimeException Java class (`java.lang.RuntimeException`) that is the parent class of every exception that doesn't require declaration in a method `throws` clause.

S

SAX *See* Simplified API for XML.

schema Formal specification of the structure of an XML document.

scope Identifier attribute that controls the identifier's accessibility to other parts of a program.

semantic event Event that includes additional logic; contrasted with low-level event.

serialize To convert a Java object into a byte stream that is formatted in a way that allows reconstruction of the object.

server Network computer that supplies resources and services to client computers.

servlet Java program that runs in a servlet container on a Web server and processes network requests (typically these are HTTP requests).

servlet container Environment in which a servlet runs. The servlet API defines a number of services that a servlet container must provide.

session In servlet and JSP applications, a session maintains information about a user during the course of interaction with an application.

Set (interface) Java interface (`java.util.Set`) that is an extension of the `Collection` interface that holds object references and that is restricted so as to prevent duplication of references; hence, every reference is unique.

SGML *See* Standard Generalized Markup Language.

shallow copy Copy produced by the `clone` method in the `Object` class that copies only the values of reference variables.

short   Java 16-bit integer primitive variable type; always treated as signed integer.

Short (class)   Java wrapper class for `short` values.

sign bit   Most significant bit in the Java `byte`, `short`, `int`, and `long` primitives, which, when turned on, causes a number to be interpreted as negative.

signature   Java method's name along with the type and order of parameters in its argument list.

Simple Object Access Protocol (SOAP)
Recent proposal for a standard way to transmit requests to objects over the Internet using XML documents.

Simplified API for XML (SAX)   Approach to processing XML documents in which the parser identifies and parses elements as it encounters them in a single pass through the document. The user of SAX must provide methods to process the parsed elements.

singleton   Design pattern that allows the creation of only one instance of a class; a `static` class method controls access to the instance.

sleep   Java `static` method of the `Thread` class, which when called, causes the calling `Thread` to sleep for a specified number of milliseconds.

SOAP   *See* Simple Object Access Protocol.

socket   On computer networks, the combination of a computer address and a port number that provides a unique channel of communications.

Socket (class)   Java class object (`java.net.Socket`) representing a single network socket connection; can supply an `InputStream` and `OutputStream` for communication.

SortedSet (interface)   Java interface, an extension of `Set`, that maintains references in a sorting order determined by the `compareTo` method.

SQL   *See* Structured Query Language.

stack trace   Formatted text output that can provide the history of a `Thread`'s execution of a method that throws an exception or results in an error.

Standard Generalized Markup Language (SGML)   Standard for annotating text documents with tags that express the structure of the document and how the content should be treated. SGML served as the basis for HTML and XML.

start (applet method)   Java method that a Web browser's JVM calls after the initial display of the applet and whenever the Web page that contains the applet is redisplayed.

start (Thread method)   Method in the `Thread` class that makes a `Thread` eligible to run.

static   Java method or variable tag that indicates that the variable or method belongs to a class, rather than to a class instance.

static fields   Member fields of a Java class attached to the class itself, as opposed to fields attached to class instances.

static methods   Member methods of a Java class that execute in the environment of the class rather than a particular class instance.

stop   Java Thread instance method (deprecated) that causes a ThreadDeath exception and brings a Thread to an abrupt halt, often with unpredictable and unwanted results.

stream   Sequence (stream) of bytes that can be read only in sequence from start to finish.

Structured Query Language (SQL)   Standard for creating and accessing the contents of relational databases via text statements.

subclass   Class that extends (indirectly or directly) another class; all Java classes (except Object) are subclasses of the Object class.

super   Java keyword that refers to parent class variables, methods, or constructors.

superclass   In Java class hierarchy, ancestor of a class; the immediate ancestor is the direct superclass. *See also* extends, parent.

suspend   Java Thread instance method (deprecated) that stops a Thread until the resume method is called.

Swing   Set of advanced Java interface components that are improvements on original AWT components; standard extensions for Java 2.

synchronized   Java keyword that activates a method's or code block's monitor mechanism.

syntax   Explicit rules for constructing code statements, including particular values and the order or placement of symbols.

System (class)   Java class (java.lang .System) composed of static methods and variables that the JVM initializes when a program starts.

T

tag   In markup languages such as HTML, XML, and JSP pages, a tag is a special character sequence that is not part of the document text but defines additional information.

taglib   In JSP technology, a programmer can define his own library of special purpose Java functions identified by tags. A special taglib directive tells JSP to use a particular library.

TCP/IP   *See* Transmission Control Protocol/ Internet Protocol.

Thread (class)   Java class (java.lang .Thread) that encloses a single thread of control in the JVM and defines its behavior.

ThreadDeath   Special type of error that brings the system resources for a Thread to a stop.

ThreadGroup (class)   Java class (java .lang.ThreadGroup) the objects of which are used by the JVM to define a set of Thread objects and to govern operations on the set.

throw   Java statement that causes normal statement processing to halt and starts processing of an exception; must be associated with a `Throwable` object.

Throwable (class)   Java class (`java.lang.Throwable`) that is the parent class of every Java exception and error class.

throws   Java keyword that is employed in method declarations to introduce a list of the exceptions that method can throw.

timestamp   Java `long` primitive variable that holds the system time for an event's occurrence.

toString   Method possessed by all Java reference types that the compiler uses to evaluate statements that include `String` objects and the + operator.

Transmission Control Protocol/Internet Protocol (TCP/IP)   Suite of communications protocols developed to support mixed network environments, such as the Internet.

try   Java statement that constructs a code block in which an exception can occur; must be followed by at least one associated `catch` clause and/or a `finally` clause.

type   Java object's class or interface. In object-oriented programming in general, an object's interface is sometimes considered separately from its implementation, resulting in a further division into class and type.

U

UDP   *See* User Datagram Protocol.

UML   *See* Unified Modeling Language.

unary   Java operators, such as ++, that affect one operand.

unchecked exceptions   Exceptions descending from `RuntimeException` for which the compiler doesn't require a programmer to provide explicit handling code.

Unicode   International ANSI 16-bit standard for the representation of alphabets (includes over 65,000 characters, including graphics). Java uses the 2.0 version of Unicode; see www.unicode.org.

Unified Modeling Language (UML)   Standard notation for drawing object-oriented designs.

Uniform Resource Identifier (URI)   Generic set of all names and addresses that refer to resources.

Uniform Resource Locator (URL)   Set of URI schemes that contain explicit instructions on how to access a resource on the Internet.

URI   *See* Uniform Resource Identifier.

URL   *See* Uniform Resource Locator.

URL (class) Java class (`java.net.URL`) that represents a Uniform Resource Locator for a Web server resource.

User Datagram Protocol (UDP) Connectionless packet communication protocol (alternative to TCP/IP) for simple communication among programs; considered unreliable because a packet can be lost completely.

user Thread Any Java Thread that has not been tagged as a daemon.

V

Valid XML XML that conforms to the vocabulary specified in a DTD or schema.

variable shadowing Java variables in the same scope that can prevent direct access to other variables that have the same identifier.

Vector (class) Java class (`java.util .Vector`) object that comprises an extensible array of `Object` references.

view Java command that creates a specific model data display in the Model-View-Controller design pattern.

viewport Logical window in which part of the Java `JViewPort` view object is viewable.

visibility Level of access a Java class grants to other Java classes.

W

W3C *See* World Wide Web Consortium.

wait Java `Object` class method that when called by a `Thread` releases the `Thread`'s lock on the object, causes the `Thread` to become inactive, and places the `Thread` on the object's wait list.

wait list List of Java `Threads` that are attached to a particular object and waiting for notification.

wait set *See* wait list.

Web application Collection of servlets, JSP pages, HTML files, image files, and other resources that exist in a structured hierarchy of directories on a server.

Web Application Resource (WAR) Collection of all files needed to create a Web application in a single file using the zip compression algorithm. Defined in the servlet 2.2 specification.

well-formed XML XML markup that meets the requirements of the W3C Recommendation for XML 1.0.

widening conversions Primitive types conversions that do not lose magnitude information or reference types conversions from a subclass to a class located higher in the class hierarchy.

widget   Programmer jargon for a component of a user interface, such as a check box or button.

World Wide Web Consortium (W3C) Organization that creates standards for the Web (www.w3.org).

wrapper classes   Java classes that correspond to each of the primitive types, providing related utility functions.

Writer (class)   Java `abstract` base class (`java.io.Writer`) of classes that write data as a stream of 16-bit characters.

X

XML   *See* Extensible Markup Language.

XSL   *See* Extensible Stylesheet Language.

INDEX

Note to the Reader: Throughout this index **boldfaced** page numbers indicate primary discussions of a topic. *Italicized* page numbers indicate illustrations.

T

W

X